The Art of the Funnies
An Aesthetic History

Studies in Popular Culture
M. Thomas Inge, General Editor

The Art of the Funnies

An Aesthetic History

ROBERT C. HARVEY

UNIVERSITY PRESS OF MISSISSIPPI
Jackson

Library of Congress Cataloging-in-Publication Data

Harvey, Robert C.
    The art of the funnies : an aesthetic history / Robert C. Harvey.
        p.   cm. — (Studies in popular culture)
    Includes bibliographical references (p.) and index.
    ISBN 0-87805-612-2. — ISBN 0-87805-674-2 (pbk.)
    1. Comic books, strips, etc.—History and criticism. I. Title. II. Series.
PN6710.H35   1994
741.5—dc20   93-45937
                                                            CIP

British Library Cataloging-in-Publication data available

CONTENTS

ACKNOWLEDGMENTS

Many of the chapters in this book had earlier, somewhat different incarnations in *The Comics Journal*, where they appeared in book reviews as lengthy historical and critical digressions in the manner of Thomas Macaulay, with whose approach I was afflicted very early in my career as a commentator on the arts of cartooning. All of these essays, however, have been re-worked and amplified in order to integrate them into the more-or-less cohesive (not to say comprehensive) aesthetic history that appears on the following pages. The first chapter expands on an article that I wrote for a special comics issue of *The Journal of Popular Culture* (Spring 1979). And some of the chapters (on *The Gumps* and syndication and on Joseph Patterson and on Milton Caniff) are taken from an unpublished biography of Caniff that I completed in 1989. But much of the material herein has been written expressly for this book—the chapters on illustrators and on the gag comic strip since 1950,

for instance. The section on Bud Fisher and *Mutt and Jeff* was also written for this volume, but it appeared prior to this in the premiere issue of *Inks: Cartoon and Comic Art Studies* (February 1994), a scholarly journal published by the Ohio State University Press.

I am particularly grateful to Gary Groth, editor of *The Comics Journal*, who has kept my byline in print for nearly twenty years; to M. Thomas Inge, who prompted me to tackle a book on this subject and whose appreciative reading of my work and perceptive comment on it have always been edifying as well as gratifying to me; and to my wife Linda, who, years ago when I had all but given up drawing cartoons, encouraged me to write about the comics, little guessing then how many of my quondom spare hours would subsequently be spent in passionate study of the medium and in devoted pursuit of the right words to describe its workings.

The Art of the Funnies
An Aesthetic History

CHAPTER I
The Aesthetics of the Comics
A Preamble through History and Form

In a world brimming with uncertainties, we must take our verities where we find them. And for whatever comfort it's worth, one of the world's more secure truths is that Homer never drew comics. It's not a profound truth, but it is secure. Fairly secure.

How secure? Well, the truth of the matter resides in the sometimes disputed authenticity of a scholarly rumor that the antique Greek was blind. Those who dispute this revered tradition say that the Bard's alleged blindness was but a poetic metaphor for his inability to read. But I say that no gentleman goes about calling one of the world's greatest storytellers an illiterate. And if they aren't gentlemen, they're not scholars either; consequently, we needn't believe one jot or tittle of their slanderous contumely.

So Homer was blind, and it therefore stands to reason that he couldn't draw comics. He could tell stories, though. And he did—at least a couple of real rousers that eventually achieved international acclaim even before we had box office receipts to tell us how good something was. In his stories of the battle of Troy and the wandering of Odysseus, Homer sometimes painted pictures with words. But he couldn't draw pictures in the usual way because he couldn't see to do it. Now I'm the last one to look a Greek telling tales in the mouth, but it seems to me that we have a lot to learn from the circumstance of a storyteller who couldn't see and who therefore couldn't draw comics. If you can't draw comics because you don't see, it's plain that you can't properly read comics if you don't look at the pictures.

Homer proved you can have good stories without pictures. And because there's nothing to look at, you can understand those stories without being able to see. But if you have stories with pictures—pictures and words, comics—then you must look at the pictures to get the most meaning out of the stories. Fact is, stories in the comics cannot be truly and deliberately considered without taking the pictures into account. If we don't take the trouble to understand the storytelling role of pictures in the comics, then we may as well be as blind as Homer. Or as illiterate. Since no one reading this book is either blind or illiterate, we all implicitly understand the role of pictures in comics as soon as we roll an eye in their direction. But to understand the art of the funnies—the craft of storytelling with pictures and words—we must try to render our implicit understanding explicit. That's the task of criticism, and that's what I propose to commit here in these pages.

The study of the comics has as its objective the same goal as that set before the student of art and literature: to promote the sort of understanding that sharpens perception and awareness, leading, ultimately, to keener enjoyment of the medium. To that purpose, in this chapter I'll offer up a few theoretical considerations for the study of comics. Then, in subsequent chapters, we can look at the way a few of the medium's masters have plied their craft in newspaper comic strips. That's where the craft of making comics was honed to an art.

To become more explicit about our understanding of how comics work, we need a vocabulary appropriate to the task, a vocabulary built upon a precise knowledge of what the comics uniquely are. In short, we need an aesthetic theory of the art of the comics that fits the art. Useful as the insights of sociology, cinematography, literature, or psychology are to an understanding of the funnies as a facet of cultural experience, those treatments of the subject apply the specialized vocabularies of disciplines essentially foreign to the medium. To articulate an aesthetic theory of the comics we need a vocabulary tailored *for* the comics—and *from* the most distinctive aspects of the art form. To find those aspects, we must look unblinkingly at the comics themselves.

And here we are liable to be stymied at the onset by the bewildering assortment of artistic styles, stories, characters, and seeming purposes that spread before our eyes when we contemplate a page of comics. By their sheer variety, the comics seem bent on frustrating serious and orderly consideration: at first, there seems to be no place to begin. But even in that variety, certain common features emerge, giving rise to a working definition of the art form. Moreover, the history of that art form's development is an orderly progression, with a beginning, high points along the way, and an end (if we can call the present the end). A definition and a smattering of history bring order and the prospect of serious study (and even evaluation) to the wild profusion before us. History first: it leads to definition.

Today's comic strip is the lineal descendant of the nineteenth century humorous drawing that accompanied the serial publication of novels like those of Dickens and Thackeray and that appeared in newspapers and other periodicals (like *Punch*, founded in 1841) as editorial cartoons, and eventually, on this side of the Atlantic, in humor magazines like *Puck*, *Judge*, and *Life* in the 1880s. Toward the end of the century, great metropolitan newspapers battled for readers, and, in the attempt to attract readers and build circulation, they began publishing extravagant Sunday supplements. The most famous of these circulation wars took place in New York, and comic drawings were on the frontlines of the battlefield.

The potential of the Sunday newspaper as a profitable venture was first demonstrated by Joseph Pulitzer, who invaded New York in 1883, purchasing the *World* with the profits from his *St. Louis Post-Dispatch*. Until this decade only a few newspapers had followed the lead of James Gordon Bennett, who had overcome religious opposition to a Sunday edition in 1841. Pulitzer fleshed out the Sunday supplement idea by concentrating entertainment features in the *Sunday World*—material for women and young readers and for sports enthusiasts, the offerings of literary syndicates, and humorous drawings and other illustrations. Inspired, doubtless, by the success of *Puck*, *Judge*, and *Life*, Pulitzer launched the nation's first regular Sunday comic section in 1889. The *World's* success in turn inspired imitation: only about one hundred newspapers had Sunday editions when Pulitzer began retooling the *Sunday World* in 1883; by 1890, there were 250 dailies publishing on Sunday.

When the *World* installed a new four-color rotary press in 1894, Morrill Goddard, who headed the Sunday staff, seized upon the new technology, using it in the way he knew would be most effective in spurring circulation: henceforth, the *Sunday World's* comics appeared in color. The popular success of Goddard's strategy precipitated a chain of events that would demonstrate the importance of comics in stimulating a newspaper's circulation, thus assuring the subsequent maturation of the comic strip form, and would contribute to the nation's lexicon a term of enduring disapprobation for the most colorful, albeit unreliable, of journalistic practices.

Among Goddard's comic artists was Richard F. Outcault, who had joined the *Sunday World* in 1894 and who, in his weekly drawings, occasionally burlesqued city life by focusing on its slums. Outcault's squalid tenements, bald-earth backyards, and cluttered alleys were infested with a manic assortment of raggedy urchins, juvenile street toughs, and enough stray dogs and cats to start a pound. In the midst of these nondescript ragamuffins, one stood out: he had a head as round and naked as a billiard ball, surmounted on either

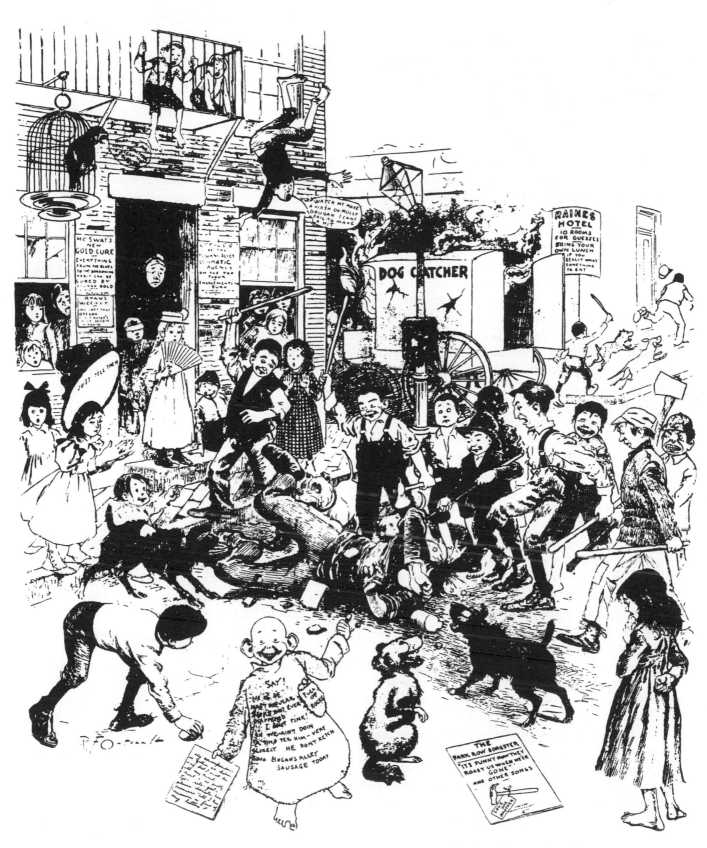

WHAT THEY DID TO THE DOG-CATCHER IN HOGAN'S ALLEY.

Figure 1. *Richard Outcault's Yellow Kid as he appeared in the* New York World *on September 20, 1896.*

side by giant ears that could have been pitcher handles, and his only raiment was a long, dirty nightshirt on which Outcault often lettered some comment about the mayhem at hand. The kid began making sporadic appearances on February 17, 1895; but soon after January 5, 1896, he became a permanent resident of *Hogan's Alley* and it became a regular feature in the *Sunday World*. On that day, the *World's* printers, experimenting with a new quick-drying yellow ink, chose the kid's shirt as the best testing ground, and the Yellow Kid was christened. He quickly became a star attraction of the *World*. No matter what the disturbance in Hogan's Alley, the Yellow Kid was there, his vaguely Oriental visage baring its two teeth at the reader in a grin at once vacuous and knowing—the capstone above whatever irreverent commentary was emblazoned on the signal flare of his yellow billboard shirtfront. So popular was the Yellow Kid that he became the first merchandized comic character, appearing on buttons, cracker tins, cigarette packs, ladies' fans, and a host of other artifacts of the age. His omnipresence could scarcely escape the notice of young William Randolph Hearst, who was just beginning to build his newspaper empire.

Hearst had studied Pulitzer's circulation-building techniques from the safe distance of San Francisco, where he had assumed control of the *Examiner* in 1887. At last, Hearst decided to assault Pulitzer's New York supremacy, and he bought the *Morning Journal* in the fall of 1895. By early 1896 Hearst's *Journal* had reached a circulation of 150,000 as a one-cent paper, forcing Pulitzer to drop the price of the *World* to a penny in order to meet the competition. The circulation war was now openly declared. The papers fought for readers with screaming headlines that sensationalized the news. Pulitzer had inaugurated this technique in New York when he took over the *World* a dozen years before, but he had balanced sensational headlines and spectacular layouts with accurate news coverage. Hearst now employed the same window dressing but without regard for facts. As the battle wore on, informing the reader became less important than luring him or her away from the opposition's paper. At Hearst's behest, journalism became a shrieking, gaudy, sensation-mongering enterprise, distorting facts to provide howling newsboys with whatever hawked best.

One of the things that proved it could sell was Outcault's Yellow Kid, and before long, the Kid's grin adorned the Sunday editions of both warring papers.

Following a practice he'd initiated in San Francisco, Hearst bought the talent he needed to beat Pulitzer. And he bought some of it from the *World* itself. With a flagrance that echoed the flamboyance of his paper's headlines, Hearst rented an office in the *World* building, and from there he raided Pulitzer's staff, starting with Morrill Goddard. Recognizing the value of a sparkling Sunday edition, Hearst offered Goddard a fabulous salary that Pulitzer couldn't counter. When Goddard protested that his staff of writers and artists were integral to his success, Hearst hired them, too—including Outcault. Knowing that a good color comic section would boost Sunday circulation, Hearst quickly put Goddard's artists to work, creating the eight-page *American Humorist* in October 1896. Testifying to the appeal of Outcault's creation, the *Journal*, on the Saturday before the *American Humorist's* debut, promised "The Yellow Kid—Tomorrow! Tomorrow!" And the next day, October 18, there he was—two-tooth grin and bilious shirtfront rampant.

Pulitzer bribed Outcault back into the *World's* fold briefly, but Hearst ultimately outbid him, and Outcault was his. So was the Yellow Kid—but not exclusively. Pulitzer hired another artist, George Luks, to continue drawing *Hogan's Alley* (starring the Yellow Kid) for the *Sunday World*. Circulation drives for both papers splashed the Yellow Kid and his vacant grin on posters all over town. Thus, Outcault's hapless waif became the most conspicuous combatant in the circulation battle. Those watching the warfare from the sidelines took to calling the two papers "the Yellow Kid journals" or "the yellow journals." And the kind of journalism the warring papers practiced was, perforce, "yellow journalism."[1]

The legacy of the Yellow Kid has thus proved a mixed blessing, a triumph whose tawdry connections tainted the future of the comics medium even while asserting its riveting appeal. That the first character of American comics should have his chromatic signature appropriated by a journalistic movement was ample testimony to the power and popularity of the comics. But because that movement was wholly commercial, embodying reprehensible ethics and sensational appeals to baser emotions, the new art form was associated with only the lower orders of rational endeavor—a circumstance that cast a shadow for a long time over any claims made for artistic merit and intellectual content in the funnies. How could anything that first surfaced in the jaundiced columns of the sensational press hold any interest for respectable, thinking readers?

Beginning with the Yellow Kid, the comics enjoyed a prized position in newspapering. They sold papers. And that was a vital consideration in the industry at the time. Until the 1920s most cities that had a daily newspaper were served by more than one paper. In 1900 915 American cities had daily newspapers, and 559 of them (61 percent) had competing dailies; in 1910 the numbers were 1,207 and 689 (57 percent). The number of cities with competing daily papers continued to climb until it peaked just before World War I; but by 1920 the number had dropped back to 552, by then only 43 percent of the cities served by daily newspapers.[2]

In the intensely competitive newspaper environment at the turn of the century—and for several decades thereafter (at least until about 1950)—the funnies were an active ingredient in a newspaper's circulation-building strategy. The reason is not difficult to discern. Apart from the political and social views of a newspaper's columnists and editorial writers (and the extent to which those views slanted the paper's treatment of the news), the only thing that distinguished one paper from another in a city with several dailies was its feature content. And the most conspicuous of the features were the comics. Granted, for a time, the headlines and the lead stories from paper to paper were different. One paper might scoop its brethren with a hot news story on any given day, and on that day that paper might be the best buy on the newsstand. Indeed, the theoretical dynamo built around this fact has driven the engines of American newspapering throughout its history, inspiring the sensational headlines of "yellow journalism." But in the second decade or so of the new century, as newspapers began to seek accuracy and comprehensiveness in their coverage of the events of the day and as national wire services began to supply much of the content of every issue, the news in one paper in a city was pretty much the same as the news in another. Only the features—and the

comics—were different, and editors exploited that difference. As a testament to the circulation building power of comics, witness that the compendious Sunday editions of most metropolitan newspapers began to be wrapped in the comics section. The funnies advertised the Sunday edition: they appeared as its distinctive, gaily colored cover on all newsstands. And they served this unique function in most cities for most of the century.

To fully appreciate the importance of the comics in newspapers during those early days, we must imagine life without radio or television. Until the advent of the broadcast media in the 1920s, the newspaper was a family's major source of outside information and amusement in the home. It was an anodyne: by informing, entertaining, and distracting its readers, it soothed and comforted. The daily newspaper gave people something to do between dinner and bedtime. And the voluminous Sunday editions furnished a day's amusement for the entire family. The comics were integral to the recreational function of the paper. Ostensibly, they kept the kids from bothering their parents on their day of rest. But it was the father who bought the paper, and he read the comics, too. The humor in many of them, in fact, would be lost on all but adult readers. From the very beginning, the Sunday funnies, masquerading as entertainment for children, entertained the grown-ups, as well.

The comics that proliferated in the Sunday supplements as the century drew to a close were not all comic strips: many were merely isolated humorous drawings, sometimes large tableaux depicting the comical capers of children or animals. Although these drawings sometimes incorporated smaller drawings showing an action in sequence, the regular use of sequential narrative panels was relatively rare until Rudolph Dirks made it standard practice in his *Katzenjammer Kids* (which began December 12, 1897, in imitation of a German work called *Max and Moritz*, by Wilhelm Busch). At first, words, when used, appeared under the pictures, not within them. But by the turn of the century the familiar combination of elements that constitutes the comic strip appeared regularly in various places. When Frederick Opper's *Happy Hooligan* appeared on March 11, 1900, the comic strip had acquired its definitive form: a narrative told by a sequence of pictures, with the dialogue of the characters incorporated into the pictures in the form of speech balloons. From its start, Opper's strip summed up all the previous experimentation and combined all the basic elements.

The technical hallmarks of the comic strip are speech balloons and narrative breakdown. Speech balloons breathe into comic strips their peculiar life. In all other graphic representations, characters are doomed to wordless posturing and pantomime—but in comic strips, they speak. And their speeches are made in the same mode as the rest of the strip: the graphic, visual, mode. We see and read the words of the characters just as we see the characters themselves and "read" their actions. Thus, the inclusion of speech balloons within the pictures gives the words and pictures concurrence— the lifelike illusion that the characters we see are speaking even as we see them, just as we simultaneously hear and see people in life.

In my own cartooning efforts (sporadic and itinerant as they are), the inclusion of speech balloons in any drawing has always seemed to change substantially the nature of the drawing. I've probably drawn hundreds of pictures of characters posturing and cavorting about, but however animated and vivid those drawings may be, it isn't until I join a speech balloon to one of the characters and make him or her talk that the drawing begins to live. Once a speech balloon points its "tail" to its speaker, that character seems more alive. Partly this is because the words spoken begin to shape the character's personality; but it is also the simultaneity and proximity of words and pictures—and their single mode of presentation—that bring the characters to life for me.

If speech balloons give comics their life, then breaking the narrative into successive panels gives that life duration, an existence beyond a moment. Narrative breakdown is to a comic strip what time is to life. In fact, "timing"—pace as well as duration—is the direct result of the second of the unique ingredients of comic strip art. The sequential arrangement of panels cannot help but create time in some general way, but skillful manipulation of the sequencing can control time and use it to dramatic advantage. The sequencing of panels controls the amount and order of information divulged as well as the order and duration of events. Managing these aspects of a story creates pace, suspense, mood, and the like. Ordinary mainstream literary prose does all of this, too; comics differ in that the pictures as well as the words ma-

nipulate time. For instance, action can be slowed down by sequences of pictures that focus minutely on each aspect of a developing action in the manner of a slow motion camera.

Comics use speech balloons and narrative breakdown to tell stories, but the art of the comics is not altogether the same as other narrative arts— despite the seeming similarities. Comics can be (and too often are) evaluated on purely literary grounds, the critic concentrating on such things as character portrayal, tone and style of language, verisimilitude of personality and incident, plot, resolution of conflict, unity, and themes. While such literary analysis contributes to an understanding of a strip or book, to employ this method exclusively ignores the essential character of the medium by overlooking its visual elements. Similarly, analysis that focuses on the graphics (discussing composition, layout, style, and the like) ignores the purpose served by the visuals—the story or joke that is being told. Comics employ the techniques of both the literary and the graphic arts, yet they are neither wholly verbal in their function nor exclusively pictorial.

In their use of words and pictures, comics are closely akin to movies, but however much these two media share, they are different in their essentials: one is a static art form, the other moves. Films are made in a hybrid, audio-visual mode. Comic strips are all visual, a seamless optic exercise: in comics, the eye takes in both word and picture. Consequently, while the language of film criticism (camera angle and distance, frame) is often directly applicable in comics criticism, comics—lacking sound and motion and functioning within a much more restricted format—cannot fairly be treated as cinema. Moreover, cinematic analysis applied to comics is blind to the special effects that can be achieved by the static medium— the dramatic impact, say, of a wordless sequence of panels, of the juxtaposition of panels, or of a large panel coupled to a series of smaller panels.

Despite the similarities comics share with these other media, critical analysis of comics requires a slightly larger vocabulary than literary or graphic or cinematic lexicons afford, a few more terms tailored to the peculiarities of the medium. Having identified some of those peculiarities, we can now begin to speak of comics in terms appropriate to their distinctive qualities.

Perhaps the most unique aspect of comic strip

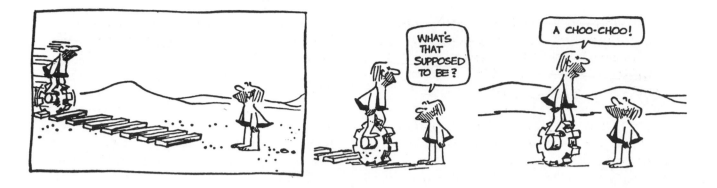

Figure 2. *In this example from Johnny Hart's* B.C., *neither the words nor the pictures make sense by themselves. In blending the visual and verbal elements in this manner, the comic strip medium achieves its unique character.*

art resides in the medium's static deployment of words and pictures. The thing that comics do that no other graphic art does is to weave word and picture together to achieve a narrative purpose. Comics are a blend of word and picture—not a simple coupling of the verbal and the visual, but a blend, a true mixture. From the nature of the medium, then, we can draw up one criterion for critical evaluation: in the usual situation, in which both words and pictures are used, a measure of a comic strip's excellence is the extent to which the sense of the words is dependent on the pictures and vice versa. In John Hart's *B.C.* strip printed here (figure 2), neither the words nor the pictures make any independent sense, they are mutually dependent.

In a humorous comic strip, the words sometimes carry more than their share of the burden in making the strip's point. Another *B.C.* strip we needn't print. Its humor is almost entirely verbal, like the ordinary joke:

FIRST SPEAKER: "Hey, waiter, there's a fly in my soup."
SECOND SPEAKER: "There can't be—I used them all in the raisin bread."

Pictures here are not at all essential to our understanding of the joke, whereas in the best examples of the art, neither word nor picture makes complete sense without the other. Consequently, our second example is, strictly speaking, less of a comic strip than the first. But that is not to say that verbal humor is wholly alien to the medium. Even in situations in which mutual dependence is not absolute, the addition of pictures to words makes our experience of the art form more "satisfying," as Stephen Becker so acutely observed in his *Comic Art in America*.[3] The merit in this argument

lies mostly in its nudging us in the right direction. With this criterion as a sort of opening gambit, it is clear that the way to fuller appreciation of the art we gather here to enjoy lies in the direction of discussing how the visual serves the verbal and how the sense of the words depends upon the pictures—in short, how storytelling is done by blending these two elements.

I don't mean to suggest that verbal-visual blending is all there is to the art of the comics. Comics do tell stories. And if the stories they tell are trivial, even the most consistently perfect blending of word and picture will not make comics great art. Great comics will be those that tell affecting and powerful stories—but they will tell those stories by exploiting to the fullest the unique potential of the art. Although the power of such stories will be rooted in plot and characterization, these elements will be realized in terms peculiar to the comics— in a blending of word and picture and in the sequential nature of that blend. What I'm going to demonstrate shortly is a way (not "the way") of looking at comics that seems to yield an understanding of the medium's unique character. And what I'm proposing is not a catechism of rules and principles so much as it is a method, a procedure—a way of coming at an understanding of comic art by beginning with an uncomplicated concept and then slowly, systematically, complicating it. I think of it as a way of "tuning up," of getting my sensibilities attuned to the special rhythms of comic art.

By applying the principle of visual-verbal interdependence, we can quickly assess the extent to which a given comic strip exploits to the fullest the specific character of the art form. While the principle is most easily exercised in consideration

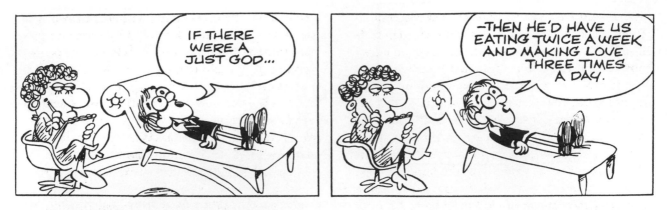

Figure 3. Inside Woody Allen, *by Allen and artist Stuart Hample, almost always gets to its punch line by verbal means alone and is therefore less of a comic strip than a strip that makes its point by blending the visual and the verbal.*

of a single daily installment of a strip, it can be brought to bear on a substantial number of strips in a title's run, too, with the object of evaluating that cartoonist's work as a whole. Clearly there are some practical constraints: a strip that has run for twenty or thirty years must be sampled judiciously throughout its run before we make a judgment. But to the degree that a cartoonist's habit of thought is predominantly verbal or visual or both, so can we characterize and evaluate his work.

Much of the cartoon humor of Sergio Aragones, for instance, is entirely visual: the tiny cartoons in the margins of *Mad* magazine that brought him his initial fame are pantomime comedy, humor without words. Carl Anderson's comic strip *Henry* starred a mute, and while other characters sometimes spoke, most of the humor was achieved without words. Mik's *Ferd'nand* was likewise pantomime humor. In contrast, Art Sansom's *Born Loser* uses words as well as pictures. It is usually a highly inferential strip: the sense of the words and the point of the joke often depend entirely upon the reader's grasping perfectly the implications of the pictures. At the other extreme, *B.C.* after its

first few years offered witticisms almost exclusively verbal. And two humor entries of 1976, *Henny* and *Inside Woody Allen*, marketed the wit of the standup comedians Henny Youngman and Woody Allen, men whose humor is conspicuously verbal (figures 3 and 4). How can such strips be examples of the art of the comic strip when they are based primarily on words rather than being visual-verbal blends? They can't. Clearly neither of these strips is a good representative of comic strip art however humorous it may otherwise be.

By way of keeping this train of thought on the track to its next destination, we might say that the visual-verbal blend principle is the first principle of a critical theory of comic strips. It is first for two reasons. It is first in importance: it derives directly from the very nature of the art. But it is first also because it is the first step in the process of evaluation, a process that involves making a successive series of "allowances" by which the principle of the visual-verbal blend is modified to accommodate special categories of comic strips. Many comic strips (those that tell continuing stories, particularly) cannot consistently meet the

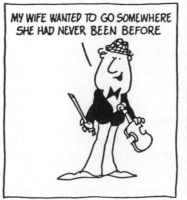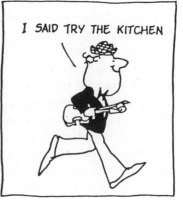

Figure 4. Henny *(drawn by Art Cumings) is almost always entirely verbal humor.*

visual-verbal blend criterion, and yet many of them are excellent strips. But their excellence derives from other aspects of the art that we have not yet considered but that must be taken into account if we are to avoid rushing to erroneous judgments about the quality of a given strip. To find those other ingredients, let me briefly resume our review of the history of the comic strip.

During the new century's first decade, the comic strip made the transition from the Sunday supplements to the newspaper's daily pages. Editorial and sports cartoonists often used their large daily allotments of space to present short narrative sequences of drawings. George McManus drew a daily version of *The Newlyweds* in the early years of the century, and other cartoonists (Clare Briggs with *A. Piker Clerk*, F. M. Howarth with *Mr. E. Z. Mark*, and Gus Dirks with *Bugville*) sprinkled the daily paper's pages with comic strips at various intervals throughout the week. Then in 1907, as we shall see in chapter 3, Bud Fisher established the comic strip as a daily feature when the popularity of his *A. Mutt* (later *Mutt and Jeff*) assured its regular appearance every day.

For the first twenty years of their history, American comic strips were largely humorous in intent. Then in the 1920s some strips began to do more than tell a joke: they told a story as well. Although such strips as *The Gumps* (1917), *Gasoline Alley* (1918; storytelling from about 1921), and *Barney Google* (1919) usually punctuated their narratives with daily punch lines or humorous conclusions, they were telling stories nonetheless—stories that continued from day to day. With that, the comics developed a second "genre," a subspecies whose purpose was slightly different from that of other comics. Henceforth, a comic strip could be classified according to genre: strips were either gag strips, ending with a punch line each day, or continuity strips, sometimes ending with a punch line but always carrying the story forward to the next day.

While the continuity strip emerged in the twenties, such early strips as *Hairbreadth Harry* (1906) and *Desperate Desmond* (1910) began the tradition of continuing stories by means of outrageously suspenseful cliff-hanger endings. These strips sowed the seeds for yet another type of continuity strip: the serious adventure strip. But both *Harry* and *Desmond*, with their heroes' exaggerated predicaments and their unrealistic resolutions, bur-

lesqued the life of adventure rather than taking it seriously. The great potential of the mechanism that these strips contained for building suspense was not fully exploited until the thirties, when "illustrators" invaded the comic pages. In chapters 7 and 8, we'll see how the realistic artwork and stories of such strips as Hal Foster's *Tarzan* (1929), Alex Raymond's *Flash Gordon*, Noel Sickles's *Scorchy Smith*, and Milton Caniff's *Terry and the Pirates* (all 1934) made the suspense keener by making it seem more real.

If these strips dealt in high adventure, other strips told continuing stories that were more concerned with domestic intrigue. Sidney Smith's *The Gumps* and Harold Gray's *Little Orphan Annie* (1924) probably began the tradition, but it found its most realistic expression in such strips as *Mary Worth*, *Rex Morgan, M.D.*, and *Judge Parker*. Thus, we can subdivide the continuity strip according to subject and/or treatment: the humorous continuity (like *Li'l Abner* and *Rick O'Shay*) that tells a comic story or concludes every day with a punch line; the soap opera continuity (*Mary Worth* et al.) that trades in domestic travail or psychological trauma; and the adventure continuity (like *Steve Roper*, *Rip Kirby*, *The Phantom*) that rambles through exotic settings and courts high-risk physical danger.

This abbreviated history suggests the way in which some order can be imposed upon the welter of strips on today's comic pages. The strips can be distinguished by genre and subgenre. And the notion of genre permits us to modify the principle of visual-verbal blend in order to take account properly of the different purposes the various genres serve. Before we examine the implications of generic divisions for evaluation, though, let me point out another lesson implicit in the history of the comics.

In that history, individual strips have acquired their reputations of excellence on the basis of the creator's ability to excel in one or more of several components of the art form: the gag, the suspenseful ending, the story itself, characterization, artwork, or dialogue. The history of the art form is marked by the "great" strips, whose authors brought one or another of the ingredients of the comic strip to a higher point of excellence, or development, than had been achieved up to that time. Hence, for example, in the early thirties the continuity comic strip—which had thus far focused on one of two extremes, exotic adventure or domestic setting—brought the excitement of adventure to the home front when Dick Tracy began fighting contemporary crime in everybody's home town (1931). Suddenly adventure was just outside the front door, not in an airplane high over the Andes. Initially, as we shall see, the reputation of Chester Gould's strip sprang from its exploitation of the criminal violence in everyday life. To this, Gould added accurate reporting of modern police methods and a gallery of ghoulish villains, caricatures of evil that underscored the moral of his strip: crime doesn't pay, and a life of crime will put you in daily communion with such creatures as *these*. The greatness of the strip resides in Gould's dramatic combination of realistic storytelling and graphic moralizing.

Milton Caniff is a giant in the history of the comics because he raised new standards for almost every facet of the continuity adventure strip. Although we'll be examining his achievement in more detail later, let me summarize it here for the sake of our present discussion. With Noel Sickles at his elbow during the early years of *Terry and the Pirates*, Caniff developed an impressionistic style of drawing that suggested realism economically, using shadow rather than painstakingly rendered detail. He enriched the fabric of the adventure story formula by weaving into an action-packed plot the threads of character development. And he polished the prose of his dialogues to a brilliant sheen of sophisticated patter. Once the Caniff years were fairly underway in the mid-thirties, every other realistic continuity strip was measured against the standards he set.

Ultimately, then, we must look to the history of comic strips for many of the criteria for critical evaluation. But on today's comic pages we can find much of that history in individual strips of various kinds, each of which reproduces—as an inheritance, as a "tradition"—various high points in the art form's history. The first to reach those pinnacles of achievement are the models in whose image today's strips are fashioned. With the history of the comics at our elbow, we can construct "family trees," tracing the lineage of a particular tradition back to its origins. The soap opera in Alex Kotsky's *Apartment 3-G* is in the tradition of *Mary Worth* and *Little Orphan Annie*; these strips in turn owe something to *The Gumps* and something to *Desperate Desmond*. And, at the same

time, Kotsky's artwork continues the standards set by illustrators. *Steve Roper* and similar "crime fighting" strips continue the tradition begun by Gould in *Dick Tracy*, and *Tracy* goes back through *Wash Tubbs* to *Desperate Desmond*. In artistic treatment, *Roper* belongs, with some qualifications, in the Caniff school. In this manner, we may arrive at a verdict of excellence as much by measuring the author-artist's ability to meet—if, indeed, he does not surpass—the standards of the tradition in which he works as by evaluating his individual combination of the ingredients that make a comic strip.

To earn the highest accolades, however, a comic strip must not only meet the standards of an established tradition, it must expand that tradition, or even create a new one. On the same page of comics, alongside the strips that continue one tradition of excellence, are strips that inaugurate new ones, employing techniques that add new dimensions to the art. Thus, the form and its aesthetic are in a state of constant creative change and development. To some extent, we must judge the new achievements by the older standards of the appropriate tradition. Conversely, we do the old standard-bearers an injustice if we judge them too harshly by the measure of emerging techniques that are creating new traditions and new standards by pushing various aspects of an overall principle to greater heights. *Mutt and Jeff* of the 1970s, for instance, falls short of the subtle anachronistic humor of *B.C.* But *B.C.* must follow the pattern set by *Mutt and Jeff*, and one measure of its achievement will be a concluding punch line day after day. The artwork in *Dick Tracy* may not meet the standard of fidelity to nature that is maintained in *Kerry Drake*, but Gould started before illustrators had completely taken over the continuity strip, establishing that pictorial standard. *Kerry Drake*, meanwhile, must tell stories that seem to be about real people facing real crises in realistic ways in order to uphold the standard set by *Dick Tracy*.

Just as familiarity with the history of the comics prevents unfair comparisons between strips belonging to different periods, so does the concept of genre prohibit comparisons between strips serving different purposes. *Dondi* and *Peanuts* are both about children, but *Dondi* is a continuity strip, seeking in its soap opera tales and realistic rendering an illusion of real life. *Dondi* can be faulted when it falls short of achieving that illusion; *Peanuts* cannot. We can look for visual-verbal blend in both strips, but if *Dondi* fails to achieve it as consistently as *Peanuts*, there may be good reasons for that failure—reasons peculiar to the continuity genre.

Storytelling strips shoulder a burden that gag strips handily avoid: plot development often requires considerable exposition, and scenes of exposition tend to be "talky." Characters are forced into relatively inactive sequences of conversation in which the sense of the words is dependent upon the pictures only insofar as the pictures identify the speakers and establish the scene. In these cases, pictures contribute to the meaning of a strip, but the sense of the words is not dependent upon the pictures as it is in a strip in which a thorough visual-verbal blend occurs. To apply rigidly the principle of visual-verbal blending under these circumstances would invariably condemn the continuity strip as inferior. Yet the principle need not be abandoned.

Despite whatever allowance must be granted to the continuity strip for accommodating the necessities of plot development, critical theory must be on guard against the genre's natural tendency toward talkiness—a tendency that threatens the integrity of a comic strip by making it proportionately less visual and more verbal. In a visual-verbal narrative whose essence suggests that neither words nor pictures are quite satisfactory alone, excessive verbiage tends to destroy the delicate balance of word and picture. Cartoonists are quite aware of the danger, and the best of them seek to restore that balance by using a variety of visual effects to offset wordy scenes. Here the terms of cinematography are useful. To avoid a parade of monotonous panels in which two or more characters are pictured (from

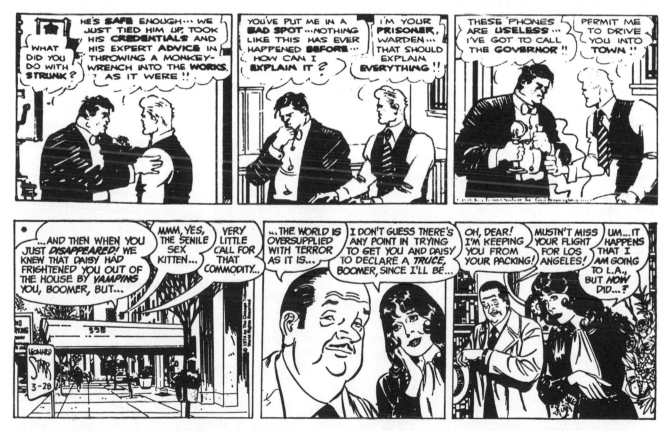

Figure 5. *To illustrate how far today's cartoonists have come in developing ways to vary the visual impact of their strips, compare expository scenes in Will Gould's* Red Barry *of 1935 (June 15) with a similar kind of scene in Leonard Starr's 1974* On Stage *(March 28). This* Barry *strip is by no means unusual: Red may stand around for panel after panel, viewed from the waist up, talking to someone for days. Mary Perkins may also engage in endless conversation, but as she does, the camera moves around—outside her apartment (where we "overhear" the conversation), then a close-up (one figure right up to the camera; the other, a little distance off), then a medium-length shot. It's a standard sequence of shots with Starr, but in each individual strip, it achieves visual-verbal balance through graphic variety.*

the waist up) talking to each other, the cartoonist may vary the "camera angle" or the distance of the "camera" from the subjects (figure 5). The objective is to make the strip as visual—that is, as pictorially lively, varied, and intense—as possible in order to balance with visual effects the verbal weight inherent in exposition. While a visual-verbal *blend* of the same order of interdependence as that in our *B.C.* example is not often possible, visual-verbal *balance* is. Moreover, a skillfully employed variety of visual effects can give even the most mundane conversation dramatic impact. A close-up, for instance, adds intensity to the speaker's words.

Some cartoonists achieve graphic variety through sheer stylistic virtuosity. In *Secret Agent Corrigan*, Al Williamson shades his figures extensively in solid blacks, creating dramatic lighting effects. Gus Arriola's *Gordo* often uses its very panels to create eye-catching patterns. And in such strips as John Prentice's *Rip Kirby*, Sansom's *Born Loser*, and Bud Blake's *Tiger*, solid black areas are spotted strategically to heighten black-and-white contrast.

Taking account of such graphic effects permits us to temper the visual-verbal blend principle in ways appropriate to the purpose of the continuity strip. But we must still be wary of continuity strips whose verbiage elbows the pictures out of the panels. And in these days of artist-writer teams, the chances of seeing verbal excesses are greater than they once were, when comic strips were produced by cartoonists alone—persons who, by definition, created simultaneously in visual-verbal terms. The writer half of the team is, after

all, a creature of words, and the temptation to write more words than are necessary for the medium is doubtless great. The tendency is conspicuously illustrated whenever we find words telling us what the picture is depicting—a kind of verbal-graphic double exposure (figure 6).

We may be tempted to evaluate continuity strips in purely literary terms because the narrative element is so pronounced in this genre. But, as I said earlier, while literary analysis contributes to an understanding of a strip, to employ this method exclusively ignores the essential character of the medium by overlooking its visual elements. The medium is better served by criticism that considers the ways in which the graphics and the story are interrelated.

Although the creative processes of the cartoonist weave the visual elements into whole cloth in which each thread's significance is bound together with all the others, we can unravel at least four distinct graphic threads useful for analysis: narrative breakdown, layout, panel composition, and style. A cartoonist is not likely to think of any of these aspects of his work as wholly separable from the others, but he probably follows a procedure in which each is associated with an individual operation. He doubtless begins with narrative breakdown, dividing his story into narrative units (into daily strips and then into panels); next he positions panels in relation to each other, allotting to each a tentative size and shape (layout); then he decides the arrangement within each panel of its various graphic elements (composition); and finally, he draws—and his style, the highly individual

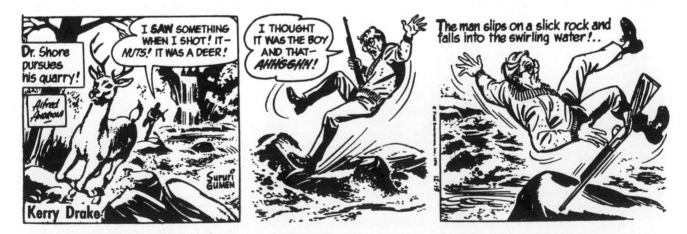

Figure 6. *In the last panel of this* Kerry Drake *strip, the words are superfluous: they tell us exactly what the picture shows us.*

and therefore characteristic way he uses pen and brush, emerges. These visual aspects of a comic strip are so integrated that any extended discussion of one of them is sure to lead to talk of the others, but such a brief consideration as I attempt here can effectively isolate each of them enough to show how they may bear upon storytelling.

In continuity strips, narrative breakdown aims first at reducing a story to intelligible daily installments. Each installment must begin with subtle reminders of the previous action and must advance the story in the next two or three panels. The installment format imposes certain restrictions: the quantity of story delivered each day is limited by the amount of space available for dialogue and picture. But there are accompanying advantages. Storytelling by installment inherently builds suspense, a vital ingredient of the continuity strip; indeed, suspense is the mechanical and emotional heart of the genre. But for many cartoonists, the inherent suspense of the serial mode of presentation is not good enough. The dedicated (not to say diabolical) craftsman seeks to enhance the suspense naturally accruing to each daily installment by working deliberately toward each day's concluding panel, creating in that last panel a springboard of suspense to carry the story to the next day. Frank Robbins's fast-paced *Johnny Hazard*, for instance, frequently ends each day on a distinct note of suspense. And there are yet other ways of judging the effectiveness of narrative breakdown.

According to one critic, cartoonists doing strips at the turn of the century "found that their task was basically the same as that of early film-makers— that is, to render a motion in sequence."[4] (In the same vein, the critic notes that some so-called cinematic techniques were developed by cartoonists before they were used by filmmakers.) Although narrative breakdown reduces all action to discrete static moments, it can be evaluated by the extent to which a smooth sequential progression is achieved. The progression embraces both visual impact and story. By the 1940s the conventions of the art form were sufficiently refined that most comic strips since then can seldom be faulted in this respect. But older strips sometimes offer examples of flawed breakdown—like the early sequences of *The Lone Ranger*.

To translate their 1933 radio cowboy creation into graphic terms, George Trendle and Fran

Striker recruited Ed Kressy from the Associated Press bull pen, where he was serving as a general illustrator. Kressy's rendering of the old West, while adequate in most respects, is glaringly incompetent in others. In the first daily strip, on September 12, 1938, for instance, he showed his hero mounting Silver from the wrong side. And Kressy insisted on putting eyeballs in the eyeholes of the Lone Ranger's mask with the result that the Lone Ranger looks pop-eyed, the expression on his face a constant grimace of wide-eyed astonishment. (Charles Flanders, who took over the strip from Kressy on January 30, 1939, learned from this mistake, and his Lone Ranger never has eyeballs unless in extreme close-up, a pose that permits the realistic rendering of eyelids and all, thus precluding the pop-eyed appearance.)

But Kressy's most serious failing as a newspaper strip cartoonist was his inability to grasp how a daily strip functioned. Instead of seeing the panels in the strip as immediately successive moments of time, Kressy treated each panel as an isolated illustration, some of which might be separated from their predecessor by the passage of as much as twenty or thirty minutes. Many cartoonists do the same, but they always signal the lapse of more than a moment of time with a caption that says, "Soon—," or "Sometime later—," or some such verbal device. Kressy gave his readers no such signals. And the results were often laughable: for example, in one panel the Lone Ranger is armed with a rifle; in the next panel, he no longer has the rifle but holds a brace of pistols instead. Kressy's explanation was that twenty minutes had elapsed between the panels, and during that time the Lone Ranger returned to his horse and sheathed the rifle. Then, when he returned to confront the captured crooks, he decided he needed to be armed again and resorted to his holstered six-guns.[5]

One effect of this attitude on Kressy's narrative is that the story seems to leapfrog key moments: we encounter the Lone Ranger popping up wholly unannounced or unanticipated, his presence explained verbally rather than visually—a lame storytelling device in an essentially visual medium. In the strip at hand (figure 7), the action vaults from the second panel to the third panel: Tonto appears at the doorway of the stagecoach office and then, in the next instant, materializes at the side of the Lone Ranger. Kressy doesn't deign to show

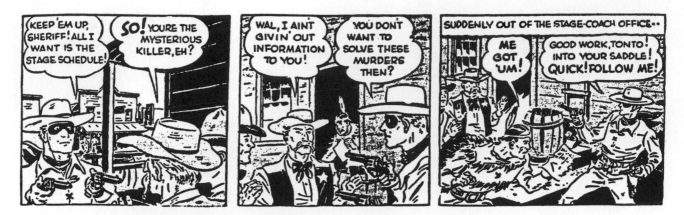

Figure 7. *Kressy's* Lone Ranger *is a trifle pop-eyed, and his breakdowns often carry the action forward in leaps and bounds, sometimes leaving out key bits of information. Here (September 20, 1938), Tonto seems magically transported from the doorway of the stagecoach office to the Lone Ranger's side.*

us Tonto's actual movement from one place to the other. But he must have realized that the Indian's figure in the doorway in the second panel wasn't vivid enough to prepare the reader for his appearance in the third panel: he wedges in a caption to make sure we understand the action. A more dramatic way of handling this turn of events might be to end the day's installment by closing in on Tonto in the doorway, showing him holding the schedule aloft and saying, "Me got 'um." But Kressy, whose understanding of the sequential nature of the medium was apparently somewhat primitive, doubtless saw no flaw in his rendering of the action.

Narrative breakdown can be translated into a kind of script—a script that has visual elements as well as verbal ones. The number of words that can be crowded into each day's speech balloons dictates the outer limits of one installment's breakdown, but this mechanical restraint is often modified for reasons arising from the story. For example, a picture is more effective for setting the scene or establishing mood, so sometimes one day's allotment of words is spread over two days to permit more pictorial display in one of the installments. In consideration of matters like this, we approach layout and composition.

The narrative breakdown of a continuity strip can be evaluated by examining the extent to which the story is delivered in intelligible daily installments that exploit and develop the suspense inherent in the serial format and by determining whether the sequential progression within each daily unit is as continuous a depiction of action or event as is possible. But narrative breakdown can

be even more fruitfully considered by evaluating the degree to which it controls the duration and focus of our attention. The succession of panels in a strip is the mechanism by which timing is achieved, and carefully controlled timing enhances the drama of every event. In gag strips, timing may be the very essence of the humor. For instance, in Sansom's *Born Loser* strip reproduced here (figure 8), it is the lapse of time indicated by the second panel that establishes Brutus Thornapple as slow-witted, a personality trait that adds another dimension to the strip's punch line.

Before considering another example, let me touch briefly upon the remaining elements of a strip's visual character. About two of these—layout and graphic style—we can say little of direct value for critical analysis. Most questions of layout for newspaper strips are determined by the restricted format. There is little room for the kind of experimentation and flexibility in size and arrangement of panels that we find on the pages of comic books. Layout in newspaper strips is, for the cartoonist, largely a matter of deciding how wide each panel should be—and that, in many instances, is dictated by narrative breakdown. Graphic style is to the visual character of a comic strip what diction is to language: each is so peculiarly distinct to every practitioner that the relation it may have to such external matters as story is very subtle. A cartoonist's graphic style is distinctly his own, his mark on his work. Although there are several "schools" of realistic drawing, there are as many styles within each school as there are cartoonists. We can describe a cartoonist's style, and we may

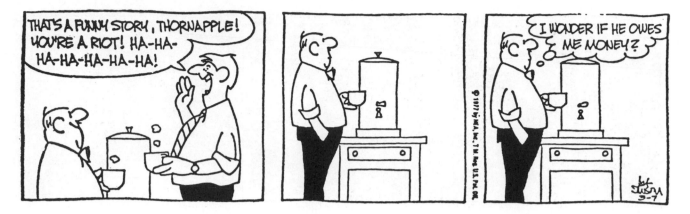

Figure 8. *In this example from Art Sansom's* Born Loser *(March 7, 1977), the timing of the strip creates the comedy.*

then determine whether his style is appropriate to his subject. Beyond that, however, evaluation based upon style becomes largely a matter of personal taste. The visual element of composition is more amenable to analysis and evaluation.

By *composition* I mean chiefly the choice and arrangement of the various visual elements within each panel of a strip. The composition of each panel can be evaluated singly, panel by panel, or in the context of that day's entire strip—the arrangement of elements in one panel being influenced by the content of panels coming before and after it. The first measure of effective composition is the standard of clarity. In one sense clarity has a purely technical reference: what is drawn must be drawn clearly enough for us to tell very quickly what it is. But clarity in another sense implies a broader objective: it has to do with choosing and arranging the elements of a panel in such a way as to clearly depict their function in advancing the story.

Some of the language of filmmaking is again admirably suited to discussing the question of what should be depicted within a panel. For the moviemaker, the question is shaped in terms of distance from the camera: a close-up focuses on one person, and mostly on that person's face; a medium shot gives us two or more people, perhaps from head to waist, and a little of the surrounding scene; a long shot includes people at full length and a good deal of the surrounding setting. The cartoonist selects, and the critic evaluates, the "camera's" distance with much the same objective in mind: each panel should frame only the minimum essentials of a scene—those elements necessary for maximum storytelling effectiveness. Maximum effectiveness may require a long shot to "set the scene," to

show the physical situation in which the characters find themselves; the first panel of a day's strip is often a long shot. A close-up, on the other hand, heightens the intensity of what a character says or thinks, serving thereby to enhance the drama of the events. The variety of distances between these two extremes may serve the story in equally various ways—or, in some instances, variation in distance and angle may aim simply at creating visual variety. Actually, as comic strips became smaller and smaller in the years following World War II, many of these considerations no longer applied— particularly with continuity strips. Such story strips as survived into the 1980s are, visually, all talking heads: there is no room for depicting much more. But in older continuity strips, artistic concerns still obtain: in these strips, the visuals serve the stories in dramatic and visually exciting ways that became impossible in the last decades of the century.

Most compositions in the graphic arts have what I call a "center of focus"—a place to which the arrangement of the elements of the composition forces our attention. This focal point is not necessarily the geometric center of the composition although in one of the world's most celebrated examples of this principle in action, Da Vinci's *Last Supper*, it is the center of the picture to which the artist directs our attention. In this case, however, the artist achieves his objective by making lines of perspective converge at the picture's center, not simply by locating the figure of Christ in the middle of his composition. Other graphic devices can similarly attract our gaze. In black and white drawings, for instance, solid blacks leap out at the viewer ahead of other elements in the pic-

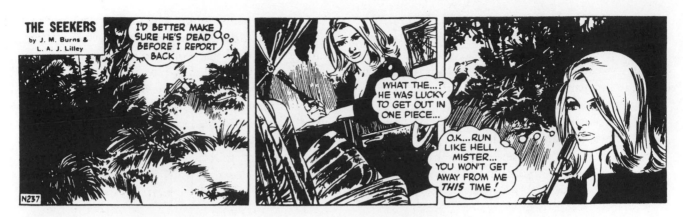

Figure 9. *Because of the composition of the last panel in this strip, we may not notice the fleeing figure in the distance.*

ture; conversely, vast areas of white can attract attention, too. And sometimes ingeniously contrived shapes can frame and thereby focus attention on selected objects in the picture. In comic strips, all such maneuvers serve a narrative purpose.

In the most effective comic strip panel composition, our attention should be focused on whatever element in that panel contributes most to the telling of the story. That place in a panel I call "the graphic center of narrative focus"—*graphic center* emphasizing the visual nature of the medium, *narrative focus* embracing the storytelling function of comic strip art. Since most cartoonists instinctively compose panels that satisfy this criterion most of the time, the concept is useful only in describing the occasional composition that, for one reason or another, fails to meet the requirement. For example, the composition of a particular panel may be influenced by the necessity for arranging speech balloons in "reading order," or by the cartoonist's felt need for varying the camera angle, or by a preference for drawing faces instead of bodies.

In satisfying one of these needs, the cartoonist may commit a blunder in composition. A British strip called *The Seekers* provides us with an example of such a panel (figure 9). The key narrative element in the last panel is the figure of a running man, but he appears in the background, a minuscule figure seen over the shoulder of the heroine. Although the positioning of speech balloons next to the running figure would seem to ensure that we not overlook it, the close-up of the woman misdirects our attention. The close-up draws attention to itself, for one thing. Moreover, the direction of the woman's glance is not clear: is she looking at the fleeing man or at the muzzle of the gun she holds? Showing the woman in profile would have removed the confusion. As it is, however, the close-up of the woman from the front flaws the composition by blurring its graphic center of narrative focus.

By way of summarizing and exemplifying the way in which a comic strip can be evaluated in terms of its visual elements, let me turn to one of

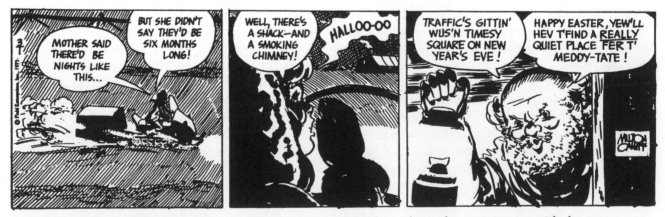

Figure 10. *Milton Caniff's* Steve Canyon *for March 1, 1975, is timed to achieve dramatic impact with the reappearance in the strip after many years of Happy Easter, once Steve's constant sidekick.*

Milton Caniff's *Steve Canyon* dailies (figure 10). As in any skillfully staged strip, narrative breakdown here times the action: the objective in this case is to delay the appearance of Happy Easter until the last panel. And the composition of the final panel enhances the dramatic effects of timing. Happy Easter could have been drawn standing, full-length, in a doorway, silhouetted against the bright interior of his shack. Instead, the camera moves in quickly, forcing our sudden recognition of him. The closeness and the suddenness combine to produce a sort of shock effect that gives this panel (and this strip) its dramatic impact. The composition of the first panel serves chiefly to set the scene, and having used a long shot here, Caniff probably wanted to avoid a second long shot in the next panel. But some kind of distance is clearly required: the narrative purpose of the second panel is to introduce the shack on the horizon, preparing the way for the concluding panel. Caniff's solution is to close in on Pipeline Polly, a close-up profile that frames the shack, forcing our attention to it. Moreover, Polly is looking in the same direction, and heavy shading and absence of detail on Polly ensure that we will not be distracted from noticing the shack. Still, Caniff must have felt uneasy about the effectiveness of his composition: Polly's words repeat the scene before us, and with that Caniff sacrifices visual-verbal blend.

Although the strip as a whole is effective in accomplishing its major purpose (the surprising reappearance of Happy Easter, absent from the strip for several years), the weakness of the second panel cannot be overlooked. This sequence might have been improved had the narrative breakdown divided the action into four panels instead of three. Panel two might then have moved in on Polly with a medium shot (for graphic variety) as she sees the shack, saying, "What's this? A glimmer in the dark." For a new panel three, the camera could have backed way off again for a long shot (Polly closest to the camera, back toward us, looking at the shack and saying, "Hallooo") before moving on to panel four, the present concluding panel. This solution would avoid the verbal-visual double-exposure of the existing panel two, but it would require extremely cramped, tiny drawings in the first three panels and the suggestion of the sweeping expanse of snowy night in panel one might well be lost. An alternative solution might be to use only three panels but to open with a medium shot of

Polly on her snowmobile, shifting in panel two to a long shot. Although the traditional scene-setting function of panel one would be forfeit, panel two could be larger—and might, by its very size and sequence, serve to establish the scene.

Caniff may have considered alternatives like these, but he discarded them in favor of a three-panel formula that he often used: an "establishing" long shot, followed by two panels that move increasingly closer, to finish with a close-up. The formula is dramatically effective because the concluding close-up gives punch-line impact to the words of the last speaker in the strip. Certainly the strategy works here, and even if the master's formula can be faulted in this strip for creating a verbal-visual double exposure in the second panel, that panel can still be seen as artfully composed for its narrative purpose.

Visual-verbal blending is not all there is to the art of the comic strip, as I've said. The notion, however, stresses both the visual and the verbal nature of the medium, and any examination of the art form must consider both if we are to achieve the kind of analytical perception that is not only appreciative but articulate, not only evaluative but appropriate. To look for a visual-verbal blend, then, is to perform a mental trick of perception by which we focus our attention on the visual character of the medium as well as its verbal content. But there's more to understanding the comics than simply appreciating and evaluating visual-verbal artistry.

The kind of analysis I've essayed thus far makes no attempt to examine or explain what makes a certain strip so peculiarly appealing to its readers. The success of a strip may arise from such things as the exotic and mysterious personality of Caniff's Dragon Lady in *Terry and the Pirates*, the indomitable innocence (or is it ignorance?) of Elzie Segar's Popeye, the brittle anachronistic wit of Hart's B.C. and company, the commanding illusion of reality of the art in Alex Raymond's *Flash Gordon*, or the masterful blend of vaudeville, allegory, satire, and caricature in Walt Kelly's *Pogo*. A thoroughgoing analysis of the medium must consider these aspects of a cartoonist's work. And we will shortly do just that with a selection of strips acknowledged as landmarks in the art form. But while the niche that such strips occupy in the history of the medium depends in part upon considerations like the ones I've just suggested, many of the greatest cartoonists achieved their stature because they expanded or exploited the visual-verbal nature of their medium.

Every comic strip artist to ply a pen since the first decade of this century has cast the product of his labors in the mold formed by such men as Dirks, Opper, and Fisher. But each pen drew a slightly different line to a slightly different purpose from a highly individualistic perspective, and the form itself was flexible enough to permit significant innovations through the years. In the remaining chapters of this book, we'll take a look at the achievements of some of the cartoonists whose work shaped the medium. Each of these strips is a milestone in the history and development of the form. Some of them extended the traditions in which they worked; others created new traditions. Still others rank in the pantheon of the history of cartooning because they are unique demonstrations of the capacities of the art form. As we pass by these milestones, we'll pause occasionally to remark upon a cartoonist's use of the visual to enhance the verbal (or vice versa), but we'll also be examining each work as a whole to discover each cartoonist's distinctive contribution to the form.

CHAPTER 2
Somnambulist of a Vanished Dream
Winsor McCay's Exploration of the Medium's Potential

Winsor McCay was the first original genius of the comic strip medium. Ditto for the medium of animated cartoons. No question. He did things in both media that no one had done before. There is a fine irony in the towering stature of his genius. He had no equals; he therefore had no imitators. And no legacy.

Much of what he achieved was simply lost: like a rocket exploding brilliantly in the midnight sky, his work illuminated a medium he worked in for a breathtaking instant and then faded into virtual oblivion as, one by one, the scintillating spangles of his achievements winked out, leaving his colleagues as much in the dark as before. He was so far ahead of his time that many of his innovations were beyond the abilities of his contemporaries: what he had discovered and demonstrated about the capacities of each medium had to be rediscovered decades later by the next generation of cartoonists.

McCay's masterpiece in the comic strip field is *Little Nemo in Slumberland*. Every Sunday the cartoonist took us into Nemo's dreams, where the young boy had fantastic adventures that ended, every week, with his startled awakening safe in his own bed. In this creation, McCay's genius, his originality, is revealed at its peak. From the very first of the Sunday pages, he was a master of the comic strip form. *Nemo* began on October 15, 1905, and by the next week, McCay was deploying the resources of the medium in an unconventional way for dramatic effect: Nemo dreams he is in a forest of giant mushrooms, and as he wanders into the forest, the panels expand vertically, emphasizing by their elongation the lofty height of the mushrooms. At exactly that point, McCay had freed himself from the inhibiting confines of the regularly rectangular grid of comic strip panels that usually prevailed on the pages of the Sunday funnies. From then on, he varied the shape and size of his panels to fit the demands of his story, using large two-tier panels (for instance) to depict the more imposing vistas of the dreamland into which Nemo wanders every week or to show an elephant or a dragon at its proper size in relation to Nemo and his friends.

McCay's use of layout and page design to give dramatic emphasis to his narrative was unusual on the comics pages of the day. Indeed, other cartoonists would not exploit this aspect of the medium with equal effect until years later. In 1916, as we shall see, George Herriman would begin to play with design on the Sunday page of *Krazy Kat*, but his strip was not widely circulated and was not therefore much admired at the time. It wasn't until the thirties that such cartoonists as Roy Crane

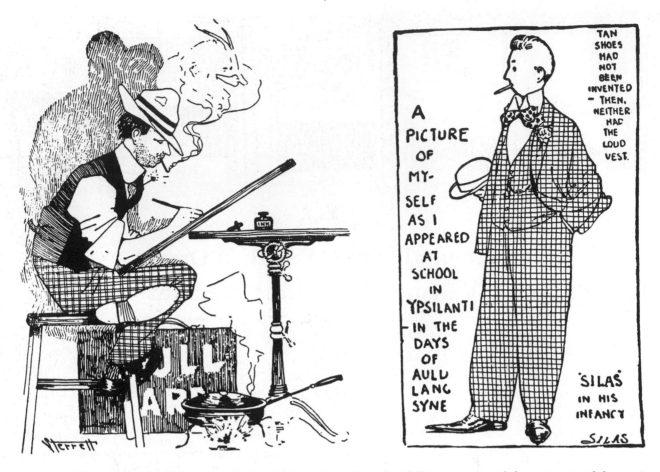

The text inside the right image reads:

TAN SHOES HAD NOT BEEN INVENTED — THEN, NEITHER HAD THE LOUD VEST.

A PICTURE OF MY-SELF AS I APPEARED AT SCHOOL IN YPSILANTI — IN THE DAYS OF AULD LANG SYNE

SILAS IN HIS INFANCY

SILAS

Figure 11. *The caricature of McCay at his drawing board was done by Cliff Sterrett, one of the cartooning laborers in the Hearst vineyards. McCay drew the nattily-attired version of himself; "Silas" was his pen name while at the* New York Herald *(c. 1907).*

in his *Captain Easy* page, Frank King in *Gasoline Alley*, and Hal Foster in *Prince Valiant* continued on Sundays the kind of visual experimentation that McCay had conducted over a quarter of a century before.

McCay was also acutely aware of the sequential art's inherent propensity for timing the action of a narrative, and he capitalized on that capacity of the medium. Sometimes he emphasized the progression of events through his panel compositions and page layouts. He might use nearly identical compositions for several panels running, varying the visuals by changing only his characters' poses slightly from panel to panel in order to indicate the key developments in an emerging fiasco, say; or he might indicate the pace of events with a series of panels all exactly the same size and shape.

And everywhere—McCay's spectacular draftsmanship. He was a master of perspective and architectural rendering, the more complex (apparently) the better. Nemo's dreamland seems filled with palatial mansions in whose vast and intricate

interiors Nemo and his cohorts luxuriate and cavort. McCay obviously loved to draw: only a person who loves to draw would have taken the time to fill up pictures with so populous a pageantry— so many people and creatures and structures, all drawn with meticulous attention to the tiniest details.

And he directed the coloring of his pages with similar precision, annotating his artwork with careful instructions to the engravers about which colors to use. As a result of McCay's instinct for color and his attention to the engravers' task, the colors of each week's *Little Nemo* evoke the mood of that Sunday's adventure, complementing both setting and action. Sometimes the colors are brilliant primaries, and the page is a riot of multihued activity; sometimes the colors are muted, pastels of the same hues—white, blue, and purple in the ice caverns of Jack Frost, for instance.

And all this—layout, design, dramatic timing, characters and settings rendered with painstaking realism, subtle coloring—worked in concert to cre-

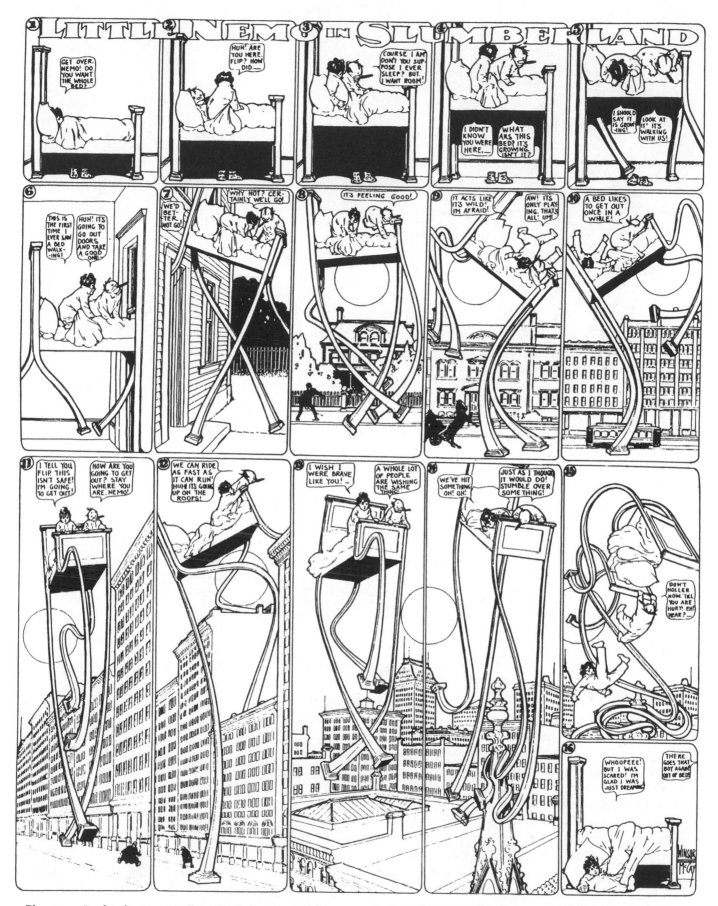

Figure 12. *In this famous "walking bed" sequence (July 26, 1908), the progressively elongated panels emphasize the height to which the bed's legs grow throughout the strip—and hence accentuate the altitude of Nemo and Flip's perch.*

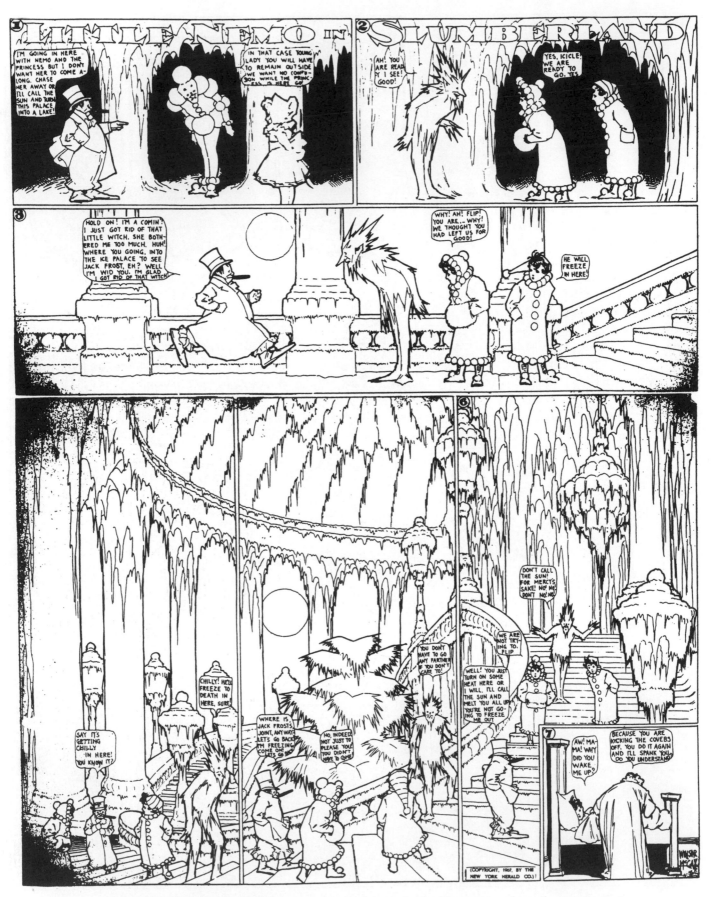

Figure 13. *McCay gives Jack Frost's ice palace grandeur and scope in the bottom tier of panels. A panoramic sequence, each panel gives us a portion of the same scene as the characters move through it; together, the three panels show us the entire cavern, and their greater than usual height stresses the height of the cavern's ceiling (January 27, 1907).*

ate the fantasy world of the little boy's dreams and to give that world a palpable reality. With his consummate artistry, McCay had indeed created a world. His *Little Nemo* of 1905 to 1911 would not be surpassed for sheer pictorial grandeur until Foster created medieval England for Prince Valiant and Arthur's knights of the Round Table in the late 1930s. But Foster's world purported to be real. McCay's was deliberately fanciful—a dream world filled with wonderful scenes marvelously detailed, a parade of foreboding creatures and fascinating artifacts that changed their shapes before our very eyes, of joyful celebrations and nightmarish terrors.

McCay's interest in the visual phenomenon that so enriched *Little Nemo*—metamorphosis, for instance, and action depicted sequentially in virtually slow-motion detail—had surfaced earlier in his career. He had been approaching Nemo's dreamworld for months before he began to delineate it. McCay came to New York in the fall of 1903 from Cincinnati, where he had drawn promotional posters and advertisements for a museum of oddities for nine years before joining the art staff

of the *Cincinnati Enquirer* in 1900. He left Cincinnati to work for the *New York Herald*. It was here that he would do his greatest work.[1]

On July 24, 1904, McCay began a series of weekly strips called *Little Sammy Sneeze*. The concept was simple but amusing: every week, Sammy sneezes. And when he sneezes, he sneezes with such ferocity that the immediate surroundings are nearly destroyed, the proximate population blown off its feet, and all adjacent equipage overturned. Every week, Sammy would start his sneeze in the first of six or eight panels, and for the next three or four panels, he would gasp ("Ah—ah—ah—ah—ah—") before ejecting his rhinal typhoon ("Chow!") in the penultimate panel. In the last panel, one of those whose lives he has so violently disrupted usually boots him off the premises. Once he sneezes while watching two men play chess; his sneeze knocks the chess pieces off the board. Another time, he sneezes while watching a couple of blacksmiths shoe horses; his sneeze knocks the horses down—and the smithy's shop, too. And then there was the time when McCay drew him all alone, and his sneeze dismantles the panel's borders.

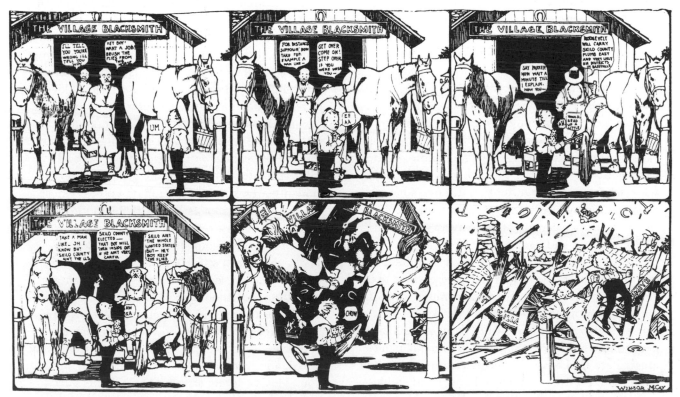

Figure 14. *Sammy sneezes—and destroys his immediate surroundings. The feature reveals McCay's fascination with the capacity of a comic strip to depict events in timed sequence: Sammy's gasping through the first four panels is the "clock" that times events, and as the boy struggles with the on-rushing sneeze, McCay shows the simultaneous actions of the two men in the background going about their business.*

The fascination of the strip—apart from discovering what would be demolished by its explosive denouement—lies with the subtle changes McCay depicted in the scene from panel to panel. The background stays the same as Sammy works up to his catastrophic sneeze, but McCay displayed his understanding of the sequential nature of the medium by running Sammy's face through changes of expression while portraying some parallel action among the accompanying adults, who conduct themselves in complete obliviousness to the disaster building under their very noses.

A few months later, on September 10, McCay launched *Dream of the Rarebit Fiend*, a feature almost as celebrated today as *Nemo*. Here the cartoonist engaged in another kind of playfulness with his medium. In each installment of the strip, its protagonist (a different person every week) is depicted in the throes of a nightmare brought on by eating Welsh rarebit just before going to bed. In the last panel, the dreaming victim awakens, vowing never again to partake of rarebit before retiring. In one strip, a father gives his infant son a teddy bear; the bear becomes real—first a cub, then an adult—whereupon the creature eats the infant and turns on the parents! In another, a man's big toe swells up until it is the size of a small sofa. In yet another, a baby playing with blocks knocks over a stack of them—which, in turn, knocks over a wastebasket and a broom that upset a table, then a chair; by the time the sequence is completed, a painter has been catapulted out of an upper-story window to collide with a safe suspended outside, causing the safe to swing into the building's side, destroying the building. Then there's the woman who, when visiting her dentist, discovers her mouth growing larger and larger until it becomes a cavern with her dentist picking away inside with sledgehammer and bar like a coal miner.

In these strips, McCay continued to indulge his fascination with the sequential progressions that comic strips seemed to encourage, metamorphosis being just another way of showing such a progression. He also showed an intuitive awareness of the psychology of dreams. Some of his rarebit fiend's dreams are frighteningly authentic: one dreams of being buried alive; another of being nearly suffocated by birds building nests in his mouth and nose.

McCay started two more strips for the *Herald* in the next year—*Hungry Henrietta* (January 8, 1905), which traced the growth, week by week, of a girl who eats her way into maturity; and *A Pilgrim's Progress by Mister Bunion* (June 26, 1905), in which the protagonist tries vainly to get rid of his suitcase labeled "Dull Care." Once again in these strips, McCay indulges his interest in sequence and progression and in nightmarish obsession. By the time *Little Nemo* began in the fall of 1905, McCay had toyed with the nature of his art form long enough. He now knew a good deal about the potential of the medium. He was ready to create his masterpiece and to sustain it for the next five-and-a-half years (until it ceased on July 23, 1911).

The first *Nemo* Sunday page establishes the theme for the next few months of the strip: Morpheus, king of Slumberland, has requested "the presence of Little Nemo," and he sends one of his minions to bring Nemo to his kingdom. Unhappily, Nemo has an accident en route and wakes up before he gets to his destination. This is the pattern that would be repeated until Nemo finally arrives at the palace six months later. On this first attempt to reach Morpheus's kingdom, Nemo is told to ride a pony named Somnus, who will take him to Slumberland safely if he is good to the animal. But Nemo is tempted into racing with various creatures he encounters as he rides across the midnight sky, and before long, Somnus is running out of control and trips. Nemo is unhorsed and falls helplessly through space—until he suddenly awakens. A couple of weeks later, Nemo is given a pair of stilts and told that they will take him to Slumberland. Along the way, the stilts start growing (and the panels on the page get taller and taller). Elevated high above the ground, Nemo is suddenly attacked by affectionate cranes, whose legs are as elongated as his stilts. Nemo loses his balance and falls—out of bed, awake.

As McCay's biographer John Canemaker observes, this was a strip "unlike any comic strip before or since . . . an exhilarating weekly fantasy adventure, a cartoon epic of sustained drama, both visually beautiful and compelling." For McCay, Canemaker goes on, "it represented a major creative leap, far grander in scope, imagination, color, design, and motion experimentation than any previous McCay comic strip (or those of his peers)."[2]

In the first few weeks, the new strip rapidly expanded the capacities of the medium as McCay deployed all the skills and insights he had developed in *Nemo's* predecessors. The strip's panels

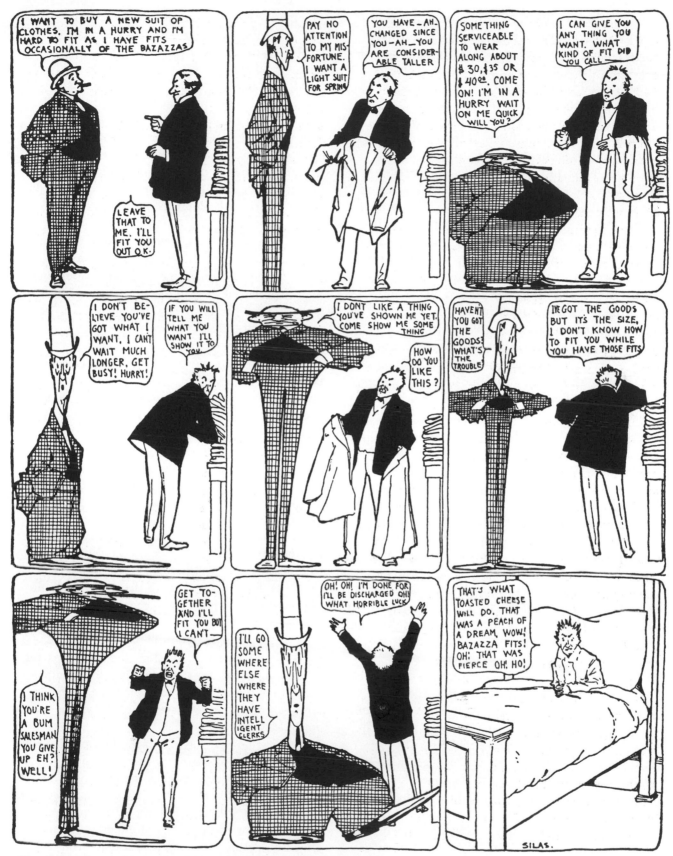

Figure 15. *The rarebit fiend's dreams display McCay's preoccupation with metamorphosis.*

changed size and shape, Nemo's surroundings metamorphosed from panel to panel, strange creatures materialized from week to week, Nemo wandered through palaces awe-inspiring in their glittering splendor and copious detail and met intriguing characters fantastically costumed. And it was all beautifully colored and beautifully printed. According to Canemaker, "*Herald* color printing was at the time superior to that of any other newspaper" in New York.[3] The Sunday funnies therefore presented McCay with the perfect showcase for his skills, and he plumbed the visual potential of the medium as no other cartoonist before him had. About *Nemo*, *Bloom County's* Berke Breathed once said: "To say that I was blown away by the quality of the art would be a shameful understatement. Blown away with the art and blown away with the fact that newspapers once featured artists of such amazing refinement. Probably more than anything else, McCay makes me angry—angry that, if he were working today, there'd be no place on the American comic page for his talent unless one accepts the microscopic space currently allotted to comics as any space at all."[4]

In addition to presenting readers with a sumptuous visual feast, McCay struck deep into their subconscious. As M. Thomas Inge observes in *Comics as Culture*, from the very first McCay skillfully exploited classic universal dream fears—falling through space, being crushed by falling objects, impalement, drowning, and having the earth beneath disintegrate.[5] Not only in incident but in structure, the strip evoked the experience of dreams: Nemo's weekly adventures had a dreamlike pattern—a cycle of anticipation and disappointment or terror and relief. But regardless of the pleasures or dangers he faces in his Slumberland adventures, Nemo always awakens.

Everything about *Little Nemo* attracted and held its readers. It was an unqualified hit. And then McCay began to explore another avenue for the exercise of his talent, one that eventually led to a detour from which he never entirely returned.

In June 1906 McCay took to the stage. In his early career, he had been close to the footlights: the dime museum in Cincinnati had featured stage shows of traveling freaks, a different show each week (for which the young McCay had drawn posters). Now in New York, McCay did what many cartoonists of his generation and the next did: he developed a chalktalk act for the vaudeville stage.

The idea was to entertain the audience with drawings and a line of patter. McCay's act was popular partly because it was a clever display of graphic talent—and partly because he also drew the *Nemo* characters, and they were becoming increasingly known and loved. His vaudeville bookings took him on the road, too—to Baltimore, Philadelphia, Chicago, St. Louis, and so forth. He would be booked for four to six consecutive weeks of shows at various times of the year, and while he was on the circuit, he continued to draw his strips for the *Herald*, working in hotel rooms and in dressing rooms backstage.

Even working amid the impersonality of these itinerant accommodations, separated from the psychic comforts of family and familiar surroundings, McCay produced masterpieces of color and design. On his *Nemo* pages, we can lose ourselves in contemplation of the cartoonist's graphic virtuosity—in the symmetry and balance of his page layouts, in the sweep of his vistas, in his daring perspective, in his command of the nuances of visual narrative, of the manipulative power of pace and scale and repetition, in his marvelously intricate renderings, in the rich fecundity of his imagination. There is so much to look at!

Only one thing blemishes McCay's execution of his vision. It is odd that an artist with his exquisite sense of design should draw such ugly speech balloons. Shapeless, chintzy expectorations of white space they are, so crammed with words (sometimes written sideways up the edges of the balloons) that they seem the tardiest of afterthoughts. Most cartoonists of the time (if not all of them) were no better at speech balloons than McCay; but you'd think a man of his graphic genius would improve upon the prevailing conventions when they so clearly disfigure his otherwise flawless artwork. But the defect is a small imperfection amid a welter of perfections and need not diminish much an appreciation of the visual splendor of McCay's pages.

Little Nemo may have been the first comic strip to have narrative continuity as well as near graphic perfection. Its story carries the reader forward from one installment to the next. For the first four months or so, the story follows a pattern: week after week, King Morpheus of Slumberland sends one of his retinue to bring Nemo to his palace, where he wants the boy to be a playmate for his daughter, the Princess. And week after week,

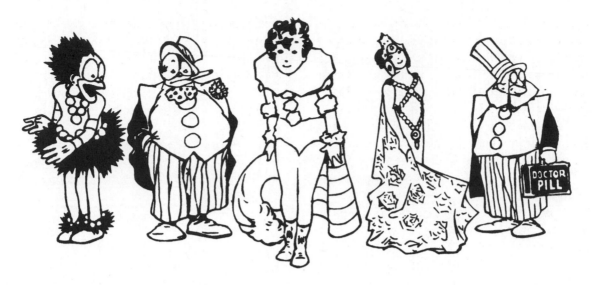

Figure 16. *The cast of* Little Nemo in Slumberland *(left to right): Imp, Flip, Nemo, the Princess, Doctor Pill.*

Nemo frustrates the King's plans by failing to follow the instructions of his guides or by sheer boyish clumsiness. Then, in March 1906, the plot device changes.

On March 4, we meet Flip, a top-hatted, cigar-smoking green-faced mischief maker in baggy striped pants, the brazen outcast member of the Dawn family. Flip wants the Princess of Slumberland for himself and is therefore jealous of the attention paid to Nemo. His role in the story initially is to wake Nemo up, thereby preventing his rendezvous with the Princess. But Flip is clearly too potent a character to waste in this single function. He soon becomes a sort of bumbling sidekick to Nemo, accompanying the boy everywhere and upsetting plans at every instance, whether intentionally or not.

Although every weekly installment ends with Nemo waking up, he doesn't always awaken because some event in his dream jolts him into consciousness. That is frequently the case, of course: Flip sometimes brings the Dawn patrol, whose brilliant lights awaken the youth; and Nemo sometimes awakens if the events of his dream frighten or startle or excite him too much. (In June 1906 another character joins the regular cast: Dr. Pill, who gives Nemo a pill the purpose of which is to keep him asleep even in the face of Flip's machinations.) But sometimes the story that week simply runs out of space, so Nemo wakes up. In any event, with the introduction of Flip, *Nemo* was established as a continuing story strip: every Sunday, the strip takes up its story at the place

that Nemo's awakening last Sunday had interrupted it.

Before McCay reached the end of this first incarnation of Nemo, his young dreamer would become a kind of savior figure in Slumberland. But at first the boy is a visitor in Slumberland—a kind of tourist—and the story line resembles a travelogue with the Princess guiding her guest to the Ocean of Rosewater, to the Carnival, to Santa's house (at Christmas), to the Snow Palace of Jack Frost, and so on. And at each of these tourist attractions, McCay created an engrossing spectacle.

In the spring of 1907 McCay converted his continuity to straight adventure: he sent his cast on a voyage, and while they are visiting the "Candy Islands" (which appear to be African jungle islands), Nemo, Flip, and the Princess are kidnapped by the natives. They eventually escape, and Flip brings a souvenir with him—one of the native kids. Christened "Imp" almost at once, this caricature of a black tribesman is a reincarnation of characters McCay had used before in the *Cincinnati Enquirer.* Imp's function in the plot of *Nemo* is to pester the pesterer, to give Flip much-needed comeuppance. This maneuver further softens the antagonistic edges of Flip's personality: by making him sometimes a victim, McCay makes him more appealing.

Then in November 1907 McCay launched one of the most memorable sequences in the strip. Nemo, Flip, and Imp wander into Befuddle Hall, where all manner of strange things happen to them. Feeling hungry, they begin to lose weight, panel by panel—

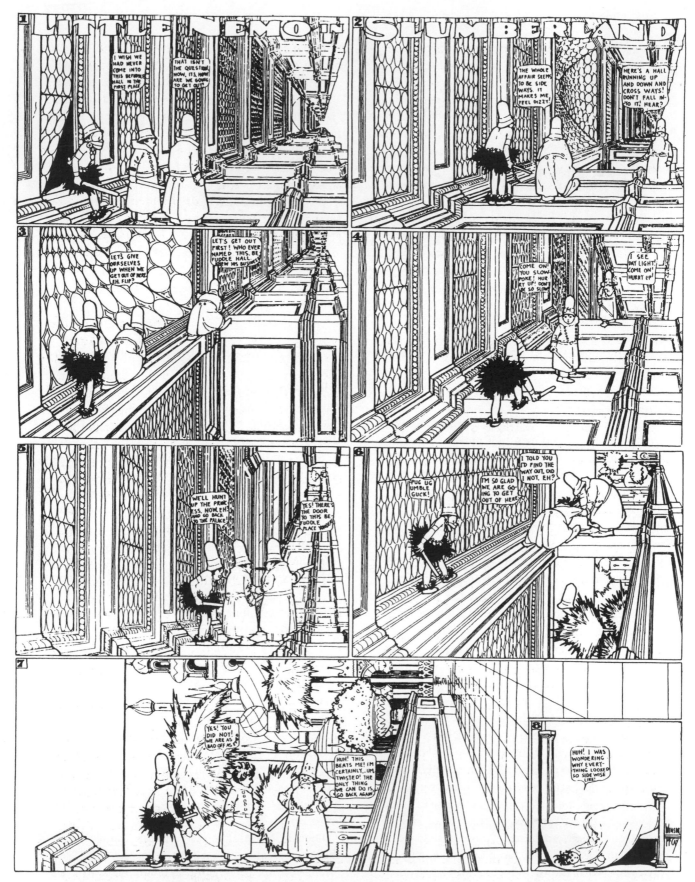

Figure 17. *McCay's consummate mastery of architectural rendering is impressively displayed in the Befuddle Hall sequence (February 23, 1908).*

wasting away to skeletons before our eyes. They knock down letters of the strip's title and eat them, at once ballooning into fat grotesques. Befuddle Hall was McCay's graphic funhouse, a comic strip palace of mirrors that he filled with kaleidoscopic images of his characters. Within its walls, Nemo and his two friends unaccountably grow to giant proportions one minute, then shrink to insect size the next. They become skinny and elongated one week, then short and fat the following Sunday. Finally, in a masterful display of architectural rendering, McCay turned Befuddle Hall sideways—then upside down. Changing the size of the panels to emphasize with perspective the vastness of the hall, McCay sent his characters clambering across the wall as if it were the floor, then across the ceiling likewise (figure 17). The sequence was a visual tour de force, extending the art form to the limit of its visual capacities.

A few weeks later, in March 1908, McCay went on a social crusade when he took his hero to Shantytown, a ramshackle ghetto of poverty and its accompanying miseries. Fittingly, the cartoonist adopted a palette of dull browns and grays to color the mean streets. Nemo is presented with a magic wand, and as he tours Shantytown, he waves the wand and dispels deprivation and misery whenever he encounters them. Christlike, he also cures the sick and the lame and the blind. Passionate as McCay would later prove to be on the issue of social justice, here in *Nemo*, with perhaps unwitting but no less telling irony, he takes us into a dreamworld: we know that poverty cannot be banished by wishing it.

With the Shantytown sequence, the creative fires begin burning a little less brightly in *Nemo*. McCay's most inventive period in this medium was now behind him. By the summer of 1908 the continuity of the strip was temporarily abandoned in favor of a series of simple one-page gags, often in the character of boyish pranksterism. Each page builds to a concluding punch line—and then Nemo wakes up. Sometimes the gags turn on visual tricks that harken back to the dreamlike character of the earliest *Nemo*s, but sustained, virtuoso hallucinatory effects are, for the most part, things of the past. And even when we see McCay performing such maneuvers again, there's something familiar about them: we've seen nightmare visions exactly like this before in *Nemo* and in *Rarebit Fiend*.

Perhaps McCay had, for the time being, exhausted the possibilities he had explored in the medium so thoroughly and with such astonishing effects. He often resumed a continuity during the remaining three years of the strip's run, and Nemo functioned increasingly in an exemplary, heroic role in such sequences. But the narrative or purely storytelling mode of the medium now took precedence over the visual pyrotechnics of those early years of untrammeled experimentation: the extravagant layouts gave way to an uncomplicated progression of uniform-sized panels. McCay, however, was scarcely through experimenting. Sometime in 1910 he had started on that detour I mentioned: he became interested in animation, a medium only just being born.

McCay later claimed it was his son Robert (the prototype of Nemo) who sparked his thinking about animation. The boy showed his father a "flip book": a little pad of paper on whose pages a succession of drawings shows a figure engaged in some activity, each drawing depicting the figure in a slightly different position; when the pages are "flipped," the figure appears to move. McCay was intrigued by the possibilities for "art in motion" that the "flipper" suggested to him. Simply photograph the pictures, one to each frame of film, and presto!—when the film is projected onto a screen, the drawings will appear to move. At once, McCay set himself to make motion picture stars of Nemo and his cohorts from the comic strip. He made four thousand drawings and had them filmed at the Vitagraph Studios near his home in Sheepshead Bay, and the resulting *Little Nemo* film, completed in the spring of 1911, was released to theaters on April 8. Simultaneously, McCay introduced the film as part of his vaudeville act. It was a sensation.

McCay's animated cartoon was not the first of its kind: one or two other attempts had preceded it. But his was the first to be entirely artwork—no footage of real people or real settings. There were no backgrounds in McCay's film, but the figure drawings were as detailed and complete as they were in the strip. Earlier animated films used drawings that were little more than stick figures.

The next year, McCay completed another animated film, *How a Mosquito Operates*, which showed the insect expanding as it sucked blood from its human victim. And then he began work on *Gertie the Dinosaur*. It took two years to complete, debuting February 22, 1914, in McCay's vaudeville act at the Palace in Chicago. Gertie was integral to the act. McCay stood on stage and interacted with the film. He introduced the lumbering creature and then directed it through a series of tricks, dismissing it at last by throwing it an apple, which the beast caught in its mouth. The blending of McCay's stage presence (reality) and Gertie's (the artist's art) was perfect.

McCay's command of the animated medium was virtually complete from the very beginning. His exploration of certain visual phenomena in his comic strips—particularly metamorphosis and other sorts of progressive action—had been ideal training for the techniques of animation. In his three films, his three experiments, he broke vast stretches of new ground. His animated characters moved with fluid ease, not with the jerks and skips characteristic of other animated endeavors of the day. And his characters had personalities: he made them perform actions or display mannerisms that gave them individuality to the audience. Moreover, McCay was able to convey the sensation that his subjects had weight and volume. No one else working in animation for the next two decades would surpass what McCay had achieved by 1914. Chuck Jones, celebrated director of Warner Brothers cartoons, marveled at McCay's achievement: "It was as though the first creature to emerge from the primeval slime was Albert Einstein; and the second was an amoeba because after McCay's animation, it took his followers nearly twenty years to find out how he did it. The two most important people in animation are Winsor McCay and Walt Disney, and I'm not sure which should go first."[6]

But by 1914 McCay had lost much of the impetus for creating animated cartoons. Apart from his fascination with the technical accomplishment that a successful animated film represented, he was motivated to create these films by the applause of his vaudeville audiences before whom he displayed his work. But shortly after *Gertie* appeared, McCay was deprived of the opportunity to make further stage appearances. In June 1911 McCay left the *Herald* to join the newspaper empire of William Randolph Hearst, who (according to his own legendary boast) did not bother to nurture talent because he could so easily buy it. Hearst bought McCay: recognizing McCay's immense popularity, he offered the cartoonist a salary that

no husband and father of two could afford to ignore.

By this time, McCay was famous as a newspaper cartoonist, the creator of Little Nemo and the fabulous Slumberland. And he was obsessed with animation. He drew several short-lived (and undistinguished) strips for Hearst, including a revival of *Little Nemo*. Published under the title *In the Land of Wonderful Dreams* because the *Herald* owned the *Nemo* title, the reincarnation ran for only a couple years. And it was a poor imitation, as John Canemaker points out: gone were the inventive layouts, replaced by a conventional grid of panels, and Flip, Nemo's nemesis, had emerged as the strip's central character. (Scarcely a surprising development: Flip always had more potential as a personality than the relatively colorless Nemo.) In this series, moreover, Nemo was but a pale imitation of the force for good that he had represented in the *Herald* version. None of McCay's work for Hearst, which now included editorial cartoons as well as comic strips, was of the calibre of his *Herald* work. According to Canemaker, preoccupied with his experiments in animation, McCay simply let the quality of his newspaper work slip.[7] But this preoccupation was the only creative indulgence McCay was permitted.

Hearst, upset by McCay's moonlighting on the vaudeville stage, demanded at first that the cartoonist restrict his appearances to New York theaters; by 1914, though, the autocratic press lord had forced McCay to give up vaudeville altogether to devote his talent exclusively to the Hearst mission. And the Hearst mission was to exercise power over public opinion. Seeking to employ the popularity of the cartoonist in ways that would advance the Hearst causes, the publisher wanted McCay to do his best work on the editorial page, producing cartoons that illustrated the moralizing pontifications of his chief editorial lieutenant, Arthur Brisbane. Hearst evidently thought McCay would do better at editorial cartooning if he were not distracted by any other assignments: he directed that McCay give up all his strips and concentrate on editorial cartoons.

Hearst's reasoning here is astounding in its wrongheadedness. It is remarkable, at least to me, that a man who formed and directed so vast an empire as Hearst eventually commanded could be so absolutely mistaken about the nature of the creative impulse. Creative talent of McCay's wide-

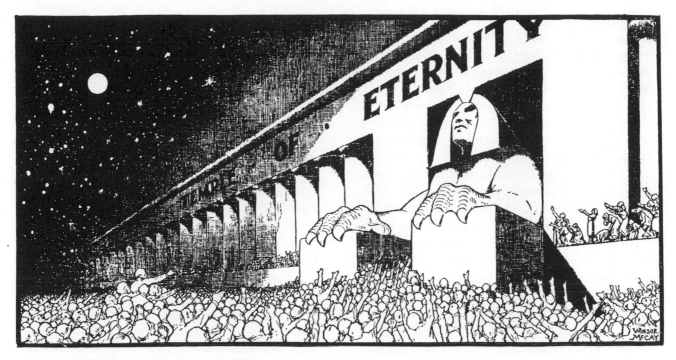

ONLY ONE IMPORTANT QUESTION, WHAT IS TRUTH?

Figure 18. *McCay's editorial cartoons for Hearst are masterpieces of pen-and-ink technique.*

ranging sort is more likely to flourish under a variety of stimuli. Not an overwhelming amount of work, mind you (McCay, Canemaker says, probably was trying to do too much), but a distinct variety of endeavors.[8] Had McCay been permitted to continue with one comic strip a week, chances are he would have been more creative, even innovative, than he was during the entire stretch of his long employment with Hearst.

Instead, McCay was hemmed in, confined, restricted, by his publisher's fiat. Hamstrung, his talent stagnated. Not only did he fail to produce any more work for the print medium of the calibre of his *Little Nemo* for the *Herald*, but, according to Canemaker, his animation work, after Hearst's prohibition went into effect, did not compare in the scope of its innovative dimensions to his earliest efforts.[9] It was still brilliant work; it just didn't take the giant strides forward that his first films had taken. McCay would begin seven more animated cartoons (that we know of), but he completed only four of them.

From the vantage point of history, we can see that McCay's best years were over. Hearst had stifled cartooning's first authentic genius.

McCay returned to the *Herald* briefly, from mid-1924 until the end of 1926. And he brought Nemo

back to the Sunday funnies then. But by that time, McCay had been too long away from comic strips: he had failed to keep up with the ways in which the comic strip had developed by the mid-1920s, and in consequence his treatment of *Nemo* was now old-fashioned, dated. If Canemaker is correct in his reading of the situation at the *Herald*, the paper's management was almost glad when McCay announced he would return to the high-paying Hearst when Hearst approached him again.[10] They would no longer have to honor McCay's past accomplishments by publishing his present feeble attempts. So anemic an attraction did they deem *Little Nemo* that they gave McCay all rights to his creation when he left.

McCay would spend the rest of his life drawing cartoons to illustrate Arthur Brisbane's platitudinous proclamations on Hearst's editorial pages. As far as we know, McCay did not object to giving up comic strips for editorial cartoons. There is ample evidence that he missed life on the vaudeville circuit, but otherwise Hearst's decree that he concentrate on political cartooning was doubtless welcome: it had the effect of reducing McCay's work substantially. With no other assignment, McCay could pour his creative energies into his sermons in black-and-white.

Winsor McCay's Exploration of the Medium's Potential   33

Technically—as pen-and-ink drawings—McCay's political cartoons were as brilliant as his other work. The drawings were powerful, dominated by McCay's commanding perspective and elaborately detailed vistas (often populated by scores of people, each rendered as a recognizable human being). But the themes of these cartoons were entirely conventional, even pedestrian (and therefore perfectly suited to Brisbane's editorials). The cartoons were morality tableaux on the plight of the poor and downtrodden or patriotic effusions celebrating the American way of life, American ingenuity and technology, and democratic principles. But however ponderous the cartoons' messages, they were superbly drawn—elaborately crosshatched to produce many shades of gray, highlighted with stark white spaces and bold solid blacks. Technical triumphs, these cartoons were still a far cry from *Nemo. Nemo* was McCay's masterpiece.

Little Nemo in Slumberland was born at precisely the right moment in the history of the comic strip. The device of the dream was perfect for showcasing the vast and as yet untapped capabilities of the medium, and in McCay's hands the strip demonstrated the art form's potential with élan and panache. And at the time McCay created Nemo and Slumberland, the concept was exactly what the cartoonist needed: the dreamworld enabled him to explore more fully his interests in the visual phenomena he had been examining in *The Rarebit Fiend* and *Sammy Sneeze*. The artist and his chosen medium were, for a time, perfectly suited to one another. They were joined in a cycle of creative invigoration: the artist followed his interests to expand the potential of his form, and the form, together with his story concept, stimulated his imagination, driving him to experiment further.

In the course of his experimentation, McCay made the haunting unreality of his dreamworld palpably real—beautiful but always resonating with a hint of nightmarish danger (of waking up?). In his hands, the comic strip became great art indeed. McCay thus showed what the funnies were capable of, although no one profited from the lesson for nearly a generation. The publishing world was changing, and fine artists—those capable of imitating McCay—were attracted to other enterprises where their talents would be coupled with better reproduction—magazines, chiefly, as well as book illustration. Not until the twenties and thirties would artists of McCay's calibre be attracted again to newspaper cartooning. And most of them would never have seen his masterpiece of the century's early years.

And so McCay left his profession no legacy, no viable model upon which those who immediately followed him could pattern their work or otherwise build upon. No one inherited his method, his secrets; for all practical purposes, they died with him in 1934—or long before, when he stopped doing comic strips. No legacy, but in the antique pages of the *New York Herald's* Sunday sections of decades ago, we can find a national treasure.

Chapter 3
Establishing the Daily Comic Strip
The Thematic Choruses of Bud Fisher
and George McManus

Mutt and Jeff attest to the visual power of the comic strip. The duo long ago ascended to the pantheon of American mythology: in common parlance, the names (seemingly forever yoked) always denote a visually mismatched pair, a tall person and a short one. Several generations of newspaper readers delighted in a daily dose of hilarity administered by the antics of the lanky Mutt and the runty Jeff, the former almost always exasperated to the point of desperation by the imperturbable ignorance (or was it beatific innocence?) of the latter. Mutt pursued every conceivable occupation and avocation in quest of a bigger bankroll; and in every endeavor, he was frustrated by Jeff's inability to concentrate on the main chance. But as a comic strip rather than a cultural and lexical phenomenon, *Mutt and Jeff* enjoys another distinction: it established the appearance of the medium, its daily format. Moreover, in the process of consolidating the art form, *Mutt and Jeff* employed many devices—such as continuous day-to-day narrative and political satire—that we normally associate with periods much later in the history of the newspaper comic strip. The author of this prototypical enterprise, Harry Conway "Bud" Fisher, was likewise something of an exemplar: in the conduct of his professional life, he set precedents that would affect the lives of other cartoonists for decades.

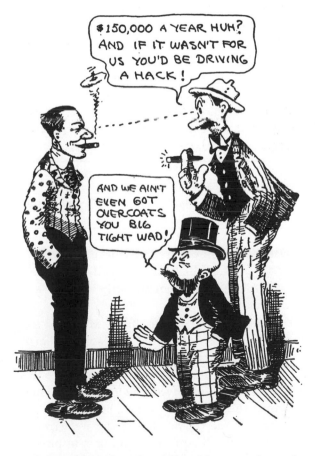

Figure 19. *Fisher drew himself and his star players for the* American Magazine *in about 1916.*

Mr. A. Mutt Starts in to Play the Races

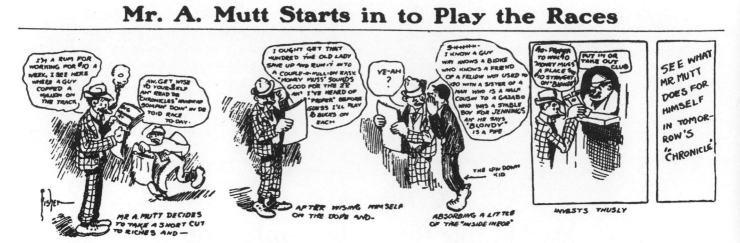

Figure 20. *A. Mutt's first appearance, November 15, 1907.*

Fisher did not invent the "strip" format for the daily comic strip. Other cartoonists before him had strung their comic pictures together in single file across a daily newspaper page before *Mutt and Jeff* first appeared on November 15, 1907. But these were isolated instances. Moreover, Fisher was not even the first to deploy the form on a regular daily basis. That distinction belongs to Clare Briggs.

Briggs, a cartoonist on the staff of the *Chicago American*, inaugurated a six-days-a-week strip late in 1903 at the instigation of his editor, Moses Koenigsberg. Called *A. Piker Clerk*, the Briggs-Koenigsberg concoction dealt with horse racing and betting. It was intended to stimulate sales of the "Final Sports" edition of the paper by serializing the gambling exploits of the title character: A. Piker Clerk placed a wager one day, and the outcome was reported in the next day's strip—so that to find out whether Clerk won, readers had to buy the next day's paper. The scheme worked; newsstand sales went up. But daily publication of the strip was discontinued after a fairly short run because William Randolph Hearst, publisher of the *Chicago American*, thought the strip was too vulgar.[1]

In contrast to these earlier efforts, *Mutt and Jeff* endured. And because it lasted—because it kept coming back, day after day after day, seven days a week—it was the first *successful* daily comic strip. As Coulton Waugh observed, the Columbus Principle obtains: the Vikings may have been the first Europeans to tread the beaches in the Western hemisphere, but Christopher Columbus inspired others with his visit and thereby earned his niche in history.[2] And *Mutt and Jeff* did the same: its

regular appearance and its continued popularity invited imitation, thus establishing the daily "strip" form for a certain kind of newspaper cartoon.

Until *Mutt and Jeff* set the fashion, newspaper cartoons usually reached readers in one of two forms: on Sunday, in colored pages of tiered panels in sequence (like Winsor McCay's famed *Little Nemo in Slumberland*, a feature intended chiefly for children); on weekdays, in collections of comic drawings grouped almost haphazardly within the ruled border of a large single-frame panel (directed mostly to adult readers). The daily cartoons were often found in a paper's sports section and featured graphic reportage and comic commentary on the doings of diamond, ring, track, and other arenas of athletic competition. In 1907 Bud Fisher was a sports cartoonist on the *San Francisco Chronicle*, and so, not surprisingly, the comic strip he launched that became *Mutt and Jeff* focused on a preoccupation of the sporting crowd—namely, betting. Maybe the similarity to the *A. Piker Clerk* venture in Chicago was pure coincidence; maybe not.[3] Fisher had grown up in Chicago, but he left long before the Briggs and Koenigsberg experiment.

Born on April 3, 1884 (or 1885), Fisher entered the University of Chicago but quit after three months and went to California to seek his fortune.[4] When he arrived at the *Chronicle*, he, like most early cartoonists, was assigned to the sports department, where for a few years he did layouts and occasionally drew pictures celebrating in humorous graphics what proper society then regarded with disdain—the dubious prowess and feats of professional athletes, their trainers, managers, promoters, and hangers-on and other alleged riffraff.

Then, on that November day in 1907, Fisher entered the history books by spreading his comic drawings in sequence across the width of the sports page. His editor's consent to this venture was not as easily obtained as we might imagine. John P. Young had turned down Fisher's suggestion for a sports page strip two years earlier because, he is alleged to have said, "it would take up too much room, and readers are used to reading down the page and not horizontally."[5]

But once the editor agreed to this departure from the usual practice, the comic strip format was on its way to becoming a fixture in daily newspapers. Fisher scarcely imagined, however, that he was establishing an art form. "In selecting the strip form for the picture," he once wrote, "I thought I would get a prominent position across the top of the sporting page, which I did, and that pleased my vanity. I also thought the cartoon would be easy to read in this form. It was."[6]

By way of introducing and describing his cast, Fisher called his strip A. Mutt (another echo of Briggs's earlier endeavor). "Mutt" was short for "muttonhead"—a fool. (In Slang Today and Yesterday, Eric Partidge even credits Fisher with inventing the clipped version of the term.)[7] And Augustus Mutt was indeed something of a fool: he was a compulsive horse-player, a "plunger." At first the strip concentrated exclusively on Mutt's daily quest for the right horse to bet on and for the wherewithal to place the wager. And Mutt had the stage almost entirely to himself: there was no Jeff at the beginning. We saw Mutt's wife every once in a while—and his young son, Cicero. But no Jeff. Jeff didn't come along until later.

In those days before national syndication, a cartoonist drew only for his own paper, and he generally drew a cartoon just the day before it would be published. (Later, syndicates would require cartoonists to submit their work weeks in advance because it took that much production time to prepare the material for distribution to newspapers all around the country.) This circumstance permitted extremely topical and local comedy: the cartoon in today's paper could be based upon the news in yesterday's paper, often news of city hall or the nearest police precinct house. Or, in the case of sports cartoons, the playing field or race track. It was a circumstance Fisher seized upon and exploited.

Whether he was deliberately or only coincidentally repeating Briggs's formula we can't say. We do know, however, that in determining which horse Mutt would bet on in the strip to be published in, say, Tuesday morning's paper, Fisher picked a real horse that would be running Tuesday afternoon at the Emeryville track across the bay. Fellow racing enthusiasts had to wait for Wednesday's paper to learn the outcome of Mutt's bet. The cartoonist's selection was entirely whimsical: he picked horses whose names inspired a gag in that day's strip.[8] Mutt mostly lost, but, given the vicissitudes of wagering, he won every once in a while. And that was often enough. Readers of the strip began to take his wagers seriously, interpreting them as inside tips. Before long they were hooked, and their addiction guaranteed the strip's continued appearance (not to mention continued sales of the Chronicle at the newsstand). Fisher was on his way to fame as well as fortune.

But Fisher did more for the comic strip medium than establish its format. According to John Wheeler, founder of the Wheeler (later Bell) Syndicate (distributor of Mutt and Jeff for most of the strip's run), Fisher, "by his guts and independence, probably did more to make the cartoon business for his more cowardly confreres than anyone else who has ever been in it."[9] To begin with, Fisher had the foresight to copyright A. Mutt in his own name—and, later, to apply for a trademark on the title.[10] And he had the audacity to go to court to secure his rights. The strip was his and no one else's. By resorting to litigation, Fisher showed other cartoonists that they could enjoy ownership of their creations if they established lawful rights to their work. (By the same token, newspapers and syndicates learned they should trademark the comic strip creations they bought.)[11]

Fisher's first legal skirmish took place within months of his strip's debut. Press baron Hearst, seeing that A. Mutt seemed responsible for his San Francisco competition's increase in circulation, did what he would do again and again over the next half century: he hired the rival's talent away by paying more. Much more. Hearst offered a weekly salary of $45, double Fisher's pay at the Chronicle, and A. Mutt began running in Hearst's San Francisco Examiner on December 11, 1907, a mere three weeks after it had started in the other paper. But it also continued to run in the Chronicle. In accordance with established practice, A. Mutt was treated as if it were the Chronicle's property: the editors simply hired another cartoonist (Russ Westover, later the creator of *Tillie the Toiler*) to draw the strip. But this time, the situation was different. The paper's presumed right to ownership of the strip had been undermined by Fisher's canny maneuver on the last day he worked for the *Chronicle*. Waiting until after his editor approved the day's strip, Fisher went into the engraving room and, before the plate was made, wrote "Copyright 1907, H. C. Fisher" in the corner of his last strip and subsequently registered the copyright in Washington.[12] The cartoonist threatened suit, and the *Chronicle*, convinced eventually of the legitimacy of his copyright holding, stopped running the strip as of June 7, 1908.

Later, Fisher went to court to protect his rights and established a legal precedent. In 1913 Wheeler offered Fisher a better syndication deal than Hearst was giving him. Hearst was then paying Fisher $300 a week; Wheeler offered the cartoonist $1,000 a week or 60 percent of the revenue, whichever was greater. It was a staggering sum, and once persuaded that Wheeler could make the weekly guarantee, Fisher left Hearst.[13] But Hearst, anxious to hold on to a good circulation builder, hired another cartoonist (either Ed Mack or Billy Liverpool; sources differ) to draw *A. Mutt*.[14] To prevent this unauthorized use of his creation, Fisher sued—this time prosecuting the issue to a final legal resolution: the strip and its characters belonged to Fisher, not to Hearst or his paper.[15] I know of no other cartoonist at the time who owned his feature. (After winning his case, Fisher hired Ed Mack as his assistant, and Mack drew the strip until he died in about 1932. Mack's assistant, Al Smith, then inherited the job and drew the strip until he retired, long after Fisher's death.)

Fisher's fights for his rights as a cartoonist were not confined to the courtroom. And the fighting began early. Stephen Becker tells us that while Fisher was still a staff cartoonist for the *Chronicle*, the paper reduced the size allotted to his cartoon without consulting him. Peeved, Fisher calmly tore up his artwork and refused to draw in the smaller format. In effect, he quit. But since he was obliged to give two weeks' notice, he came to the office every day for the next week or so. He did not, however, touch pen or paper. After several days of this, his editor relented, and Fisher's cartoon resumed at its usual dimension.[16]

Fisher was perfectly constituted for doing battle.

According to Rube Goldberg and others who knew him well, Fisher was an inlet of self-assured independence in a churning sea of whimpering egos.[17] He was antagonistic and belligerent—a cocky, scrappy, dapper, hard-drinking, carousing denizen of city rooms and saloons. His was the sort of personality that generates legends. For example, there was his penchant for using his apartment as a target range, an incident recounted by Wheeler in his autobiography, *I've Got News for You*.[18]

While waiting for his contract with Hearst to expire, Fisher was doing no strips. To fill his idle hours, he went with Wheeler on an expedition south of the border to interview Pancho Villa, the bandit who had somehow become the savior of his country. Villa gave Fisher a six-shooter that he'd taken from the body of a man whose execution Fisher and Wheeler had been invited to watch. Fisher took the pistol back to New York, and sometimes when he returned home late at night feeling frisky, he'd take the gun out and fire it at selected targets in his rooms. The first time it happened, other tenants complained to the superintendent, and that worthy naturally warned Fisher about the noise.

"You're too damn strict around here," Fisher said. "It is getting so you can't shoot off a pistol in your own place at four in the morning without someone complaining. I'll move out tomorrow."

"You bet you will," said the superintendent. And he did.

The soaring popularity of *Mutt and Jeff* made Fisher rich beyond his wildest dreams. By 1916 popular magazine articles were reporting that he earned $150,000 a year; five years later, *Mutt and Jeff* animated cartoons and merchandising, as well as the constantly growing circulation of the strip, had increased his annual income to about $250,000. Fisher was without a doubt the profession's richest practitioner. He was also famous. And he quickly habituated himself to both wealth and renown.

His celebrity made him welcome in circles that were normally closed to newspapermen and other lowlifes (such as actors and professional athletes, all of whom were social outcasts for at least the first twenty years of the century). The first truly famous cartoonist, Fisher relished his position in high society, and he worked hard on his public image (tainting the world's perception of cartoonists in the process). Fisher bought a stable of race horses, drove about town in a Rolls Royce, and prowled nightclubs with a beautiful showgirl on each arm. The flood of publicity attending the production of *Mutt and Jeff* animated cartoons (beginning in 1916) claimed that Fisher did all the work himself; the Raoul Barre–Charles Bowers studio was never even mentioned. Fisher had divorced his first wife, Pauline, years before, and although he enjoyed the license of a bachelor life, in 1924 he married a titled European whom he met on a voyage home from France, the Countess Aedita de Beaumont, only to be legally separated four months later (with the countess inheriting 62 percent of his estate).[19]

By the 1920s Fisher was enjoying his social life so much that he left most of the work on the strip to Ed Mack. In this respect, too, Fisher may have set the mold. For a long time, most average newspaper readers, who acquired their perception of the world from what they read in the paper, believed that the famous cartoonists whose escapades were so frequently related in the society columns spent most of their time lolling around in fancy nightclubs while their strips were being drawn by underpaid, starving teenagers, who slaved away in secrecy in some obscure garret. In Fisher's case, this perception was probably close to the truth (as it was with another Fisher, Ham, whose *Joe Palooka* was drawn by others even if it was written by its creator of record). Bud Fisher soon became a gambling, womanizing night owl, who seldom handled a pen anymore. And the more he moved in society's salons, the less use he had for his erstwhile brethren of the inky-fingered fraternity. He regularly snubbed his onetime friends. "He squandered his life and was a very unhappy man," Wheeler wrote.[20]

Fisher died in 1954 at the age of seventy. He spent his last years desolate and alone in a huge museum of a Park Avenue apartment. He had purchased rooms from historic European houses and had them dismantled and installed in his New York residence. There was an English manor room of the Elizabethan period and a French Provincial room. Another room was Oriental, a trove of Chinese treasures. Sick and solitary, Fisher spent his final days amid this splendor but probably not enjoying it much. Toward the end, he seldom left his bedroom, where he slept on a bare mattress and pillows without cases, while the rest of his abode slipped into shabby decay, its hallways lined with stacks of unopened envelopes from his bank. He had few visitors: his treatment of his fellow cartoonists had been so high-handed for so long that none except Rube Goldberg and Bob Dunn would have anything to do with the man who had established the format of the medium in which they worked. Occasionally, though, young aspiring cartoonists would visit, and Fisher, desperate for company, would keep them entertained for hours with stories of his travels in European society and his dockside welcoming parties. Like Miss Havisham, Fisher died amid the faded remnants of a once opulent lifestyle as cartooning's first millionaire.[21]

The strip that made Fisher a wealthy celebrity graduated from pedestrian race-track touting to classic comedy when the tall and gangling Mutt acquired his diminutive sidekick. Mutt had encountered Jeff among the inmates of an insane asylum in late March 1908, but it wasn't until a year or so later that Fisher brought Jeff back into the strip as a regular cast member. The skinny tall man sort of adopted the short fellow, and the historic team was born. By then, the strip was appearing in Hearst's *New York American*, well on its way to national distribution. Even before Jeff's arrival, however, Fisher had explored another of the medium's conventions—narrative that continues from one day to the next.

Fisher had recognized at once the potential of the daily comic strip for bringing readers back day after day after day: the central device of *A. Mutt* virtually forced the cartoonist into day-to-day continuity. Mutt places a bet one day, the outcome is reported the next day, and Mutt promptly places another bet. To learn whether Mutt won or lost, we must buy a paper every day. Here again, Fisher seemed to be repeating Briggs's performance. But Fisher soon began to bait his hook with other lures.

In early January 1908 Fisher insinuated another story line into the daily ritual. Mutt's wife divorces him, and Mutt begins paying court to another woman. Even in the throes of courtship, however, the plunger makes his daily dash to the betting window. Despite his addiction, he wins the lady's hand—only to lose her once and for all when he deserts her at the altar in order to place a wager on a horse named Lazell running in the

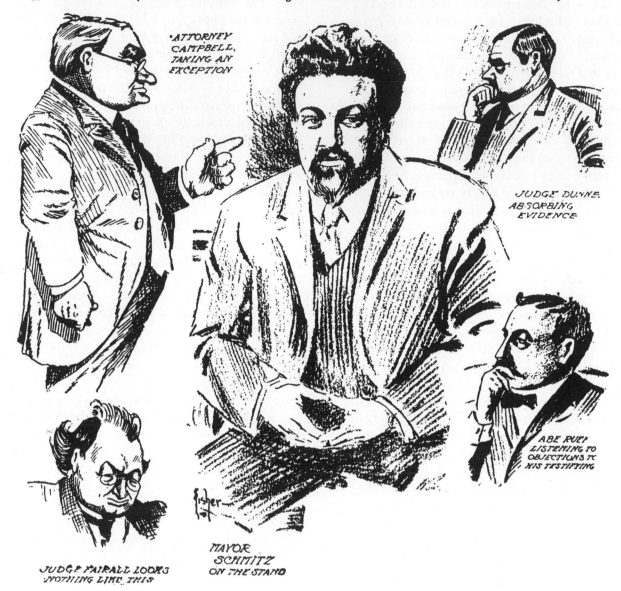

Figure 21. *Done before* A. Mutt *began, these drawings of assorted San Francisco politicians reveal that Fisher's artistic ability was considerably greater than it appeared in the comic strip.*

third race that day. Subsequently, his wife takes him back, telling him that the divorce had been faked, a tactic she cooked up with the aid of a judge to jolt Mutt into dependable domesticity. The scheme, clearly, didn't work. They resume their marriage, but Mutt is as devoted to the track as ever.

Obviously, Fisher's strip was aimed over the heads of children at adult readership. Wagering is, after all, an adult diversion. And the strip appeared on the sports pages of the paper, a section reflecting adult preoccupations. So obvious is the strip's

appeal to adults that no one to my knowledge has remarked much upon it, apart from comics historian Bill Blackbeard, who mentions the fact but makes little of it.[22] But Fisher's courting of adult readers is worth emphasizing because it contradicts the traditional belief that comics are for children. It's quite accurate to say that the Sunday funnies were conceived at least in part as entertainment for children. Not Fisher's strip. At first he did seven strips a week, one for Sunday and six for the weekdays. But the Sunday strip ran in black-and-white on the sports page, not in the colored comics section. Fisher knew his audience. In deliberately appealing to adult readership, he once again set the pace for the medium. Although in the popular mind, the funnies still remain "kid stuff," in their daily format they never were directed at youngsters: from the very beginning, cartoonists wrote and drew their weekday comic "strips" for adults.

In yet another way, Fisher may have shaped the medium, albeit this time, less commendably. There is ample evidence to indicate that Fisher deliberately assumed a rudimentary drawing style for rendering the adventures of Augustus Mutt. As Blackbeard observes in his introduction to the Hyperion Press volume in which the strip's first year is reprinted, Fisher's other cartoons for the *Chronicle* (some drawn before he started *A. Mutt*; some after) display a drawing ability that, while not spectacular, is nonetheless accomplished, certainly better than merely adequate (figure 21).[2,3] In fact, some of the pen portraits of Mutt that the strip's continuity occasioned in 1908 show a command of the nuances of cross-hatching and shading that is a cut above the skill otherwise revealed in the strip (figure 22). Fisher apparently believed that cartoons of the sort he was inventing with *A. Mutt* should be drawn in a crude, almost inept manner. I'm not referring to Mutt's heronlike appearance—his beaky, chinless visage and tall rangy build or his rawboned, loose-limbed all-elbows-and-knees mode of locomotion. No, I'm talking about basic anatomy and other artistic fundamentals such as simple perspective. In giving his protagonist human dimension, Fisher was apt to change Mutt's proportions from one panel to the next: when Mutt bent his arms and legs, they got longer. And the characters very often looked as if they didn't quite fit the surroundings Fisher gave them: chairs and doorways were too small, and various furnishings tilted wildly to conform to Fisher's idiosyncratic understanding of perspective.

To the extent that *A. Mutt* provided a model for others to emulate—and as the first successful daily strip, its influence must have been considerable—Fisher demonstrated the way a comic strip should be drawn: crudely. His influence in this regard was not, fortunately, pervasive. Cartoonists who, like Winsor McCay, had a towering talent drew in the way their talent dictated and produced art works of great beauty. Even artists with less skill were driven mostly by their gifts,

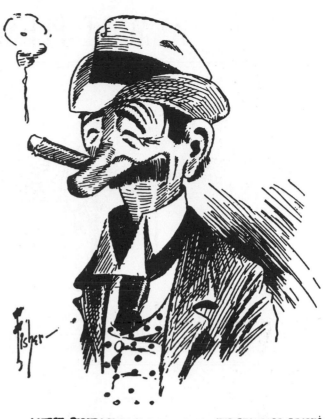

LATEST PORTRAIT OF AUGUSTUS MUTT, THE STANDARD BEARER OF THE BUGHOUSE TICKET, WHOSE NOMINATION WAS THE SIGNAL FOR A WILD DEMONSTRATION WHICH LASTED 23 HOURS AND NINETY MINUTES.

Figure 22. *Even this rendering of A. Mutt himself shows a more sophisticated artistic talent than was on display in most of the daily installments of the strip.*

and, drawing as well as they could, they created reasonably accomplished pictures. But Fisher had opened a door, and through that door, many less talented artists could now pass. More significantly, Fisher, perhaps unwittingly, gave the reading public the impression that comic strips should be ineptly rendered. It was an image the medium would carry for years. Regardless of how popular comic strips became (and they were very popular indeed from the very beginning), for much of their early history comic strips were seen as sensational, amateurishly drawn appeals to the baser instincts of newspaper readers. And for that, the Yellow Kid was partly responsible, as we have seen; and Bud Fisher must surely shoulder his share of the blame, too.

Whatever Fisher's impact upon comic strip graphics and upon the public perception of the artistic merit of comic strips, it's clear that when Fisher started *A. Mutt*, he launched it as a fairly mature art form. *A. Mutt* presented itself as a

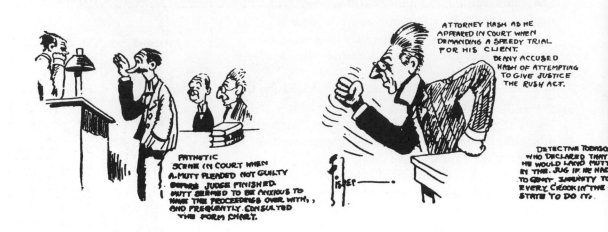

Figure 23. *When Mutt went on trial, Fisher converted the strip to a miniature newspaper, with daily "photographs" and their "captions" carrying the narrative—and building suspense.*

"strip" of pictures, its narrative continued from day to day, and it aimed deliberately at an adult audience. At this late date in the study of newspaper comic strips (we've been pondering them seriously at least since about 1970), it may come as a surprise that the first successful example of the daily breed burst upon the pages of a San Francisco newspaper with nearly all of the medium's conventions in place virtually at the outset. Upon reflection, though, it is not quite so astonishing. As Samuel Johnson said of Jonathan Swift's *Gulliver's Travels*, "When once you have thought of big men and little men, it is very easy to do the rest." With newspaper cartoons, once the decision had been made to format them in "strips" and run them daily, the rest—continuity, even adult readership—follows logically. And these elements were not the last of Fisher's explorations. He continued to play with the medium, and over the next year he pioneered many facets of the form that others would eventually take up again.

For the first two months of his new strip's run, Fisher repeated essentially the same gag every day, seven days a week. The punch line was Mutt's daily bet, and the last panel in every strip showed Mutt dashing up to the betting window, knees and elbows a-flap with the exertion of his desperate haste, a few dollars clenched in his fist. Fisher varied the daily drill in one of two ways: Mutt's pre-

dicament on one day might be determining which horse to bet on; on another day, his dilemma might be how to acquire enough money to place a bet.

Mutt often overhears a phrase in the discourse of passersby and, taking the phrase as some sort of omen, he bets on a horse whose name he hears in that conversational fragment. Mutt's compulsion is overpowering. He can be diverted from any endeavor by chancing upon a phrase or a word that suggests which pony to play that day. He jumps in the bay to rescue a woman from drowning, and when she drops a word of gratitude, Mutt abandons her to her fate in order to get to the track in time to bet on "Thanks Be." He has a heart attack as the result of some betting misfortune, but, on his sick bed, he hears his doctor recommend rest and "sea air," so he leaps out the hospital window to place a bet on "Sea Air" to win. He even arises from the dead to get to the track. Stricken by "apoplexy," Mutt dies and is buried. In the grave, he overhears the grave diggers discussing that day's races, and when they mention Pullman as a sure thing, Mutt bursts out of the earth and makes his customary last-panel sprint to the betting window. To get money to bet, Mutt finds employment as a policeman, the first of many miscellaneous jobs he'll hold over the years. But he can't keep the job: he runs off to the track every time he hears the

SECURING JURY TO BE BEGUN TO-MORROW

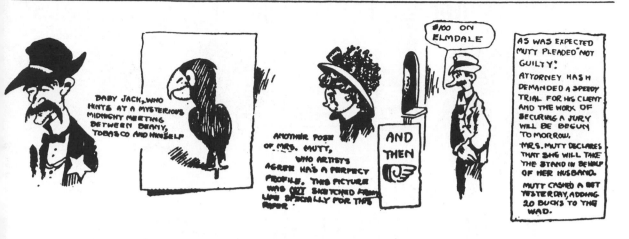

name of a horse. Eventually, he steals from Cicero's piggy bank, sells the family parrot, hocks the bathtub and, ultimately, the clothes off his back.

The comedy in these early strips arises entirely from Mutt's run of bad luck and his overwhelming obsession. But Mutt doesn't always lose. Because Fisher was picking the names of real horses that ran in real races, Mutt sometimes wins. And when he does, Fisher keeps track of the size of Mutt's bankroll, recording its dwindling (or increasing) amount in the last panel of each daily installment. Fortunately for the strip's comedy, Mutt loses more often than he wins, so he never has a stake large enough to quell for long the general feeling of frantic desperation that seems to animate him. Then, on a fateful day in early February 1908, the "great plunger," as usual in need of cash, steals money from a pay phone. This development started Fisher on a fresh course for his strip—and, as before, he ventured on to new ground for the medium.

For a week or so, Mutt remains a fugitive from justice. He eludes the police, but he still makes his daily dash to the track to place a bet. Caught at last, he is brought to trial—and Fisher stretched the proceedings out for the next six weeks. Mutt still makes a wager in the last panel on most days, but the real interest in the strip is generated by the trial. And to the natural suspense that a trial might create, Fisher added a titillating device: the prosecuting attorney and the various minions of the law surrounding him are devised to remind

readers of several local politicians who were recently implicated in a case of corruption in the city government of San Francisco. The references by which Fisher jogged the memories of his readers are obscure today, but in the winter of 1908 they were doubtless clanging alarm bells in the minds of those who read the strip. And Fisher rang the bells every day, day after day, mentioning "$30,000," "curl papers" (which someone used to curl his moustache), and one dignitary's "goat" (which Fisher "got"). As political satire, this sort of thing was pretty thin. But as outright ridicule, heavy-handed though it was, it probably delighted Fisher's readers: the barely veiled references amounted to public name-calling, a sensationalized novelty for the embryonic comic strip form (even if the same techniques were common practice in the news columns of many newspapers of the day).

Our concern at the moment, however, is with the manner Fisher chose for presenting his daily jabs. He toyed with the incipient form, capitalizing upon its daily recurrence and the medium in which it appeared. He converted his strip from a narrative of sequential visuals to a miniature newspaper: each daily installment featured a succession of "newspaper photos" of the principals with accompanying captions, as Fisher reported the daily developments in the Mutt Case (figure 23). The strip assumed a new "voice"—the voice of the front-page headlines of a daily newspaper. Fisher would use the device again later in the year;

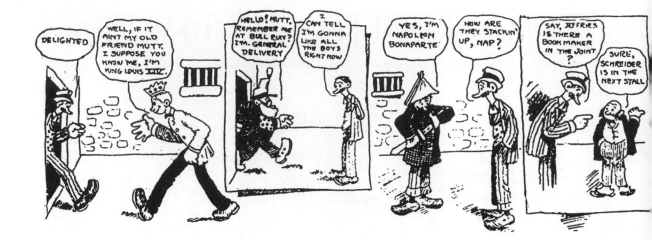

THE JEFFRIES OF THE BUGHOUSE GETS PESTY AND MUTT

Namesake of heavyweight champion suffers awful indignity.

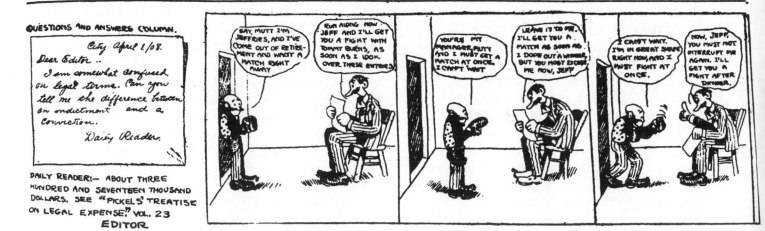

and the technique would be refined twenty years later by Roy Crane in *Wash Tubbs*.

The trial sequence is of interest today for yet another reason: it brought us to the immortal Jeff. Mutt is found guilty, of course (he *was* guilty, after all), but he is released after serving only a couple days because of suggestions of malfeasance among the officers of the court. (The constant references to the corruption of the real city government thus opened the way for Fisher to free his protagonist.) But Mutt's sanity was brought into question during the trial, and as soon as he is released from jail, he finds himself committed to a local insane asylum, although Fisher skimps on the reasons for this development (and so, therefore, must we). In the "bughouse," Mutt meets such historic personages as Shakespeare, George Washington, the

Czar of Russia, and assorted millionaires, poets, kings, and captains of industry. Among these deluded souls is a short bald fellow with muttonchop whiskers who believes he is James Jeffries, the heavyweight boxing champion of contemporary notoriety (particularly on the sports pages where *A. Mutt* appeared). Little Jeff has at last arrived, wandering onto stage on March 27, 1908 (figure 24).[24]

Jeff (called Jeffries in many of his earliest appearances) is the bughouse fall guy. The other inmates are always playing tricks on the poor boob. But he doesn't seem to mind. As Fisher put it in one of the strip's captions, "What's the diff? He's just as happy as if he had good sense."

Jeff did not immediately become Mutt's ever-present sidekick and comic factotum. He was,

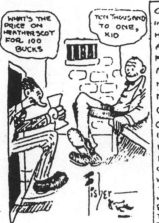

PUTS THE CRUSHER ON HIM

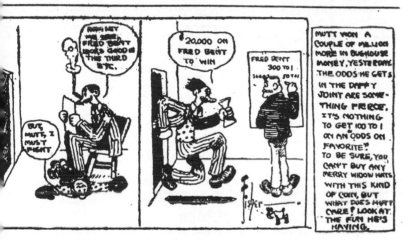

Figure 24. *One of the most historic moments in comic strip history, Mutt's first meeting with Jeff among the other inmates of the local insane asylum (the top strip is a portion of the install- ment for March 27, 1908; the other portion dealt with the courtroom personalities at Mutt's trial). It wasn't until April 2 (the bottom strip) that Fisher clarified Jeff's delusion—the little man's identification with the heavyweight champion; and the clarification was made mostly in the typeset overline above the panels.*

rather, just another member of the strip's growing cast. When Mutt is released from the asylum, Jeff occasionally visits the plunger—usually in the company of "General Delivery," another of the in- mates. Through most of April and May, however, Fisher resumed his ridiculing of the city's corrupt politicians, using the same "newspaper format" approach as he had used during Mutt's trial. For a time, the strip ceased to be a "strip"—a narrative sequence of drawings—becoming instead a series of daily tableaux that poked fun at the foibles of local politicians.

When the 1908 presidential campaign began heating up that summer, Mutt was again linked with Jeff. Mutt is the Bughouse Party nominee for president, and Jeff is the other half of the ticket. This may be the first time a comic character ran

for the U.S. presidency (and Mutt and Jeff will do it again several times), but Fisher did not greatly exploit this rich vein of material. In fact, he used the campaign as an excuse to reprise his now- familiar needling of San Francisco politicos. He must have enjoyed this sort of thing a great deal, and he probably was encouraged by the public re- ception of the maneuver, but the constant chorus of the same material ($30,000, curl papers, the goat) makes dull reading in later years.

On election day in November, Jeff returns to the strip (as does Mutt), and he makes periodic reap- pearances over the next year, eventually proving himself the ideal foil for Mutt. By 1910 Jeff is a regular cast member, appearing frequently. By the end of the year, he has become virtually indispens- able to the strip—so much a part of Fisher's enter-

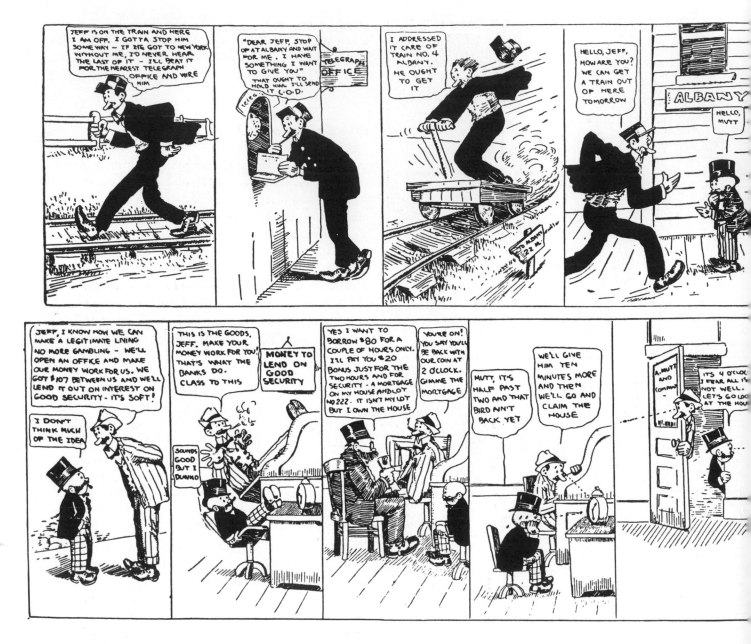

prise that when a booklet reprinting a selection of 1910 strips was published that year, the booklet was called *The Mutt and Jeff Cartoons*. This is the first pairing of the duo's names in print. The strip itself did not assume its historic title formally until September 15, 1916, after Fisher had joined Wheeler's syndicate.[25]

Fisher had widened the scope of his strip's focus very early in its history, as we've seen, by turning from horse-playing to politics (from one kind of horseplay to another, we might say). He did it deliberately: he aimed to broaden the appeal of the strip. And he continued to search for ways to make *Mutt and Jeff* interesting to the widest possible readership. He saw that many entertainers

achieved success by appealing to the special interests of a particular group. He reasoned that "if *Mutt and Jeff* appealed to *everyone*—high-brow, low-brow, man, woman, and child—their value to me would be much greater."[26] Although he subsequently determined that "the high-brow sense of humor does not differ much from the low-brow," he decided his other distinctions were valid. "So I worked out a scheme," he wrote in 1920, "which I have followed ever since. Mutt and Jeff do something one day that will tickle the women; the next day, the kids; the next day, I try to give the old man a laugh. If Mutt hits Jeff across the face with a fish, Father says, 'That isn't funny!' Mother sniffs and looks away without a grin. But the small

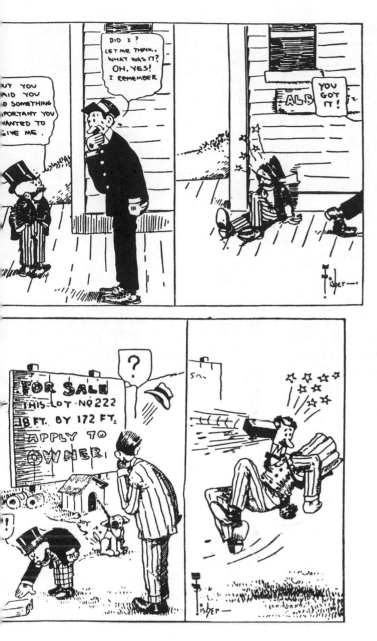

Figure 25. *The daily punch line was often a punch (or a pie in the face or a brick to the head), a tradition that began almost as soon as Jeff arrived. These examples are from 1910.*

tions perpetually frustrated by Jeff's benign and well-intentioned ignorance. Frustrated by the little man's uncomprehending bumbling, Mutt often responds with classic vaudevillian exasperation: the strips' punch lines are frequently precisely that, punches. In the best slapstick tradition of the stage, Mutt lets his pesky partner have it in the face with a pie, a dead chicken, a brick, or whatever object he happens to have in his hand when he realizes that the little fellow has scuttled yet another scheme with his literal-minded stupidity. Being beaned with a brick was a classic *Mutt and Jeff* finish long before George Herriman took the same device and turned it into poetry in his masterwork, *Krazy Kat*.

Often deploying gentle Jeff as his shill in a succession of joint careers and enterprises, Mutt sometimes conceives plans that have the incidental effect of victimizing the little fellow. But we always root for Jeff: visually, the short guy is the underdog, and most American readers cheer for the underdog out of cultural habit. As usual, Fisher was perfectly aware of what he was doing: "Mutt is a big, simple-minded boob who is always trying and always blundering," Fisher once said. "The great majority of people like Jeff much more than they do Mutt, but Mutt always has been my pal and friend. Mutt is trying, and making mistakes, just like the rest of us, and he is a rough worker at times. People like Jeff because he is smaller, and almost every person in the world is for the little guy against the big one."[28]

And Little Jeff in his innocence and kindliness justifies our faith. Regardless of Mutt's machinations, Jeff invariably winds up on top, unwittingly victorious over whatever traps or pitfalls may have lain in his path. So does the benevolent nature of humankind seem somehow to triumph eventually over its baser instincts in the long, long run. We laughed at them both, but we merely tolerated Mutt and his schemes; we loved little Jeff.

Fisher and his assistants were able to work endless variations on their simple theme. It wore well: the strip ran for over three-quarters of a century.[29]

boy yells. The next day, Mother gets the laugh. And finally, I squeeze a grin out of Father. After a while, it gets to be a habit."[27]

With the emergence of Little Jeff as Mutt's partner, the strip acquired the humane dimension that made it a classic: it ceased to be solely a daily chorus about crass money-grubbing and became instead a cautionary tale about the human condition. Mutt remained the scheming conniver that he'd always been as a horse-player: his role in the strip was to come up with ways to make a buck. And Jeff's seeming mental deficiency made him the perfect innocent, the ideal foil for Mutt the Materialist. Thus the strip's comedy soon acquired its vintage form, with Mutt's avaricious aspira-

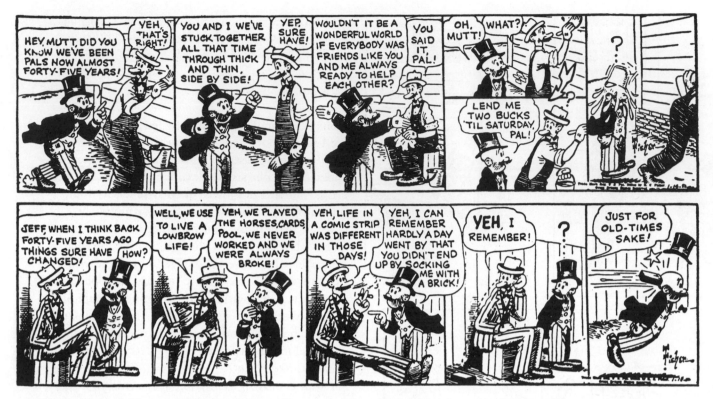

Figure 26. *Both Mutt and Jeff have clear recollections of the role of the brick in their history. These strips are from a 1952 sequence in which the history of the feature is recalled by the characters themselves (January 14 and 15).*

Early strips were frequently single-theme enterprises of this sort. Their humor resided in little more than a single situation, presented time and time again, each presentation a variation of the first, and basic, situation. We call them "one joke" strips in the more sophisticated years in the last decades of the twentieth century, but at the century's beginning, such single-minded thematic choruses, repeated day after day, were awaited eagerly by avid readers. And the themes often proved mar-

Bringing Up Father

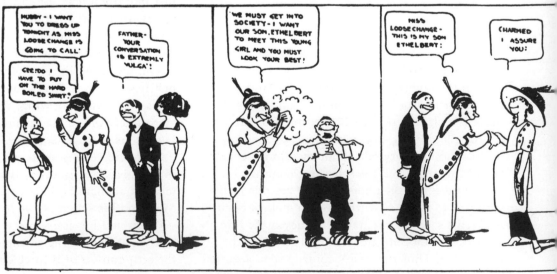

velously adaptable, susceptible of countless mutations. *The Katzenjammer Kids*, with its endless parade of juvenile pranks, comes immediately to mind, as do others of its turn-of-the-century contemporaries—*Foxy Grandpa*, about a sly oldster turning the tables on youngsters, and *Her Name Was Maud*, about a stubborn mule that outwits the humans around her. Such strips were continuous replays of some aspect of the human predicament. They succeeded because the predicament was so fundamental to the human condition and because the attitude toward it that was displayed in the strip was so absolutely refreshing.

One of the most enduring of these strips is George McManus's masterwork, *Bringing Up Father*. None of us has ever called it by its proper name: we called it "Jiggs" (after its male protagonist) or "Jiggs and Maggie" (including his wife). And only *The Katzenjammer Kids*, which began December 12, 1897, and *Mutt and Jeff* can claim comparable longevity. The first strip to bear the title *Bringing Up Father* appeared on January 2, 1913, a Thursday (figure 27).[30] It ran only daily for the next five years, albeit not every day at first, and then on April 14, 1918, it began appearing in Sunday format, too. And it ran continuously after that, seven days a week, until at least 1993 (as this is being written)—an eighty-year run.

But Jiggs and Maggie did not burst upon the comics page fully formed in January 1913. Their origin, in fact, reveals something about the nature of newspaper cartooning in the early decades of

the century. Beginning at the *Republic* in his native St. Louis and then at the *World* in New York, McManus had created several comic strips—*Panhandle Pete*, *Nipsy the Newsboy in Funny Fairyland* (in imitation of McCay's *Nemo*), *Spareribs and Gravy*, and *The Newlyweds*, to name a few. When Hearst recruited the twenty-eight-year-old cartoonist in 1912, McManus brought *The Newlyweds* with him as a Sunday page and retitled it *Their Only Child*. Then he started cranking up other features for the daily pages.[31]

His first creation for Hearst was *Outside the Asylum*, a daily strip with no recurring characters that ran for only a month, beginning December 10, 1912. Then came *Bringing Up Father*. It ran three or four days a week at first, alternating with another domestic comedy strip, *Ah, Yes! That Happy Home*, in which the husband, after proclaiming his everlasting preference for married life in the opening panels of the strip, discovers a thorn in his bed of roses by the last panel. Meanwhile, for Sundays, McManus created a second page, *Love Affairs of a Muttonhead*, which accompanied *Their Only Child*; in tandem, they explored romance and marriage among the young and naive. *Father*, however, focused on the problems a family has in adjusting to life in higher society. McManus never explained in the strip how Jiggs gained his wealth, but it is apparent that the family fortune was rather suddenly acquired, catapulting them all forthwith into a social whirl for which they had very little preparation. Jiggs's wife and daughter are socially ambitious and eager to be accepted by the "better people," but Jiggs, wholly unpretentious, perpetually frustrates their parvenu social aspirations by behaving as if he's still a hod-carrier on a construction gang. This theme proved the most provocative for McManus's sense of humor: by January 1914 he had discontinued all the daily strips except *Father*, and by the end of the decade his other Sunday features were subordinated to "Jiggs and Maggie."

McManus was not unique in producing a variety of comic strips for his newspaper. Other early cartoonists did the same, creating features on impulse; some of them lasted only a few days or

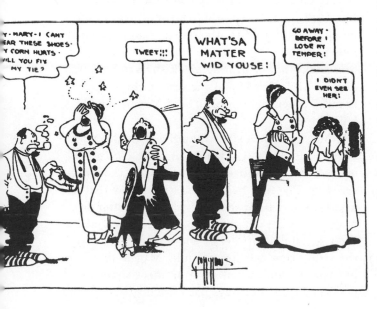

Figure 27. *The first strip to bear the title* Bringing Up Father, *which appeared on January 2, 1913.*

weeks before giving way to yet another inspiration of the moment. Many of these features appeared as aspects of a sort of daily or weekly anthology of graphic humor. Billy Ireland at the *Dispatch* in Columbus, Ohio, for instance, did a weekly page called *The Passing Show*, in which he presented a miscellaneous array of panel cartoons on various subjects.[32] Such weekly features were common during the century's first two decades, although history tends to remember only those that yielded long-lived characters. Some of Ireland's *Passing Show* cartoons featured recurring country characters, the Jedge and Uncle Jerry, but Ireland never felt the urge to produce a cartoon or comic strip about them on a daily basis. Frank King, though, found his life's work while doing a similar weekly feature for the *Chicago Tribune* during and after World War I—but more about *Gasoline Alley* later.

McManus was also producing an anthology, but his appeared in daily installments, as it were—finite variations on aspects of a subject appearing in rotation as a series of individually titled comic strips. But if McManus worked in the mainstream of the current conventions of newspaper cartooning, he was somewhat unusual in having so focused an anthology. Most such features were genuine hodgepodge collections of comic commentary; McManus concentrated on a single subject.

Although the tack taken in *Father* was the most distinctive of the domestic situations that McManus was experimenting with at the time of its inception, it was nonetheless of a piece with his other work. All his strips dealt with relations between the sexes, chiefly marriage. And Jiggs and Maggie were part of the larger ensemble that McManus created in order to explore the human potential for domestic bliss, an exploration that had been the principal preoccupation of McManus's career to date. Not surprisingly, then, characters resembling Jiggs and Maggie had appeared earlier than 1913 in one or another of the miscellaneous domestic comedy strips that McManus had been doing. Indeed, according to McManus, the characters who eventually became Jiggs and Maggie first appeared in November 1911.[33] But their personalities were presumably not yet fully formed, nor was the concept for *Bringing Up Father* well defined.

Once McManus hit upon the title for his concept, Jiggs and Maggie began to emerge. Their personalities were almost completely articulated by

the concept, but McManus hadn't quite settled such matters as their names or their appearance when they debuted. Maggie was called "Mary" in one of the early strips; and Jiggs was spelled "Giggs" at first. (It was initially used as a surname, although McManus later claimed he didn't know whether it was a first or last name. He also said the name was intended to invoke the gaiety of the Irish dance.) Their daughter Nora was first called "Katy." McManus was clearly feeling his way. Initially, Maggie's figure was matronly, even a little dumpy. Fairly soon, however, she developed the figure of a chorus girl but retained her painfully plain (even ugly) visage. (McManus once described her as the "composite of all the beautiful women in the world when they are angry.")[34] With a figure like that, Maggie was the perfect clothes-horse, displaying women's fashions throughout the years. McManus saw to it that she was always dressed in the styles of the moment.

In the beginning, the baboon-faced Jiggs sported a goatee. (And his simian physiognomy partook of a long-standing racial stereotype of the immigrant shanty Irish—a little surprising to the racially sensitive in the closing years of the twentieth century, considering that McManus was himself distinctly Irish.) When he first appeared, Jiggs was almost the same size as his wife, his burly build bespeaking his former career as a hod-carrier. By the mid-twenties, though, he began to grow shorter and wider. Perhaps Maggie was taking her toll, wearing him down, or perhaps, as McManus remarked somewhat in jest, it was due to "the evolving process of creating him in my own image." But McManus gave yet another reason: "Jiggs is short now for contrast with Maggie. It is simply ridiculous to believe that Maggie could do what she does to a husky, powerful roughneck such as Jiggs was originally."[35] The visual rhetoric of the strip demanded a Jiggs who looked as if Maggie could bully him.

If McManus was still tinkering with the appearance of his characters when *Bringing Up Father* started, he had no hesitation about his thematic territory. The first half-dozen strips show that he knew his way from the very start. Day after day, Maggie and her daughter are rudely interrupted at their social obligations by the uncouth Jiggs. On the strip's first day, for example, Maggie tells her husband to don formal attire to meet some distinguished guests, but Jiggs has difficulty getting into

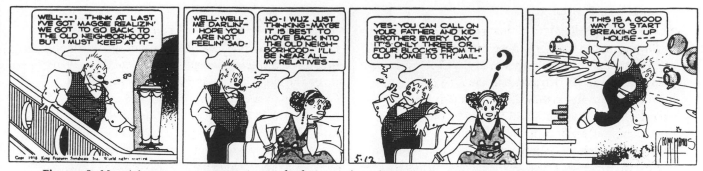

Figure 28. *Maggie's customary corrective—a hail storm of crockery.*

costume and isn't ready when the guests arrive. After a futile struggle with his tie, he comes to get Maggie to help him. Maggie is just finishing the introductions with her guests when Jiggs wanders into the strip's fourth panel—in shirtsleeves and stocking feet (shocking!). His clothes cause consternation again a couple days later when he bursts a suspender button while bowing to meet a visiting count. On his next appearance, Jiggs arrives during one of Maggie's fancy dinners—bringing with him his "old boyhood friend, Bill Maloney," who looks suspiciously like a tramp. Everyone is appalled. The formula was quickly established. Aspiring to acceptance on a higher social plane, Maggie concentrates on decorum and appearances. The uninhibited Jiggs bursts her bubble the minute he appears.

And Jiggs remains wonderfully oblivious to his sinning. Maggie chases him away from the breakfast table because he is still in his undershirt and stocking feet and she's invited a guest. Jiggs dutifully leaves but returns a few moments later—after the guest has arrived—to retrieve the morning paper he'd left at the table. Maggie and her guest gasp in alarm, and the guest, shocked and insulted, leaves. Jiggs is baffled: "What's the matter? Did she want the paper?" The next day, Maggie asks him to carve the turkey for a dinner party. Jiggs takes off his coat and rolls up his sleeves to perform this duty, thereby outraging the guests so much that they all leave. "What's the matter?" he asks Maggie, "Don't they like turkey? I'd rather had corn beef and cabbage, myself."

At first, Maggie reacts to Jiggs's gaucheries by gasping in shock or sputtering in exasperation—or, sometimes, by fainting with fright at the thought of the social humiliation she is sure will follow. But before the end of the inaugural decade, she has adopted her classic tactic: whenever Jiggs strays from the prescribed behavior, she lets him have it

with whatever missile was handy. She throws kitchenware and other household furnishings at him. The last panel of many a *Father* installment is a picture of Jiggs in a blizzard of platters and dishes, a wordless punch line that proclaims the comic conclusion with vaudevillian certainty.

McManus's graphic style evolved to match the ethos of the strip. Deploying a meticulous line of unvarying width, precisely placed, the cartoonist drew clean, uncluttered pictures. No hatey cross-hatching or shading. From this uncomplicated but careful way of rendering, McManus developed the mannered style that characterized his mature work. McManus's penmanship was elegant, his line fine and delicate, and once his style matured (by the early twenties), *Father* was distinguished by its fine-line detail in backgrounds and props, the filigree of a city skyline, the graceful curlicues in the design of a stair railing or of the pattern in Maggie's dress, the judicious and telling placement of solid blacks.

Above all else, McManus had a marvelously inventive graphic imagination. The variety of things he drew in his panels—not to mention the copious decorative detail of his work—amuses the eye endlessly (even as it boggles the mind to think of the time and energy he devoted to producing the drawings).

McManus's tricks with silhouette were striking (figure 29). A silhouette of Jiggs is always accented by the stark white of his shirt collar and cuffs. In silhouette, Maggie frequently stands with the light behind her, which renders her dress nearly transparent, a lacey network of lines, with her figure showing through. (At least once, syndicate editors were offended by McManus's daring to reveal Maggie's "superb figure": they filled in the dress, thereby inking the silhouetted figure away. "I think that was being overly proper," McManus said, "but that's the business of the office.")[36] By the thirties,

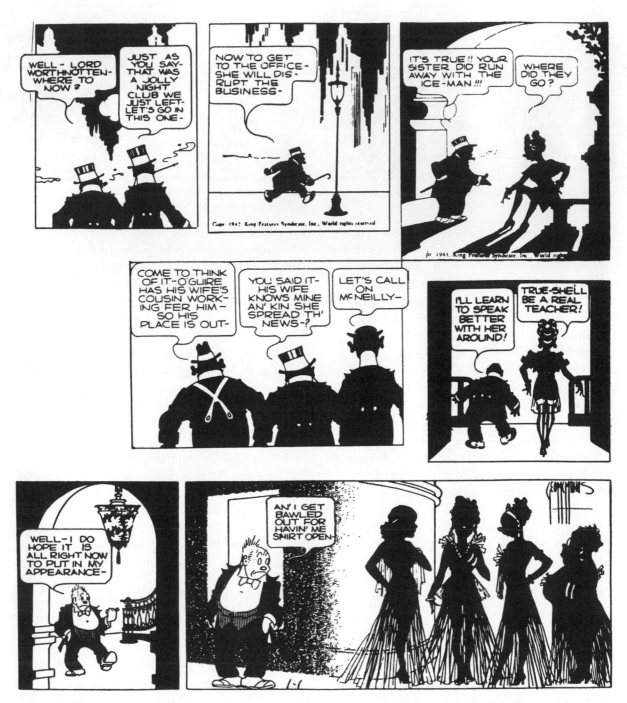

Figure 29. *McManus's use of silhouette is striking—and sometimes downright spectacular—as this montage of miscellaneous panels shows.*

McManus was using Ben-Day shading—a mechanically applied gray tone made with tiny dots—in daily strips, but he also varied the tonal quality of his strip with intricate hachuring and boldly patterned black-and-white designs.

The fecundity of McManus's graphic invention led him occasionally to play with the form of his medium. Once on a Sunday page in 1938 a wayward character slips in and out of panels, descending the page from tier to tier as if he were climbing down the facade of a building from window to window, say, or from ledge to ledge. Another time, in a daily strip, Jiggs coils up the "lines" of the panel borders. A similar spirit of playfulness doubtless inspired the antic visual device that McManus originated and that became a sort of trademark in *Father*: in prop pictures on the wall, figures emerge beyond the picture frames—even tossing things from one picture to another. "The more burlesque they are, the better," McManus

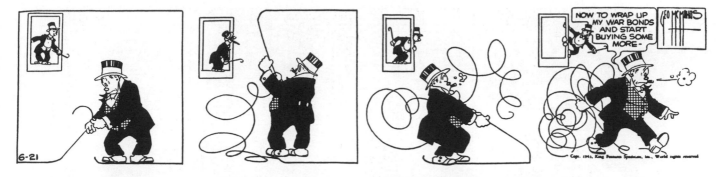

Figure 30. McManus occasionally made his characters conscious of the medium in which they appeared. Notice also the antics of the figure in the picture on the wall.

said. McManus developed the trick accidentally. Once, he said, "when I was drawing a forgotten strip called *Ready Money Ladies*, I had an annoying problem: there were a couple of figures I wanted to get into a picture frame hanging on the wall, but for balance and design, the frame couldn't be large enough to accommodate them. So I simply drew them outside the frame as well as inside."[37]

The cartoonist met a graphic challenge of a different sort when he took his characters on a tour of the country in 1939–40. The tour took better than six months (dailies as well as Sundays) and so

taxed McManus that he once said doing this sequence was "probably the toughest job of my career." He explained: "When it was announced that Jiggs and family were to make the tour, there were demands from everywhere, it seemed, that they visit this or that town. Since it was excellent promotion, I acceded to the demands. The result was that Jiggs and Maggie and Nora went from New York to California via practically every state in the Union and through the Dominion of Canada as well. . . . The backgrounds had to be accurate and the work was prodigious."[38]

These tour strips demonstrate McManus's con-

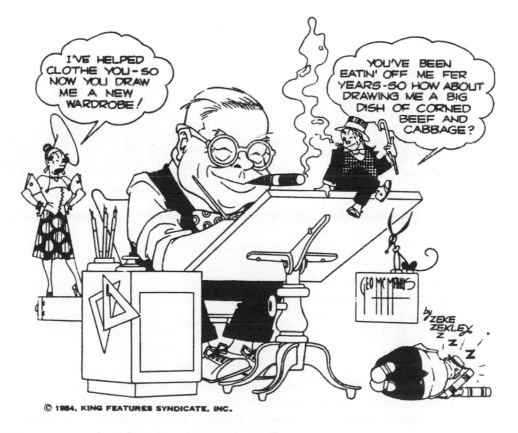

Figure 31. McManus as seen by Zeke Zekley, his longtime assistant.

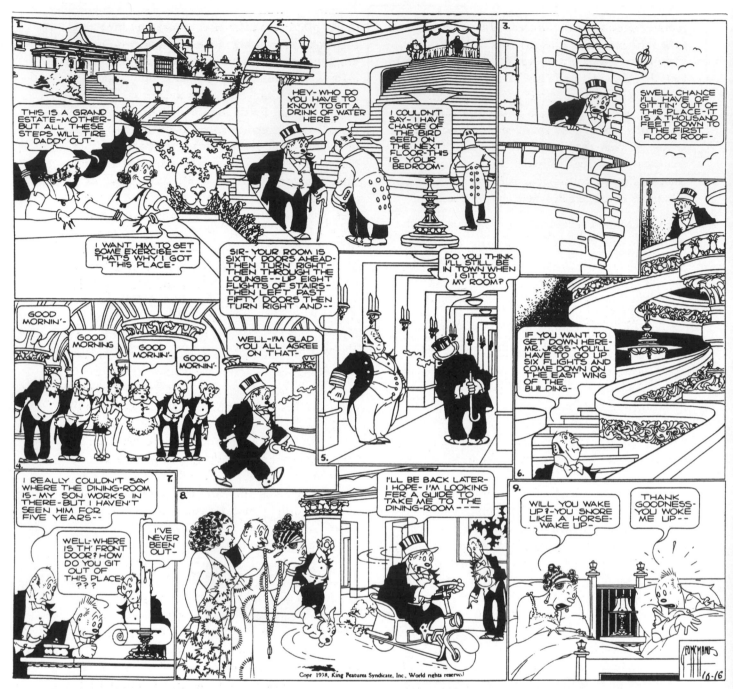

Figure 32. *The interiors of the mansions Jiggs and Maggie inhabited display McManus's extraordinary design facility.*

summate skill as an artist. He was not only skilled: he was passionate about background detail. He said he spent two weeks on a single panel of the Sunday page for December 31, 1939: "This was New Year's Eve," McManus said, "and I had Jiggs looking north in New York's Time Square with the Square faithfully pictured in every detail."[39] The Sunday pages of *Bringing Up Father* were often elaborately designed, the panels shaped to suit the narrative purpose of the day, their varying sizes and shapes fitting together like jigsaw pieces.

McManus's elegant linework was perfectly matched to his subject. The atmosphere of opulence that pervades the world in which Jiggs and Maggie live was virtually created by the rococo style of McManus's renderings. His graceful line gave substance to artifact and architecture. And the same line was masterful at suggesting a lush female figure with the drapery of fashionable feminine raiment. Jiggs, like any reasonably healthy male animal, was not above ogling pretty girls. (In fact, doing so was perfectly in character for him, contributing to his portrait as an unabashed fellow. But ogle was all he did: no philanderer he.) And McManus made these young women simply gorgeous. He neglected no detail in rendering these beauties: their faces were delicately delineated, their coiffures luxuriously curled and coiled and piled, their figures full, their legs long and curvaceous.

But McManus did not confine himself to drawing the world of the wealthy. Periodically, he produced Sunday pages that reminisced fondly about the life of the laboring classes that Jiggs and Maggie had left behind. Jiggs would lean back and say: "Remember, Maggie me darlin', when we kids used to call at Wun- Lung-Gon, the Chinese laundry, to get your daddy's shirts—I mean, shirt . . . and how we envied Jerry McGuire when he had the mumps an' didn't have to go to school . . . and th' women always had a fancy apron to put on when they answered the front door . . . and how cold it used to get in the morning—we used to get the ice-pick to break the ice in the water pitcher so we could wash."

The pictures usually complemented the prose, providing an ironic gloss. "Remember when the boys would go on a fishing trip to get away from the congestion in the city," Jiggs would say—and the picture showed a boat jammed, bow to stern, with fishermen. "Remember, Maggie, the day your mother gave Willie a dime to clean the attic where your father used to take his daily nap—and nip"— and the picture exhibited little Willie contemplating an enormous stack of empty liquor bottles. The comedy was created by the juxtaposition of words and pictures. "And Willie Gitwell tried to show off to Maxie Hazy by smoking a cigar"—and in the picture, Willie is clearly sick. And sometimes the coupling of word and picture yielded a poignant insight into a character's past: "And how proud you were when I took you up on th' avenue an' we mingled with the elite," Jiggs says, and the picture reveals that, at the time, he and Maggie were but seven or eight years old, young lovers indeed.

These strips capture the quality of life for immigrants in turn-of-the-century urban America. In them, McManus celebrates communal life along the back alleys of big cities, the numerousness of brothers and sisters and cousins and aunts, the distaste for school among the young, the scarcity of luxuries, the drudgery of the common labor by which they all lived, and the delinquency of fathers (who seemed to spend as much time drunk or in jail—with all their other relatives—as they did on any job). In these strips more than in any other category of his work, McManus's gift for comic art runs rampant, unfettered. His comic figures cavort on these nostalgic pages entirely uninhibited by any purpose other than to be humorous. And that they are. No one ever equaled McManus in portraying the hilarious aspect of an unlettered laborer attired in his Sunday best, celluloid collar choking him to such an extent that his ears stand straight out from his head.

But if these strips deal with the immigrant experience in America directly, they do not embody it as profoundly as does the central theme of McManus's strip. It seems to me that the recurring chorus of Father's formula accurately captures the essence of the immigrant experience—culture shock, all the more disorienting because the rise from rags (metaphorically speaking) to riches (ditto), from the poverty of the Old World to the relative prosperity of the New, was so rapid. The strip epitomized the consequences of this transformation.

The inspiration for the strip came to McManus seventeen years before he drew it. Growing up in St. Louis, young George saw a play in 1895 in the theater his father managed. The play, The Rising Generation, featured a poker game scene, during which, for twenty minutes each night, the actors played a real game of poker for real stakes and ad-libbed throughout. One of the poker players, the hero of the play, was a little Irish laborer who'd struck it rich and moved to Fifth Avenue. As McManus tells it: "His socially ambitious wife and daughter were ashamed of his uninhibited naturalness and they could not abide his old pals (leftovers from the days before he was rich). Therefore, he had to sneak off to the poker game, which was in the back room of a saloon run by an old friend in the district from which the Irisher came."[40] In the Irish poker player's "uninhibited naturalness" and in his consequent unflagging desire to escape (for however brief a time) from the pretensions of

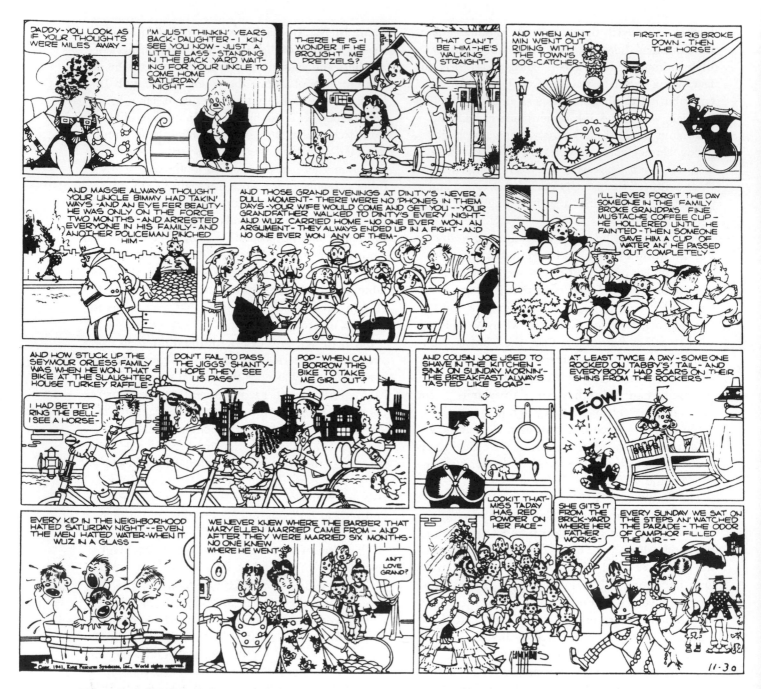

Figure 33. *When Jiggs reminisced, McManus reconstructed a turn-of-the- century past that provided insight into the immigrant experience of most Americans.*

the social world into which his wealth has flung him, we find the quintessential Jiggs—and the formula that is central to most of the humor in *Bringing Up Father* as well as the theme of the immigrant experience in America. Although the formula involves but a single, basic situation, which was expressed in only about a dozen different ways, McManus multiplied that one times twelve to produce an infinite number of variations

upon his basic theme. But each of those modifications restates the central conflict of the informing formula.

Jiggs's abiding affection for a game of cards, a drink, the fellowship of his old cronies at Dinty Moore's corner saloon, for corned beef and cabbage (the strip's ubiquitous symbol of a simpler, more natural life), and for pretty girls pits him forever against Maggie's tyrannical efforts to reform him, to mold him into a dignified shape appropriate to their new status and to her social ambitions. As often as not, Maggie is defeated in her efforts by her own bad taste or by her fundamental ignorance of the ways of high society. By far the bulk of *Bringing Up Father* deals with situations that exemplify these traits in Jiggs or Maggie. In the forty-one years he drew *Father* before he died in 1954, McManus never entirely abandoned his "single-situation" formula. It faded into the background for one or two strips, but it soon emerged again, an unending restatement of the strip's enduring theme. In this regard, McManus carried far into the twentieth century the essential character of the early comic strip.

Because *Father* presents so often the situation that embodies its basic theme, the daily strips often seemed to end without a punch line. That impression is due partly to the fact that we've seen that punch line—that situation itself—before. But even if we hadn't, we don't really need a punch line. The situation itself is the mainspring of the humor in the strip—not any punch line at the end. Given a ready-made comic conclusion of this sort in the very situations he depicted, McManus developed the humor in a given installment by weaving witty repartee into its panels throughout. The kind of humor we have come to associate with the last panel of a humor strip was often found in the first, second, or third panels of *Father*. Here's a sample bit of dialogue from the first panel of a 1939 strip:

NORA (in a riding costume): Why, Daddy—this is my English riding habit. I intend to wear it a great deal when I get to England.
JIGGS: I hope I don't form any habits like that. It looks like a fit to me.

This strip concludes when Jiggs sees Maggie in her version of the same English riding costume. And the visual nature of the medium creates the final punch line. Nora looks beautiful and dignified in her costume, but that's because she's beautiful and dignified looking—not because the costume contributes anything. Jiggs sees the costume; we see the costume and the girl. On Maggie, who hasn't the saving grace of physical beauty, we see the riding costume as Jiggs saw it on Nora: as an outlandish and therefore ridiculous outer covering. Maggie puts on the costume in the simple, misguided belief that appearances are all: her clothes

will prove she belongs in English high society. To assure the success of the effort, she's added a monocle. It is the appearance of status, to be sure. But Jiggs knows Maggie—and Nora—and the nature of their origins, who they really are. In his startled reaction when he sees Maggie we find the hint that clothes do not, despite appearances, make the man (or woman). Maggie is wrong again: she falls short of her pretentious ambitions.

Here's another dialogue sample, this time from 1919:

MAGGIE (who is thinking of her birthday): Do you know what day tomorrow is?
JIGGS: Sure—it's Dugan's chowder party. Kin I go?
MAGGIE: You insect. I married you to reform you.
JIGGS: You've succeeded: I'll never marry again.
MAGGIE: I wish I'd never met you.
JIGGS: Yes—now when it's too late, you are sorry for me.

There are at least two good punch lines in the foregoing—and we haven't come to the strip's last panel yet. In that last panel, Jiggs is shown in a hail of crockery, Maggie's customary corrective for his unrepentant uninhibitedness. We've seen it before, and we'll see it again: the punch line is built into the situation, and, seemingly, we never tire of seeing that situation replayed.

Jiggs's unceasing attempts to escape from Maggie's world to Dinty Moore's were given heroic dimension by McManus. Throughout the years he demonstrated convincingly that Jiggs would do anything to escape, resort to any device, follow any route. In the classic Sunday routine, Maggie locks Jiggs in his room, and he leaves by an upper-story window, creeps along the cornice twenty floors above the ground to a telephone wire, walks the wire, swings to a steel girder suspended high above the street, and finally gets lowered to a convenient back alley from which it is but a few steps to Dinty's tavern and the goodly fellowship he craves. The pictures create the comedy as well as the illusion upon which the comedy depends: we laugh because the extremes to which Jiggs resorts are so outlandish, so exaggerated, and yet we believe it is happening because we can see it with our own eyes, right there before us on the page.

After witnessing a performance or two like this, readers could reasonably be expected to be bored by further repetition of the maneuver, the humor in it exhausted. Not so. Jiggs did all these things countless times for over forty years, and he kept

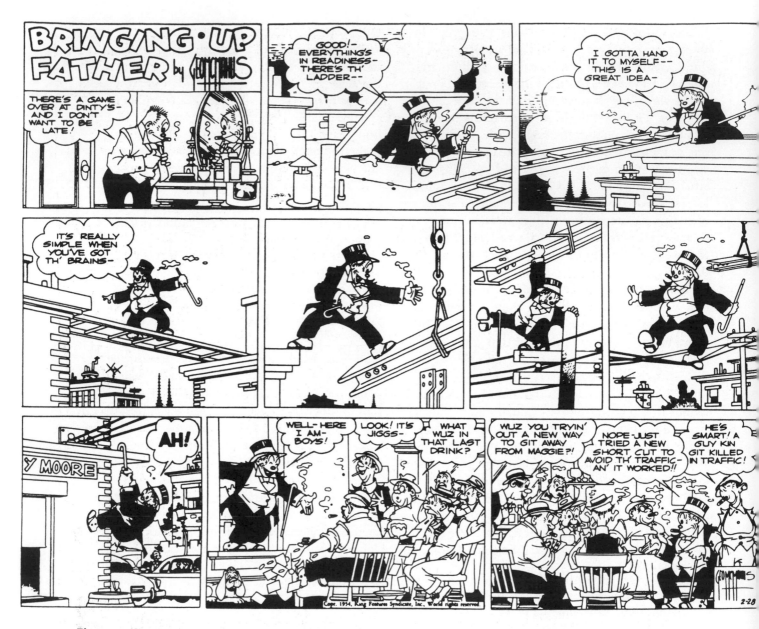

Figure 34. *Jiggs's escape routes to Dinty Moore's are legendary.*

his readers with him all the way. By the time McManus died, Jiggs was repeating his escape act in five hundred newspapers in forty-six countries— an estimated audience of eighty million people. The inexhaustible humor in the situation lay in Jiggs's marvelous ingenuity—and that, in turn, spoke of the unquenchable resourcefulness of human aspiration. But it is in the nature of that aspiration—in its fundamental message—that we find the basic, unyielding appeal of the strip.

In Jiggs's unrelenting effort to escape and in Maggie's frequent failure to live up to her own pretensions, we see the seemingly endless elaboration on the theme that people *will* be themselves—and

that they are the better for so being, regardless of social pretensions. It was, for countless immigrants, the message of America. In one of the oft-repeated reversals found in *Bringing Up Father*, Maggie discovers that Jiggs is already the intimate companion of some social lion whom she wanted him to meet. And Jiggs has done it by being himself.

In later years, McManus recognized explicitly the simple message of his strip. In an article in *Collier's* (from which I've been quoting him), McManus wrote: "My own conclusion is that Jiggs and Maggie are burlesques of basic human characteristics. I say 'conclusion' because only in rela-

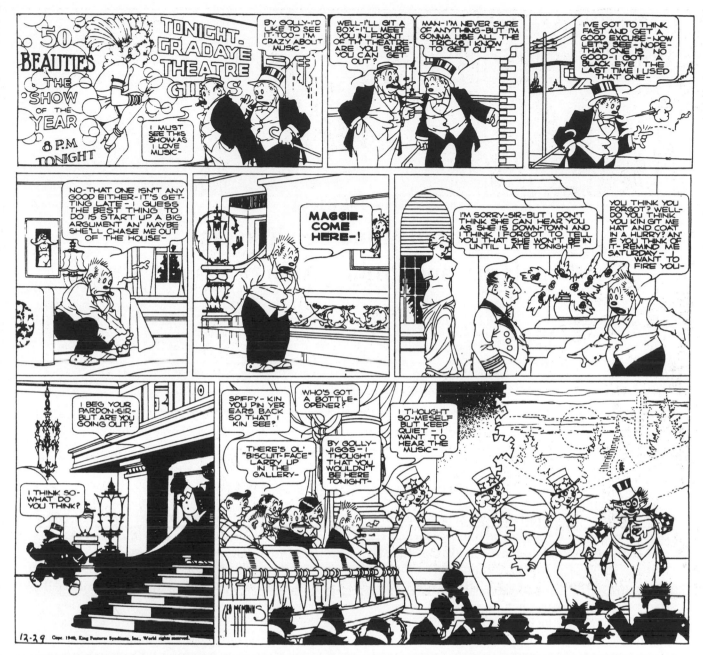

Figure 35. *The finale—architectural opulence, dramatic silhouette, a clutch of gags and witticisms, and a bevy of pretty girls (December 29, 1940).*

tively recent years have I thought much about it. Most of the time, I just drew characters I thought were amusing in situations I thought were funny. It was as simple as that. . . . Jiggs represents man's eternal struggle to be himself in this modern world. Always he strives against what he considers feminine domination and a womanly desire to mold him into an ideal image. His resistance is constant, but so are his respect and tolerance, so he usually fights back obliquely.[41]

"Jiggs and I enjoy being ourselves," McManus

concluded. "Hedda Hopper says (doing the strip) should be easy for me. 'George,' she wrote once, 'draws Jiggs the way he wants to act himself.' Maybe. Anyway, we both like people. We like restaurants and round tables, with people sitting around them enjoying themselves."[42]

Enjoying themselves by being themselves—the message McManus dinned into his readers for nearly two generations, a vivid demonstration of the power of the single-situation comedy that so often characterized early comic strips.

Thematic Choruses of Bud Fisher and George McManus   59

CHAPTER 4
Continuity and Syndication
The Popularity and Proliferation of Comic Strips

Mary Gold died on April 30, 1929. The public outcry when her death became known was gratifying in both its precipitousness and its volume. Switchboards at major metropolitan newspapers were clogged for hours. Mail rooms quickly overflowed with letters expressing sympathy and outrage. Her doctors would offer no medical explanation for her death. They merely muttered shamefaced speculations about the vagaries of the human mechanism, and many of her friends consequently concluded that the cause of death was a broken heart—the tragic and tattered end of a labyrinthine love story that should have ended happily.

The body politic had been following the ups and downs of Mary Gold's love life for months. She'd been courted by a young inventor, Tom Carr, but on the eve of their wedding, he'd been arrested for absconding with his backers' money. After a long trial, he was found guilty and sentenced to ten years in prison. Mary Gold came to public attention in the sensational aftermath of the trial. Grief-stricken, she nonetheless consented to marry a friend of her family's, a wealthy banker named Henry J. Ausstinn. On the day of the lavish wedding, the ceremony was spectacularly interrupted by Tom Carr's brother, who produced evidence that not only established his brother's innocence but fingered Ausstinn as the man who'd stolen the money and framed Tom. The strain of these events

was too much for poor Mary. Her health broken, she took to bed with a high fever, and in a week or so she was dead. The outburst of popular sentiment promptly exploded all across the country.

Public preoccupation with the affairs of private citizens was scarcely novel in the twenties (or in any other period, for that matter). But during that decade, the mass media were coming of age, and newspapers learned to play upon the nation's curiosity with all the skill of a pied piper fingering his flute. Editors seized upon every scandal or sensation that seemed to capture the public fancy and kept it on the front page for weeks. In addition to the daily doings of such luminaries as Waxey Gordon, Al Capone, Legs Diamond, and Dutch Schultz, there was the Fifi Stillman divorce case (in which her husband maintained that their fifth child was illegitimate), the Fatty Arbuckle scandal (featuring the trial of the popular film comedian for accidentally killing a starlet during one of his typical Hollywood orgies), the Hall-Mills murder mystery (the unsolved killing of a pastor and a female member of his choir), and the Sydney-Gray sex-and-homicide epic (in which Ruth Snyder and her lover, a corset salesman, were brought to book for the murder of her husband).

Still, Mary Gold was different. The Mary Gold who died had never lived. She was only a paper doll. A character in a comic strip. Her sole distinc-

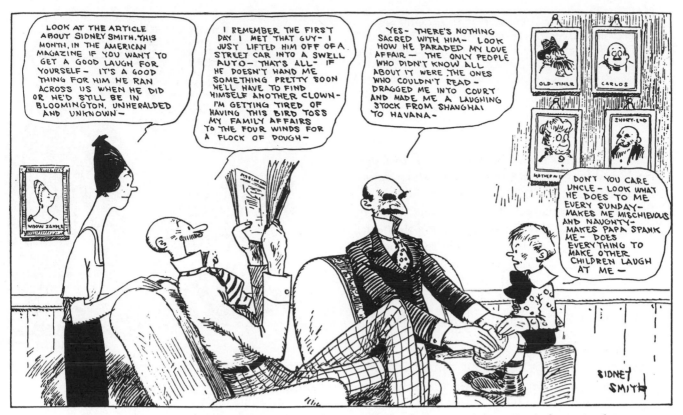

Figure 36. *By 1923, the date of this family portrait (made especially for the* American Magazine*), the main characters of Sidney Smith's* The Gumps *had been firmly established (left to right): Min and Andy Gump, their fabulously wealthy Uncle Bim from Australia, and their son Chester.*

tion was in being the first major comic strip character to die. And the overwhelming public reaction to her death testified to the popularity of the comics with an authority difficult (if not impossible) to dispute.

Not that there was any dispute. The comic strip in which Mary Gold lived and died was *The Gumps*, written and drawn for the *Chicago Tribune* by Sidney Smith. The strip dwelt with melodramatic excess on the opportunistic yearnings of Andy Gump, a creature whose bizarre, chinless physiognomy set him apart from every other comic strip character in the popular mind (which conveniently overlooked, apparently, that Augustus Mutt was identically endowed). Andy's avaricious middle-class aspirations struck a chord—whether sympathetic or antithetic—among newspaper readers. The strip was a resounding success, inspiring the kind of fanatical following that grieves over fictional death.

The Gumps began in the *Tribune* in 1917, and within a few years the strip had created such a stir that it was syndicated for distribution in every major city in which there was a newspaper with any

pretensions to greatness. The combined circulation of the newspapers in which *The Gumps* appeared eventually reached twelve million. So valuable a property was the strip that the *Tribune* was moved to extraordinary financial largess when cartoonist Smith's contract came up for renewal in March 1922. To retain his services, the *Tribune* made him a million-dollar deal—$100,000 a year for the next ten years. It was not as much as Bud Fisher was making, but news of the million dollar-contract was widely circulated, fueling interest in the strip among both its fans and those who might become fans. At the time, the publicity was certain to point out, President Harding earned but $75,000 annually. And Babe Ruth wouldn't sign his heralded $80,000 contract for eight more years. Sidney Smith manipulated the daily doings of Andy, his wife Min, Uncle Bim, and all the rest—but the strip was created, named, and guided by Captain Joseph Medill Patterson, who had a genius for knowing what the public wanted.

At the time of Mary Gold's death, Captain Patterson was in command of the largest daily newspaper in America, the *New York Daily News*,

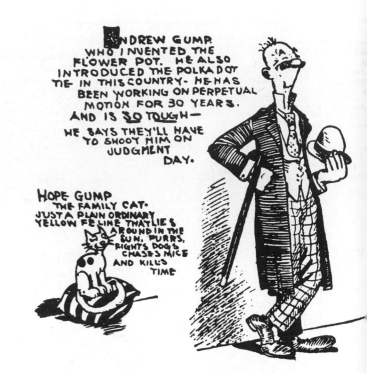

Figure 37. When The Gumps *began in 1917, the cast, depicted here in Smith's introductory strip of February 12, didn't look much different than the ordinary people they were supposed to be. Andy's chinlessness wasn't quite so noticeable as it became within weeks of this drawing's publication. At the upper right, a glimpse of Andy without his moustache (from a strip drawn in the early 1920s).*

which he and his cousin, Colonel Robert McCormick, had founded ten years earlier, using profits from their *Chicago Tribune* to invade the New York newspaper market. The *Daily News* began on June 26, 1919, starting at the bottom of the heap with the lowest circulation of New York's eighteen daily newspapers, but in less than five years, it surpassed Hearst's champion, the *New York Journal*. Patterson had beaten the king of the hill at his own game, and he had done it by giving the public what he knew it wanted—sex and scandal, games and contests.

Along the way, it is often said, Patterson also invented the continuity comic strip. Probably, he didn't. But even if he didn't invent the story strip, Patterson certainly midwifed at its birth and nursed it into healthy infancy.

Patterson's inspiration for a continuity strip may have arisen from his earlier experiences while in charge of the *Sunday Chicago Tribune*. He'd started running a directory of current attractions in Chicago's movie theaters, and, noting the favorable reader response, he soon hit upon another way to capitalize upon the public's fascination with the flickers. Making a deal with William Selig, the producer of one of the first movie serials, *The Adventures of Kathlyn*, Patterson began on January 4, 1914, to publish the written version of each week's installment the week before the film version appeared. Readers could win prizes by guessing the solutions to mysteries in each week's printed episode. *Kathlyn* ran for twenty-six weeks, and each week the *Tribune's* circulation department had to increase news agents' orders by hundreds of copies.

The lesson was not lost on Patterson. He continued to run written versions of serial thrillers, and the success of these features (together with that of serialized popular fiction, which he also published in the *Sunday Tribune*) doubtless lodged in a corner of his brain an idea that he would later introduce into the medium of comic strips. A basic ingredient of the installment stories he was pub-

lishing was *continuation*: the reader, the newspaper buyer, had to buy next week's *Sunday Tribune* to see how the stories came out—and he had to go on buying the next week's edition as long as the story continued.

Comic strips that told continuing stories had been around long before Captain Patterson took an interest in the idea. As we've seen, *Little Nemo* frequently continued a narrative from Sunday to Sunday, and Bud Fisher had done it from day to day at various times in the early days of *Mutt and Jeff*. And these two strips were not alone. C. W. Kahles introduced *Hairbreadth Harry* in 1906, a Sunday strip that carried its story forward from week to week. And Harry Hershfield used daily continuity in his *Desperate Desmond* (1910) and its sequel, *Dauntless Durham* (1913). Patterson can scarcely be said, then, to have invented the concept. But he (and Smith) refined it in a way that opened the door to the future, to continuity strips of exotic adventure: *The Gumps* made suspense the driving mechanism of the continuing-story strip. And because *The Gumps* was syndicated and distributed to many papers around the nation, it had a greater impact upon the medium than any of the earlier attempts at continuity strips.

The earlier continuities were not altogether serious about suspense. *Little Nemo*, in fact, was not even particularly suspenseful. Nemo woke up in

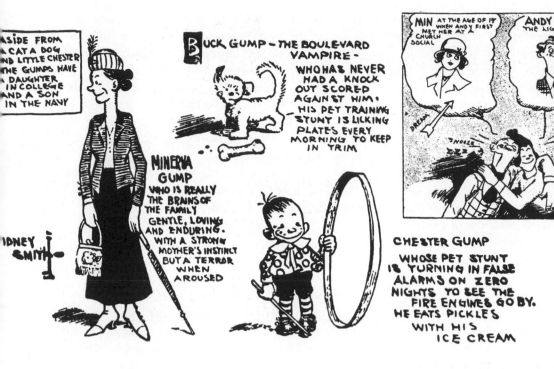

bed at the end of every Sunday episode, so we were hardly on tenterhooks about what would happen next. Still, a narrative is inherently suspenseful: it is, after all, the nature of a story to make us want to know its outcome. And the suspense is enhanced when the story is told in installments, a little bit of narrative each day or week. But McCay did not capitalize upon the serial nature of his medium by deliberately constructing suspenseful conclusions to each installment. He permitted his story to be interrupted as a matter of necessity, the following week's installment merely resuming the story at the point of interruption. Fisher and Kahles and Hershfield used the medium more deliberately, particularly the latter two: they contrived suspenseful conclusions for every installment of their strips. (Fisher did so only occasionally.) Their strips were also forays into farce, mock heroic adventures that burlesqued popular melodrama (itself little more than a burlesque). The stock characters of stage productions—stalwart and stoic hero, beautiful and cringing damsel, mustache-twirling villain—were exaggerated and the cliff-hanger narrative mechanism similarly overdrawn for comic effect.

When Patterson began thinking about a new comic strip in early 1917, he envisioned something considerably more in touch with reality than either Kahles or Hershfield had achieved. And that's what the Captain got—and then some. Once Sidney Smith warmed to his task, he soaped his stories with every sudsy bubble of melodrama he could lay his pen to, but the people in his stories were ordinary people and their predicaments those of ordinary people, recognizably the fellow creatures of the strip's readers. "I wanted everyday things to happen to them," Smith once said. "I was not so much concerned about making them terribly funny, but I did want them to be *true*. I thought I'd get what I wanted if I could draw something which a wife would read and hand to her husband with the remark, 'There, that's *you!*'"[1] And that was precisely what Patterson desired—a strip about real people who would become involved in situations with which *Tribune* readers could identify.

Doubtless in conceiving the strip Patterson harkened back to the novels he had written in his youth when influenced by the social realism of Theodore Dreiser. The strip would achieve both comedy and catastrophe by focusing on an average lower-middle-class family—father, mother, and children (one young son at home, one in the Navy, and a daughter in college; the elder offspring were mentioned in the strip's introduction, but Smith never brought them into his stories). In its aspirations and adventures, the family would mirror the ambitions and appetites of the *Tribune's* readers as

Patterson imagined them. Patterson christened his family "the Gumps," employing a slightly derisive term he and his sister Cissie had applied as children to loudmouthed adults. In Andy Gump's case, the name was a self- fulfilling prophecy.

Having conceptualized his new strip, Patterson looked for someone to produce it. It was probably the shortest talent search on record. In those early, unsophisticated days of comic strips, Patterson probably thought anyone who could draw cartoons could draw *The Gumps*, so he simply turned to the *Tribune's* staff of cartoonists—which, at the time, was minuscule. The Sunday comics section printed only four strips: in addition to *Hans and Fritz* by Rudolph Dirks (Patterson's favorite), there was *Mama's Angel Child* by Perry Ross, *Bobby Make Believe* by Frank King, and *Old Doc Yak*, Sidney Smith's offering. Only *Yak* and a Clare Briggs's feature of rotating titles ("Ain't It a Grand and Glorious Feeling?" "They Can't Arrest You for That," "Days of Real Sport," and the like) ran in the daily paper.

Why Patterson picked Smith to do *The Gumps* is something of a mystery. *Old Doc Yak* certainly bore no resemblance to the kind of strip he imagined: a silly slapstick romp about a goat and his son, Yutch, it was about as far from Dreiser's gritty realism as vaudeville is from Shakespearean tragedy. Maybe Patterson merely elected to discontinue the strip that he liked least—in effect, reassigning the cartoonist to *The Gumps*. Or maybe he saw in Smith's goat strip an almost imperceptible quality that he felt Smith could translate effectively into the realization of Patterson's idea. Whatever the case, Smith got *The Gumps*, and he turned out to be an inspired choice.

Given Patterson's proprietary, almost paternal, feeling about *The Gumps*, it would be difficult to imagine Smith doing a continuing story without Patterson's approval—if not at his express suggestion. And while *The Gumps* eventually told a continuing story, with Smith, as I said, pitching suspense at fever levels, at the beginning the continuity was more thematic than narrative.

Before Smith introduced the Gumps to his readers, he devised an exit for Old Doc Yak. On Thursday, February 8, 1917, Smith announced to *Yak* readers that "Old Doc Yak has been served notice that if the rent for this space is not paid by Saturday, he and his son Yutch will have to leave this page and it will be rented to another party." Yak

fails to come up with the rent, of course, and on Saturday the landlord appears to confide: "Between you and me and the lamppost, I was going to put him out anyway—whether he paid his rent or not—there's a new family goin' to move into this space on Monday." And on Monday, the 12th, the Gumps are introduced. The slender continuity of these last *Yak* strips was prolonged through the following week, which featured jokes about the Gumps' moving in. But the strip was essentially a daily gag strip, its continuity deriving entirely from the moving-in theme. In March the daily gags perpetuated thematic continuity in Andy's on-going battle with a mouse in his new house. And so it went for the rest of the year and the next two.

At first, Andy's adventures were the mundane preoccupations of the average American of the times, and Smith aimed to provoke laughter in his readership. Andy had mother-in-law troubles for days on end, went fishing on his vacation, and railed in endless monologue against the minor evils and irritations of the world, those that particularly festered in the middle-class mind: taxes, waste in government, the rising cost of living, women's fashions, food, family life, and so on. His diatribes were often so heated as to inflate speech balloons at the rate of eighty to a hundred words per balloon, a heroic accomplishment. But no story line emerged.

By January 1920 Andy's rich Uncle Bim was on the scene, and there was much discussion of Bim's settling on little Chester Gump as his heir (with Andy's accompanying flights of fantasy at the prospect of being thereby enriched himself). But it wasn't until the following year that *The Gumps* began a strong narrative, a story line that was continued suspensefully from day to day. In February 1921 Uncle Bim starts to fall into the clutches of the Widow Zander, a gold-digging damsel whose marital intentions for Bim threaten Andy's hopes for fortune. The laughter went out of the strip as the suspense heightened. The Widow Zander affair continued into 1922, and that year Andy ran for Congress. The blowhard had found his calling, and Patterson and Smith had captured their audience.

By this time, people were asking newsdealers for "the Gump paper," not the *Tribune*. During the Widow Zander affair, feelings ran high, as some of the letters Smith received reveal: "I have read the *Chicago Tribune* for about twenty long years. If

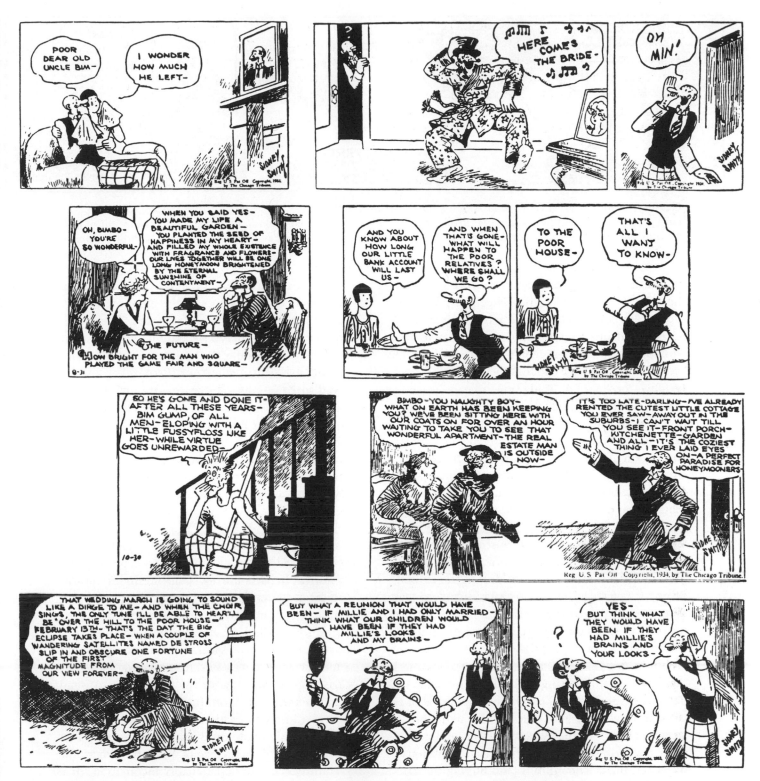

Figure 38. *Andy and Minerva Gump's avaricious aspirations became pinned to Uncle Bim almost as soon as the Australian relative showed up in late 1919. These panels, all from the early 1930s, suggest the ups and downs the couple's hopes suffered through the years. Once (upper left) they thought Bim had died, and their grief at losing a cherished relation was typically short-lived. Beginning with the famous Widow Zander sequence in 1921, Bim was the object of every gold-digging young woman's schemes, and he frequently fell into their snares. Bim's hopes for matrimonial happiness doom Andy's expectations for inheriting Bim's fortune through Chester—a fact that neither Andy nor Min was very adept at concealing whenever it appeared Bim's wealth would find its way into someone else's bank account.*

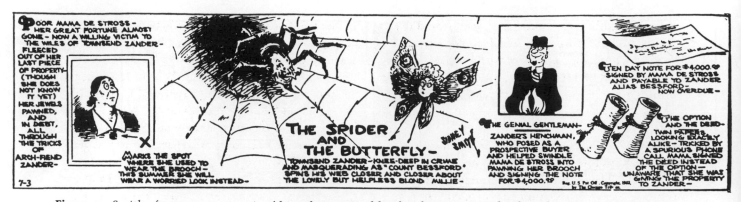

Figure 39. *Smith often gave a synopsis of his tale in strips like the above. A virtual political cartoon in format, the strip prolongs suspense by postponing further developments while the emotion-laden images add to the pall of tragedy and disaster hanging over the affairs of Mama De Stross and her daughter Millie (who would eventually marry Bim).*

you let that Zander female marry poor old Uncle Bim, I am off your blooming sheet for life. Final notice." Another letter came with eighteen co-signers: "If this engagement isn't broken very soon, the undersigners won't buy the Tribune any more!"[2] On the day Uncle Bim was to wed the Widow, the Board of Trade in Minneapolis (according to report) suspended operations for several minutes during the busiest part of the day in order to give the brokers a chance to read the early edition of an afternoon paper carrying *The Gumps* so they could find out whether Bim escaped the Widow's clutches or not. (Bim does: on the way to the church, he discovers the Widow's diary in the recesses of his automobile's back seat, and in the diary he reads uncomplimentary things that she has written about him, things that reveal her true opinion of him. Instead of driving to the church, Bim goes off into the country.) The strip's growing popularity resulted in the *Tribune's* monetary tribute to Smith's value—his celebrated million-dollar contract of 1922.

While Andy Gump's pedestrian interests and his opinionated trumpeting probably contributed in large measure to the rapidly growing appeal of the strip during its earliest years, it was undoubtedly the continuity of the Widow Zander episodes that sent the strip soaring into the public consciousness and made *The Gumps* (and buying the *Tribune* every day) a habit if not an addiction among its readers. Suspenseful continuity as a device for building a successful comic strip had been established.

Smith played upon his readers' addiction mercilessly. He began to pull out all the stops of melodrama, and *The Gumps* stepped back several paces

from reality (although not so far that readers could no longer see themselves in the dilemmas of Smith's characters). The villains, at first merely grasping, became heartless and vicious. The predicaments of the good folks became more and more pitiful, and Smith ladled out the purple prose: "And so Zander escapes again—through his lies and deceit, he has made another innocent man victim to an unjust fate. How long can this fiend's amazing luck hold out?" And, two days later: "Oh, Townsend Zander, could you but see this brave, pathetic little figure trudging down toward the cold icy gray swamp, even your icy heart would be melted."

Smith milked the crises in the strip for every last dribble of suspense, slowing his plots by postponing developments for days. To keep suspense at hysterical heights during such interludes, Smith sometimes employed a maneuver unique for a comic strip: for a day or two, he would turn the strip into an editorial cartoon, with the villain portrayed variously as a vulture preying on his victim, a hungry cat eyeing a bird (the heroine) in a bird cage, a spider waiting for the heroine-fly to wander into his web, and so on (figure 39). No other cartoonist I know of so blatantly exploited the resources of his medium. But in no other strip I know of would the device of an editorial cartoon installment fail to be laughably incongruous. It is more than a bit too much. But *The Gumps* was so excessive in every way that Smith's novel means of protracting the suspense seemed entirely appropriate.

Smith's artwork was crude by today's standards —his line often shaky, his compositions cluttered with cross-hatching as slapdash as his plotting seemed. But his style, crude as it was, suited his subject, underscoring with its hayey appearance the seamy ambiance of many of the stories. All of it—the melodramatic plots, the bathetic perils, the purple prose, the transparently mechanical drawing out of suspense—kept readers coming back for more.

The full dramatic potential of continuity would not be achieved until realistic illustration transformed the funnies pages in the thirties. But the operative principle of comic strip continuity as a mechanism for building suspense as well as newspaper circulation could not have received a more effective demonstration than the one Smith gave in *The Gumps*.

The immense popularity of *The Gumps* helped establish the Chicago Tribune Syndicate (which later became the Chicago Tribune–New York Daily News Syndicate). Out-of-town papers began requesting to buy the strip for their readers. Since 1910 the *Tribune*, like many large metropolitan dailies of the time, had been selling its features to other papers. But in 1918 Patterson gave the word from Europe (where he was earning his military rank in the American Expeditionary Force in France) to form a subsidiary marketing organization and put Arthur Crawford in charge. A few years later, the reputation of *The Gumps* would give Crawford's salesmen a commodity that virtually sold itself, enriching the *Tribune's* coffers beyond the possibilities attainable through increasing the paper's circulation alone. And syndication gave Smith a national audience. It also enabled him to pour his creative energies solely into the strip, a benefit of syndication that would have a profound effect upon the comic strip medium.

The modern feature syndicate began in the 1860s by supplying small-town newspaper editors with newsprint already printed on one side with "evergreen" material (feature stories and illustrations that were timeless, without topical or local reference). Country editors who bought the service then printed local news and advertising on the blank sides of the sheets. The first syndicate was started by Ansel Kellogg in Wisconsin, and it quickly acquired a large list of subscribers. During the Civil War there was a shortage of manpower: those who might otherwise be setting type in country newspaper shops were engaged in the conflict in the South. For a comparatively modest user fee, the syndicate service filled in the vacant ranks

in the print shops by doing half the work the absent printers would have done. This economic attraction of syndicate service was later improved upon when a growing number of syndicates began to supply small papers with material they could not generate locally—reports on the New York social scene, for instance, and serialized fiction. The service gave small-town newspapers a sophisticated content beyond the capacity of their tiny staffs' abilities and with the same stroke freed those staffs to devote their time and energies entirely to the pursuit of local news stories.

With the growth in 1890s of the Sunday editions of great metropolitan dailies, the services of syndicates were even more appreciated—this time, even in the big cities. Syndicates supplied much of the feature material used in the swelling Sunday supplements, developing a contractual system that gave a client paper exclusive rights to publish the features it bought: the syndicate would not sell the same features to any other newspapers in the same circulation territory. Once the exclusive contract was conceived, syndicates were almost compelled to develop a great variety of similar features so that they would have something available for purchase by several clients in the same territory. Technological developments kept pace with the expanding content of the services. By the end of the century, syndicated features were available in four delivery media: printed sheets, plates, matrices ("mat," paper-pulp molds pulled from metal plates), and typewritten copy.

Big-city papers had the financial resources to hire staffs to develop their own feature material, too, of course. And before long many of the large newspapers started their own subsidiary syndicates in order to supply the papers in other cities with popular features that they requested. Syndication added to a newspaper's prestige and financial standing by selling the work of its most popular writers and artists to clients nationwide. Hearst's papers began the first of his syndication operations in 1895 in response to out-of-town requests. Other metropolitan papers in New York, Philadelphia, Chicago, Boston, San Francisco, and St. Louis did the same over the next ten years. In 1914 several of Hearst's related syndicate services were merged as King Features, and two years later King Features became a producing concern, buying and selling its own staff-generated feature material.

In 1865 there were only three syndicates, but by

1935, when syndication was approaching its peak in circulation and client papers, there were over 130 syndicates offering to 13,700 papers more than 1,600 separate features covering a wide range of topics that would appeal to every interest of the newspaper-reading public.[3]

The comics could have been tailor-made for syndication: they were an entertaining feature that could easily be produced without topical or local references, making them ideal for distribution and sale to newspapers anywhere in the country. Fontaine Fox, whose *Toonerville Trolley* had been syndicated a few years before *The Gumps*, recognized the change he had to make in his approach when drawing for papers all across the nation instead of only for the paper in his city. "I realized," he said, "the need of identifying myself in the minds of my following with a series of characters so as to make each cartoon's appeal as sure in San Francisco as in New York."[4] It was an adjustment any cartoonist could handily make, and the benefits were more than worth the slight effort.

The market was clearly ready for syndicated comics: indeed, it had been moving rapidly into a state of eager readiness for forty years. Over five thousand new papers had started in the decade from 1870 to 1879; and from 1880 until 1890 newspapers multiplied at the rate of two new publications a day. Many were small operations that could scarcely afford a staff artist, let alone a cartoonist. But by paying a syndicate a modest weekly or monthly fee, these papers could publish comics just like the big- city papers with their populous art departments. And the accumulation of hundreds of such small weekly or monthly fees netted huge financial rewards for the syndicates— and for the cartoonists whose work sold best.

Comics went into syndication almost as soon as they had demonstrated the kind of appeal that increased circulation. Comics were a part of the Hearst syndicate's package from the beginning; in 1898 the *World* was selling its comics to other papers (although it didn't set up a separate syndication operation until 1905). By 1906 comics were in nationwide circulation: even small-town papers were offering weekly comic supplements in full color. Syndication proved a bonanza for cartoonists, but—more important—it stimulated the growth and refinement of the comic strip medium.

Until the advent of syndication, a cartoonist's earning power was limited to the salary his paper chose to pay him. Whopping salaries were paid, naturally, to those cartoonists whose work was deemed vital to building and maintaining circulation. But the earning power of a syndicated cartoonist was, by comparison, nearly unlimited: syndicate contracts guaranteed an annual salary and eventually developed a sliding scale by which the cartoonist increased his income in proportion to the number of papers that bought his comic strip. Both the cartoonist and the syndicate stood to gain by increasing a feature's circulation. In the usual arrangement, the syndicate fielded a sales force to sell the feature to papers across the country, and it also distributed the feature (supplying mats or proofs) and kept the books. After the costs of distribution were deducted, the syndicate split the profits with the cartoonist. (When the cartoonist was guaranteed a salary, as most were, there were no "profits" to divide until a strip's circulation was great enough to earn more than that salary.)

In return for the financial commitment it made to selling and distributing a feature, a syndicate took ownership of the feature. This policy protected the syndicate's interests: if the cartoonist of a popular strip died, say, or failed to produce his work on schedule, the syndicate could continue to supply the feature to its clients by hiring another cartoonist. But the policy made the cartoonist, in some sense, a hired hand. Contractually, a syndicate could dismiss a cartoonist at whim. But few (if any) ever did: it was clearly in the best interests of the syndicate to retain the services of a cartoonist of a popular feature since it was his creative imagination that made the feature popular.

Syndication was a mutually beneficial enterprise, but it pinched both parties to the arrangement. In the hope of great financial return, the syndicate risked its resources in a double gamble that a new strip would sell and that the cartoonist would then continue successfully to produce it; in order to reap the initial rewards, the creator of a comic strip had to give up all rights to his creation—including, usually, any share in the revenue generated by merchandising his characters (a circumstance that, once the merchandising mill began to grind for a popular strip, grated more and more on cartoonists, leading ultimately to contractual modifications). Uneasy though the relationship might have been, it was nonetheless better for most cartoonists than working in a single newspaper's art department, their historic niche before the era of syndication.

The compensation from syndication had other implications than the purely financial, both for the cartoonist and for the medium. Unsyndicated cartoonists in the early days of comics were usually required by their papers to produce a great variety of comic illustrations. They may have produced a regular full-page feature for the Sunday edition, but the rest of the week they drew sports cartoons, editorial or political cartoons, column decorations, ads, and miscellaneous fillers and features of all kinds. Once syndicated, a cartoonist escaped this gamut of illustrative labors and could devote his whole energy to the feature that was syndicated. With his creative energy thus focused on—even confined to—a single enterprise, the cartoonist was bound to improve the product: his imagination and invention had no other outlet.

Syndicates became the forcing bed, too, for the growth of comics. The exclusive nature of the syndicate's contracts with their client papers encouraged a proliferation of comic strips. Not only did a given syndicate need a variety of strips to satisfy the variety of needs editors imagined for their readers, but rival syndicates had to have similar offerings. When *The Gumps* proved so popular, for example, other syndicates came up with their own "family" strips to sell in Chicago to the *Tribune's* competitors. Thus we find *The Nebbs* offered by Bell Syndicate, beginning May 22, 1923, and *The Bungle Family* by McNaught in 1925. (Incidentally, *The Nebbs* strip, while doubtless picked up by Bell in order to compete with *The Gumps*, did not ape Smith's strip expressly to provide an alternative to it. Drawn by Wally Carlson, *The Nebbs* was written by Sol Hess, a Chicago jeweler who had supplied Smith with material for years without pay. When Smith signed his million-dollar contract, he offered Hess $200 a week to continue writing for him, but Hess, miffed at his piddling portion, turned Smith down and sought a more rewarding outlet for his gags and situations.) Eventually, every major syndicate felt it had to have a science fiction strip (in imitation of *Buck Rogers*), a cops and robbers strip (*Dick Tracy*), a domestic gag strip (*Blondie*), and so on. Some of the imitations were but pale reflections of original conceptions that were, in the last analysis, inimitable. But a few—like *Barney Google* (which began as a strip about a racing tout, following in Fisher's *A. Mutt* footsteps) and *Flash Gordon* (King Features' answer to *Buck Rogers*)—were classics in themselves. Without the competition among syndicates, comic strips would never have multiplied as they did, and the art form wouldn't be nearly as rich in invention and variety as it is.

CHAPTER 5
A Flourish of Trumpets
Roy Crane and the Adventure Strip

Once the principle of continuity had been established on the funny pages, the stage was set for the curtain to go up on the adventure strip. Strips that told a continuing story from day to day were inherently suspenseful: the serial format could not help but create a daily cliff-hanger. And it did not take cartoonists long to realize that a cliff-hanger gained in emotional power if the characters left dangling were in danger of losing life or limb. Life-threatening danger in turn meant life-threatening action: in short, adventure—action-packed and danger-laden. And the adventure strip was made-to-order for service in the circulation battles of daily newspapers. What better inducement could an editor contrive for getting the public to buy his paper every day than to promise readers, each day, the resolution of yesterday's comic strip cliff-hanger?

Al Capp, who produced the burlesque adventure strip *Li'l Abner* for forty-three years beginning in the summer of 1934, understood the mechanism perfectly. Once, his tongue in only one cheek, he described it as follows:

> Newspaper publishers had discovered that people bought more papers, more regularly, if they were *worried* by a comic strip than if they were merely amused by one. A citizen who laughed delightedly at one of Rube Goldberg's great "inventions" could put his paper down with a

chuckle, eat his dinner with a calm and unworried mind, and sleep the sleep of the peaceful.

> The same citizen, however, who read Chester Gould's magnificent *Dick Tracy* didn't laugh when he reached the last panel of that strip. He moaned, or gasped—as who wouldn't?—at the sight of a bullet whizzing out through his favorite detective's forehead (Tracy had been shot from behind, of course) accompanied by a fine spray of Tracy's brains and bits of his skull. You may be sure that *that* reader didn't eat *his* dinner in peace; he didn't spend any restful night. *That* poor soul couldn't wait until dawn came, and with it the next edition, to relieve his agony. And then, while the next strip revealed that it was an unimportant section of Tracy's skull that had been shattered—and that he could get along just as well without those particular brains—the reader's relief was short-lived, for in the last panel of that strip, the walls of the room into which Tracy had been lured began slowly and relentlessly to *close in on him*, with no escape possible, and with the maniacal laughter of the criminal fiends operating the death-dealing levers outside ringing in Tracy's helpless ears.

> And so there was no peace again for the reader until he could rush out and buy the next day's paper—and the next and the next. Now, when you multiply this by several million readers, and when you realize that newspaper publishers *love* to have millions of people rushing

out to buy their papers, you can understand why—having discovered that worrying the hell out of people paid off a lot more in circulation than did simply amusing them—publishers declared a New Order for the comic page. Out went the simple fun, the pratfalls, the gentle satire—in came the "Suspense Continuity." . . . Out went the laugh, the guffaw, the chuckle, that were the end purpose of the old-time comic strips—and in came the gasp, the shudder, the cold sweat on the brow, the sick feeling in the pit of the stomach that was the *new* end purpose of the new "Suspense Continuity" comic strips.[1]

Clearly, what Capp means by "suspense continuity" is the action-adventure comic strip. And he successfully lampooned the genre for over four decades.

Among the first to seize upon this fiendish device for compelling newspaper readers to turn to the funnies as soon as they picked up the day's paper was Harold Gray, whose *Little Orphan Annie* (launched in the summer of 1924) we'll meet in the next chapter. Gray's plucky waif was popular enough to inspire a score of imitators. One of them, borrowing from the rags-to- riches tradition of Horatio Alger, Jr., was *Phil Hardy*, which began in November 1925. Written by Jay Jerome Williams, the strip starred a spunky youth who, in the first sequence, runs away to sea. George Storm made the strip one of the most visually appealing of its day, drawing with a confident albeit simple line, spotting blacks generously and effectively. Despite the attractive appearance of the strip, though, it lasted less than a year, disappearing in September 1926. Storm went on to create *Bobby Thatcher*, which he wrote and drew for about ten years, beginning in mid-May 1927. In every notable particular, this strip was a continuation of *Phil Hardy*. Bobby was a blond Phil.

Apart from featuring orphans, however, the strips had less in common with Gray's strip than it would seem at first blush. Neither strip was, strictly speaking, in the soap opera tradition being ushered in by *The Gumps* and *Little Orphan Annie*. Both boys were thrown immediately into life-threatening circumstances. No domestic crises for them: they had Adventures. Their roles required them to take actions to extricate themselves from dangerous situations. Their lives were at risk. Death stalked both young heroes. And as Bill

Blackbeard has convincingly argued, "It is the imminence and actuality of real (not comically exaggerated or spoofed) suffering, hardship and death that form the crux of the realistic adventure strip emerging in the 1920s."[2] *Phil Hardy* was the first comic strip to portray death on stage in a realistic fashion. It was, therefore, the first adventure strip.

But *Phil Hardy* was short-lived. And *Bobby Thatcher* fairly soon became less adventuresome and more like *Little Orphan Annie*—a heart-rending urchin epic. Bobby often wandered into adventurous settings: he dabbled in aviation, detective work, seafaring. But by this time, Annie was doing the same sort of thing. Both kids had adventures, but the spirit of both strips was soap-opera continuity not adventure continuity—emotional travail rather than physical action.

Effective as Storm's pioneering endeavors may have been technically, neither of his strips was successful enough to establish the adventure genre. And it was probably a good thing, too: adventure strips patterned after Storm's example would have produced a much grimmer genre than we eventually got. Indeed, Storm's work was unrelentingly humorless. Adventuring in Storm's strips never looked like it was much fun for the adventurers. And somehow, adventuring ought to be fun: adventuring promises excitement, and excitement is an aspect of fun. To cultivate fully this dimension of the adventure strip genre, we needed Roy Crane.

Roy Crane is undoubtedly the most unsung of the cartoonists who shaped the medium. His historic achievement was to set the pace for adventure strips in the thirties by showing the way in the twenties. Many of those who drew the earliest adventure strips were inspired and influenced by his work. We recognize the milestones in the history of comics that mark the accomplishments of such creators as Chester Gould, Alex Raymond, Hal Foster, Noel Sickles, Ham Fisher, Zack Mosley, Milton Caniff—even Mel Graff. But we forget that Crane preceded them all onto the stage they later filled with their presence. And most of them, as they felt their way in developing adventure storytelling skills, looked to Crane for hints about how to do it.

Crane's magnum opus, *Washington Tubbs II*, debuted in the spring of 1924, a few months before *Little Orphan Annie*. A nearly undistinguished strip about an exuberant young man with soaring ambitions for amorous conquest and financial

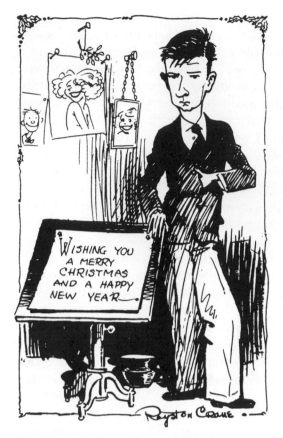

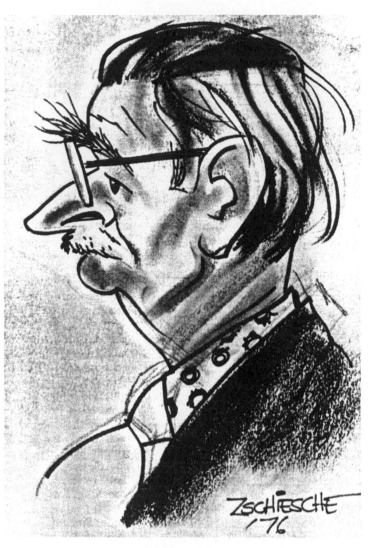

Figure 40. *Crane's self-portrait, on the left, was made in about 1925, shortly after* Wash Tubbs *was launched. Bob Zschiesche did the portrait of the artist as an older man in 1976, the year before Crane died.*

gain, there was little in the inaugural sequences to suggest that it was the vanguard of a new genre in the medium. Within a very short time, though, Wash would be plunged into globe-circling adventure, the likes of which the funny pages had never seen before. And by the end of the decade, Crane would achieve the pinnacle of his accomplishment with the introduction of that rugged and savvy soldier of fortune, Captain Easy. Easy would inspire a generation of cartoonists. "Dynamite Dan" Flynn in Milton Caniff's *Dickie Dare* was an incarnation of Crane's Easy. And Pat Ryan in Caniff's *Terry and the Pirates* was Easy. Uncle Phil in Mel Graff's *Patsy* was Easy.

It is almost impossible to overestimate the impact of this character on those who wrote and drew adventure stories in comic strips and comic books in the thirties. Cartoonist Gil Kane, who began his comic book career in the early forties, once chanted a litany of credit to Crane before an audience at the San Diego Comic Convention:

"Superman was Captain Easy," he said; "Batman was Easy." And he listed several more characters before he stopped.[3] Kane may have overstated the case in order to make his point. But anyone familiar with the earlier work of Superman's creators, Joe Shuster and Jerry Siegel, will recognize Easy in Slam Bradley, a character the two invented a year or so before Superman saw print. Bradley even had a diminutive sidekick like Wash Tubbs. And Superman/Clark Kent looked a lot like Slam Bradley. While the facial resemblance may have been due more to Shuster's limitations as an artist than to Crane's influence, it is clear that Captain Easy was in the minds of virtually everyone who was doing adventure stories in comics in the thirties. For the medium's adventure genre, whether in strips or books, Easy was an archetype.

How Crane chanced upon this seminal creation is anyone's guess. If we take the other important moments in Crane's creative life as a guide, Easy was probably no more than the accidental by-product of plot machinery cranking out story. Crane was the beneficiary of many such accidents. He had achieved syndication through a happy coincidence and subsequently had simply fallen into doing a new kind of strip—more through frustrated disinterest in his own work, it would seem, than by conscious design.

Crane was born in 1901 in Abilene, Texas, and raised in Sweetwater, forty miles west. An only child, he drew to amuse himself. By the time he was ten, he was drawing comic strips. At fourteen, he signed up for the correspondence course in cartooning offered by the legendary Charles N. Landon. When he was nineteen, he found himself in Chicago at the Academy of Fine Arts, where Carl Ed, who had just sold his *Harold Teen* to the *Chicago Tribune*, was one of his instructors. Crane didn't stay in Chicago long: Ed had told him his work was excellent, so he returned to Texas, worked on a couple of papers, and then tried college. He wasn't good at college. The dean of the University of Texas told him he was unsuited to remain a student. That life closed to him, Crane went to sea, serving on a freighter that went to Europe and back, docking in New York on its return. There, Crane jumped ship to try newspapering again. He was hired by the *New York World*, where he worked for a couple of years in the art department and assisted H. T. Webster, inking his Sunday page. Crane tried a panel cartoon, *Music to the Ear*, and sold it to United Feature Syndicate. But when only two papers bought the feature, Crane had to agree with syndicate officials that it wasn't worth the effort of continuing to produce it. Sympathetic to his desire to draw a syndicated cartoon, a friendly United Feature editor suggested that Crane try to sell his panel to another syndicate among whose features his small town humor might be more at home. Try NEA, he said. Enter, happy coincidence.

The Newspaper Enterprise Association was based in Cleveland, and its art director was none other than Crane's former mail-order maestro, Charles N. Landon. Still operating his correspondence course on the side, Landon had developed an interlocking, reciprocal relationship between the course and the syndicate. When he saw a talented student submitting work in the course, he waited until the youth graduated and then tapped him to do a feature for NEA. If the feature was successful, publicity for the Landon course would point with pride to another graduate who'd made it big in cartooning. Merrill Blosser with *Freckles and His Friends* in 1915 was the first beneficiary of this system, according to Landon's promotion, and he was joined over the years by Martin Branner, Paul Fung, Ralph Hershberger, Gene Byrnes, and others.

Crane knew nothing of this, of course. He simply sent his panel cartoon off to Cleveland. He heard nothing for six months. Then one day, he got a phone call from Landon. The master was in New York and asked Crane to come and see him. Crane went. And he took with him samples of a comic strip idea he was working on, *Washington Tubbs II*. "Landon seemed to like the strips well enough," Crane said, recalling the interview in later years. "But when I mentioned that I was one of his graduates, he got enthusiastic and exclaimed, 'Crane, I like your stuff!'"[4] *Wash Tubbs* was launched forthwith. And shortly after the strip debuted on Monday, April 21, 1924, a Landon course ad listed Crane as another graduate who had made good.

Wash Tubbs was a shrimp of a fellow with spectacles and a curly wad of hair, who quickly emerged as a slang-slinging, girl-chasing opportunist, a brash version of Harold Lloyd. "He's at that restless age," the introductory strip revealed, "too big to act like he's a kid any longer and too immature to take life seriously." Under a picture of Wash strolling the beach, ogling pretty girls, the caption advised that to Wash "a girl is like a pair of hinges—something to a door."

The immediate inspiration for the strip may have been Walter Berndt's *Smitty*, a gag strip about an office boy that had started in November 1922; or perhaps *Jerry on the Job*, another humorous feature about a youth in the world of work that Walter Hoban had been doing since 1913. Like these strips, *Wash Tubbs* told a joke a day, and Crane strung his gags along the frail thread of a tenuous story line. In the first strip, Wash takes a job in a grocery store in order to pursue the owner's pretty daughter. In between pursuits, he hatches plots to make money quick. But Crane quickly found he didn't like thinking up jokes. He didn't much like what Wash was doing either. And it showed in the strip's feeble humor and plot. Dissatisfied, Crane was bored. He dreamed fondly of the excitement of his seafaring days. "I wanted to be a hell of a long way off," he said.[5] And about the furthest way off he could think of was the South Pacific. Since he

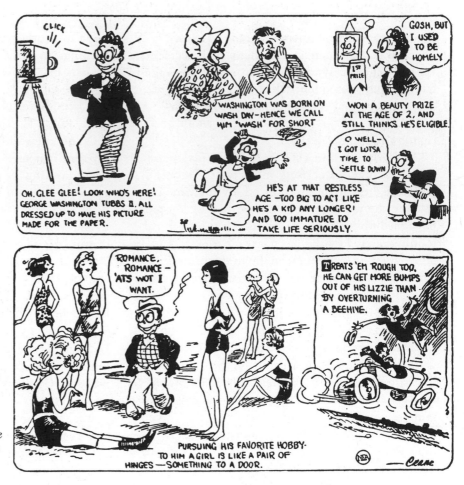

Figure 41. *Nothing in the introductory strip of* Washington Tubbs II *suggested the life of wild adventure that Wash would eventually lead. Incidently, Crane always drew the strip in "halves" so that it could be cut in two and "stacked," as shown here. The intention was to enhance the marketability of the strip by making it possible for an editor to use it as either a strip or as a square "panel" cartoon. Note, too, that the flappers are all fashionably slim.*

couldn't go himself, he sent Wash. He sent him on a treasure hunt—a device he would employ again and again. It was a romantic, simpleminded machination, but Crane made it work time after time. By the end of the fifth month in the strip's run, Crane had moved from pallid gags about his pint-sized Romeo to high adventure with a comic emphasis. Marooned on a South Sea isle, Crane's diminutive protagonist, surrounded by pretty native girls, finds buried treasure. Unknowingly, in following his fantasies, Crane had struck it rich, too. Wash didn't hold on to his fortune long; he never did. But Crane had found a successful formula for his strip—one that pleased and interested him and, as it soon proved, comic strip readers, too.

Wash is stranded for four months on a South Sea island, but when he returns in early January 1925, he's rich—rich enough to attract the attention of the gold-digging movie starlet he's been pursuing all along, Dottie Dimple. Wash fritters away thousands to impress this shallow beauty, and he loses the rest of his fortune to an assortment of conmen who prey upon his naïveté. He recoups a little by

going into the movie business, then returns to his hometown in financial triumph, whereupon he gives away most of his money to charity. After that, in July 1925, he takes up with a philosophical hobo named March McGargle, and the two set off on a transcontinental race as a promotional stunt for a soap manufacturer.

Crane would later be acclaimed for the graphic treatment of his stories, particularly his evocative use of gray tones. But that, as we'll see, didn't occur until the mid-thirties. When *Wash Tubbs* began, Crane's visuals were not especially noteworthy, although his distinctive style was in evidence. His line was tentative at first, but his symmetrical sense of composition is already on display, balancing figures and solid blacks in each panel. By the tenth week, Crane's linework is more confident. And by the end of 1924 the strip had begun to mature graphically, its clean lines and uncluttered compositions distinctively Crane. Crane's tendency toward innovation is already apparent, too. At the beginning of the treasure hunt, he drew Wash against realistic San Francisco backgrounds, establishing mood as well as locale with visual authen-

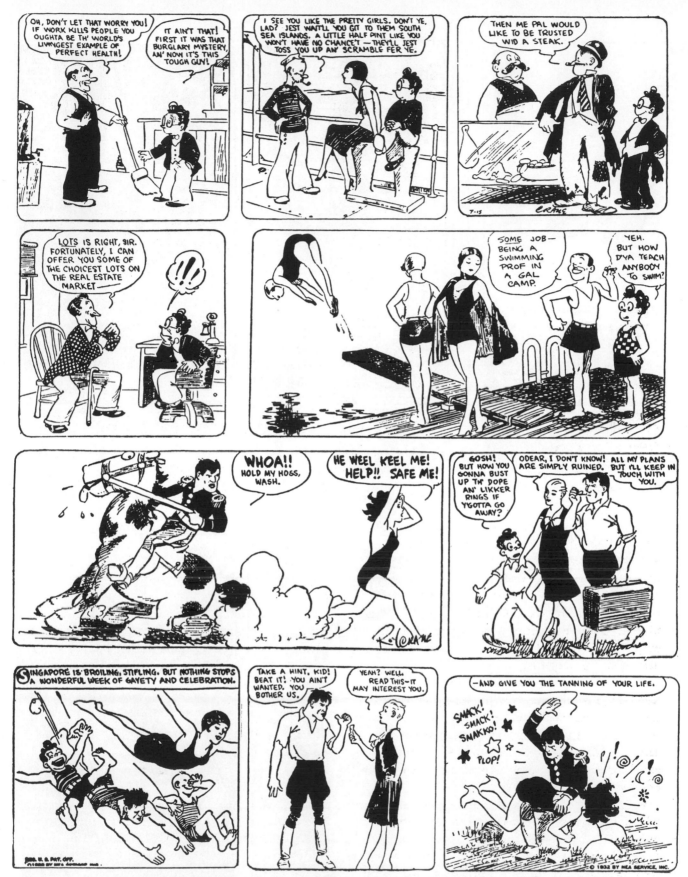

Figure 42. *Virtually from the very beginning (the panel at the upper left is from the first month of Wash Tubbs), Crane, composing his panels as individual pictures, displayed a sense of symmetry that would inform his work throughout his career. Figures and solid blacks were balanced or centered in each composition. This miscellany of panels, incidentally, includes pictures of several members of the cast from the early days of the strip. At the upper left, the man with Wash is his boss at the grocery store where he's working when we first meet him. At the upper right, the hobo is March McGargle; and the fellow in the swim trunks with the puffed-up chest is Gozy Gallup. With the horseback rider, we get to Captain Easy.*

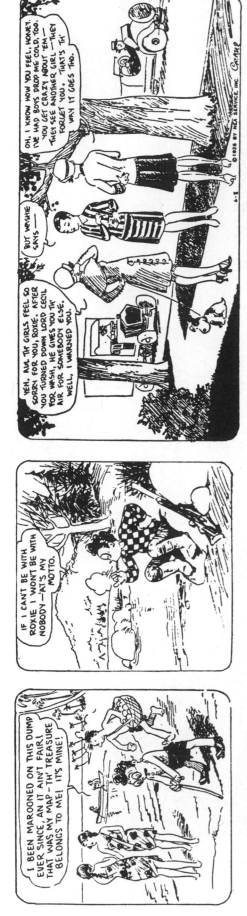

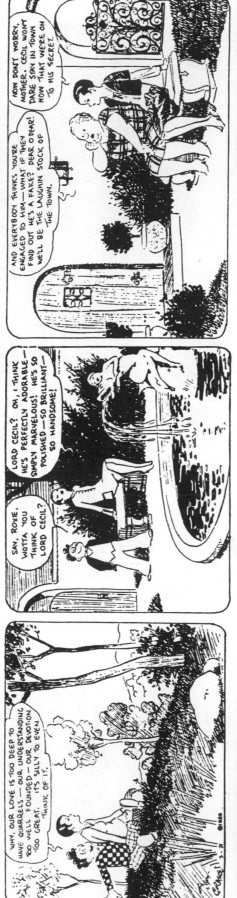

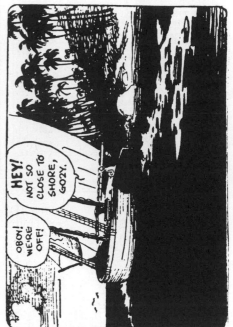

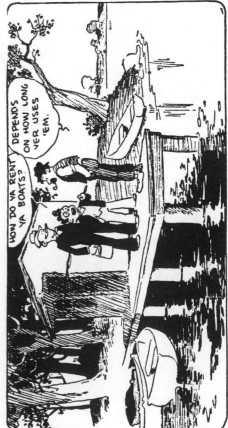

Figure 43. *The evolution of Crane's background treatment goes from the simplicity of 1924 at the upper left through the increased complexity of the 1926 panels at mid-page to the greater sophistication of the 1927 panel at the bottom left and the 1928 scene at the right.*

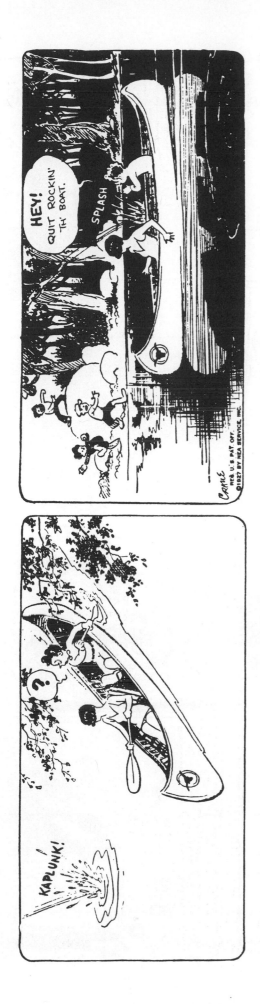

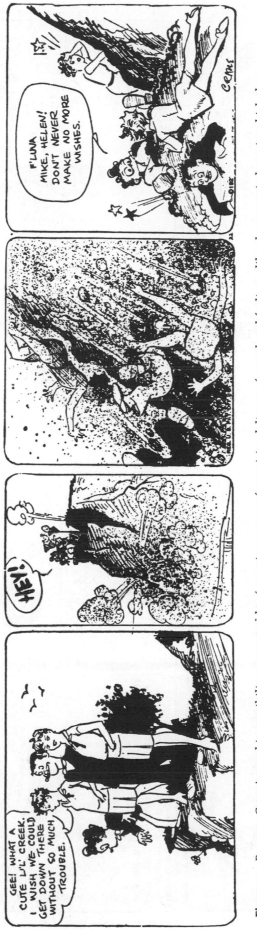

Figure 44. By 1927 Crane's graphic sensibility was capable of creating scenes of exquisite delicacy of mood and feeling—like the top strip here, in which the placid lack of detail in rendering the water in the first panel evokes the silence of the idyllic moment itself; and the second panel, in which the glassy surface of the water is suggested with the mirror image of the canoe. In the bottom strip, he spattered ink on the drawing to create the grit of the landslide. He was always experimenting with tonal values.

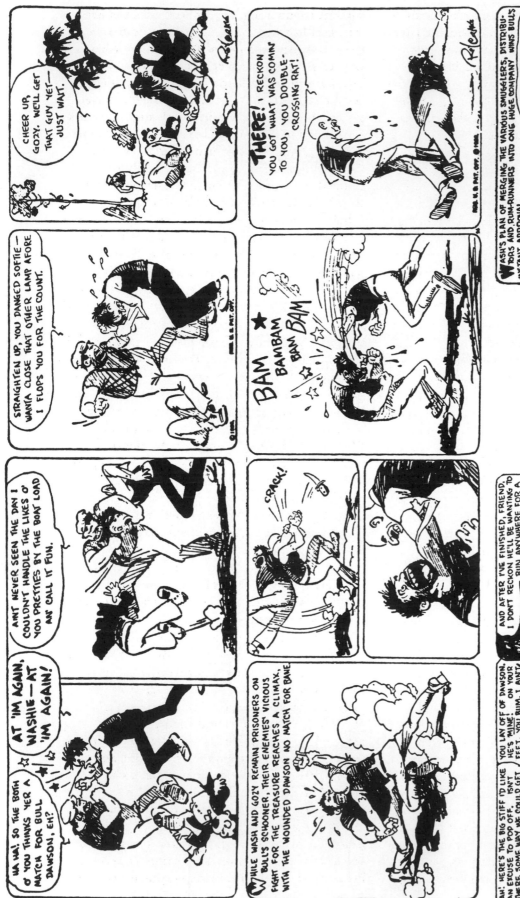

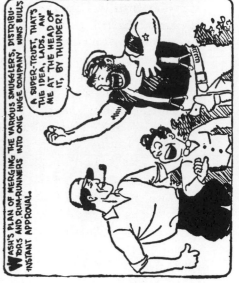

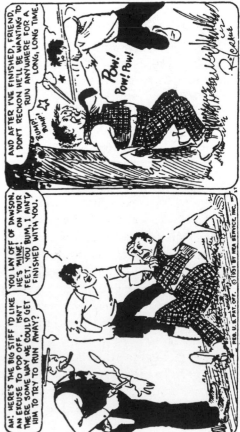

Figure 45. *Bull Dawson didn't kid around: when he got physical, it hurt (top). And when he met Bane in combat (middle), there was genuine bloodshed. Bull beat Easy the first time they tangled, but later (bottom left), Easy evened the score. They were always bitter enemies, although once (bottom right), Easy and Wash posed as fellow smugglers in order to apprehend the old pirate.*

ticity. Eventually, Crane would use backgrounds as the chief means of giving the strip a realistic aura. As 1925 drew to a close, he was lavishing attention on outdoor scenes—mountains, lakes, ornamental gardens, and the like (figure 43). By shading with diagonal linework and cross-hatching and by spotting blacks dramatically, he gave the strip textural variety and realistic atmosphere.

The characteristic Crane women also emerged in the first year of the strip. Dottie Dimple, in her first appearance in the spring of 1924, evoked the flat-chested flappers of John Held, Jr. But by the fall of the year, the plumply curvaceous Crane cutie has arrived. Crane's girls are cuddly girls next door. In drawing women, Crane said he looked for "the graceful, flowing line." He drew them with small hands and feet, and he emphasized curves without making his women buxom. Crane's girls are sex symbols, but they don't know it. They pout and dimple with engaging innocence.

Throughout the first years of the strip's run, Wash bubbles with boyish enthusiasm, flitting like a summer butterfly from emotional high to emotional low at every turn of his fortune. In this, he is doubtless an original conception, but he is not very interesting. And in spite of Crane's occasional tries at pathos with his protagonist, Wash is chiefly just the flywheel of the plot, a personality too lightweight to long hold our interest or regard. Crane seemed to sense this flaw in his hero: he brought in a succession of secondary characters, each more intriguing than Wash, until he arrived at last at Easy. March McGargle is the first in this long line. And he is interesting. But he's no Easy.

Wash Tubbs remained a thoroughly humorous strip: with its ebullient hero, reaching always to fantastic heights quite above his stature, it could scarcely be anything else. But by 1927 deliberate daily gags had all but vanished from the strip. Crane played the stories for the merriment he could provoke, but not for a daily punch line. He also saw to it that Wash scampers rapidly from one exotic locale to another, engaging in a succession of desperate gambles to strike it rich again and, at the same time, to capture the undying affection of the latest "bonbon" that catches his ever-roving eye. Excitement rather than laughter was the quarry in Crane's pursuit. In search of it, Wash wanders the world. He joins a traveling circus (and so did Crane, to research the sequence), gets stranded on

a desert island again, tangles with Mexican bandits, gets lost in the Sahara, rescues women in distress, and goes on another treasure hunt. Along the way, Wash picks up a sidekick named Gozy Gallup. Taller than Wash and furnished with a city slicker's moustache, Gozy shares Wash's hunger for action, his get-rich-quick motivations, and his fascination with dimpled damsels. Two of a kind, the pair prompt nothing particularly new from Crane. But on the treasure hunt in early 1928 Crane developed a new kind of character, and with that, he added another dimension to the strip.

Bull Dawson is the captain of the ship Wash and Gozy engage to take them to the desert island where the treasure is supposed to be. Dawson is a burly modern version of Long John Silver; he hasn't Silver's charming guile, and he has two perfectly healthy legs, but in occupation and malevolent menace, he's Robert Louis Stevenson's pirate reincarnated. A swaggering, boastful, cunning, and unfeeling brute, Dawson is the uncrowned prince of roughneck villains. He meets and surmounts every crisis with his fists. "Ain't never seen the day I couldn't handle the likes o' you pretties by the boatload an' call it fun," he roars, pummeling Wash and Gozy into submission. No physical abuse is too savage or murderous for Dawson; no underhanded trick too vile. He simply radiates evil. Dawson did not arrive unheralded on Crane's stage. During their Mexican adventure at the end of 1927, Wash and Gozy had encountered a bald bandit chieftain named Brick Bane. Bane is every bit as serious about committing crimes as Dawson. But Dawson outdoes Bane in unremitting unscrupulousness and brutality. Crane would bring him back repeatedly for encores.

The presence of Dawson and his ilk did not alter entirely the essential nature of *Wash Tubbs*. Even as Crane introduced serious villainy into his formula, he preserved the strip's high-spirited joie de vivre. For all the menace of its villains, *Wash Tubbs* remained a boisterous, rollicking, fun-loving strip, full of last-minute dashes, free-for-all fisticuffs, galloping horse chases, pretty girls, and sound effects—Bam, Pow, Boom, Sok, Licketywhop. When Crane's characters ran, they ran all out—knees up to their chins. When they were knocked down in a fight, they flipped backwards, head over heels. These old-fashioned comic strip visual conventions gave to the action the pace of a headlong sprint. Bull Dawson heightened this excitement by adding an ingredient vital to an adventure strip: he made the threat of danger real. Dawson wasn't fooling around. He was no joke. We could see that when he beat up Wash and Gozy, they were hurt. They ached; they had bruises. With Dawson's arrival, Crane's adventure strip matured. The horseplay now produced hors de combat.

The aura of adventure in the strip was enhanced by Crane's increasingly realistic backgrounds (figure 46). His seascapes were dramatic renderings, the water a brooding solid black with white foam flecking the caps of the waves; his jungles, shaded and ominous tangles of vines and underbrush. Crane began experimenting with graphic techniques. For the Sahara Desert scenes, he used crayon shading to give sandy, gritty texture and tone to his pictures. In other sequences, he began to shade more extravagantly, drawing diagonals through substantial portions of many scenes. In the fall of 1926 it is Crane's treatment of the setting that gives an incident its emotional impact. Wash is off on another voyage—shanghaied this time—and the vindictive sea captain throws him overboard to silence his protesting. In the last panel of the October 30 strip, Crane shows Wash's head and shoulders bobbing in a patch of water—all alone, surrounded by a vast and turbulent sea. No caption; no words. Just the picture. The waves are dark and ominous. Wash is isolated graphically in a sort of moonlit eddy. We see the ship disappearing over a distant horizon. And for a moment, we catch our breath. This is no prankish pratfall. It smacks of real danger for our hero: he could drown in this dark and trackless sea. The death knell sounded for the first time in the strip.

Crane heightened the drama of his stories with realistic detail. In June and July 1928, Wash and Gozy go on a world cruise, and Crane gave the sequence a travelogue realism with almost photographically accurate renderings of the harbors through which the duo pass. But the details were not restricted to backgrounds. When Bull Dawson fights the Mexican bandit king Brick Bane in May 1928, it's a grisly encounter, both combatants splattered with blood. In the emerging ethos of *Wash Tubbs*, Crane could even sound a note of tender sorrow without its seeming false. Wash is mauled by a tiger during his circus adventure, and Gozy, working as a clown, can't visit him in the hospital right away because the show must go on.

"Poor li'l fella," he mutters, head hanging as he stands in the wings in his outlandish costume, "and I must be funny and make people laugh at a time like this."

Crane's combination of the fantastic and the authentic—cartoony-looking people capering through realistic scenes, whimsical plots jammed with life-threatening dangers, humorous heroes with real feelings—made *Wash Tubbs* unique on the comics page. It was the comically rendered characters that gave the strip its distinctive appeal. The funny-looking cast underscored the light-hearted ambiance of the strip. No one could take such characters altogether seriously, so the strip radiated a fellowship of carefree excitement and of good times had by all. And in so doing, it gave the adventure story strip an aura the genre would not have otherwise had. *Wash Tubbs* was high-spirited and often laugh-provoking; its sole reason for being, to tell entertaining adventure stories. Infected with a fun-loving spirit, the strip was every boy's dream of what adventure should be—and the dream of every man who still harbored the boy he had been within him. Adventure should be exciting and dangerous, but not too dangerous: the idea was to have some fun in an otherwise mundane life.

Milton Caniff read the strip avidly while in college at Ohio State University. "I admired it," Caniff said. "I felt then and still do that Crane was the greatest in his field. He combined almost big foot comedy with magnificent drawing. I think I leaned in that direction myself then, without being fully aware of it. I was bending toward my natural way to go."[6] And Caniff, following Crane's lead, would show the way to the next generation of adventure strip cartoonists.

Incorporating the threat of real danger into the strip had given *Wash Tubbs* an edge it had lacked before, but Wash was too frolicsome a personality to sustain the feeling of reality over the long haul. Besides, he was neither bright enough nor rugged enough physically to surmount the dangers he now encountered. The strip still needed something— something serious, something capable. Finally, on May 6, 1929, Crane introduced the character who would complete the transformation of his strip (figure 47).

For a couple of months, Wash had been in the comic operetta country of Kandelabra, trying to restore to the throne its rightful heiress, the Princess

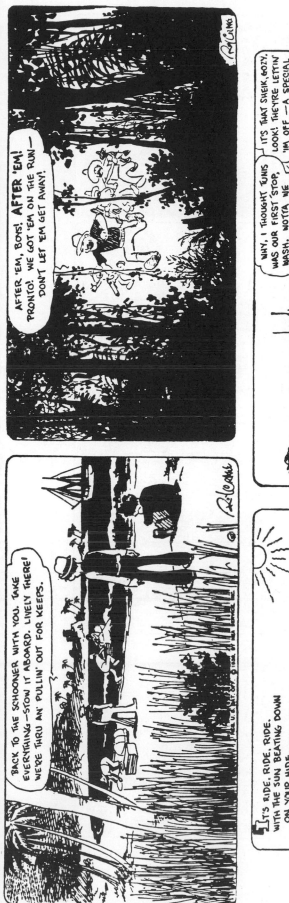

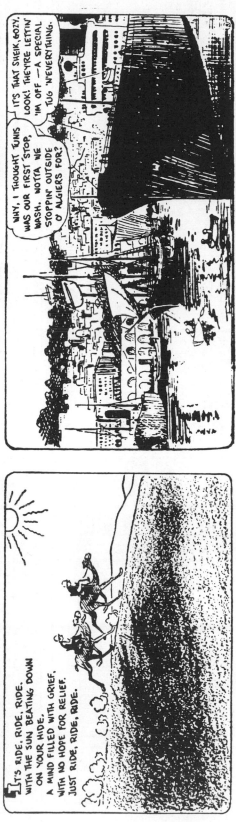

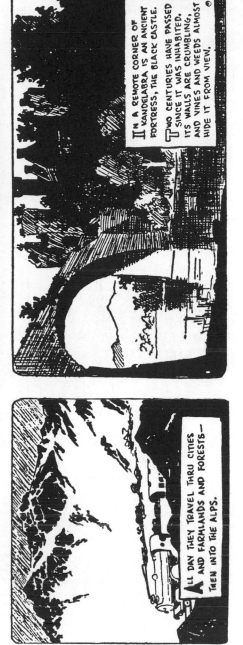

Figure 46. By 1928–29, Crane's renderings of the strip's locales lent Wash's adventures a palpable reality. And Crane continued to experiment with techniques, too—as in the desert scene above, where he used a crayon to give the picture texture as well as to vary the tone. Crane's way of drawing mountains in 1929 (bottom left) was appropriated years later by Milton Caniff (with equally spectacular results).

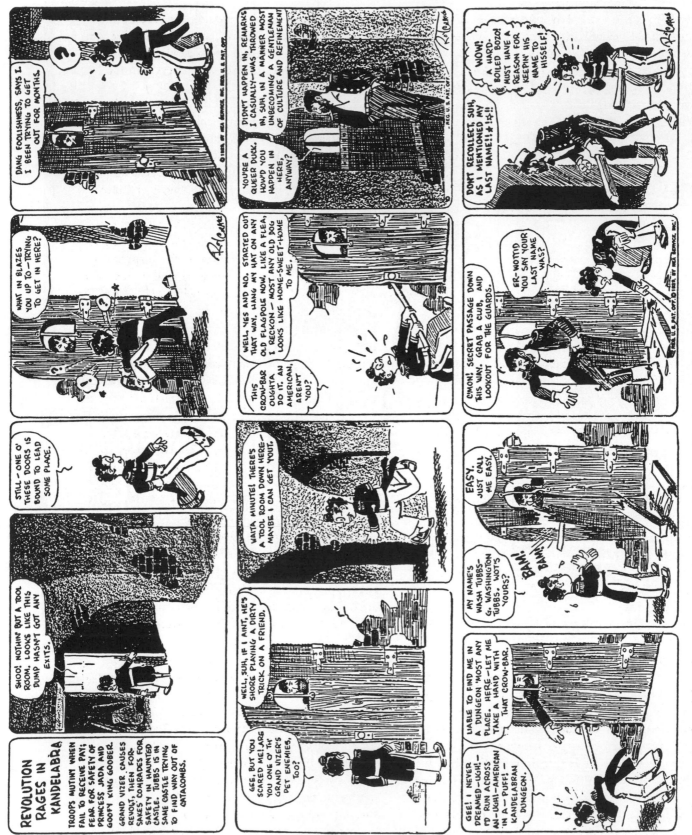

Figure 47. *Another of those famous moments in comic strip history: May 6, 1929, when Captain Easy arrives. Note the mixed media—pen strokes and crayon for varying tonal effects.*

Jada. The grand vizier has matrimonial as well as monarchical designs involving Jada, so he drops Wash into the castle dungeons, a maze of booby-trapped doors and dismal corridors. After wandering the passageways for days, opening doors and narrowly escaping death, Wash finally tugs on the door of a cell that he quickly finds is occupied by a hawk-nosed, squint-eyed, lantern-jawed hard-case dressed in what passes for a military uniform in Kandelabra. "Easy. Just call me Easy," he says. And when Wash presses him for his last name, Easy snaps: "Don't recollect, suh, as I mentioned my last name!"

Easy is the classic soldier of fortune. A wanderer ("Hang my hat on any old flagpole now. Like a flea, I reckon—most any old dog looks like home-sweet-home to me"), he will one day give his occupation as "beach-comber, boxer, cook, aviator, seaman, explorer, and soldier of artillery, infantry, and cavalry." And he's a champion brawler. When he and Wash fight their way out of the dungeon, Easy demonstrates his superiority over Gozy Gallup as a two-fisted sidekick. Gozy was no better than Wash in a fight, but Easy handily dispatches three guards and then, seeing Wash in trouble with his opponent, he disposes of him, too, with one punch. As Wash begins to rave about his new acquaintance's prowess, Easy interrupts.

"Lucky I'm good then. You're terrible. Thought you said you could fight. Blazes! You couldn't lick a postage stamp. That little runt hit you so many times he—why, what's the matter? Hurt your feelings, didn't I? Aw, kid, I'm sorry. Honest I am. You're O.K., son—a game kid. Bum fighter, maybe, but dead game."

Here was something novel: a hard-bitten down-and-outer of heroic cast who's also sensitive. It's the beginning of a friendship that will last more than five decades.

When Wash leaves Kandelabra, Easy goes with him. They embark upon an ocean liner bound for New York, and Wash meets a countess and falls in love. Easy is suspicious of the countess and her "father," the duke, but shortly after the ship docks in New York, Easy disappears, apparently leaving Wash to his fate. The countess and the duke are actually wife and husband, partners in whatever confidence game comes to hand. Just as they finish separating Wash from his fortune, Easy returns, telling Wash he's spent the interval investigating the countess and her husband. But before Easy can

retrieve Wash's money, the duke is found dead by the railroad tracks. When the police find out that Wash is the aggrieved party in a swindle, they assume he killed the duke and arrest him for murder.

Crane handles the continuity of the murder trial sequence in newspaperly fashion: almost every day's strip begins with a caption block of headlines that announce the latest developments. Sidney Smith had used the same device the year before during the trial of Tom Carr, as had Bud Fisher, during the first six months of *A. Mutt*. It was an extremely effective mechanism for advancing the story while hyping the excitement in daily bulletin style. And Crane heightened the suspense by implicating Easy. It was early enough in Easy's career that Crane could dangle before his readers the possibility that Easy might be the real murderer. Despite his apparent friendship for Wash, Easy is still pretty much a man of mystery—a man without a past. (Crane once gave him a past, explaining in a 1931 sequence that Easy was the scion of an aristocratic southern family who had fled his heritage because he believed himself in disgrace. His real name: William Lee. But the cartoonist later regretted having invented a personal history for his hero, and he contrived to have everyone forget it by never mentioning it again. In 1939, however, temptation apparently got the better of him, and Crane had Easy allude to an affair of the heart that "messed up" his life.) The murder story subsequently unfolds in all seriousness, with Easy solving the mystery ingeniously but realistically. (The countess shot her husband in the belief that he was double-crossing her.) Throughout, it's clear that the threat to Wash's life is nothing to joke about.

Stories like this established the fundamental realism that underpinned Crane's big-foot graphic style and his frequently indulged penchant for broad comic effects. After the trial, Crane took his heroes off on another treasure hunt, and they wind up on a desert isle where they find and rescue the obligatory beautiful damsel. (Crane's desert island plots are wonderfully predictable.) And during the desert island sequence, we find Crane doing the kinds of things that riveted the attention of his contemporaries in cartooning, inspiring them to develop the adventure strip by refining Crane's techniques and reapplying them.

If Crane wasn't the first cartoonist to use the de-

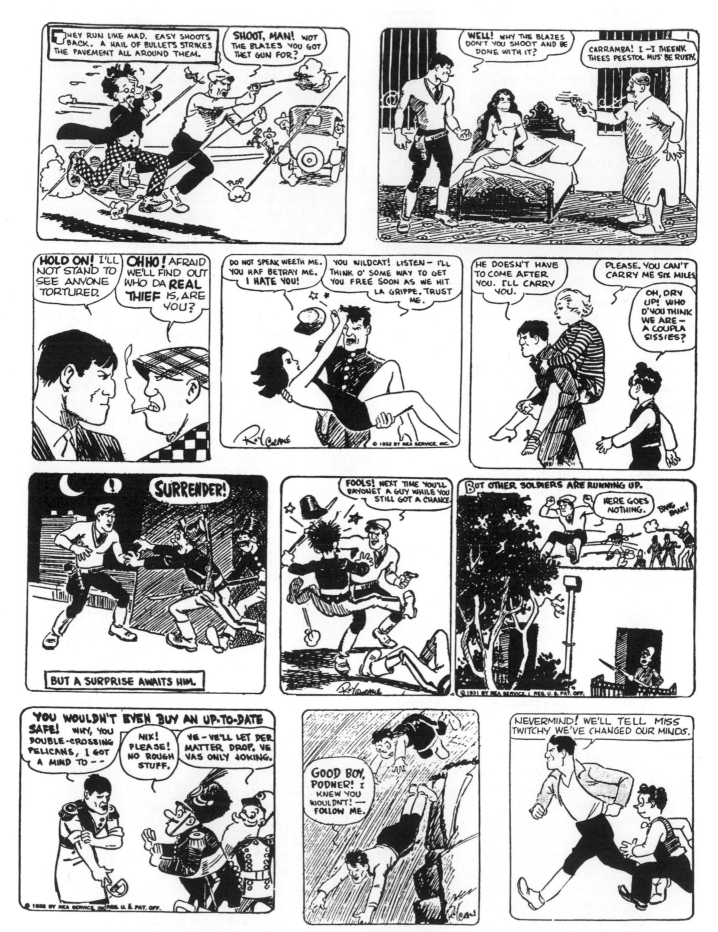

Figure 48. *Easy is the archetypal action hero—always on the move in the service of some mission or other. But Crane's "big-foot" drawing style for rendering people gives the strip a comic flavor and reminds us that all the action is still in fun.*

vices of the cinematographer in telling his stories, he was among the very first. He didn't shift his camera angles much more than some of his fellows did in those days, but he varied the camera *distance*—first (probably) for simple graphic variety but sometimes with dramatic narrative effects, too. But Crane's most striking use of cinematic technique was in setting the scene for a daily strip with an establishing shot of the locale. He had devoted considerable creative energy to realistic background detail in outdoor scenes since at least 1928, and in the 1930 desert island adventure he again pulled out all the stops in depicting the setting for his story. Beach scenes are bleak and desolate; the island jungle, lush and dark. His careful attention in the first panel to environmental details gave to the exoticism of his story a convincing realism. Crane was probably the first to experiment successfully with achieving realistic narrative effects through purely visual means.

Crane may not have been more conscious than some of his colleagues of the graphic aspects of his art and of the effects that could be achieved through visual means alone, but he was more willing than many of them to explore the possibilities. That willingness led him to draw pictures and compose panels and time the action chiefly for the impact produced upon the narrative. He wasn't just drawing pictures: he was telling a story, and the pictures had to serve that purpose. And his pictures did more than simply advance the story by identifying speakers and depicting actions and scenery: they also provided dramatic emphasis. Establishing shots set tone as well as depicting locale; and close-ups stressed the emotions of the speaker being pictured. Crane also contrived his breakdowns for narrative effect, pacing the action for maximum excitement and suspense. His daily installments did not end where they did because he ran out of room: they were deliberately built toward suspenseful conclusions. Those years Crane had spent constructing sequences that ended in comic punch lines had not been wasted. Whether consciously or unconsciously, the impulse to give each daily installment an ending—a concluding impact, whether cataclysmic or comic—shaped Crane's art. He may not have been the first at any of these endeavors, but he was the first to attract the attention of his colleagues—the first to make these devices so effective that they were worth emulating.

However much Crane's graphic devices may have attracted the attention and admiration of fellow members of the inky-fingered fraternity, it was Captain Easy that won their unalloyed admiration—and that of all of *Wash Tubbs*'s readers. Easy was an inspired invention. (Even the name is absolutely apt. Crane almost called him Early.[7] Good but not quite as perfect as the laconic Easy.) A swashbuckler of the old school, Easy wore jodhpurs and boots for most of his early adventures. He looked the part of a soldier of fortune. And he was supremely capable. With his wits if not his fists (and usually by deploying both), he won through every time, no matter what the difficulty. Not that he was invincible: Crane knew better than to make his hero a superman. In his first encounter with Bull Dawson, for instance, Easy loses the fight. And that makes his victory the next time they meet all the more satisfying a triumph.

Easy provided precisely the right ingredient to take the strip the last step from simple exuberant horseplay to suspenseful high adventure. The adventures were still lighthearted, and they were undeniably life-threatening whenever their plots required. And now, with the addition of Easy to his cast, Crane succeeded in convincing us to take those threats seriously. Easy took them seriously. And Easy was a serious fellow, not a featherweight like Wash. The overarching formula was simple: Wash pursued his effervescent dreams of love and wealth until he got himself (and Easy) into trouble; then Easy, both fists flying, got them both out again. But the spirit of adventuring—an essentially fun-loving spirit—still pervaded the strip. Coulton Waugh put it best:

> In the old days, tubby Tubbs and lanky Easy were loose-footed soldiers of fortune, a big and a little stone rolling through the romantic places of the earth, usually broke, sometimes fabulously wealthy, but always ready for fight, frolic, or feed. The special quality that set off the strip was that it had the appeal of a child's box of fascinating toy soldiers, painted in bright red and green, and marching to battle, all gay and flashing, to the inspiriting rattle of tiny drums.[8]

Easy was so popular that he eventually took over the strip. Oddly enough, however, Crane apparently did not realize what he had in Easy right away. After letting Easy share adventures with Wash for a couple years, Crane wrote him out of the strip in July 1931. Wash ventures forth solo briefly but then acquires another comrade-in-arms. Crane clearly recognized that Wash was too much the perpetual underdog to be a convincing adventurer all by himself. Wash's new sidekick is Rip O'Day. Like Easy, Rip is handy with his fists. Perhaps too handy: he likes nothing more than a good brawl. And he likes them so much that he often provokes them; he is always scrapping with someone. He is virtually out of control most of the time, a loose cannon threatening the safety of those he seeks to assist. In short, he is not the stuff of heroes. He is essentially a comic character, not a serious enough creation to carry Wash through realistic, life-threatening situations. Wash needed more than an accomplished brawler. He needed Easy.

Crane brought Easy back on April 29, 1932, and from then on the strip is his, for all intents and purposes. In 1933 Crane abandoned all pretense and retitled the strip's Sunday installment (with drum roll and trumpet) *Captain Easy—Soldier of Fortune*. And the Sunday strip began to retail a continuity separate from the daily adventures.

On Sundays, Crane concentrated on Easy, and these pages soon absorbed him. The art chores on the dailies were assigned to others in the NEA bull pen so that Crane could pour his imagination into the weekly installments of Easy's adventures. Crane loved the spacious potential of the Sunday page—as would any graphic artist; and he spent most of his energy here rather than on the less visually challenging dailies. And on the Sunday pages Crane did some of his finest work. Since he was drawing for the addition of color, Crane shaded these pages very little, so his artwork here is refined to its unembellished essence. And in its essence, Crane's work demonstrates the marvelous precision and telling efficacy of a line so simple it seems naive. But appearances in art are as often deceiving as they are in life. The simplicity of Crane's linework is the ultimate sophistication— irreducible economy, the absolute in purity of graphic expression. It is pure because it does its job all alone, no helps, no crutches, no cross-hatching or other embroidery. A simple line is not only the purest; it is the most authoritative of lines. It is an unhesitating declaration of visual intent. When a simple line fails, it is the ugliest of all lines; but when it succeeds—as it does on Crane's Sunday pages—it sings.

Crane's Sunday pictures are carefully, lovingly, drawn, every panel composed to tell the story while sustaining the illusion of time and place. And the pages themselves are often artful designs, irregular albeit nonetheless pleasing patterns of panels rather than uniform grids. But these layouts are not simply designs: they were devised to give visual impact to the story. When Crane drew Easy at the brink of a cliff, he gave depth to the scene by depicting it in a vertical panel that is two or three tiers tall. When Easy leads a cavalry charge or paddles a canoe down a lazy river, the panel is as wide as the page, giving panoramic sweep to the scene depicted.

And the old *Wash Tubbs* excitement courses through Easy's Sunday adventures, too. The stories are rambunctious, fast-moving gallops. Nobody walks on these pages: everyone runs, knees up, elbows pumping. Scarcely a page passes without a fistfight or some similarly vigorous knockabout action. And despite the comic opera countries and the caricatured villains, these pages pulse with the authentic excitement of real adventure swashbuckled into lively entertainment.

Toward the end of the 1930s Crane added a new arrow to his creative quiver—Craftint doubletone illustration board. As we have noticed, Crane had been experimenting for years with ways of giving his pictures different textures and tones. Late in 1936 he chanced upon Craftint doubletone, and within six months he had adopted exclusively this method of achieving tonal effects. Doubletone illustration board is a chemically treated drawing paper. The chemical on the surface of the paper makes a pattern of lines or dots in light blue (which does not photograph for reproduction). By applying a foul-smelling liquid developer with a brush or pen, an artist can make the blue lines or dots turn black (or dark brown, which, photographically speaking, is just as good). Crane used the lined variety of doubletone paper. The lines created one of two patterns: parallel diagonal lines or cross-hatching. In reproduction, the diagonal lines gave a drawing a light gray tone; the crosshatched lines, a dark gray tone.

Crane had dabbled briefly with the use of Ben Day shading as early as the spring of 1936. Ben Day shading, a gray tone of tiny dots created mechanically in the photographic stage of reproduction, produced a single, uniform gray tone. Crane used it sometimes alone, sometimes augmented by

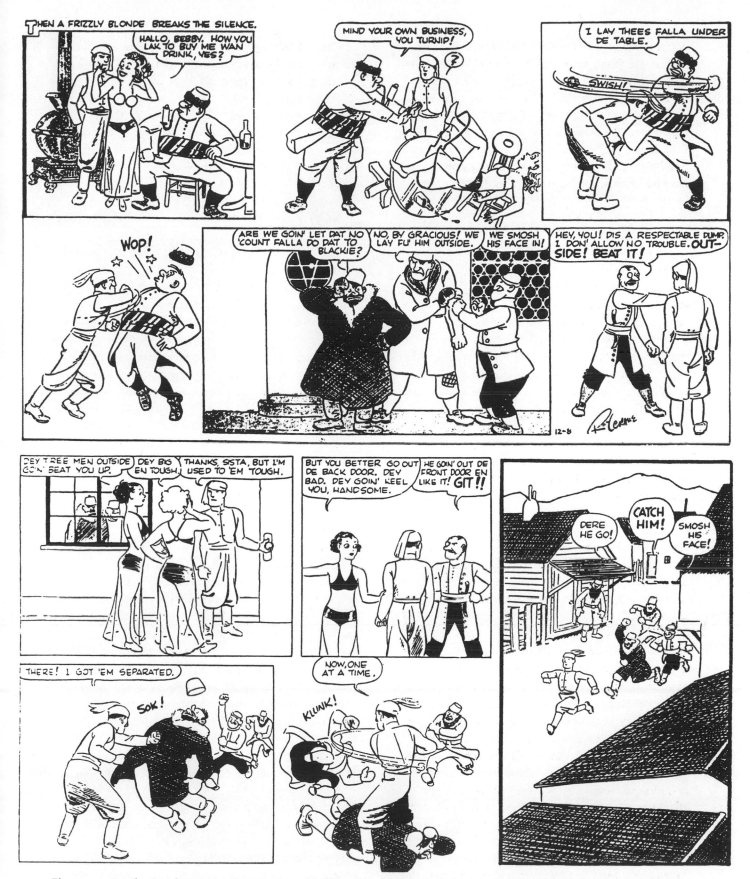

Figure 49. *On the Sunday pages,* Captain Easy—Soldier of Fortune *kept the action lively. Drawing for the addition of color, Crane didn't embellish his linework at all, and the purity of his line is sheer poetry. (This is not a single Sunday page but two halves from successive weeks.)*

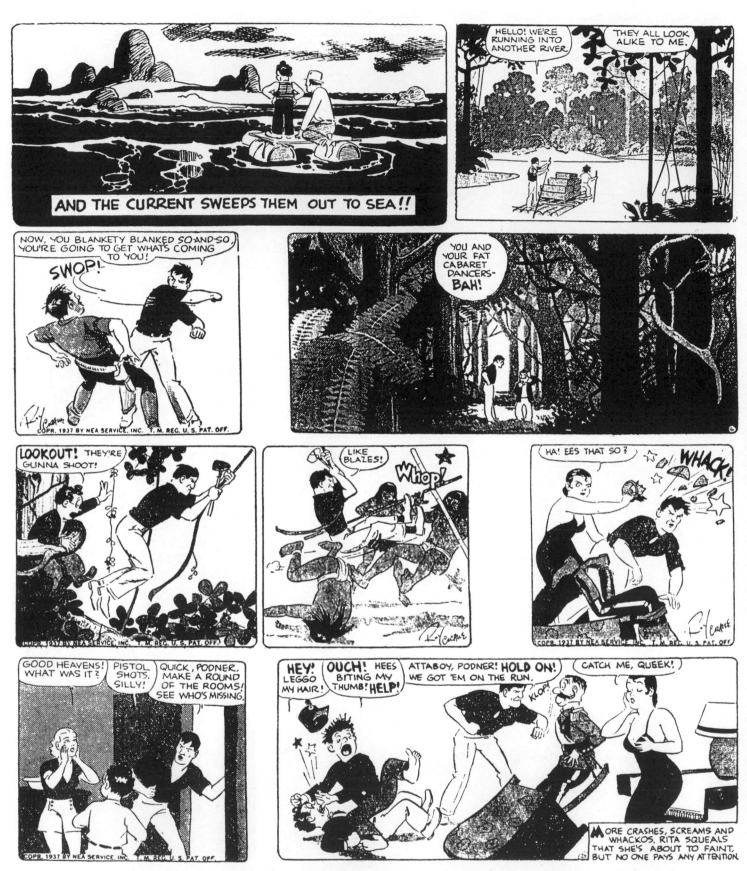

Figure 50. *In the daily strips, Crane was using Craftint doubletone extensively by 1937. Earlier, he had demonstrated his dramatic use of solid black (upper left), but now he was able to give his pictures an almost photographic depth by deploying black, white, and the two tones of gray that could be chemically developed in Craftint illustration board.*

hayey cross-hatching with a pen. During 1936 he was deploying every method he could think of for creating variety in texture and tone—grease crayon, splattered ink, Ben Day, and cross-hatching and shading with a pen. He was searching. Once he found Craftint doubletone, the quest was over. With twice the gray-tone capability of Ben Day, Craftint was clearly the superior product. By April 1937 Crane was employing doubletone on a daily basis. Grease crayon and all the other textural effects were abandoned for good.

Using Craftint doubletone, Crane created some of the most beautiful scenes in comics (figure 50). With solid black as a third "tone"—progressively, the darkest of the three—he produced pictures with photographic gradations of gray, giving his strip a visual depth no other strip on the funnies pages had. He is noted for the exquisite delicacy of shade and tone in his outdoor scenes. Distant objects he rendered in the lightest gray tone; closer to the camera, he added the dark gray. With doubletone, he could give the backgrounds against which he played out his stories a photographic realism—dramatic seascapes, moody wind-swept swamps, majestic mountain ranges, brooding jungles festooned with foliage and vines and mysterious shadowy somethings. As always, the realism of the settings added an aura of actuality to the otherwise sometimes fantastic events.

Just about the time he had mastered doubletone, Crane acquired a full-time assistant. Sometime in the summer or early fall of 1937, Crane wrote an old friend, a fellow Texan who'd been born two years earlier than Crane, and asked him if he'd help him out on the strip. Despite the proximity of their birthplaces—only eighty miles apart—Roy Crane and Leslie Turner didn't meet until they went to classes at the Academy of Fine Arts in Chicago in 1920. The two returned to Texas, where they entered different colleges. They also did a certain amount of bumming around together during this period, according to cartoonist Bob Zschiesche, who knew them both in later years when they lived in Florida. Some of their adventures hopping freights and riding the rails would later turn up in *Wash Tubbs*. They parted ways soon, though, when Crane dropped out of college and went to sea. But they kept in touch. Turner eventually made his way to New York and a career as an illustrator and was reasonably content. Then

in 1937 he got that letter from his old rail-riding chum.

Crane had been doing the strip for nearly fourteen years without a break. It was a grueling pace—albeit no different than that endured by every syndicated newspaper cartoonist. Until Garry Trudeau astounded the syndicate world in 1982 by taking an eighteen-month sabbatical (during which his strip *Doonesbury* simply languished, undrawn, unwritten, uncirculated), the only way a syndicated cartoonist got a vacation was by working ahead: if a cartoonist drew two weeks' worth of strips in one week, he could take the next week as vacation. It might take a month or more of cranking out a few extra strips a week to create enough surplus to get that week off, but that was the only way it could be done. By 1937, Crane needed a rest. He wanted to escape the deadline-meeting ordeal for an extended period—say, six weeks—without having to double his rate of production. He could do it if he had an assistant who could draw like him well enough to sustain the strip. His old friend Turner was his choice.

Before leaving for his European vacation, Crane finished writing the story he was in the middle of. Then he left, and Turner drew the strip. Turner's work was published from October 17 through December 1, 1937. When Crane returned, Turner stayed on as his assistant, having decided he liked cartooning better than illustrating. In 1938 the two cartoonists broke an NEA tradition: they moved out of Cleveland, flouting the dictum that required them to work in the office. They moved their families and studio to Florida, where they worked together until 1943.

In the summer of that year, Crane left NEA to create a new strip for Hearst's King Features. It was the old story: Hearst offered Crane a sweeter deal (including, I assume, ownership of his feature). Crane was only the second major cartoonist in the medium's history to leave a successful feature to create an entirely new one. (The other rebel had also been an NEA cartoonist—Gene Ahern, who had abandoned Major Hoople to create a similar character, Judge Puffle, for King in 1936.) On November 1, 1943, Crane's *Buz Sawyer* debuted. Crane expected Turner to join him on the new strip, but NEA apparently made him a better offer to stay on and continue *Wash Tubbs* over his own signature. Turner is one of the few cartoonists to

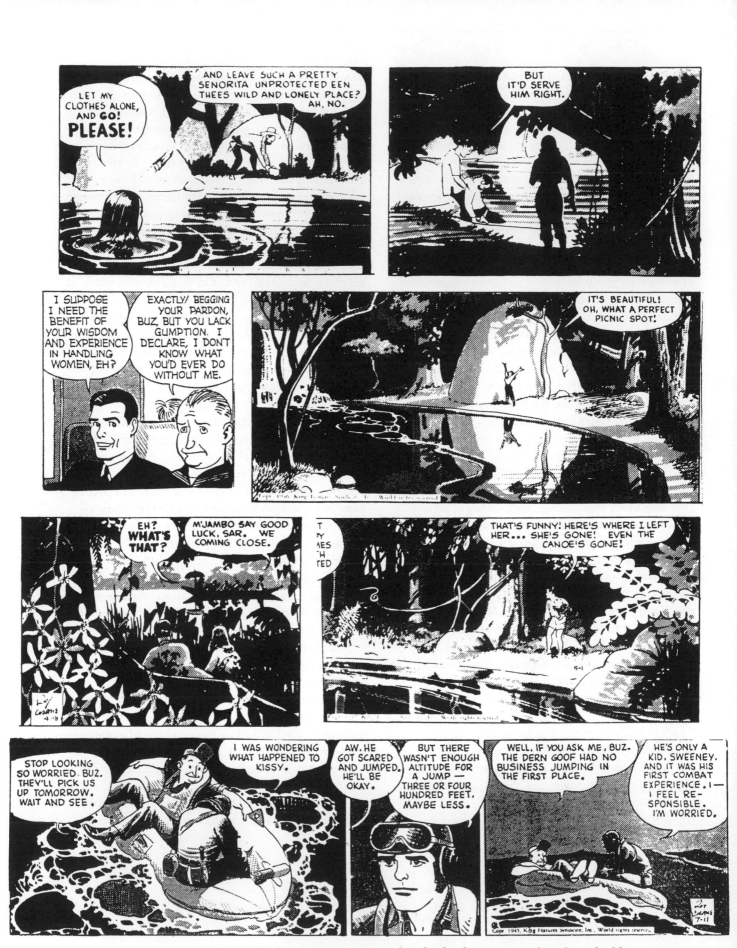

Figure 51. *As this miscellany of panels shows, Crane continued to display his mastery of Craftint doubletone in* Buz Sawyer, *which started November 1, 1943. The girl in the pond is Christy, a home-town girl whom Buz eventually married. With Buz in the third panel is his Navy sidekick, Roscoe Sweeny.*

continue another's creation successfully—equaling and sometimes, as Ron Goulart says, surpassing his mentor's achievements. His *Wash Tubbs* (which became *Captain Easy*, finally, in 1949) was every bit as lively and exciting as Crane's *Wash Tubbs* had been.

Crane's new strip was another masterpiece of doubletone shading, and the pace and the action were in the tradition Crane himself had established. But Buz Sawyer is a younger man than Easy. (And he's prettier—too pretty, as it turned out. Crane broke his hero's nose in July 1946. And it was an improvement: with a flattened proboscis, Buz seems a more rugged character, better suited for the roundhouse adventures Crane put his heroes through.) Taking advantage of the opportunities for action and adventure offered by World War II, Crane put Buz in the Navy. The strip remained a military strip for most of its run, with Buz in Naval Intelligence after the war. In the postwar strip Crane was soon up to his old tricks, echoing the lighthearted operetta ambiance of his prewar ramble with Wash and Easy. But that's another story.

Buz Sawyer was an accomplished piece of work by a master of the medium, but Crane broke little new ground here compared to the vast tracts he had opened in the 1930s. Curiously, by the time *Buz Sawyer* was launched, the tables of inspiration had turned: Crane was now clearly influenced by a cartoonist he had once inspired, Milton Caniff. Buz, like Caniff's Terry, is a pilot. And Crane now strove for authenticity in military details with the same zeal as Caniff. Then, when Crane conjured up a beauteous sultry female guerrilla leader in the South Seas and gave her the codename Cobra, the character (not to mention the serpentine nom de guerre) could not help but evoke comparisons with Caniff's celebrated Dragon Lady. Later, Crane also introduced a blonde bombshell in the mold set by Caniff's Burma. Crane's work continued to be impressive in its own right, too, but *Buz Sawyer* never had the magic that animated *Wash Tubbs* in those halcyon prewar years.

Crane was doubtless not as intrigued by the character of Buz Sawyer as he had been by Captain Easy. When creative artists are stimulated by their creations, they do their best work. And while *Buz Sawyer* was by no means any kind of a slouch of a strip, it lacked the fire of Crane's earlier achievement. The invigorating excitement of discovery, of innovation day by day in a medium not yet fully formed, wasn't there at the drawingboard anymore. Still, *Buz Sawyer* was the work of a master who knew all the tricks of his craft and who put his characters through their paces with the sangfroid of an experienced ringmaster, an old trouper who never made mistakes because he had seen and done it all before.

Bob Zschiesche too thinks Wash and Easy enjoyed a place in Crane's heart that Buz never approached. "The last drawing Roy drew—a week before he died—," he wrote, "was of Wash and Easy in Jim Ivey's Wash Tubbs book, which Roy sent to Dick Moores in Asheville, North Carolina." Zschiesche continued: "I got the feeling he took greater delight in his Wash Tubbs work. Perhaps he felt that in the early days the comics looked their best in six- or seven-column wide format. 'In the early days,' Roy said, 'cars and planes were more simply designed—and a cartoonist could make 'em look funnier. The cars today, they're big, wide, enclosed things. You can't do a thing with 'em!'"[9]

In the 1930s illustrators would make the adventures in comic strips seem more real by accurately depicting enclosed automobiles—not to mention jungles and spaceships, soaring skyscrapers, office furniture, ladies' fashions, people in general, and every other thing under the sun. But before illustrators brought serious authenticity to comics, there was Roy Crane. And it was the work of Roy Crane—those often funny stories of treasure hunts and melodramatic villainy and pretty girls and a hook-nosed soldier of fortune—that an entire generation of cartoonists sought to equal as they invented and refined the adventure comic strip. All of them, like Crane, were seeking adventure for the fun of it.

CHAPTER 6
The Captain and the Comics
How a Noncartoonist Shaped the Medium

If circulation is what makes a newspaper great (and that is surely one of the measures of greatness in newspapering), then Joseph Medill Patterson knew more about how to achieve greatness than any other man of his time: in circulation battles in both Chicago and New York, he soundly defeated the champion of the previous generation, William Randolph Hearst. Like Hearst, Patterson recognized the importance of comics in selling newspapers. One of his first acts upon assuming control of the *Sunday Chicago Tribune* in 1910 had been to add to the Sunday funnies his favorite strip, Rudolph Dirks's *Hans and Fritz*. (Retitled *The Captain and the Kids* in the national fit of anti-German feeling during World War I, the strip was Dirks's reincarnation of his famed *Katzenjammer Kids*.) But Patterson was otherwise much different than Hearst when it came to publishing comic strips. Hearst purchased established or proven talent; Patterson developed talent. Hearst's success as a press lord had rested almost entirely upon the size of his bankroll (which derived more from inherited mining interests than from the newspapers he published); Patterson's was founded upon his uncanny understanding of what appealed to the ordinary citizen.

Patterson had been born to wealth and influence, but he gained his extraordinary insight into human nature through the variegated experiences of a

youth that only his wealthy peers might say was misspent. He had learned disdain for members of his class at Groton, a tony school for the scions of the rich and famous where his classmates had sneered at his midwestern accent. Henceforth, he had no use for snobs, young or old. And disdain fostered a reformer's spirit. Moreover, he acquired by the experience a dread of ostentation that lasted throughout his life.

He entered Yale in 1897, interrupting his tenure there for a year to serve an apprenticeship in the family calling. But his baptism in journalism was not performed at the family font: when he went to cover the Boxer Rebellion in imperial China in the summer of 1900, he went as an aide to a reporter for Hearst's *Chicago American*. In China he doubtless witnessed the last flaunting of old-style imperialism, the final flourish of traditional, premechanized military campaigning, as the multinational force wound its way from Tientsin to besieged Peking under a rainbow of fluttering guidons. A wondrous sight—the mounted and trudging might of historic colonialism in full martial panoply.

After his adventure in the Orient, Patterson returned to Yale, graduated in 1901, and joined his father's *Tribune* as a reporter. But he found the work dull and left in order to throw himself into local politics, campaigning for municipal reform in Chicago. His performance eventually earned him a

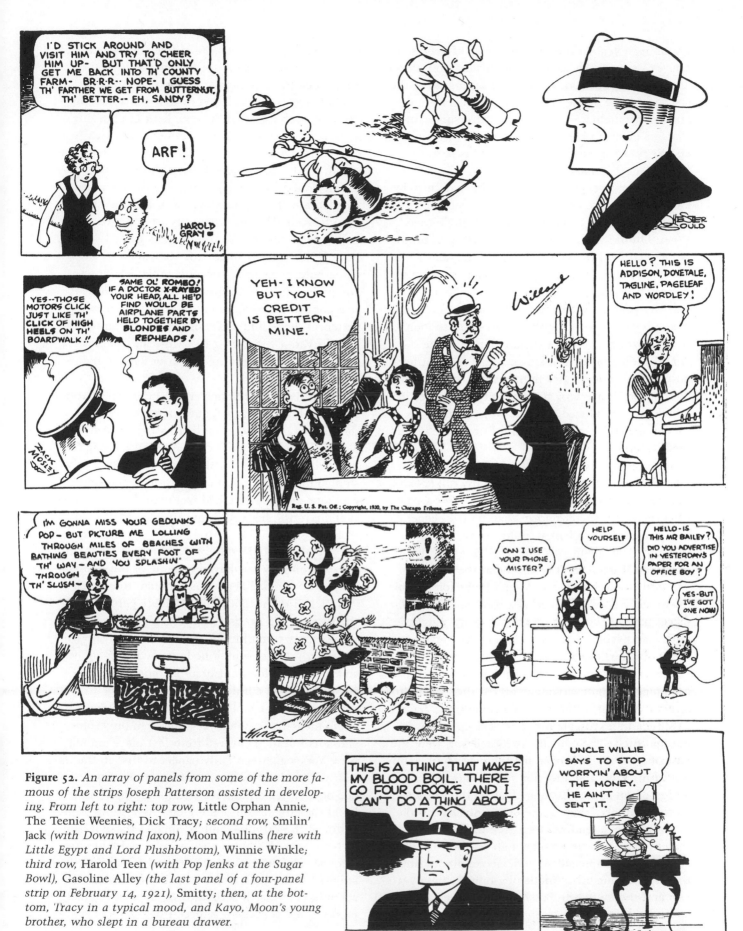

Figure 52. *An array of panels from some of the more famous of the strips Joseph Patterson assisted in developing. From left to right: top row,* Little Orphan Annie, The Teenie Weenies, Dick Tracy; *second row,* Smilin' Jack *(with Downwind Jaxon),* Moon Mullins *(here with Little Egypt and Lord Plushbottom),* Winnie Winkle; *third row,* Harold Teen *(with Pop Jenks at the Sugar Bowl),* Gasoline Alley *(the last panel of a four-panel strip on February 14, 1921),* Smitty; *then, at the bottom,* Tracy *in a typical mood, and* Kayo, *Moon's young brother, who slept in a bureau drawer.*

Republican seat in the Illinois House of Representatives in 1903. There he distinguished himself on at least one occasion by throwing an inkpot at the speaker of the house during a heated debate on streetcar franchises. Then when Patterson learned that his election had been engineered by his father and Republican bosses, he resigned his seat, the fires of rebellion again banked.

Patterson promptly scandalized his paternity by switching parties and working for Democrat Edward J. Dunne's campaign for mayor of Chicago. When Dunne won, Patterson served in his administration. Then in 1906 he shocked his family once again: in a dramatic letter of resignation, he expressed a loathing for himself and all other wealthy persons who enjoyed the fruits of others' labors without working themselves and announced that he was becoming a socialist and that he would thereafter earn his own living. To that purpose, he became a dairy farmer and a writer, producing socialist tracts, novels, and plays (three of which were produced on Broadway); in 1908 he served as campaign manager for Eugene Debs's bid for U.S. president.

By 1910, however, Patterson had become disillusioned with socialism: with too many talkers and too few doers, the movement was no more a practical means to social reform than politics generally had proved. Coincident with his growing disaffection with socialism was the death of his father, Robert W. Patterson. The throne at the *Chicago Tribune* stood empty, and Joseph Patterson and his aristocratic cousin, Robert McCormick, took their places at it. The newspaper community watched with fascination as the cousins assumed management of their legacy: disruptive quarrels between the Pattersons and the McCormicks were a Chicago legend, and everyone expected the cousins to provide juicy entertainment by ripping the *Tribune* to shreds in a struggle for control. Everyone was disappointed. The cousins, it turned out, were the best of friends. Each regarded the other with genuine admiration and affection, and although they disagreed on some matters affecting the *Tribune's* editorial stance, they were determined to end the historic family feuding. As a step in this direction, they made a unique arrangement on the editorial page: by the unprecedented device of alternating the top responsibility month by month, the Bourbon and the erstwhile Bolshevik shared editorial control while at the same time managing to avoid

daily disputes. (They also modified the extremities of their differing views so the paper would not have an editorial policy with a split personality.)

While the cousins shared overall control of the *Tribune*, each followed his own bent in choosing an aspect of newspaper management in which to concentrate his energies. McCormick devoted himself to the business side. To the editorial side, Patterson brought the perspective of a disillusioned idealist, a man born to power who had thus far been frustrated in his rebellious attempts to exercise it. He brought also the insights gained through his associations with state and city machine politicians and with blue-collar socialists and parlor pinks and through his modest success as a popular playwright and novelist. To these experiences, he would add those of a war correspondent in Vera Cruz during the Mexican troubles of 1914 and of commanding officer of Battery B during World War I.

When the United States entered the war, Patterson joined up. He turned down a commission in the Illinois National Guard, enlisting instead as a buck private, but by the time his unit (among the first called up as part of the famous Rainbow Division comprised of guard units from all the states) was sent to France, he had worked up the ranks to captain, a title he would invoke the rest of his life. Working side by side with his men, he impressed them with his understanding and regard for them.

Patterson may not have been one of the ordinary people, but he had been close enough to enough varieties of them to acquire an acute perception of their wants and needs. That understanding he would apply to building the circulation of the *New York Daily News*, which he launched after the war, and to the development of an astonishingly successful series of comic strips.

America's first tabloid, the *Daily News* grew phenomenally, as noted previously: in only four-and-a-half years, it moved from last place among New York's eighteen daily papers to first in the nation with a daily average circulation of over 600,000. Patterson had learned much about how to build the circulation of a big-city newspaper while editor of the *Tribune*, and he applied those lessons in New York. Believing that people wanted more romance and adventure than their lives ordinarily afforded them, Patterson produced an outrageous, sobby, glamorous sheet featuring sex and scandal, pictures and contests—a three-ring circus of sensation and entertainment. At first, he managed the paper from Chicago, making frequent visits to the New York offices. By 1926, though, when the *Daily News* had achieved the financial success the cousins imagined for it, Captain Patterson could restrain himself no longer. He moved to New York to assume direct daily control of the tabloid, retaining only a financial interest in the *Tribune*. At last, the somewhat uneasy editorial partnership the cousins had endured while sharing the helm of the *Tribune* was dissolved: now each cousin had his own paper and could follow his editorial instincts unencumbered by considerations of the other's views.

Although nothing in the *Daily News* was too trivial to evade the Captain's attention, he concentrated, as he had in Chicago, on improving and increasing the paper's feature material—including, especially, the comics. Because Patterson's specialty was features, he also ran the Tribune-News Syndicate, which was therefore headquartered in New York. Arthur Crawford, whom Patterson had named head of the syndicate, was little more than an administrator: Patterson made all the important decisions. And the day-to-day implementation of his decisions was entrusted to his assistant, Mollie Slott, who, in the normal course of events, became the de facto manager of the syndicate.

The war had interrupted Patterson's program for developing new comic strip features for the *Tribune*. In May 1914 he had introduced William Donahey's *Teenie Weenies*, a Sunday illustrated text feature aimed directly at kids. It was the first comics section feature that Patterson selected for its juvenile appeal—and it would be the last. He quickly realized that comics, like everything else in a newspaper, had to attract adults: it was adults who bought the papers. His next comic strip, *The Gumps*—as we have seen—reflected this conviction. And as he began in the postwar years to develop new comic strips, he continued to design them with adult readers in mind.

The first of his new comic strips was developed while Patterson was still editor of the *Tribune*, before the *Daily News* was started. Although the strip was about youngsters, it was aimed at adults. Booth Tarkington's novel *Seventeen* had been published in 1916, and its popularity was of sufficient intensity and duration to make Patterson pause when he saw a comic strip submission with the same title cross his desk in 1919. He was on the verge of expanding the *Sunday Tribune* comic section from four to eight pages, and this strip looked promising: at the time, there were no strips about teenagers. He renamed the submission *The Love Life of Harold Teen*, and Carl Ed's long-running strip debuted as a Sunday page on May 4, 1919. Ed was soon producing a daily version, too. The strip was slow to generate reader enthusiasm, but once the twenties began to roar, *Harold Teen* became a national pastime, popularizing such expressions as "shebas" (girls), "sheiks" (boys), "Yowsah!" "Yeh, man, he's the nertz!" "pantywaist," and "Fan mah brow!" Ed's highschoolers congregated at Pop Jenk's Sugar Bowl soda shop to imbibe Pop's "gedunk sundaes"—a confection that so captured the imagination of readers that Ed had to invent a recipe for it. Ed continued the strip for fifty years.

In 1921, perhaps at the same time as he was discussing the introduction of the Widow Zander with Smith, Patterson tinkered with another *Tribune* cartoon: *Gasoline Alley*. The feature had been inspired by his McCormick cousin's conviction that people needed help in learning how to care for their automobiles, which were becoming increasingly available to a middle-class public. Drawn by staff cartoonist Frank King, *Gasoline Alley* was scarcely a self-help feature, although it did talk a good deal about the problems people had with cars. "Cars had character in those days, and there was plenty to discuss," King once remarked.[1] Set in an alley where men met to inspect and discuss their vehicular difficulties, *Gasoline Alley* had first appeared on November 24, 1918, as one of several panel cartoon features boxed together on a black-and-white anthology page King had been doing for several years for the *Sunday Tribune*.[2] Called *The Rectangle*, the page was a conglomeration of cartoons like Billy Ireland's *The Passing Show*. It offered comic commentary under a rotating series of headings—"Familiar Fractions," "Pet Peeves," "Science Facts," "Our Movies," and the like. The *Gasoline Alley* panel appeared routinely after its debut, but only on Sunday until August 25, 1919, a Monday, when it began to run daily as well. It didn't appear in strip form, though, until about a year later: up to then, although it was occasionally a series of panels, it was usually just a single picture, which nonetheless sustained a modest (mostly thematic) continuity.

Reflecting on the feature, Patterson decided all the talk about cars left out the interests of women

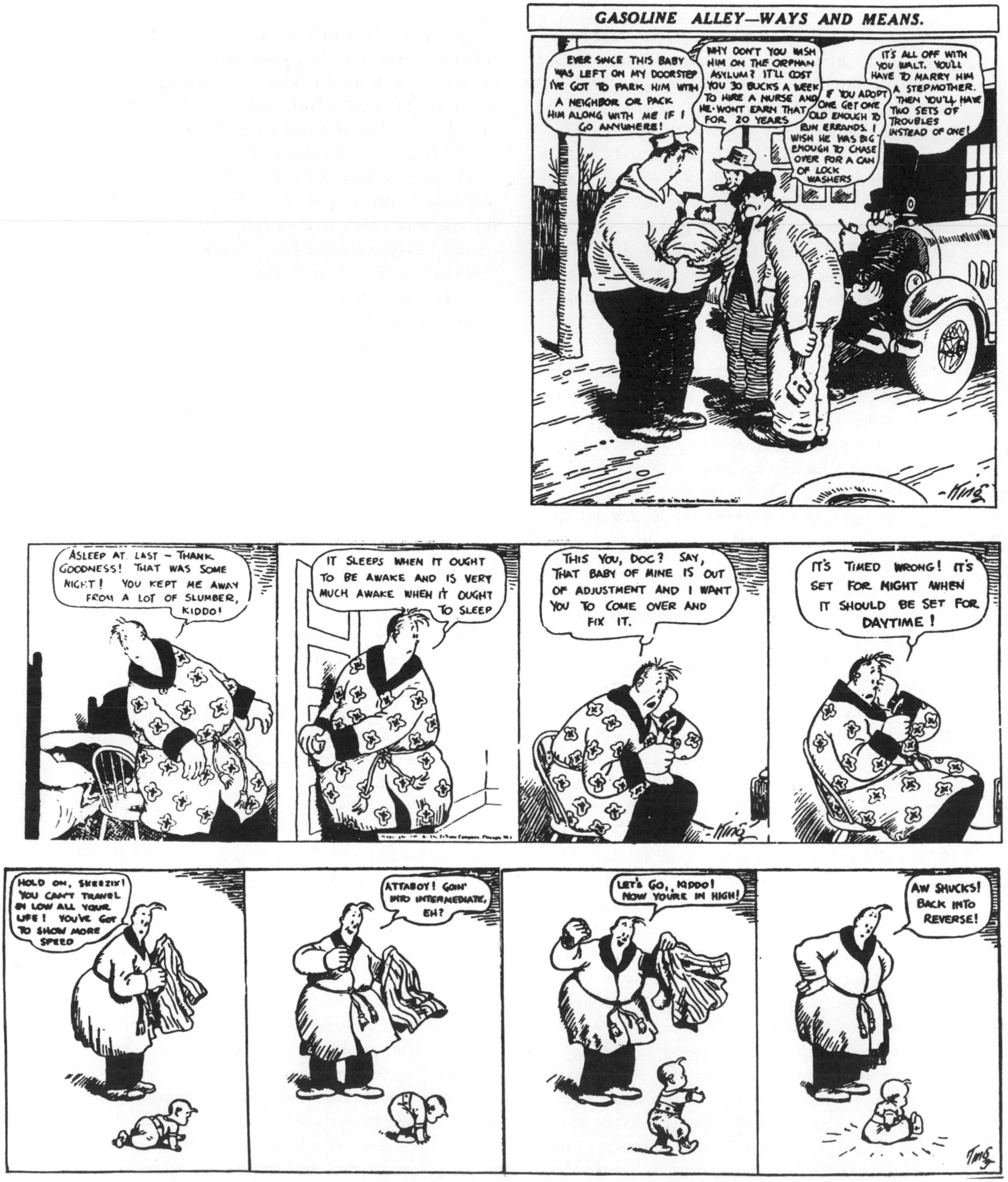

Figure 53. *Frank King's* Gasoline Alley *was sometimes a comic strip and sometimes a single panel even after Skeezix arrived in 1921. Much of the charm of the humor in the strip at this time arose from the predicament of the bachelor father, Walt, who, knowing nothing about child-rearing but a lot about automobiles, treated the infant as if he were some new make of car.*

readers. "Get a baby into the story fast," he commanded the flabbergasted King, who protested that the main character, Walt Wallet, was a bachelor. It was then decided to have Walt find a baby on his doorstep—which he did on Valentine's Day, 1921.

With the arrival of Skeezix, the strip developed a stronger story line. (Walt took several days just to get the neighborhood's approval of the name he chose for the infant boy.) Subsequently, almost accidentally, the strip evolved its most unique feature: its characters aged. The children grew up, and the adults grew older. To King, this innovative aspect of his strip was simply logical: "You have a one-week-old baby, but he can't stay one week old forever. He had to grow."[3] By logical extension, so did everyone else in the strip. Patterson concurred. This attribute of Gasoline Alley added a dimension of real life to the strip, and King went on to convert everyday concerns about automobiles into a larger reflection of American life in a small town. The strip quickly took on familial overtones, and the setting, with Walt's subsequent marriage to "Auntie" Blossom, became thoroughly domestic, the situations those of ordinary life, the humor warm, pleasant, low-keyed.

For most of the readers of the Tribune and the Daily News, the mirror of small-town life that King held up so faithfully in Gasoline Alley probably evoked nostalgia, with its fond reminders of the way things used to be. Both papers were big-city papers, whose readers dwelled and worked in a world far removed from King's comfortable idealization. When Patterson began looking for his next new comic strips after Harold Teen, he had his metropolitan readers foremost in his mind. Particularly, he wanted something for the working women who crammed the streets in Chicago and New York. Winnie Winkle the Breadwinner was his choice.

Arthur Crawford captured Martin Branner, a former vaudeville hoofer who was then drawing two Sunday strips—Louie the Lawyer for Bell Syndicate and Pete and Pinto for the New York Sun and Herald—and in September 1920 Winnie Winkle began. Winnie wasn't the first career girl in comics (Somebody's Stenog earned that distinction in 1906), but she was the first of the post World War I "liberated women." Branner started with a daily gag strip but eventually developed a continuing story. Winnie's struggle to make her way in the world, supporting her father and mother and kid

brother Perry, made the strip a great attraction among women readers. And Branner enhanced the strip's basic appeal by dressing his heroine in contemporary working-girl fashions. The strip was so popular that it earned the Daily News its nickname—"the working girl's paper."

Two years later, Patterson found a male counterpart for Winnie in a strip called Bill the Office Boy. The strip had been developed for the New York World, but its cartoonist, Walter Brendt, had been asked to leave after two weeks ("because of the way I addressed my boss," he later explained).[4] On the same day he left the World, Brendt dropped by Patterson's office and showed him the strip. Patterson liked it but asked Brendt to come up with a different name for his thirteen-year-old protagonist. Brendt grabbed a phone book, opened it, and saw a page of Smiths. So Smitty was born. He first appeared in print on November 29, 1922.

Brendt initially drew upon his own experiences for Smitty's stories and gags: after only six months of high school, he started as an office boy at the New York Journal. But, he learned to listen to Patterson, too. By this time, Patterson had established himself as a canny story counselor for his cartoonists. His letter to Brendt on November 23, 1923, is typical of the kind of direction he gave:

> Dear Mr. Brendt;
> I believe it would be proper to try an experiment. That is, put a little pathos in the Smitty strip. This came to me: Suppose Smitty is unjustly suspected of stealing. Things disappear from the office, which he doesn't take, but the boss, very much against his wish, is convinced of his thievery and that Smitty is light-fingered. So, reluctantly, he fires Smitty who goes home in disgrace and everybody points the finger of scorn at him. Eventually, of course, he is exonerated and all is well.
> I believe that you could get some Jackie Coogan appeal by this method.
> Sincerely yours,
> J.M. Patterson[5]

Brendt, who subsequently became an unofficial talent scout for the Captain, learned to squeeze suspense out of his continuities with the best of them, but Patterson had to continue his search for comic strip pathos until he found its epitome in an orphan girl a year later.

In the meantime, looking over his comics lineup, Patterson decided it was missing another element of big-city life: nowhere among his strips were there any real roughnecks, any genuine denizens of the lower strata of society who made their way with their wits and pure gall, in total disregard (or ignorance) of the Puritan work ethic, books of etiquette, and every other refinement of social intercourse. "We need a low-life strip," he told Crawford, and Crawford put the word out. Before long, a cartoonist named Frank Willard came to see Patterson. Willard was doing a not-too-successful strip for King Features when he heard that Patterson was looking for a new strip. He came to hear what Patterson had in mind.

According to Ferd Johnson, who assisted Willard on *Moon Mullins* from almost the very beginning, Willard had been fired by King. Willard and all the King cartoonists at the time had to submit their strip ideas in advance to the editor, and the editor regularly tossed Willard's submissions into the wastebasket as the hapless cartoonist watched (and fumed). Willard got even angrier a few weeks later when he saw some of his ideas appear in George McManus's strip. "The editor was feeding Willard's ideas to the Syndicate's big star," Johnson explained. "Later Willard and McManus were very good friends, but at the time, Willard got so damn sore that he went and had a couple of drinks and then went after the editor. He found the guy sitting in his chair and he let him have one that knocked him onto the floor. Willard knew he'd get fired for that—and he did. But the story got around, and when Captain Patterson, who was looking for a tough-guy strip, heard about it, he said, 'That's my man.' He called Willard in. And that's how *Moon* got its start."[6]

After a few minutes of conversation, Patterson knew Willard was the man to limn the lowlife of the city. He described what he wanted, and Willard went off to develop that classic comedy of conniving, brawling, uncouth social pretension, *Moon Mullins.*

Starting on June 19, 1923, Moon quickly proved himself to be an unabashed freeloader, a "whadda we get" con man, always on the look out for a free lunch and a quick buck and willing to let anyone take the risks but himself. His only redeeming quality is his endurance: he keeps at it. Nothing gets him down. Disappointed at the outcome of one con, he immediately goes on to the next—not bothered one whit by failure. Moon's motives are undisguised by the usual veneers of civilization's

respectable society. And he is entirely unabashed. His honest embracing of his own self-interest is refreshing. And perhaps that is his charm.

Willard surrounded Moon with kindred souls— Lord and Lady Plushbottom, Uncle Willie and his wife, the cook Mamie. Moon's kid brother Kayo was the only realist (and he was a full-blown cynic). As Stephen Becker says, the strip was

> the greatest collection of social pretenders ever assembled. . . . *Moon Mullins* might be subtitled The Quest for High Life, or the Imitation of Glamour. The impulse is always upward—to fame, riches, dazzling lights. But the culmination is always a descent to reality, via the nightstick, the pratfall, or the custard pie. Always, earthly reality wins out over the ideal, the pretension; beef stew defeats poetry. Perhaps the key to the strip and to its popularity is this: nobody works. This family is a collection of con artists; that they con themselves, or each other, as often as they do anyone else is the meat of the strip. What we admire is not this family's virtues; it is their tirelessness. They are the indefatigable pretenders to a shaky throne.[7]

Willard's graphic style was wonderfully attuned to his subject: he drew his characters with a bold outline, but he shaded them with hayey cross-hatching, giving to every scene a seedy appearance entirely suitable to the moral leanings of his cast.

Patterson was right about Willard: he was exactly the man for the kind of strip the Captain wanted. In the brief autobiography that appears in Martin Sheridan's *Comics and Their Creators,* Willard unveils (mostly for laughs) a personal history that might have been a blueprint for Moon's. While a partner ran a hamburger stand at county fairs, Willard played the horses and they split the profits. One day his partner "became interested in trains" and took all the receipts to California. As a claim tracer in a Chicago department store, Willard conned a friend into doing all his work by supplying lunch—free sandwiches that Willard appropriated at a nearby bar. If Patterson hadn't given him the idea for *Moon Mullins,* Willard might have wound up as Moon always did, with the title of his faltering King Features strip as his epitaph: it was called *The Outta Luck Club.*

Another cartoonist who hadn't been running in luck very much was a former *Tribune* staffer named Harold Gray. He'd quit the *Tribune* in 1920 to operate his own commercial art studio, and then Sidney Smith hired him to assist on *The Gumps*. Gray soon aspired to doing a strip himself (Smith's million-dollar 1922 contract may have helped inspire him), and he began sketching characters and imagining situations and talking to Smith about them. When Gray came up with a concept they both agreed was promising, Gray showed his idea to Patterson. The Captain wasn't interested, but Gray kept at it. The ensuing parade of ideas was followed by a parade of rejections. It went on for months.

One day while going over some of his sketches with Smith, Gray pointed to a drawing of a small gamin and declared that the boy would be an orphan. "Not bad," Smith said, intrigued by the simplicity of the idea of a strip about an orphan, who must start out without relatives or friends or other complications. "But make the kid clean and cute and sweet to appeal to women readers." Gray dutifully made the kid cute, gave him a head of curls, drew up a dozen sketches of the boy in various poses, and showed them to Patterson, calling his strip idea "Little Orphan Otto." For once, Patterson was interested. Probably still searching for pathos, the Captain decided to try the orphan strip. But he wanted Gray to alter Otto: "The kid looks like a pansy to me," Patterson growled. "Put a skirt on him and we'll call it 'Little Orphan Annie.'"[8] It may have been the head of curls that did it, recalling to Patterson's mind the image of Mary Pickford in her early films.

Patterson worked with Gray to plot the first few strips, telling the cartoonist to aim for adult readers. "Kids don't buy papers. Their parents do," Patterson explained. They devised a Dickensian tearjerker of an introductory sequence: little Annie (smaller and therefore cuter at first than in her heyday) was forced to labor for her keep at the orphanage, which was as grim and oppressive as any Oliver Twist ever endured. Her fate was presided over by Miss Asthma, whose rotten disposition ringed every childish hope for adoption with a nimbus of gloom. The first strip appeared on August 5, 1924, and concluded with Annie's bedtime prayer: "Please make me a real good little girl so nice people will adopt me. Then I can have a papa and mama to love. And if it's not too much trouble, I'd like a dolly. Amen." But Annie wasn't just a cute, sweet little girl. Gray quickly added dimension to her character: in the next day's strip, when a rude boy teases her, Annie wallops him in the kisser, establishing immediately that she has a certain independence of spirit in spite of her straitened circumstances.

In a short time, *Annie* was a popular feature, and the spirit of independence that pervaded Gray's work eventually enlisted a devoted readership. At the end of the second month of the strip's run, Gray introduced the character who would shape the philosophy of independence into a political stance: Annie is adopted by Oliver "Daddy" Warbucks, a millionaire industrialist. Warbucks became Gray's example of the self-made man, the self-reliant individualist who made himself what he is through purposeful enterprise. The epitome of this culture hero, Warbucks is the larger-than-life version of what all the "little people" in the strip inevitably become if they follow Annie's example of hard work and canny capitalism.

But to be exemplary, Annie can scarcely be a rich man's daughter. As soon as Gray had established bonds of affection between Annie and "Daddy," he sent Warbucks off on a business trip, and Annie is returned to the orphanage by the spiteful Mrs. Warbucks (who soon disappears from the strip forever). Annie is adopted again, this time by a slave-driving couple who make her life miserable. She runs away, accompanied by her only friend, a pet dog named Sandy, whom she acquired in January 1925. The two eventually take refuge at a farm owned by the poor but kindly Mr. and Mrs. Silos. But Annie is no burden to them: through hard work and her own ingenuity, the eleven-year-old waif is able to contribute to the couple's welfare and happiness. After a few months, though, "Daddy" Warbucks finally locates Annie and takes her and Sandy back to live in splendid comfort with him. Thus did Gray inaugurate the cycle of separation and hardship, rescue and reunion that framed Annie's adventures, along with the quest motif that animated them throughout the strip's run. Separated from "Daddy," Annie must find the means of survival; through her unflagging diligence, she always does.

Oddly enough perhaps, *Little Orphan Annie* reached the zenith of its popularity during the thirties. "Oddly" because it was the decade of Franklin D. Roosevelt, the man who gave government a social conscience. FDR's mission ran in directions diametrically opposed to Gray's ideas. Under Roosevelt's tutelage, the downtrodden and the poor, the halt and the lame were encouraged to

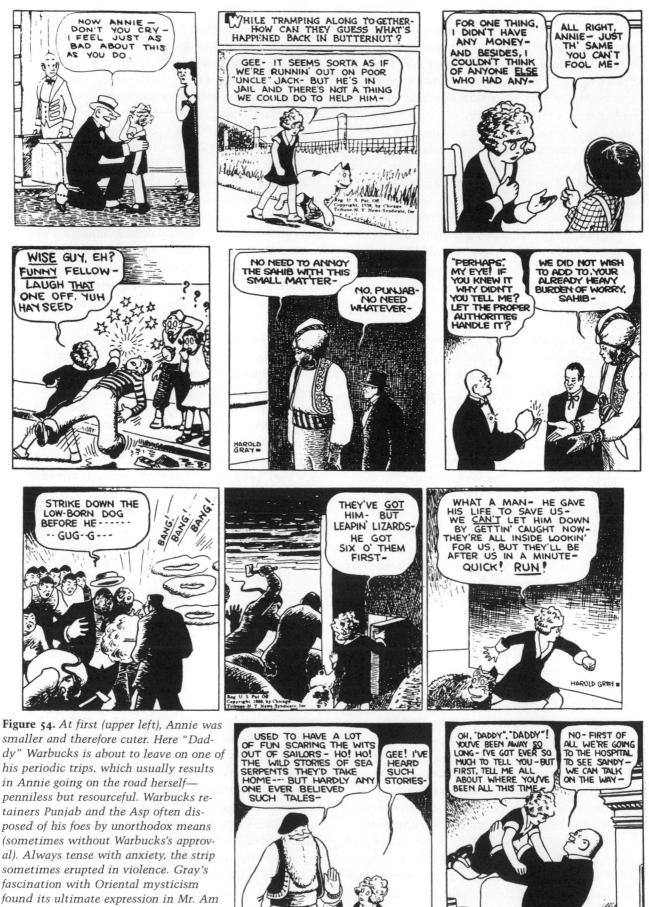

Figure 54. *At first (upper left), Annie was smaller and therefore cuter. Here "Daddy" Warbucks is about to leave on one of his periodic trips, which usually results in Annie going on the road herself— penniless but resourceful. Warbucks retainers Punjab and the Asp often disposed of his foes by unorthodox means (sometimes without Warbucks's approval). Always tense with anxiety, the strip sometimes erupted in violence. Gray's fascination with Oriental mysticism found its ultimate expression in Mr. Am (bottom left). Whatever Annie's adventures, though, she was eventually reunited with her beloved "Daddy."*

look to government for help rather than exhorted to help themselves by working hard and exercising diligently the principles of free enterprise. Gray's message was precisely the opposite—although it was as much an accident of his story as it was a matter of political conviction.

The best way for a little orphan girl to make her way in the world without being simply a weepy milksop is for her to be self-reliant. As a good storyteller, Gray knew that: Warbucks and the rest of Annie's entourage were natural outgrowths of this central notion. As Gray's exemplar, Warbucks could scarcely espouse self-reliance and free enterprise during the Roosevelt years without, at the same time, attacking FDR's policies. And so *Little Orphan Annie* became the first nationally syndicated comic strip to be unabashedly, unrelievedly, "political." *Annie* was not the first political strip: as we've seen, *A. Mutt*—the first successful daily strip—was the first to take political potshots in its panels. But Fisher's strip was published only in San Francisco at the time: it could reflect the opinions of its host paper to a fare-thee-well and suffer no more consequences than the editorials in the same paper (that is, the paper would presumably not be purchased by those who disagreed with the views expressed). Gray's strip, on the other hand, was distributed nationally, and, by tradition, syndicated strips steered clear of politics for fear of offending client papers who might cancel their subscriptions in retaliation. *Annie* was the first to break with this custom, but it did so because the very essence of its story demanded it. Gray's celebrated conservatism was hardly negligible in the development of the strip's political thrust. But neither was the strip's political content artificially superimposed upon an otherwise simple tale of a wandering orphan girl and her dog. The strip's politics were organic—integral to its story and its heroine's personality.

Throughout the decade, Annie drifted from place to place, into "Daddy's" care and out of it, spending most of her time with the ordinary folk and reviving by precept and example their faith in the values of hard work and economy. Sometimes the villainy she faced would be too much to be overcome by such simple virtue, and then "Daddy" Warbucks would show up and rescue Annie and everyone else.

In the thirties Gray introduced another element into the harsh reality of his rendition of the Depression—the element of fantasy. Increasingly, Annie was encountering villains that were not merely greedy landlords or corrupt small-time politicians: some of them were criminals of the most unconscionable nastiness, unscrupulous schemers and plotters of the vilest sort, some with plans for world domination. "Daddy" always arrived in time to save Annie, but not even he, powerful as he was, could punish these villains enough for their crimes. So Gray gave Warbucks aides adequate to the task. Gray had always been fascinated by the Orient (one of Warbucks's earliest cohorts had been a Chinese Mandarin named Wun Wey), and he now began to employ Oriental magic against his villains. On February 3, 1935, a giant, turbaned Indian, eight (perhaps nine) feet tall, showed up as Warbuck's new right-hand man. Punjab was that paragon, a kindly man of enormous strength and vast intelligence. And he could also supply an appropriate punishment for the most unsavory villains, villains too unspeakable for ordinary legal disciplining: throwing a magic blanket over them, Punjab muttered an incomprehensible incantation and banished them from this world (presumably sending them to another, much more unpleasant, plane of existence). Two years later, on February 21, 1937, Gray gave Warbucks another memorable assistant, a black-garbed, hooded-eyed agent of vengeance much more single-minded in purpose than Punjab and entirely humorless—the Asp, whose homeland was (appropriately) in the Middle East, where the term *assassin* originated. Gray's fascination with the mysteries of the Orient culminated later in the same year with the introduction of the cryptic Mr. Am, a fatherly, bearded sort of sultan, who, Gray hinted broadly, had lived since the dawn of time and who could enter the fourth dimension and restore the dead to life.

Fanciful as Gray's fantasy element was, it was not at all lighthearted. At first glance, his drawing ability seemed too crude for rendering either his reality or his fantasy convincingly, but upon longer acquaintance his artwork cast a spell that enhanced his story. In maturity in the late thirties, Gray's drawings were filled with solid blacks, heavy shadows, darkly shaded nooks and crannies. It was a comfortless world, vaguely sinister. And in that world, Gray's people stood around rigidly, posturing woodenly, as if inhibited, restrained, in their movements—perhaps because they were fearful. They seemed, in effect, nearly paralyzed with fear

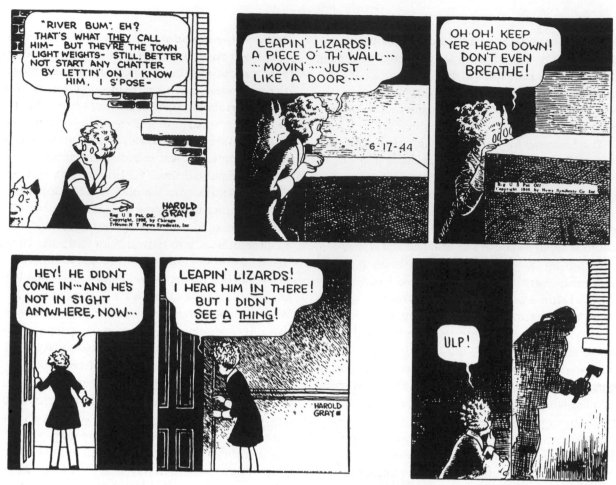

Figure 55. Annie's surroundings were always, it seemed, vaguely threatening. She moved through life forever looking over her shoulder in fearful apprehension. This unspecified anxiety was perfectly symbolized by her blank and therefore unseeing eyes. At the lower right, Warbucks stops Punjab just as the giant is about to send another miscreant to "join the Magi," as Punjab often puts it.

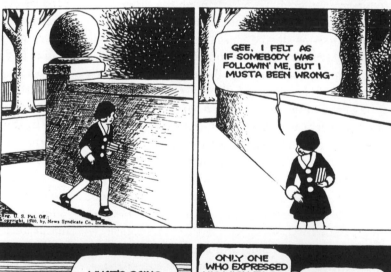

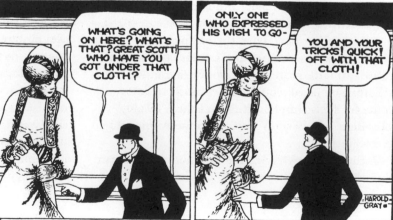

and apprehension. And the blank eyeballs for which Annie is celebrated were integral to the mood of this fearful climate.

Although there was little action in many of Gray's tales, most of them erupted in violence sooner or later. Consequently, Annie seemed perpetually immersed in a sinister nighttime world that threatened to assault her at every street corner. And her blank eyeballs were marvelously appropriate to her situation. We walk through a threatening night gingerly, never looking behind or to the side for fear of seeing a sinister presence there. We keep our eyes focused resolutely, rigidly, ahead of us, in a kind of unseeing stare—precisely the effect that Annie's eyeballs have. In such an atmosphere, when violence breaks out, we are not surprised. It belongs there. We have been led to expect it—to fear it. The blank eyeballs would have been an inspired graphic touch had Gray invented the device expressly for the purpose just described. But, as it happens, he was merely following one of the conventions of early comic strip art: George McManus drew Jiggs's and Maggie's eyes in the same way in *Bringing Up Father*, where the effect produced was quite different. In Gray's strip, though, the convention contributed substantially to the impression Gray clearly intended.

Some readers and critics—mostly avid supporters of Roosevelt's New Deal—saw *Annie* as a political mouthpiece for Colonel McCormick's conservative views masquerading as entertainment, a not-too-subtle indoctrination attempt by the *Chicago Tribune*. Not likely. Although the strip's political diatribes during the thirties echoed the Colonel's on the editorial pages of the *Tribune*, they didn't, for a long time, reflect Patterson's views. Patterson became a strong supporter of FDR early in the New Deal, and Patterson ran the Tribune-News Syndicate and directed the efforts of the cartoonists. (It wasn't until 1940—when Patterson, a passionate isolationist and advocate of neutrality, came to believe that Roosevelt intended to get America into the European conflict—that the Captain broke ranks and became as bitter a critic of FDR's policies as his cousin had been for nearly a decade.) No, *Little Orphan Annie* reflected her creator's opinons, no one else's—opinions born of both political conviction and narrative necessity.

Even while attacking FDR, *Little Orphan Annie*

addressed profound concerns among its readers. The events of the Great Depression unfolded gradually: the world did not collapse overnight. And as the economic institutions slowly crumbled, one after another, the dominant emotion among the population was fear—fear that an entire way of life, the American way, was falling apart. Gray's strip not only addressed but assuaged that fear. Annie's adventures proved again and again that the historic American ethic of hard work was not bankrupt and that capitalism could still work. Readers were reassured and comforted.

Testimonials to the success of Patterson's strips began appearing almost immediately—in the usual flattering form. I've already mentioned *The Nebbs*, which, while not an outright imitation, was at least an offshoot of *The Gumps*, and Harry Tuthill's *The Bungle Family*, with more direct praise in the Gumpish upward aspirations and social criticism of its protagonist, George Bungle. *Harold Teen* doubtless prompted the birth in 1925 of *Etta Kett*, King Features' teenage-manners strip by Paul Robinson. *Winnie Winkle* obviously inspired Russ Westover's *Tillie the Toiler*, which King launched in 1921. And *Smitty* may have had something to do with Roy Crane's sale to the Newspaper Enterprise Association in 1924 of *Wash Tubbs*, since Wash initially worked as a sort of office boy (actually, a clerk in a grocery store). *Little Orphan Annie* immediately provoked United Feature into getting Charles Plumb and Bill Counselman to do *Ella Cinders*, which appeared in 1925, the same year that *Phil Hardy* began—less than a year after Gray's strip debuted. Two years later, Hearst entered two strips in the waif lists: *Two Orphans* and *Little Annie Roonie*. If two strips were better than one, then two orphans (a boy and a girl, both with blank eyeballs—and a dog) were also better than one. Drawn by Al Zere, this double-trouble entry had but a short life. But *Little Annie Roonie* (an echo of the original in title as well as heroine and constant canine companion) lasted longer. Drawn at first in the simple cartoon style of the day by Ed Verdier, *Roonie* was eventually rendered in superb illustrations by Darrel McClure.

Of Patterson's great strips, only Willard's *Moon Mullins* proved, in the long run, inimitable. Although, strictly speaking, no such great works of imagination as those the Captain fostered could be

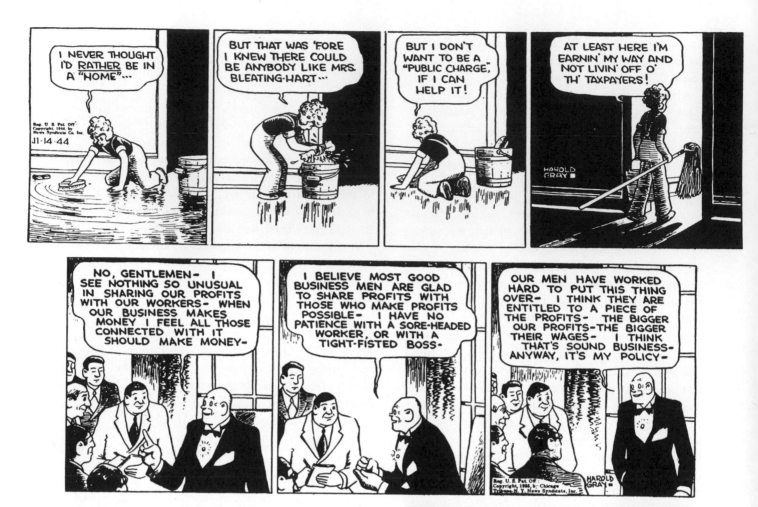

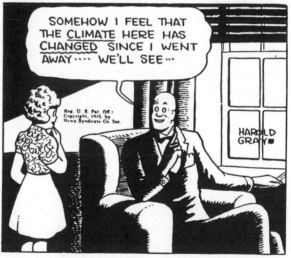

Figure 56. *Annie's work ethic and Warbucks's were expressions of their self-reliance as well as their creator's conservatism. But Warbucks wasn't greedy: he shared his company's profits with those who made the profits possible. No war profiteer, he. His philosophy was in direct conflict with the social programs of Franklin Roosevelt, however, and so strongly was Gray opposed to the New Deal that he killed off his champion in 1944; Warbucks simply couldn't survive in FDR's welfare state. After Roosevelt died, though, Gray brought Warbucks back to life: now that the "climate" had changed, Warbucks could presumably thrive.*

truly duplicated, all except *Moon* inspired notable attempts, and many of those were successful enough, even if a trifle pallid in comparison with their originals. Sincerely meant as all these encomiums doubtless were, they were to fade into insignificance in the face of similar praise that would be tendered the strip Patterson restyled

from a submission by Chester Gould in 1931. *Dick Tracy* would be so widely imitated that it could correctly be said the strip started an entire genre in the medium. And Tracy himself would come to share a place in the history of detective fiction hitherto occupied in solitude by Conan Doyle's Sherlock Holmes.

Gould came to Chicago in 1921 to take courses in commerce and marketing at Northwestern University, but he had his eye on a cartooning career and so took night courses in art, as well. And he began to bombard Patterson immediately with ideas for comic strips, keeping up the barrage steadily for ten years with more than sixty different strip ideas. He tried everything, he recalled later: "the beautiful girl strip, the office boy, the smart aleck, the oddball, the believe-it-or-not cartoon, even a comic feature on sports. But none of them quite clicked."[9] After leaving Northwestern in 1923, Gould worked for Hearst's *American*, doing a strip called *Fillum Fables* in imitation of Ed Wheelan's *Minute Movies*. Six years later, Gould left to do advertising art for the *Chicago Daily News*. It was there that he had his brainstorm.

The country was awash in a coast-to-coast crime wave. Prohibition had given gangsters a socially approved mission: to supply illegal adult beverages to a thirsty populace. With that approval as a foundation, gangland thrived. One thing led to another, and gambling, vice, and other rackets soon proliferated. Johnny Torrio took over Chicago as early as 1920, finally surrendering his turf to a former lieutenant, Alphonse Capone. The infamous Valentine's Day Massacre took place in 1929. By 1931 national public opinion polls identified the paramount problems of the era as Prohibition, inadequate administration of justice, and lawlessness. Bribery, extortion, graft, corruption, arson, and shoot-outs in the streets kept the criminals in control and in the public eye.

"A known gangster would be arrested in the morning," Gould recalled, "and late that afternoon, he'd be back out in the streets." Gould, like a lot of Americans, had had enough; unlike most Americans, he decided to do something about it. What was needed, he felt, was the kind of incorruptible cop who would shoot known hoodlums on sight. He promptly sat down to create just such a stalwart as a comic strip hero. Gould wanted "a symbol of law and order who could 'dish it out' to the underworld exactly as they dished it out—only better. An individual who could toss the hot iron back at them along with a smack on the jaw thrown in for good measure."[10]

The hard-boiled detective had been flourishing in the pages of such pulp magazines as *Black Mask* throughout the twenties. Gould appropriated the persona and, in visualizing his hero, gave him

the chiseled profile he associated with Sherlock Holmes. Calling his hawk-nosed, razor-jawed private detective Plainclothes Tracy, Gould did some sample strips and shipped them off to Patterson in June 1931. He heard nothing for nearly two months. Then, on August 13, he received a telegram:

> YOUR PLAIN CLOTHES TRACY HAS POSSIBILITIES STOP WOULD LIKE TO SEE YOU WHEN I GET TO CHICAGO NEXT STOP PLEASE CALL TRIBUNE OFFICE MONDAY ABOUT NOON FOR AN APPOINTMENT J M PATTERSON.

Patterson began the interview by telling Gould his strip's title was too long. "Call him Dick Tracy," he said; "they call plainclothesmen 'dicks.'"[12] He also felt that the gangbusting activities of Gould's hero needed to be legally validated to prevent the strip's being accused of championing vigilantism, combating one sort of lawlessness with another. Tracy would not be a free-lance operative: he would be a professional police officer. Patterson quickly outlined an introductory story that would provide both motive and legitimacy for Tracy's dogged crusade against crime. Tracy would begin as an ordinary fellow, but when his girlfriend's father is murdered by thugs and she is kidnapped, he would dedicate himself to her rescue and the hoodlums' apprehension. (Patterson named the girl, too: Tess Trueheart.) The police take advantage of Tracy's determination and enlist him in the plainclothes squad. Tracy infiltrates the gang, rescues Tess, and finally brings the crooks to book. Having proven his prowess as a hard-hitting crime fighter, Tracy becomes a career policeman.

Dick Tracy began in the *News* and the *Detroit Mirror* (the Tribune Company's second tabloid undertaking) on Sunday, October 4, 1931. It appeared again the following Sunday, with the dailies starting the next day, October 12. The first Sunday page retains vestiges of Gould's initial conception of his hero as a slangy, tough-talking private detective (figure 57). In adjusting to Patterson's directives, though, Gould presents Tracy as a private citizen, an amateur flatfoot perhaps, whom the police call in to identify an alleged robber. When the lineup fails to produce anyone Tracy can finger, he notices a woman in a cell and asks to talk to her. He fakes a punch at the woman, and when "she" dodges like a man, Tracy snatches off "her" wig, revealing the robber he'd seen in action the night

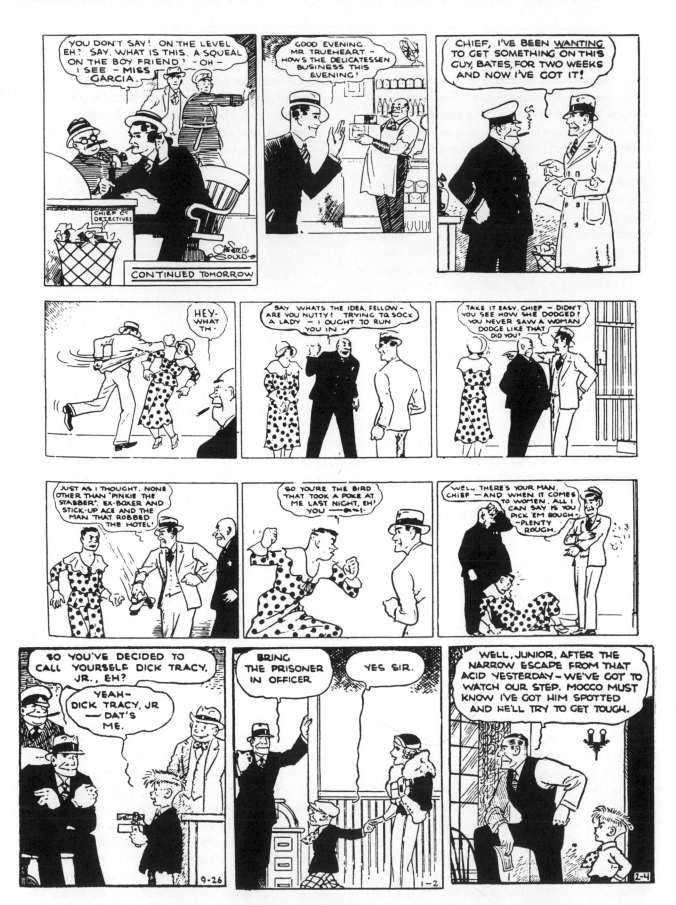

Figure 57. *At the upper left, a panel from Gould's* Plainclothes Tracy, *the strip that Patterson bought and renamed* Dick Tracy. *The next panel is from the first daily strip; in the next, we meet Chief Brandon and see how Gould is already beginning to simplify his way of drawing people in order to present them as moral emblems. The two tiers in the center are from the very first Dick Tracy, the Sunday page. Across the bottom tier, Tracy's juvenile charge appears in 1932 and, nameless, takes Tracy's name while Brandon and Pat Patton look on; Junior meets Tess Trueheart, and then helps his guardian dope out a case.*

before. In one brief sequence of twelve panels, Gould presented the essential Tracy—a no-nonsense crime fighter whose superior deductive powers are satisfyingly amplified with a two-fisted modus operandi. The formula was set, and Gould would spend the next forty-six years applying it.

Until the debut of *Dick Tracy*, the continuity strip had focused on one of two extremes, exotic adventure or domestic intrigue. *Tracy* brought the excitement of adventure to its readers' front doors when Gould's cop began fighting contemporary crime in everyone's home town. Initially, the popularity of the strip sprang from its overt exploitation of the harsher realities of everyday life. It was the beginning of raw violence on the comics page: until *Tracy*, gunplay and bloodshed had been nearly taboo. But Gould changed that. On Friday of the strip's first week, we see a thug shoot and kill Tess's father, bullets drilling into his chest before our eyes. Gould knew he was breaking a precedent. "At the time," he recalled later, "no cartoon had ever shown a detective character fighting it out face to face with crooks via the hot lead route. This detail brought certain expressions of misgivings from the newspapers that were prospective customers. However, within two years, this sentiment had faded to the point where six other strips of a similar pattern were on the market, and the gunplay bogey had disappeared into thin air."[12]

Some of those first imitators also disappeared pretty quickly, but among the ones that lasted a reasonable time were *Dan Dunn* by Norman Marsh (1933), *Pinkerton, Jr.* by Charlie Schmidt (1933; becoming *Radio Patrol* in 1934), *Red Barry* by Will Gould (no relation to Chester; 1934), *Secret Agent X-9* (1934), written by Dashiell Hammett and drawn by Alex Raymond, who would achieve greater fame drawing *Flash Gordon* and later *Rip Kirby*, another detective strip that started in 1946; *Inspector Wade* by Lyman Anderson (1935), *Jim Hardy* by Dick Moores (once an assistant to Gould; 1936), *Mickey Finn* by Frank E. Leonard (focusing on a policeman's family life; 1936), *Charlie Chan* (1938) and *Kerry Drake* (1943), both by Alfred Andriola, and so on. Virtually every comic strip about cops and robbers is a descendant of *Dick Tracy* (including, natcherly, Al Capp's patent parody, *Fearless Fosdick*, in which Gould delighted, saying he was pleased to be the only cartoonist in the world who had a great comic strip artist for a press agent—absolutely free).

The shock of seeing foul crimes committed and retribution dealt out in equally detailed panels undoubtedly accounted for the sensation *Tracy* caused and the almost immediate popularity it enjoyed. But Gould's strip was more than a string of violent shoot-'em-ups. Tracy was much more than a quick-draw and fast-punch artist. He combined intellect with action. Drawing upon current events for inspiration, Gould was quick to incorporate into his strip the realism of police procedure as well as the reality of contemporary crime. He kept himself up-to-date on modern police methods, even hiring a retired Chicago police officer on a part-time basis for weekly conferences on new developments. Tracy quickly emerged as the world's first procedural detective of fiction, his exploits illustrating in painstaking detail the techniques of contemporary crime detection. Gould even anticipated some developments: the use of closed-circuit television (to monitor potential criminal activities in such places as banks, to detect burglars) and two-way wrist radio communication. (Gould once said he found he'd bought some "laughing stock" when he introduced the wrist radio in 1946.[13] But he had the last laugh: his science fiction became fact.) The authenticity of Tracy's methods elevated the strip above most of its imitators.

But Gould's achievement as a cartoonist arises from his pictures as much as from his stories. His drawing style is deceptively simple. Backgrounds are rendered with geometric precision and have a ruler-and-pen linear quality; figures are outlined with a single bold stroke. Wrinkles in clothing are indicated with but a few lines. Gould was a master of the black-and-white daily medium. He laced his strip with solid blacks. Every panel has a huge black area. Ceilings, walls, streets, the sides of buildings or furniture—any of these might be solid black if there were no other possibility for using black in a panel. Tracy always wore a black suit, which Gould presented as a solid shape, virtually a silhouette. And there are plenty of other characters in black suits if Tracy isn't around. Surprisingly, though, all this black does not create a mood of foreboding and pending disaster as it does in *Little Orphan Annie*—perhaps because there are no grays, no ambiguities, in Gould's artwork. Shadows are seldom created in graduated shades: objects have a solid black side (the side away from the light source) and a delineated side (the side facing the light). Nor are people ever in shadow: they are

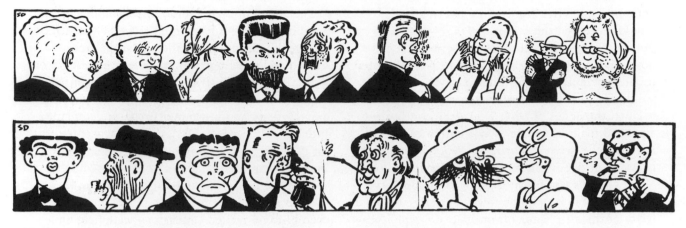

Figure 58. *Some of Gould's rogue's gallery: (top) Little Face, B-B Eyes, Mrs. Pruneface, Boris Arson, Laffy, Shakey, Breathless Mahoney, Jerome Trohs and Mamma; (bottom) Flat Top, Pruneface, Influence, Blow Top, Vitamin Flintheart, B. O. Plenty, Gravel Gertie, and Itchy.*

either fully depicted or completely silhouetted. The result is a stark rendition of reality—planes of black giving definition to planes of white (and vice versa) with uncompromising contrast. The strip is an exercise in black and white both graphically and philosophically. There are no grays in Gould's moral convictions either.

Despite the precision of his technique, however, his graphic treatment is not photographic in the illustrative manner; it is only semirealistic. It is a style that permitted Gould a dramatic deviation from naturalism. And he took full advantage of the opportunity: he created a gallery of ghoulish villains, caricatures of evil that underscored the moral of his strip: crime doesn't pay, and a life of crime will put you in daily communion with such creatures as *these* (figure 58). Pruneface, Flattop, the Mole, Shoulders, B-B Eyes, the Brow, Shakey, Mumbles—none of them are realistically rendered. All are grotesques, gargoyles of criminality. Hence the greatness of the strip: Gould's unique achievement was to combine realistic storytelling and graphic moralizing. It is a combination none of his throng of imitators could successfully duplicate or sustain.

Gould's gratitude to and admiration for Patterson remained undiminished throughout a long career. "I owe everything that came to me in those days to the faith Patterson had in the strip," he once said.[14] And Patterson's counsel did not end with their initial meeting. He continued to give advice—on everything from broad plot outlines to tiny transitional maneuvers for getting from one

story to the next—as he did the same with all the Tribune-News Syndicate cartoonists. Sometimes the ideas came to the cartoonists by memo or phone call. Sometimes they came out of the special forum Patterson conducted to nudge his strips to continued success.

Patterson had regular monthly meetings with his Chicago cartoonists, commuting from New York after he'd moved there permanently. All the cartoonists had offices along the same hallway in the Tribune building, and Patterson would call them all together in one of the offices. Then he would make suggestions about stories and characters, and about whole ranges of reader-grabbing, suspense-building devices. He helped cartoonists fine-tune continuity and kept them abreast of his views on what would interest readers. If someone had drawn his story into a corner from which he saw no escape, Patterson would offer solutions. He usually began by questioning each cartoonist about his progress and intentions on his strip's current story. Then the Captain would take his turn. "He would invariably have something to contribute," Gould recalled, "a story outline, a finale to a plot. He had a fantastic mind. He could talk to five cartoonists and give every one of them a terrific idea."[15] Frank Willard agreed:

> I worked for a syndicate manager once who got everybody in the place together once a week and jumped on a desk and gave us "pep talks." In fact, I believe he was the original pep talker. He didn't give us any ideas, but, oh boy, how worn out we were after those pep talks. The guy

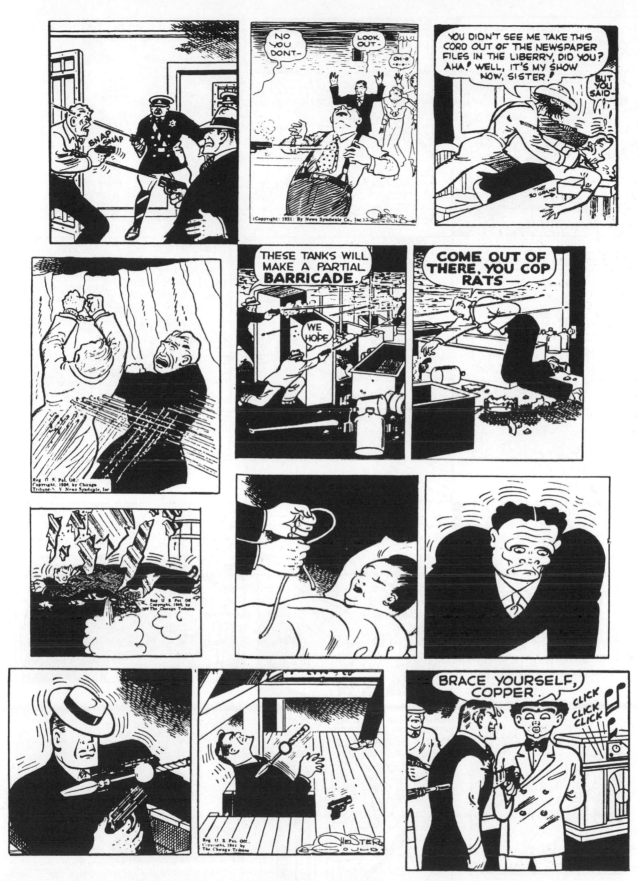

Figure 59. *Gould wanted his hero to trade hot lead with the hoodlums, and he wasted no time in sending the bullets flying. The center panel at the top, the murder of Tess Trueheart's father, is from the fifth day of the strip. The lead seldom stopped flying for the next four decades. The strip offered other violence, too—the criminal acts of those Tracy pursued. Some of them came to grisly albeit picturesque ends, like Gargles, who was skewered by falling shards of plate glass. Tracy himself was scarcely immune from violence. At the lower right, he's about to be "wasted" by Flat Top and a couple of the hood's confederates, all pointing their guns at him. Tracy escaped by lunging at Flat Top.*

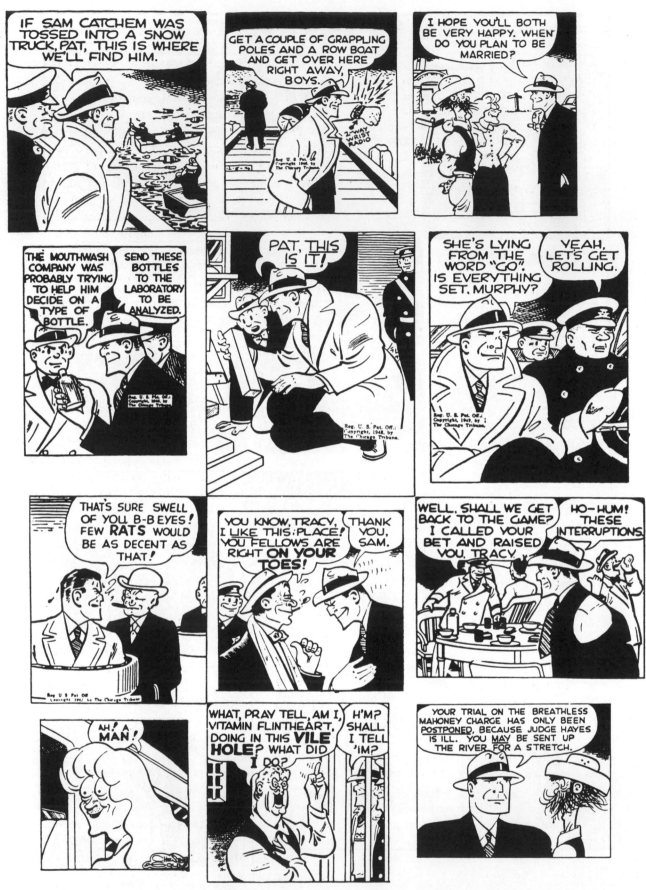

Figure 60. *Some familiar scenes from Tracy's career—dragging the river, communicating via two-way wrist radio, following accepted police procedures. Tracy virtually adopted the eccentric farmer B. O. Plenty, who began his strip life as a would-be criminal. B. O. married Gravel Gertie, and Gould delighted in bringing the colorful couple back for encores. Their daughter, a beautiful baby called Sparkle, was relentlessly merchandised in the 1950s. The ham actor Vitamin Flintheart was another favorite. When Tracy's sidekick Pat Patton became chief of police in 1948, Sam Catchem took his place at Tracy's elbow.*

who applauded the loudest got the most money, and I didn't get much as he found out who it was who gave him the bird. So I've never been accused of waving flags for the boss. But when you ask me what influenced me most in making *Moon Mullins*, I've gotta put the Captain in the Number One position, and I hope he never learns to draw, or I know about five or six comic artists who'll be looking for jobs.[16]

Patterson knew the value of comics in building the circulation of his newspaper, and he treated his cartoonists accordingly—always allowing for the fact that their value would be even greater once they had enjoyed the benefit of his own insights into the minds and hearts of readers. Mostly, his instincts were right. But sometimes he was dead wrong. Once in 1925 he yanked *Little Orphan Annie* when he disapproved of the direction in which Gray was going. Patterson thought Annie had no business leaving the Silos' humble farm to stay in Daddy Warbucks's sumptuous mansion. And when she got mixed up in international finance and foreign intrigue, the Captain had had enough. But when the paper came out on October 27 without *Annie*, reaction from readers quickly told Patterson he'd made a serious mistake. He hastily reinstated the strip and apologized in a front-page editorial.

On at least one other occasion, Patterson revealed his fallibility. The takeoff of Zack Mosley's *Smilin' Jack* was so wobbly and prolonged as to suggest that the Captain's fabled instinct had bailed out to attend to other pressing matters while he was buying the strip. *Smilin' Jack* is one strip that Patterson launched without apparently having a clear idea about what he wanted it to be.

Those who remember *Smilin' Jack* doubtless recall a strip with lots of pictures of airplanes and a string of bizarre adventures. It's true that *Smilin' Jack* always had airplanes in it: Mosley was so fond of drawing them that he decorated his panels with airplanes, putting in pictures of them even when the action didn't require it. But it didn't begin as an action adventure strip. It started on October 1, 1933, as a humorous Sunday-only feature called *On the Wing*. Five weeks after it started, Mosley got a telegram in Chicago from Patterson: "Change the name of *On the Wing* to *Smilin' Jack*," it said. Mosley wired back: "The name of the main character is Mack not Jack." But Patterson was not deterred by details: "Change name to *Smilin' Jack*," he responded.

"Naturally I did," Mosley recalled, "but I wondered what the readers would think when they saw that 'Mack' was suddenly 'Jack.'" Readers apparently thought nothing of it: not one complained when the new name appeared on December 30. Mosley never found out why Patterson changed the name. Maybe the Captain was inspired by Mosley's own beaming countenance, the autobiographical nature of the strip, and the profusion of soundalike names—Zack, Mack, and Jack.[17]

Mosley occasionally strung his weekly gags together on a slender plotline, but the strip's chief function was to make people laugh—a fact of which Mosley had to be rudely reminded almost immediately. Shortly after the strip began, he insinuated some hair-brained adventuring into it. Mollie Slott wired the Captain's displeasure, and Mosley went back to drawing about the high-spirited training field antics of a bunch of young pilots and bided his time. After a couple years, he thought he'd waited long enough. In the spring of 1936, Mosley sent Smilin' Jack into the South Seas in search of a famous missing aviator, Major McCloud—a continuity that ran for several months. The strips still had punch-line endings rather than cliff-hangers, but Mosley's execution of the story apparently convinced Patterson to rescind his dictum against adventuring. *Smilin' Jack* was converted to a seven-day strip, the daily beginning June 6, 1936, and Mosley's aviator was thrust into one harrowing scrape after another for the next thirty-seven years.

Mosley proved himself adept at telling an adventure story—albeit in his own haphazard, eccentric, almost zany, fashion. He subjected his hero (whose last name, for trivia collectors, is Martin) to more hair-raising cliff-hangers per week than any other strip around. His offhand plots were held together by a rapid-fire series of increasingly desperate situations from which Smilin' Jack extricated himself by a succession of maneuvers whose ascending ingenuity of contrivance gave every story the breathless spontaneity of catch-as-catch-can invention. Once into this tangle of cliff-hangers, we lose all sense of a plot in the headlong progression of stratagems by which Mosley advanced his stories day by day. Despite the artifice of these inventions, Mosley's plots seldom clanked: they were so flaccid as to lack working parts. But we never noticed because we were having such a marvelous time.

Smilin' Jack was the only aviation strip in which the techniques and skills of flying functioned actively in the stories. A licensed pilot himself, Mosley used his flying experiences to create both technical dilemmas and their solutions for his hero, scattering them liberally along every storyline with a propwash of aviator's jargon. By letting his zest for his hobby spill so constantly into his work, Mosley cast a mantle of authenticity over the strip thereby rescuing it from the realm of the fantastic to which its often preposterous incidents would otherwise have consigned it.

Soon after the adventures started, Smilin' Jack was battling a succession of Gouldish grotesques who handily surpassed all of Tracy's crooks for unrelenting villainy: Mosley's monsters were champion fiends, committing atrocity after atrocity for the sheer sadistic pleasure of it. One of the more noteworthy evildoers was the Great Toemain, who was fond of dropping his opponents into a pool of piranhas ("my man-eating minnows," he called them affectionately). But there is justice in *Smilin' Jack*: in fleeing the forces of law and order, Toemain stumbles into the pool himself and suffers the inevitable consequences. A couple of weeks earlier, one of his chief henchmen is decapitated before our eyes when he gets too close to the propeller of Jack's low-flying plane. (Ever authentic and always ready to throw a complication into the story, Mosley quickly passes from this grisly scene to the cockpit of the plane, where Jack notices immediately that the impact on the prop has made it vibrate. "It's ripping the motor loose," he exclaims and quickly adjusts to meet the crisis: "I'll feather the prop so the blades won't turn," he says, and a footnote explains that *feathering* turns the prop control so the blades knife the air.)

A steady diet of this kind of grim stuff could be depressing, but Mosley's imagination was too boisterous to sustain a long run of unrelieved fiendishness. The strip had been thoroughly infused with the horseplay sense of humor of its training field days, and Mosley never resisted a frequently recurring impulse to pull a prank for laughs, even in the midst of the most dire circumstances. And many of Jack's adventures were far less bloodcurdling than the Toemain tale (although just as harrowing). Mosley also ornamented his strip profusely with fuselages other than the purely aerodynamic: the

runways endlessly attracted shamelessly curvaceous pretty girls (whom Mosley christened "li'l de-icers"), and Jack was forever becoming entangled in their coils. He seemed always to be either falling in love or grieving over the (often falsely) reported death of a fiancee. He even got married—twice: first to Joy Beaverduck, who died; then to Sable.

Among Mosley's most memorable characters, perhaps typifying his creative eccentricity, was Downwind Jaxon, whose face we never saw. In early 1939 Mosley was rushing to complete a batch of strips so that he could take a vacation in Cuba. He needed a handsome skirt-chasing character, but since handsome men were difficult for him to draw distinctively, he couldn't come up with a good face quickly. Mosley decided to postpone the moment of creation until he returned from Cuba, but he had to introduce the character before he left. So he faked it. When we first see Downwind, we see him almost from behind: only the side of his forehead and rounded cheek and chin are visible in a sort of profile.

When Mosley returned two weeks later, he still couldn't come up with a face for Downwind, so he continued to draw him in profile as seen from behind one shoulder. Pretty soon, the mysterious Downwind began to draw mail. Patterson complimented Mosley on his perspicacity and suggested waiting about two months before showing Downwind's face. "Well, if it's getting such a good response," Mosley said, "how about never showing his face?" The Captain thought for a moment and then concurred.[18] And so Downwind was condemned to a faceless existence. Patterson's instinct converted Mosley's fumbling and groping into a firm grip on his readers, and letters asking for a glimpse of Downwind's permanently averted visage came in a steady stream for the next three decades.

But the Captain wasn't always right about his comic strip readers, as I said, and not every strip he touched was Midasized. He'd stumbled at the starting block with *Smilin' Jack* (perhaps it was only its creator's unquenchable enthusiasm for excitement that prodded him at last into rectifying his error by recognizing that the cartoonist was uniquely equipped to do a slam-bang adventure strip). And none of the other strips Patterson introduced with *Smilin' Jack* in his expanded comic section in 1933 lasted as long as Mosley's strip or

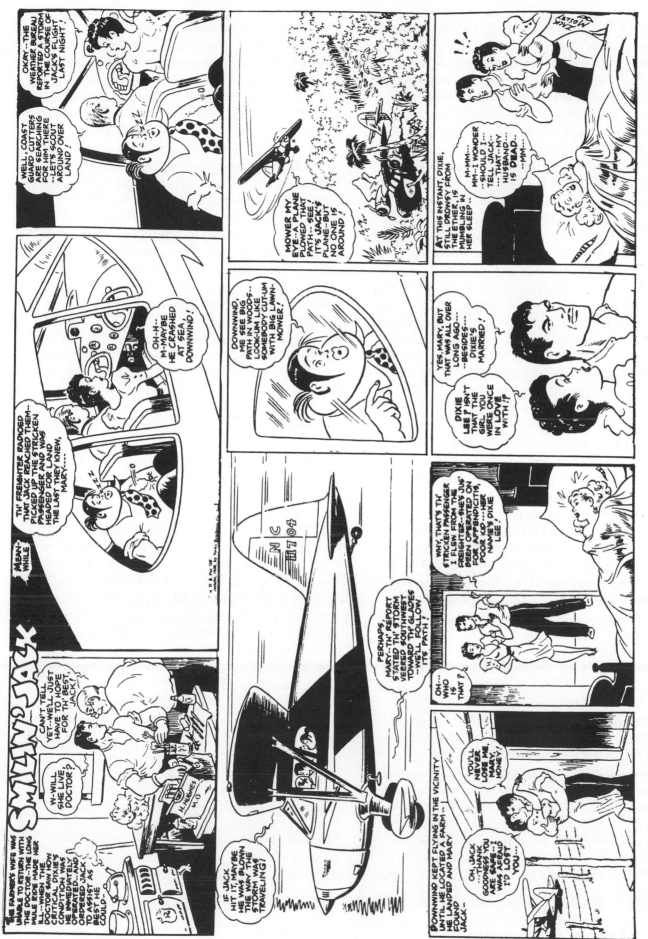

Figure 61. *Mosley crammed his clanking plots with suspense-building devices. Here on a single Sunday page, we are tantalized by the possibility that Dixie might die; that Downwind, Mary, and Fatstuff won't find Jack alive in the jungle near his wrecked plane; and that if Dixie lives, she might take Jack away from his newfound love, Mary. Just last week, we found out that Dixie's blind. Notice how quickly Downwind lands and gets Mary into Jack's arms—all done by caption.*

attracted as faithful a following. Al Posen's *Sweeney and Son* and Ed Leffingwell's *Little Joe* were solid efforts and ran at least half as long as *Smilin' Jack*. But neither strip had mass appeal. Garrett Price abandoned *White Boy* after three years to concentrate on magazine illustration and *New Yorker* cartoons (a sure indication that *White Boy's* circulation was not remunerative enough). And Gaar Williams's *A Strain on the Family Tie* and Gus Edson's *Streaky* both sank without a ripple. Even the last of his new package, a revamped *Teenie Weenies*, didn't do well in the new strip form the Captain had recommended to Donahey. (Patterson replaced this feature as soon as he found something he thought suitable for the *Daily News* readers. The replacement was a sex-and-action adventure strip, *Terry and the Pirates*, another work of genius, which we'll take up in chapter 8.) Patterson had launched other strips that had faltered and, finally, failed: Tack Knight's *Little Folks*, starting in January 1930, lasted only a few years before it was discontinued.

And then there was Ferd Johnson's *Texas Slim*. The strip's beginning could inspire legends; it's demise, ditto. Working for Willard in one of the offices along cartoonists' row in the Tribune building, Johnson adopted an ingenious strategy for getting a strip of his own. All the *Tribune's* department heads regularly played deck tennis on a court that had been devised on the roof just outside the windows of the cartoonists' offices. "They had to climb over my desk to get to the court," Johnson said, "so I made sure I had a cartoon of my own on my desk every time they came through. Finally, Patterson took notice of them and said, 'I think you can do a Sunday page.' He took six cartoons. One was a cop strip. After about six weeks, he called me up to his office and said, 'I don't think that strip is the one for you. What I'd like to have you do is a cowboy strip.'"

"Patterson loved cowboys," Johnson continued. "He went to every cowboy picture that ever came out. And so he had me do *Texas Slim and Dirty Dalton*. He named them. He named all the comics. It ran for a couple years. Patterson was still nuts about cowboys, and he went out to Wyoming to be on a ranch one time. He got on a horse, and the damn horse bucked and threw him off and damn near broke his neck. He came back madder than hell and threw me out of the paper."[19]

Johnson's experience may be unique. And in the last analysis, *Texas Slim* was scarcely a failure. Although Patterson discontinued it in 1929, after it had run only about three years, the strip was revived in 1940 and ran for another eighteen years until Johnson retired the title to devote his full energies to *Moon Mullins*. But the cowboy strip proves that the Captain simply wasn't infallible. He could be wrong. He was wrong about *Brenda Starr*. Brenda is undoubtedly the most frilly-witted heroine in comics, and perhaps for that reason, Patterson wanted nothing to do with her.

Brenda is the creation of one of cartooning's most celebrated female cartoonists, Dahlia Messick. Messick, knowing that a woman cartoonist would have small chance of success in the male-dominated world of the thirties and forties, changed her name to Dale when she signed her cartoons, thinking that most editors to whom she submitted her work by mail wouldn't suspect she was female. But by the time she got around to peddling her strip about a girl reporter to Patterson, he knew Dale was a woman. Patterson didn't like the strip. Perhaps he was guilty of simple male chauvinism, or of sexism. But anyone hoping to make the charge stick will have to explain Mary King and Mollie Slott. King was Patterson's first assistant on the *Sunday Tribune*, and he gave her credit for "at least half of every good idea I ever had." (He eventually married her.) And Slott was Patterson's astute right hand on Tribune-News Syndicate matters. It seems doubtful that a rampant sexist would give such power and responsibility to women. In any case, Slott overcame Patterson's objections to *Brenda Starr* and prevailed upon the Captain to buy the strip. He agreed—but only so long as *Brenda Starr* would never appear in *his* newspaper, the *New York Daily News*. And it didn't. Not until after Patterson's death in 1946.

Messick's chronically romantic newspaperwoman first appeared June 30, 1940, in the *Chicago Tribune's* newly launched Sunday *Comic Book Magazine*. The cutout paper dolls that distinguished the Sunday *Brenda* for so many years were not yet in evidence, but in almost every other respect the early adventures are vintage Brenda— fluffy nighties and lounging pajamas, low-cut (for that day) gowns, and plots governed only by the whim of Messick's breathless imagination, which often ignored logic and reason in favor of such purely feminine diversions (in the traditional male chauvinist sense) as a fresh hairdo or a new pair of shoes. Yes, I know: that sounds sexist. But consider the evidence. On March 30, 1941, for instance, a doctor speculates that he'll have to amputate Brenda's legs, so badly have her feet been frozen in a Sun Valley winter storm. The next week, we're still waiting for a verdict on the projected amputation. But by the following week—happily, Easter Sunday—Brenda has miraculously recovered so she can waltz down the avenue in her Easter finery.

By the end of her first year, Brenda is the fashion plate she'll be for the rest of her run under Messick (who stopped drawing the strip in 1980). In her first adventure, the redhead is a little more fiery than she eventually became for the duration, but otherwise she lacks only those stars in her eyes to be the Brenda we've always known (and, yes, loved). The stories are fast-moving adventures—fast and even a little dizzying. But that is always part of the pleasure of reading Messick's strip. The woman with a man's name kept us on the edge of our chairs for forty years, and a cartoonist doesn't do that without being a teller of good, suspenseful tales, however dizzy they sometimes are.

No, Joe Patterson wasn't always right. To make the comic strips that he adopted succeed, he doubtless needed the chemistry of collaboration with just the right kinds of cartoonists. Willard was probably correct: Patterson was only half of a creative team. He was the spark that kindled the tender, but without the proper combustible, the flame wavered and expired. Nonetheless, the Cap-

tain's successes far outdistanced his misfires.

If not all the strips he midwifed attracted the fanatical followings achieved by *The Gumps* or *Little Orphan Annie* or *Dick Tracy*, all of the others I've described acquired large and devoted readerships, garnering wide circulation and running so long as to outlast their creators. Each of these strips is, moreover, a unique creation. Each bears the individual signs of its cartoonist's creative personality, and they all carry the stamp of their co-creator's generative invention and imaginative intervention. And Patterson's continued participation in the production of these strips not only helped assure their success but perpetuated his reputation. It is clear that he had a peculiarly valuable gift for knowing what his readers would like—for story lines, characters, incidents, and gimmicks. And when his genius as a story editor and idea man was coupled to the genius of a graphic storyteller—when the cartoonist was another kind of genius—the combination produced strips of remarkable originality and longevity. Patterson got the strips started, but his ideas, valuable as they were, could not have flourished without cartoonists. To make the long haul, the cartoonists needed ingenuity of their own to complement Patterson's contributions, to put his notions into successful motion. For all the inspiration and advice he gave his cartoonists, theirs were the individual creative talents that took his suggestions and molded them into distinctive and memorable works of narrative graphic art.

CHAPTER 7
Exoticism Made Real
The Advent of Illustrators

January 7, 1929 is a date that resonates in the minds of historians of the comic strip. It rings with import. Alas, the note it sounds is false. What is supposed to have happened on that date did not, in fact, happen. Early historians of the comics commonly gave January 7, 1929, as the date that the adventure strip was born. On that propitious day, the adventure strip seemed to burst, full-blown, onto the funnies pages of the nation's newspapers. On that date, two new comic strips started. The synchronous coincidence of this double debut doubtless had something to do with making the launch date portentious. Perhaps (we might have thought) something magic resided in the simultaneity itself. And there was more than mere magic here: neither *Buck Rogers* nor *Tarzan* was quite like any other strip. They regaled their readers with exotic locales, and they subjected their heroes to high-risk physical dangers. That was not so new. As we have seen, Roy Crane was doing much the same in *Wash Tubbs*—and had been for at least a year before either Buck Rogers or Tarzan appeared on the scene. No, the adventure strip had begun long before January 7, 1929. But something else started on that date.

Crane drew in a big-foot cartoony style. And the men who rendered the adventures of Buck and Tarzan sought to convince us of the reality of their heroes' circumstances by the accuracy with which they depicted the natural world. Both attempted, one more successfully than the other, to draw realistically. And this was different. This was new. And it was probably this—the coupling of realistic drawing styles to stories of high adventure—that made the debut of these two strips stand out in the history of the medium, stand out to such an extent that Crane's earlier achievement was completely overshadowed in the history books. But Crane was not the only cartoonist whose work in the adventure mode was overlooked.

Adventure strips had loomed briefly on the comics horizon early in the century, and then they sank out of sight, leaving the field entirely to joke-a-day strips. As I mentioned earlier, *Hairbreadth Harry* and *Desperate Desmond* had deployed the cliff-hanger as a narrative device, but the objective was comedy not suspense. The great potential of this mechanism for building suspense would languish unexploited until "illustrators" (not, strictly speaking, "cartoonists") invaded the comic pages. Then adventure strips would tell their stories in deadly earnest, and the realistic artwork of the men who illustrated them would make suspense keener by making people and events seem real. Realism was vital to a good adventure strip.

The heady brew of a good adventure strip traditionally includes several ingredients. A good adventure strip tells a story that is, at the least,

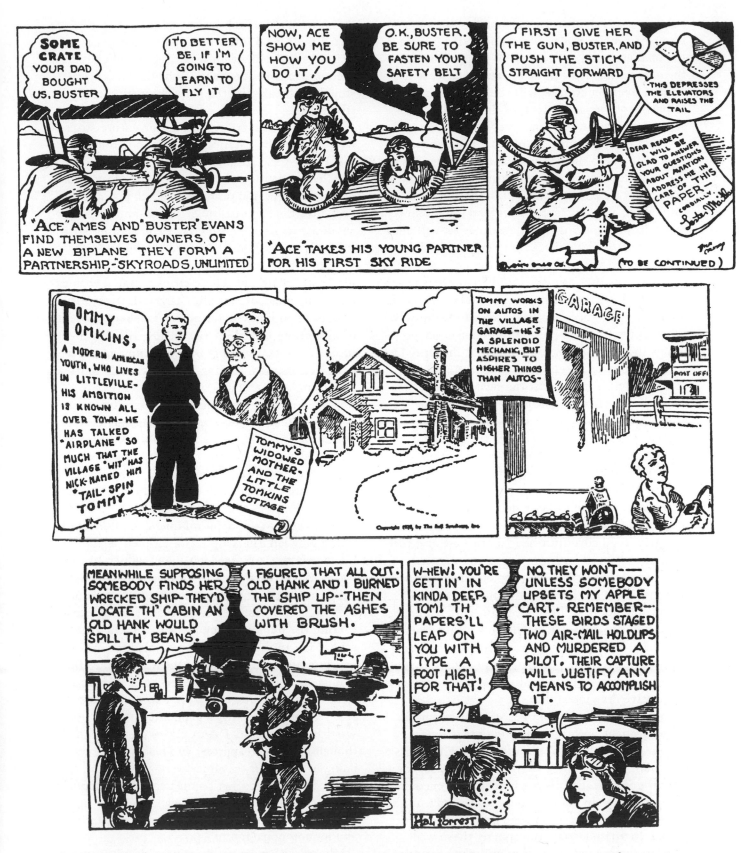

Figure 62. *In an effort to make the early adventure strips look realistic enough to be serious, artists tried to mimic the elaborate shading techniques they saw in pulp magazine illustrations of the day. But all that penwork couldn't disguise the clumsiness of the drawings. At the top, panels from the first Skyroads (May 27, 1929); then, the opening panels from the first Tailspin Tommy (July 19, 1928). The artwork in the latter had become slightly more sophisticated by 1930 (bottom panels), but Hal Forrest's command of his medium was still shaky.*

exotic—that is, it involves characters in events far removed from everyday life. And the story includes the challenge and excitement of physical danger, the adventure strip's stock in trade. Suspense is a natural by-product: how will the hero extricate himself from today's dilemma? In the adventure strip, then, the storytelling or continuity genre finds its most gripping expression. And what the punch line is to the gag strip, the cliff-hanger is to the continuity strip—particularly, to the adventure continuity strip. The classic cliff-hanger poses an immediate and apparent danger, and only tomorrow's strip—or, perhaps, the next day's—will allay the reader's anxiety about that peril. And by then, a new hazard will threaten. But the necessity for creating, day after day, one cliff-hanging episode after another, each as menacing as the last, is too demanding to be successfully sustained indefinitely. What's more, an ever-present cliff-hanger undermines the seriousness and realism of the story by seeming to mock itself. Consequently, although the cliff-hanger remains at the heart of the adventure strip mechanism, suspense finds its usual expression in more muted forms, in the construction of a story that continually poses the general question: What's going to happen? This question alternates with another, more specifically about the heroes: How will they survive? And these questions become urgent only when the dangers faced seem real.

Hence, good adventure strip stories are also realistic: the effect of both exoticism and danger is heightened if the situations depicted have about them the aura of "history"—of actual events, of real people doing real things. Stories are realistic when one event leads logically to another (even if the initiating force is somewhat improbable). And realistic storytelling is enhanced in a visual medium like comic strips by realistic artwork—by an illustrative drawing style.

The comics pages didn't get straight adventure stories fraught with real dangers until Crane started sending Wash Tubbs off on treasure hunts. But Crane's stories were fun-loving escapades, despite the very real perils his heroes were encountering by 1928. In comparison, the new adventure strips of subsequent years were grim enterprises indeed. In attitude and atmosphere, they owed more to the soapier operas found in such strips of urchin travail as Gray's *Little Orphan Annie* and its imitators in which waifs with hearts of gold pitted their good intentions and fervent hopes against a malevolent universe that mercilessly beat them down time after time—the drama of hardship, heartbreak, and the heroism of simple resilience.

The first of the grimly serious adventure strips were inspired by Charles Lindbergh's heroic solo flight across the Atlantic. *Tailspin Tommy*, written by Glenn Chaffin and drawn by Hal Forrest (a former flyer), appeared on July 19, 1928, just about a year after Lindy's historic accomplishment. And about a year later, on May 27, 1929, another strip about flyers, *Skyroads*, debuted, drawn by Dick Calkins (or his assistants) and written by an aviator, Lester Maitland. These strips pulsated with excitement: incident was all; characterization, nil. According to Ron Goulart in his excellent account of the action-packed thirties' strips, *The Adventurous Decade*, the plots were fast-moving and a little hair-brained, leaping with willy-nilly motivation from airplane races to crazed scientists to treasure hunts to smugglers. Although the artists attempted realistic illustration, their talents were not up to the task: the panels are filled with pen-scratch shading that tries but can't quite manage to mask the distorted anatomy and awkward perspective that parades before us (figure 62). *Buck Rogers* belongs in this company.

Buck Rogers took aviation into space. Written by Philip Nowlan, the strip was a scripted version of his novelette, "Armegeddon 2419," which had appeared in the August 1928 issue of *Amazing Stories*. The strip was the first to seriously attempt science fiction, and it was successful enough to capture the public's fancy. In fact, as Goulart observes, the impact of the strip on popular culture was profound and lasting: to this day, science fiction is often called "Buck Rogers stuff." The novelty of the strip's futuristic vision was doubtless the sole reason for the strip's popularity: its artwork was barely adequate. Dick Calkins drew it, and although he tried to approximate reality as he was doing in *Skyroads*, his lines were sketchy and tentative, his figures often seemed caught in painful if not impossible poses, and his panel compositions —his camera angles and distances—were static and monotonous (figure 63).

Like the other artists drawing early adventure strips, Calkins made a valiant try at realistic illus-

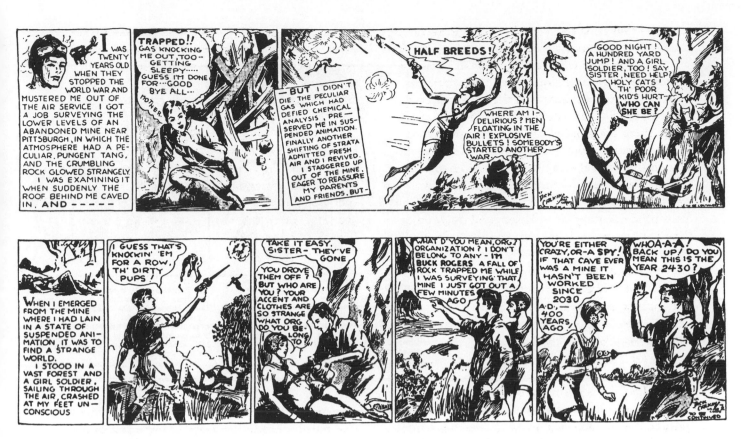

Figure 63. *The first two strips in the saga of Buck Rogers showed, again, the influence of pulp magazine illustration. Although artist Calkins simplified his style a little within a few weeks, his drawings were still as stiff and awkward looking as they appear here.*

tration. Valiant but not convincing. The drawing was so poor that it could scarcely be said to foster the illusion of reality (and thereby to enhance the drama of the story). This earliest crop of wholly serious adventure strips earned a niche for the genre on the comics page, but it took Harold Foster to show how adventure stories should be rendered.

Foster's *Tarzan* was introduced on the same day as *Buck Rogers*, but there ended the similarity of the strips. At first, *Tarzan* was simply an illustrated version of Edgar Rice Burroughs's novel. And it wasn't even a true comic strip: Foster's drawings merely illustrated the typeset narrative beneath them, and speech balloons weren't used (figure 64). An experimental venture, it ran six days a week for ten weeks (January 7–March 16, 1929), following the plot of the book faithfully. It proved popular enough, though, to warrant continuing the Tarzan saga through Burroughs's other novels, and eventually the strip told original stories. After the first sixty strips, the art was handled by Rex Maxon, Foster having returned to advertising illustration

at the conclusion of what he thought had been a single, ten-week assignment. He would return on September 17, 1931, to draw the Sunday version of *Tarzan* until May 2, 1937, when he left again to launch his acclaimed *Prince Valiant*.

An epic of the days when knighthood was in flower, *Prince Valiant* started February 13, 1937. Writing as well as drawing the feature, Foster would achieve an excellence in both story and illustration that would never be surpassed on the comics pages. But the feature was not, strictly speaking, a comic strip. Like the early *Tarzan*, it was an illustrated narrative, Foster's luxuriant and marvelously detailed pictures appearing above blocks of his terse, languid prose. The illustrations were deliberately separated from the verbiage and were unmarred by the intrusive element of speech balloons. Although not a comic strip, *Prince Valiant's* presence in the Sunday funnies gave the medium indisputable class, and Foster's illustrative style illuminated the possibilities for others working in comic strips.

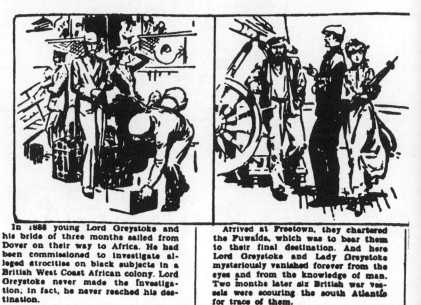

In 1888 young Lord Greystoke and his bride of three months sailed from Dover on their way to Africa. He had been commissioned to investigate alleged atrocities on black subjects in a British West Coast African colony. Lord Greystoke never made the investigation; in fact, he never reached his destination.

Arrived at Freetown, they chartered the Fuwalda, which was to bear them to their final destination. And here Lord Greystoke and Lady Greystoke mysteriously vanished forever from the eyes and from the knowledge of man. Two months later six British war vessels were scouring the south Atlantic for trace of them.

Figure 64. *From the very first installment (January 7, 1929), it was amply evident that Harold Foster's* Tarzan *was being drawn by a thoroughly accomplished illustrator (even when, as here, the reproduction is not very good).*

But Foster was more admired than imitated. His impact was not achieved by providing an example that could be copied in any slavish way. His influence was simpler, more direct—absolutely unequivocal. He showed what quality illustration could do to enhance the narrative of continuity strips, adventure strips. The most persuasive of his demonstrations, however, was probably not conducted in the daily *Tarzan* strips of 1929: Foster's sixty-day stint was simply too short to have a lasting impact. Clearly, it was the Sunday *Tarzan* that provided the opportunity for Foster to shine with such inspirational effect.

By 1931 the Depression had begun to cut into Foster's income as an illustrator, and he therefore quickly accepted the *Tarzan* Sunday page assignment when it was offered. The Sunday page had started March 15, 1931, under Maxon's auspices, and in replacing Maxon, Foster saved Burroughs's creation from further desecration by this undistinguished artist. Foster was an accomplished craftsman, and his artwork was realistic, confident, masterful—the perspective and proportions cleanly and clearly rendered. But even though Foster's *Tarzan* is better drawn than Maxon's, it is scarcely better written. At least, not the early pages.

At first, Foster simply illustrated the syndicate-furnished script. And it was a script laden with unintentional gaffs and syntactical awkwardnesses.

The Arab maiden who frees Tarzan in one adventure bids him to follow her: "I have a fast camel waiting," she says, sounding like a fugitive from an S. J. Perelman scenario. (Even worse, we never see the camel: Foster chose a close-up, relatively rare for this period of his work on the feature, to depict their flight across the desert, and the camel isn't shown at all. Probably Foster didn't like drawing camels.) The writers were inordinately fond of a *Time*-style sentence structure that runs backwards, beginning with modifiers and ending with the verb: "Swiftly did Tarzan strike." "Long had it been . . . ." "Desperately the Ape Man fought." After a while, this kind of poetry palls.

In some of the early sequences, Foster's visualizations were no better than the scripts. His drawings were competent enough, but they hadn't yet been fully enlisted in service of the story. Once Foster committed a cardinal sin of comic strip storytelling: from one Sunday to the next, he changed the setting from outdoors to indoors, even though the second Sunday begins in the middle of a fight that was in progress when the preceding Sunday concluded. One minute, Tarzan is fighting on a mountain pass; the next, he's slashing away in a barracks room. And then there's the page on which, for several panels, Foster shows Tarzan swinging through the jungle, from tree to tree, vine to vine, all the while holding some spears in

| Beyond sight of land, the Fuwalda's captain, with a terrific blow, felled an old sailor who had accidentally tripped him. The swarthy bully's brutality caused big Black Michael to crush the captain to his knees. This was mutiny. The enraged captain suddenly whipped a revolver from his pocket and fired. | Lord Greystoke struck down the captain's arm, saving Black Michael's life and thus forged the first link of what was destined to form a chain of amazing circumstances ending in a life for one then unborn such as has probably never been paralleled in the history of man. | With suspicion of organised mutiny confirmed, they hurried to their quarters. Even their beds had been torn to pieces. A thorough search revealed the fact that only Lord Greystoke's revolvers and ammunition were gone. An undefinable something presaged bloody disaster. |

one hand. Think about it.

In later years, Foster admitted that his work on the strip was at first merely perfunctory. But after he began to receive fan mail, he realized there were actually readers out there—people before whom he was performing every Sunday. With that realization, he began to take more care with his work. And he also realized how badly written the scripts were. Perforce, he began to revise them, tinkering a little here, a little there.[1]

In the artwork of the earliest pages, there is little detailing and fine linework; all is outline—anatomically correct, beautifully proportioned, but nothing, whether body or background, is rendered in any more detail than the story absolutely demands. Except for an occasional double-wide panel, Foster used a twelve-panel grid for most of his first year on the feature. And most of his pictures over the first six months are composed of full-figure drawings seen from about the same perspective: eye-level. Although Foster has been acclaimed in some quarters for his cinematic approach to illustrating a story, we don't see much evidence of it in the first six months.

By March 1932, however, Foster was devoting more effort to Tarzan's jungle surroundings, detailing foliage and trees. Close-ups are more frequent, too; and by summer, Foster was using close-ups to intensify drama as well as to vary the visual appearance of the strip. He was also devoting more attention to anatomical detail. Tarzan's body, for the first time, has the enhanced musculature of a physically powerful individual—not the extreme, perpetually flexed muscular renditions of latter-day superheroes in comic books, mind you, but something a notch above the simple outlined physique Foster started with in the fall. And facial expressions are more attentively depicted. Then, in August, Foster displayed the first sign that he felt confined by the rigid twelve-panel grid: he produced his first large display panel in order to capture the towering grandeur of the canyon entrance to an elephants' graveyard (figure 65).

Early in 1932 the stories began to hint at the kind of storytelling Foster would bring to fruition in *Prince Valiant*. The action is occasionally interrupted by interludes of domestic tranquility at Tarzan's jungle plantation. Sometimes several panels are devoted to depicting Tarzan's ingenuity at some activity essential to his survival or to his conquest of an enemy. In June, two whole Sunday pages are devoted to a prank Tarzan's son plays on his father—scarcely the sort of thing the scripters in the syndicate bull pen would concoct.

In short, by the summer of 1932 it's clear that Foster was in control of the feature. And it is equally clear that, once in command, Foster produced art and story in a way that would have a

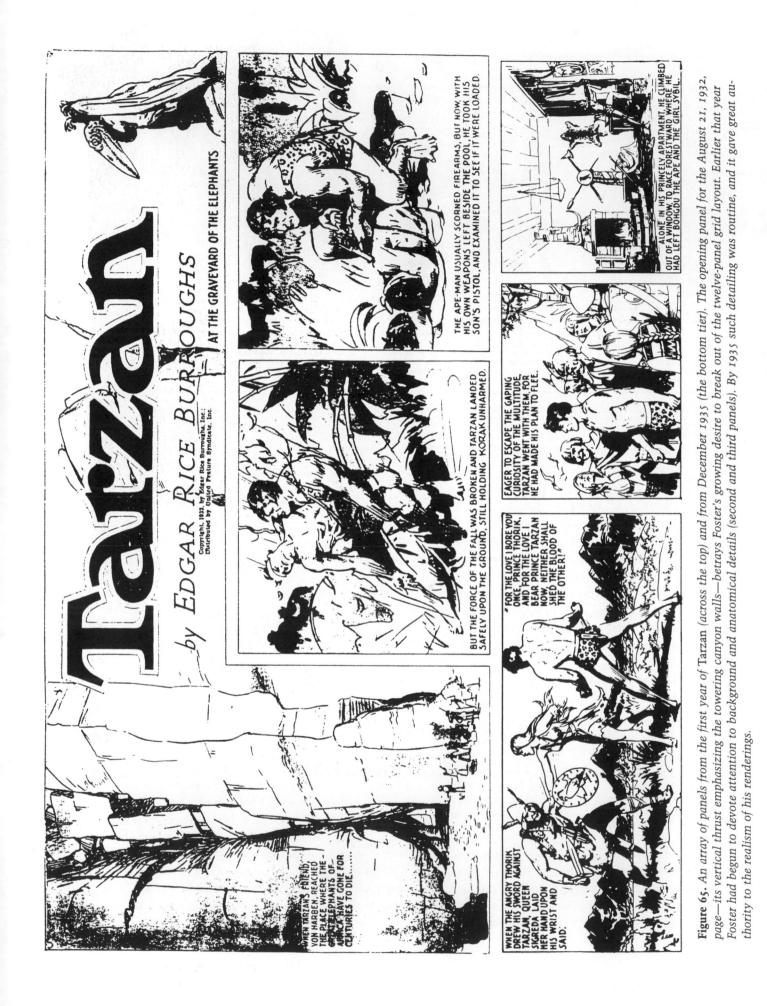

Figure 65. *An array of panels from the first year of Tarzan (across the top) and from December 1935 (the bottom tier). The opening panel for the August 21, 1932, page—its vertical thrust emphasizing the towering canyon walls—betrays Foster's growing desire to break out of the twelve-panel grid layout. Earlier that year Foster had begun to devote attention to background and anatomical details (second and third panels). By 1935 such detailing was routine, and it gave great authority to the realism of his renderings.*

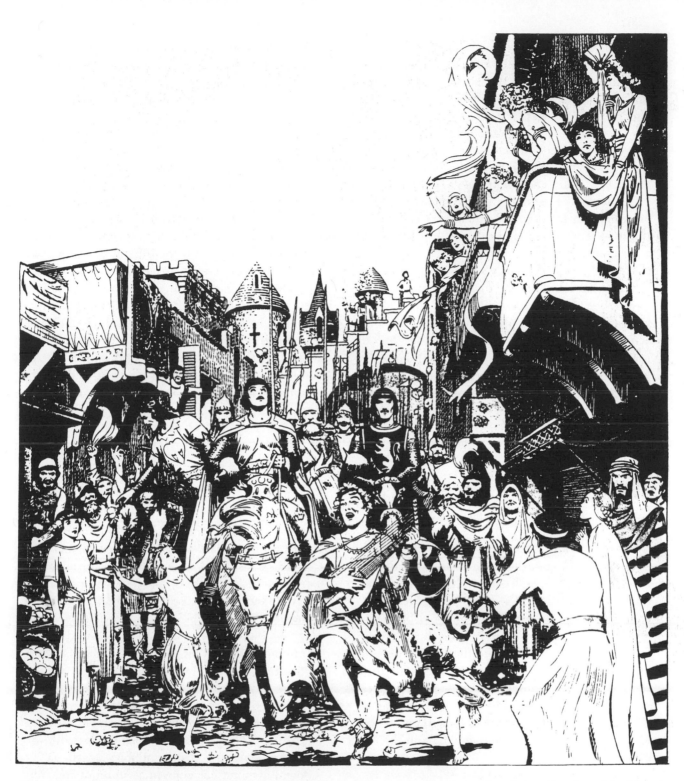

Figure 66. *In* Prince Valiant, *Foster evoked the putative court of King Arthur by recreating the medieval world with his meticulously accurate drawings of the life, costumes, and architecture of the period.*

lasting influence on how comic strip adventure stories would be rendered thereafter. After having been exposed to Foster's *Tarzan*, the reading public would no longer be quite satisfied with less than adequate illustration in realistic comic strip sto-

ries. The clumsy approximations of Dick Calkins on *Buck Rogers* would no longer serve. By the mid-thirties, a host of comic strips were being drawn in the illustrative manner, following Foster's lead.

The advent of illustrators on the comics page

marked the last stage in the development of the modern comic strip. Until their arrival, all comic strip artists could be classified as "comic artists" or "cartoonists." The work of the illustrator is distinguished from that of these traditional cartoonists by being realistic, a difference readily apparent in a comparison of *Tarzan* to *Mutt and Jeff* or to *Minute Movies*, or of *Mary Worth* to *B.C.* But how about *Li'l Abner* and *Dick Tracy*? In the final analysis, the details make the fine distinctions. The grotesques of *Li'l Abner*—caricature faces and diminutive bodies and big feet—make it the work of a cartoonist, despite realistic touches. No one could find a jaw like Tracy's in real life either—or villains that look like the ones he pursues. This strip too is the work of a cartoonist, albeit one who aims at realism in most of his art and achieves it ultimately through his stories. Indeed, many cartoonists approach realism in their artwork without being entirely, photographically, realistic. Even before the coming of the illustrator, some strips were more realistic in appearance than others.

The earliest of those to follow in Foster's footsteps were former illustrators of fiction in pulp magazines, although they hadn't his facility. In strips like *Fu Manchu* (introduced in the early thirties), the conventions of pulp illustration flourished briefly—sketchy penwork, matted crosshatching, labored shading, stiff and theatrical poses. Something of the same clumsy treatment (with a little less emphasis on shading) could be found in the medium's second space adventure, *Jack Swift*, by Cliff Farrell and Hal Colson, which began August 28, 1930. Not all the illustrative-style strips were badly drawn, though. *Connie*, for instance, was rendered with great verve in a lively sketchy style by Frank Godwin. Beginning May 13, 1929, this was the first adventure strip to star a woman, and Godwin, a skilled illustrator, made his heroine the most attractive female in the funnies (figure 67).

Meanwhile, in strips like Ham Fisher's *Joe Palooka* (starting April 19, 1930) and Chet Gould's *Dick Tracy* (October 4, 1931) and Ernest Henderson's *Flying to Fame* (November 4, 1929) and John Terry's *Scorchy Smith*, another aviation strip (March 17, 1930), cartoonists approximated the illustrative manner by adapting traditional cartoon styles to a more realistic depiction of people and scenes, without entirely abandoning the simplicity of the earlier style. Milton Caniff started doing *Dickie Dare* in this "adapted" manner on July 31, 1933 (see figure 78, next chapter). But when comic strips began to be drawn by illustrators, a new variable was introduced by which the storytelling effectiveness of a comic strip was evaluated. And with the advent of this new measure, the adapted cartoon style soon lost favor altogether.

For the artwork in a continuity strip that attempted to tell its story realistically, the standard quickly became faithfulness to reality, to nature—a standard which, until the illustrator's time, had not plagued comic strip artists. Now, however, if they chose to render their story in realistic terms, their work could be faulted if it fell short of photographic fidelity to the actual appearance of things. The illustrator opened new vistas for the comic strip: a strip could always tell stories of exotic adventures in faraway places, but now it could give credibility to its tales via the authority of realistic artwork. (But the illustrator, almost by definition, could never create a character like Snoopy in *Peanuts*.)

By 1933 the adventure strip had been safely launched, but the armada would arrive the next year with Alex Raymond's illustrative Sunday strips, *Jungle Jim* and *Flash Gordon* (January 7), and his daily strip, *Secret Agent X-9* (January 22); Rube Goldberg's *Doc Wright* (January 29) and Will Gould's *Red Barry* (March 3), both in the adapted cartoon style; and others, most drawn in an illustrative manner less accomplished than Raymond's —including such strips as *Don Winslow of the Navy* by Frank Martinek, Leon Beroth, and Carl Hammond (March 5) and *Mandrake the Magician* by Lee Falk and Phil Davis (June 11). And, at last, Caniff's *Terry and the Pirates* (October 22). Raymond and Caniff, particularly, would consolidate in their work all the previous experimentation, establishing the standards by which the artwork in all future adventure strips would be judged.

Alex Raymond has enjoyed an unremitting and entirely deserved chorus of acclaim. His work on *Flash Gordon*, *Jungle Jim*, *Secret Agent X-9*, and, later, *Rip Kirby* won him an idolatrous following and a secure place in the history of the medium. But Raymond earned idolatry solely as an illustrator of other men's scripts. He was not, strictly speaking, a cartoonist: a cartoonist (by definition)

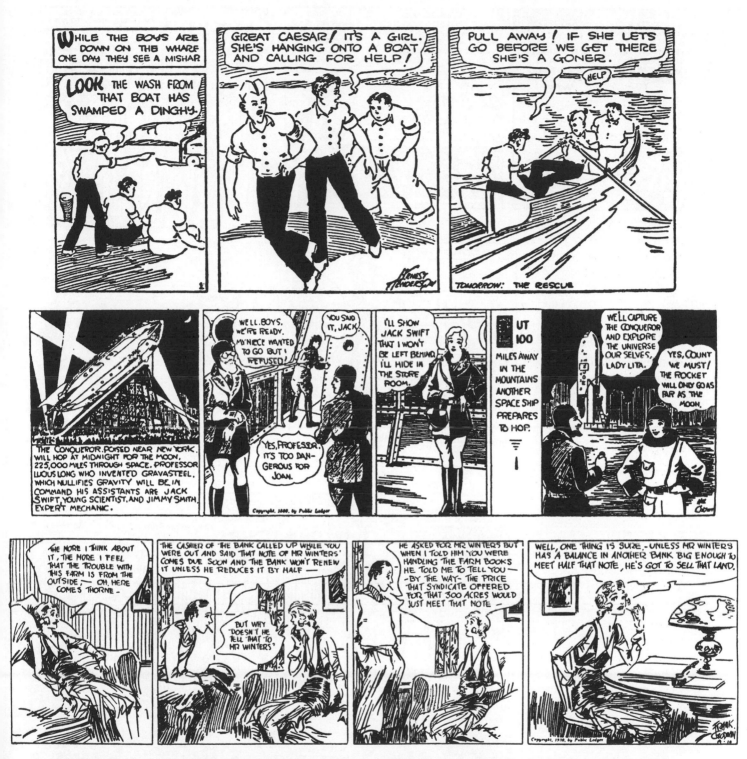

Figure 67. *More adventure strips for which the artists attempted an illustrative manner: at the top, panels from the first installment of Ernest Henderson's* Flying to Fame *(November 4, 1929); next down, the first day (August 28, 1929) of* Jack Swift *by Cliff Farrell and Hal Colson; and, bottom, the August 10, 1930 installment of* Connie, *Frank Godwin's superbly drawn girl adventurer strip (which had started the previous year, every bit as well drawn then as in this example).*

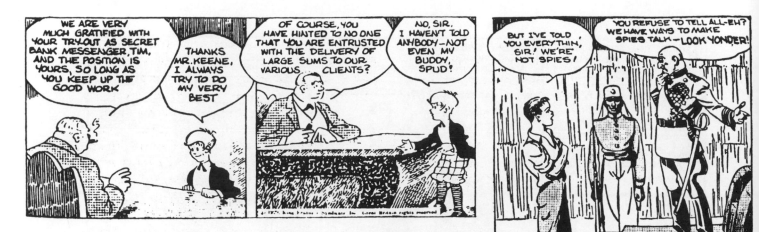

Figure 68. *When Tim Tyler's Luck began April 1, 1929 (first two panels), it was drawn in the cartoony manner that prevailed on the funnies pages at the time. Soon, however, the strip was being drawn in an illustrative style. The remaining panels are from two dailies of May 1933, when Alex Raymond was ghosting the strip, and display a craftsmanship that was even then superior to most of the work in comics at the time.*

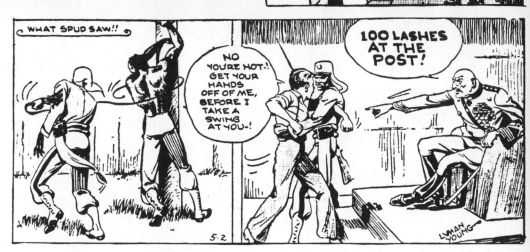

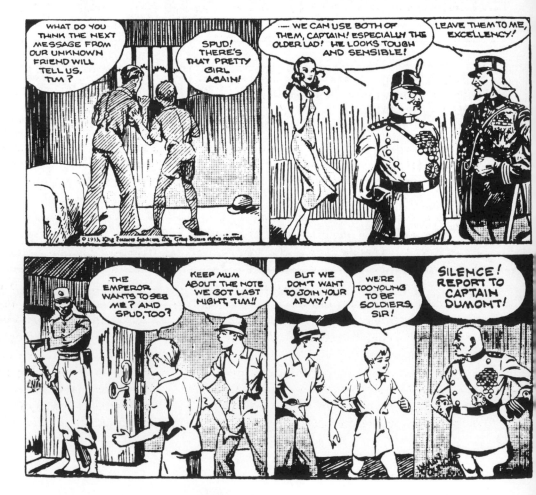

both draws and writes his material, and all four of the great strips with which Raymond's name is associated were written by others. Still, it was his consummate artistry that elevated the strips above the mundane. They were not all of equal excellence. *Flash Gordon*, which was intended to be King Features' competition for *Buck Rogers*, is unquestionably Raymond's masterpiece, but his great skill in executing the other strips magnified his impact upon the profession.

Raymond's first employment was about as far removed from the drawing board as possible. At eighteen, he went to work as an order clerk in a Wall Street brokerage. In the wake of the 1929 crash, he lost this position and fell back upon his drawing ability to earn a living. At first, he worked for Russ Westover, a former neighbor in New Rochelle who had been producing *Tillie the Toiler* since January 3, 1921. Westover secured additional work for Raymond in the King Features bull pen, where the youth assisted Chic Young on *Blondie* after it started on September 8, 1930. Raymond also helped Chic's brother Lyman on *Tim Tyler's Luck*, a boys' adventure strip. Cast initially in the mold of *Bobby Thatcher* and others of that ilk, *Tim Tyler's Luck* had started August 13, 1928, as an aviation strip with a kid hero. A few years later Young took his cast to Africa, and the strip became a kind of jungle strip. It was shortly thereafter that Raymond joined Young; he ghosted the strip for most of 1933. By this time, the strip was being drawn in a much more realistic manner than it had been when it first appeared (figure 68). Initially, Young had rendered it in a cartoony style, but he later employed assistants to draw it in an illustrative manner. Raymond, too, drew realistically, using a confident outline style with virtually no shading or cross-hatching; it was thoroughly competent but undistinguished linework. By now, Raymond knew he wanted to pursue a career in cartooning. From the launching pad of the King Features bull pen, Raymond would soon start three comic strips—that is, a daily feature and two Sunday features.

In devising the daily strip, *Secret Agent X-9*, King Features hoped to steal some of the thunder Gould was drumming up with *Dick Tracy*. Publishers Syndicate had a *Tracy*-inspired strip in *Dan Dunn, Secret Operative 48*, and William Randolph Hearst wanted a crime strip "with a hero who'll combine the toughness of a detective like Tracy with the mystery of a secret operative like Dunn." This tall order, Hearst thought, could be delivered only by the writer of the day's popular hard-boiled mystery stories, Dashiell Hammett. Hammett was at the moment riding the crest of his popularity and fame, but he went through money fast. Needing cash, he took the assignment. Securing an artist for the strip was a secondary concern—but nonetheless important. "We were after top-notch talent," Joe Connolly, King's president, later recalled; "Hearst himself would make the final choice."[2] The talent search was exhaustive. Hearst finally settled on Raymond, who had just sold King his Sunday science fiction page. *Flash* debuted on Sunday, January 7, 1934—accompanied by Raymond's other Sunday feature, *Jungle Jim*, which ran in two tiers on the top third of the page (a "topper" in the argot of the trade). Two weeks later, on January 22, *X-9* began.

Hammett wrote the strip for a little over a year. His last scripted story ended March 9, 1935. He reportedly outlined the next adventure (which ended April 20), but he had lost interest in the assignment—perhaps because of the more lucrative prospect awaiting him in Hollywood, where MGM wanted him to develop a sequel to *The Thin Man*. (After leaving *X-9*, Hammett would never again write fiction that was published.) Until a replacement could be found for Hammett, Raymond, it is presumed, wrote the strip. His stories ran from April 22 to September 22, 1935, and are perhaps the only evidence of his comic strip writing ability (about which, more in a moment). Hammett's replacement was Leslie Charteris, creator of the Saint. The Charteris-Raymond collaboration (from September 23 to November 16, 1935) was the last *X-9* adventure Raymond drew. That fall, he quit *X-9* to concentrate on *Flash* and *Jungle Jim*.

Hammett, it turns out, was a pretty good writer of comic strips. For one thing, he successfully translated his prose fiction detective persona into comic strip form. Hammett's X-9 is Sam Spade and the Continental Op all over again: tight-lipped and grim, he's a humorless, ruthless, and nameless man ("Call me Dexter—it's not my name, but it'll do"), dedicated without personal reservation to the fight against crime. (We eventually find out his family was murdered by gangsters, so he had sworn venegeance.) Raymond's visualization of Hammett's tough guy grates a little: his X-9 is a bit too dapper, more of a fashion model than a street fighter. But Hammett's dialogue reinstates his hero. When the femme fatale in the first adventure tries vamping X-9 to get her way—"I like you," she purrs, "I really do"—the agent cuts her short with a characteristically hard-boiled Hammett rejoinder: "I don't like you," he growls, "I really don't."

Hammett's first *X-9* adventure ran for seven months. And the action never flags, nor does the suspense dwindle. As one of Hammett's biographers, William F. Nolan, observed: "In the pulp tradition of action, Hammett kept things moving. The opening adventure is full of gun fights, car crashes, gold shipments, piracy, explosions at sea, mysterious coded messages, and multiple murders."[3] Hammett's handling of his new medium shows a sure hand. His breakdowns pace the action coherently and build suspense. Action scenes are staged across several panels, capitalizing on the visual excitement that the medium is capable of creating. I credit Hammett for these aspects of the strip's storytelling because after he left, the storytelling began to lurch markedly.

In contrast to the first three episodes by Hammett, the plots of the two by Raymond stumble along with motiveless actions, and the narrative breakdown leapfrogs from one event to another, continuity gaps filled in with huge chunks of narration (figure 69). Both these adventures rush to conclusion, much of the action taking place offstage so that it must be narrated to us in captions, thereby weakening the drama of events. If Raymond did write these two sequences, they reveal clearly how badly this gifted illustrator needed a writer. Charteris, alas, was no more suited to scripting comic strips than Raymond. His *X-9* story (his only work on the strip) offers a story line that is too complicated for reading in installments, on top of which he confuses his staggering story with too many characters and too little characterization.

If Raymond's handling of the writing for five months reveals his shortcomings for all to see, his visual treatment reaffirms his status as the leading illustrator in the comic strips of the period. All of his characters are fashion plates, and the women are particularly attractive. Raymond's surpassing achievement as an illustrator is highlighted by the four weeks of the strip that he did not draw. Doubtless feeling the pinch on his time by having to write the strip in the spring of 1935, Raymond

took on an assistant, Austin Briggs, and the initial twenty-four strips in the first Raymond-written sequence were drawn by Briggs. The styles, although similar, are clearly distinguishable: Briggs was a more than competent illustrator, but his work hasn't the delicacy of line and grace of figure composition that marks Raymond's work.

Despite Raymond's great talent as an illustrator, however, his use of the comic strip medium was ultimately undistinguished. His strips often lack the variety of panel composition—such things as varying camera angles and distances—that would lend visual drama to the story. Compared, say, to Caniff's work on *Terry and the Pirates* a short time later, much of Raymond's stint on *X-9* seems a monotonous parade of panels in which the characters appear always the same size, always seen from the same angle (figure 70). Moreover, Raymond's people never change expression: X-9's grim, albeit handsome, visage seems carved in stone, and his facial expression is repeated on the head of every male character in the strip. Likewise, Raymond's women, although superbly drawn and seductively beautiful, all look alike, and when he makes both young women in a story dark-haired, we can't tell one from the other—with much resulting confusion about the story's plot (particularly after Hammett left). Raymond fared much better on the Sunday pages. The mode of storytelling there—by weekly installment—lends itself to his illustrator's talents without revealing his failings as a visual storyteller. And on the Sunday page, Raymond had more room in which to exercise his graphic skills.

But it was more than format that fired Raymond's imagination. *Jungle Jim* alone, although every bit as well-drawn as *Flash*, would not have secured Raymond a place in the pantheon of cartooning's greatest practitioners. Invented, we assume, as King's answer to *Tarzan*, the strip followed the exploits of a hunter named Jim Bradley as he righted wrongs in the jungles of southeast Asia. But Raymond's heart was clearly not in this work: after a couple of years, his pictures appear almost dashed off. For weeks in mid-1936 the strip's panels were almost wholly devoid of background detail: the strip consisted entirely of pictures of Jim and the other characters talking (figure 71). They are all attractively drawn. Raymond's technical virtuosity was so great that his figure drawing alone rescues the strip visually. But

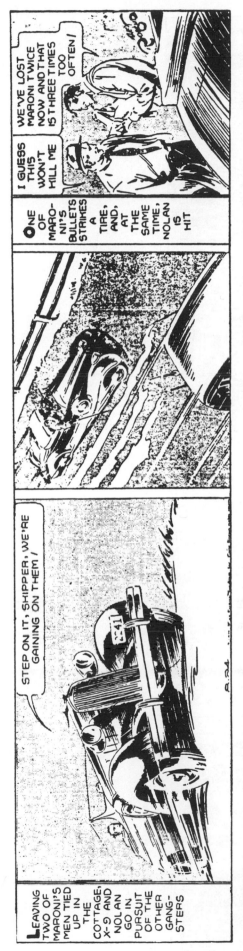

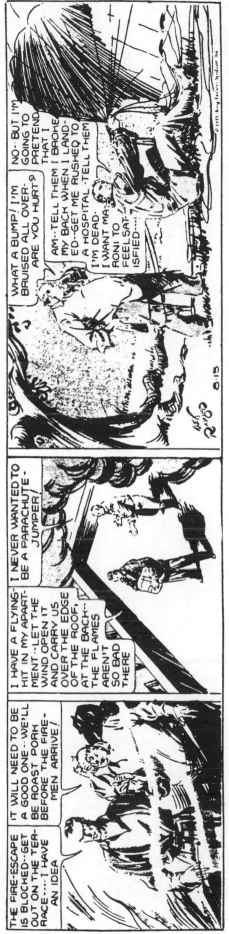

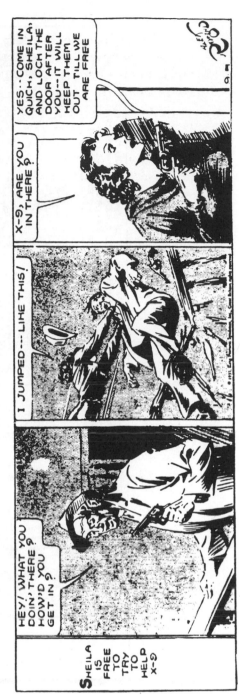

Figure 69. Secret Agent X-9 strips written by Raymond revealed his tenuous grip on the conventions of the medium. In the top strip, all the action takes place between the second and third panels; the verbiage of the caption that describes what has taken place is scarcely as exciting as pictures would have been. Again, the parachute jump in the strip above is omitted entirely from the visual narrative, which leapfrogs from the rooftop to the ground below. And at the right, whatever happens to the hoodlum and to Sheila between the second and third panels is left out completely.

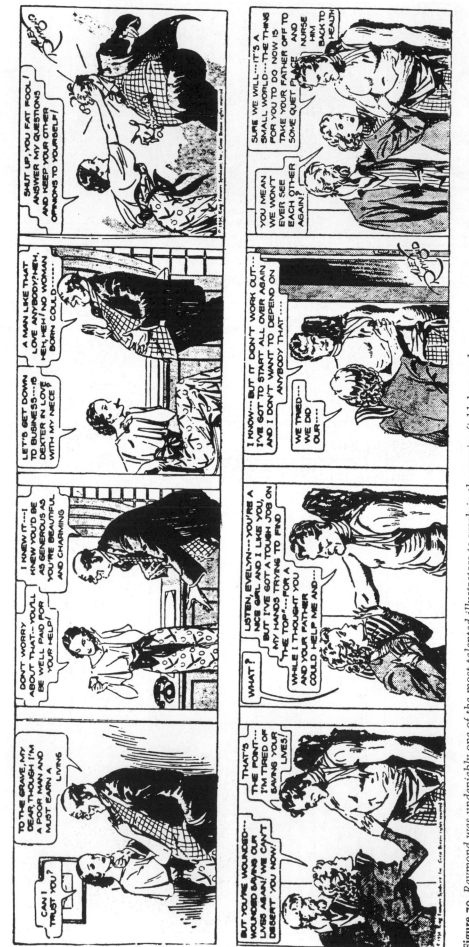

Figure 70. *Raymond was undeniably one of the most talented illustrators to work in the comics field, but as the monotonous compositions of these early Secret Agent X-9 strips reveal, he had little understanding at the time of the storytelling dynamics inherent in the visual medium.*

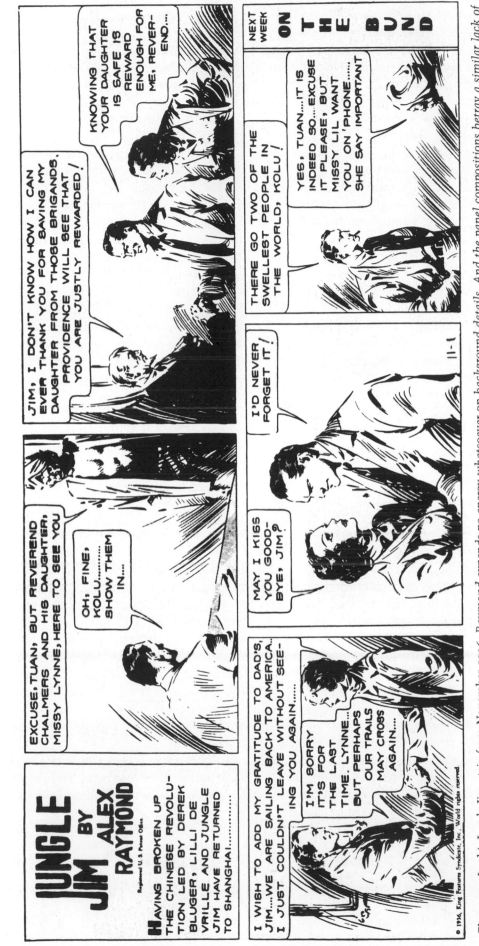

Figure 71. In this Jungle Jim strip from November 1936, Raymond expends no energy whatsoever on background details. And the panel compositions betray a similar lack of interest—especially when compared to the spectacular work he was then doing on Flash Gordon, which was appearing at the bottom of the same page in the Sunday funnies.

he was obviously not putting much work into the feature. His effort—his creative energy, his imagination and skill and dedication—was being poured into the feature at the bottom two-thirds of the Sunday page, *Flash Gordon*.

Flash's story begins with the end of the world. In the inaugural Sunday page, the first panel shows a newspaper headline that proclaims: "World Coming to End: Strange New Planet Rushing Toward Earth—Only a Miracle Can Save Us, Says Science." In the face of certain destruction, one scientist—Dr. Hans Zarkov—still works to save the Earth. Zarkov plans to launch a rocket ship at the approaching planet, hoping that a direct hit will deflect the "comet" from its course. As he works desperately, we meet a world-renowned polo player named Flash Gordon, who is flying over Zarkov's laboratory in a small plane. An attractive young woman, Dale Arden, is the only other passenger. Suddenly, a meteor, "torn loose from the approaching comet," roars past the plane, shearing off a wing. Flash bails out, taking Dale with him in his arms; Flash seems, unaccountably, to have the only parachute. They land near Zarkov's lab, and the scientist, now slightly mad under the strain of his endeavor, forces them to accompany him on board his rocket ship, which he promptly launches toward the approaching comet. (Naively, the rogue planet is alternately termed "planet" and "comet" throughout the opening episodes.) At the last moment, however, Zarkov weakens in his resolve: he can't bring himself to commit suicide. Instead of striking the planet like a missile, he lands his rocket on it. It is the planet Mongo, ruled by Ming the Merciless, the tyrant of the universe. And thus begin Flash's adventures as the leader of all opposition to Ming. (Since the adventures go on for years, we must assume that Mongo did not smash into Earth, as foretold in the strip's first installment.)

The graphic excellence that would distinguish *Flash Gordon* did not spring, full-blown, from Raymond's pen with the strip's debut. At first, he drew in the same unembellished illustrative style he had used on *Tim Tyler's Luck*. But before long, he began to feel the influence of other styles of illustration, and the artwork in *Flash* began to change (figure 72). In using the work of other artists as models for changing his style, Raymond was scarcely unique. Most artists are influenced by what their fellows do, and they borrow freely this technique and that. When the borrowing is well done, however, it goes beyond mere imitation and gives to the borrower's work a new dimension wholly his own. His work becomes an amalgam of all he has borrowed, unified by a single creative consciousness into something distinctly his—his own style.

It is not clear who influenced Raymond's emerging style the most, although there are several candidates; he probably borrowed a little from them all (and from others we don't know about). In rendering the futuristic architecture of Mongo, Raymond was obviously imitating Franklin Booth, a turn-of-the-century artist. And Ron Goulart notes that Raymond's contemporaries, Matt Clark and John LaGatta, were also among the models he employed. "From Clark's slick illustrations," Goulart wrote, "Raymond borrowed a good deal, including the prototype for the new improved version of his other hero, Jungle Jim."[4] The influence of LaGatta, who painted beautiful women elegantly gowned in ways that revealed rather than concealed their figures, can be seen clearly in Raymond's increasingly sexy renderings of Dale Arden and the other women in the strip, all of whom started wearing exotic and skimpy garments.

By May 1934 Raymond was feathering his linework and modeling figures more extensively, and he began brushing shading into the landscape of Mongo, giving the scenery texture as well as topography. And by the end of the year Raymond's drawings showed the influence of the dry brush technique of pulp magazine illustrators: his brush strokes were orchestrations of tiny parallel lines, suggesting thereby the stroke of a brush nearly dry of ink. Although Raymond sometimes let his brush go dry, he normally kept enough ink on the implement to give his drawings a liquid sheen. The appearance of dry-brushing, however, gave his pictures great depth and textural beauty, and he employed the same techniques in *Jungle Jim* and *Secret Agent X-9*.

In the summer of 1934 Raymond began to vary the layout of the *Flash* page. The strip had been designed in a four-tier format—four stacked rows of panels. But as Raymond's imagination became more and more engaged with the feature, this format seemed increasingly restrictive. In July he started using an occasional two-tier panel—a pic-

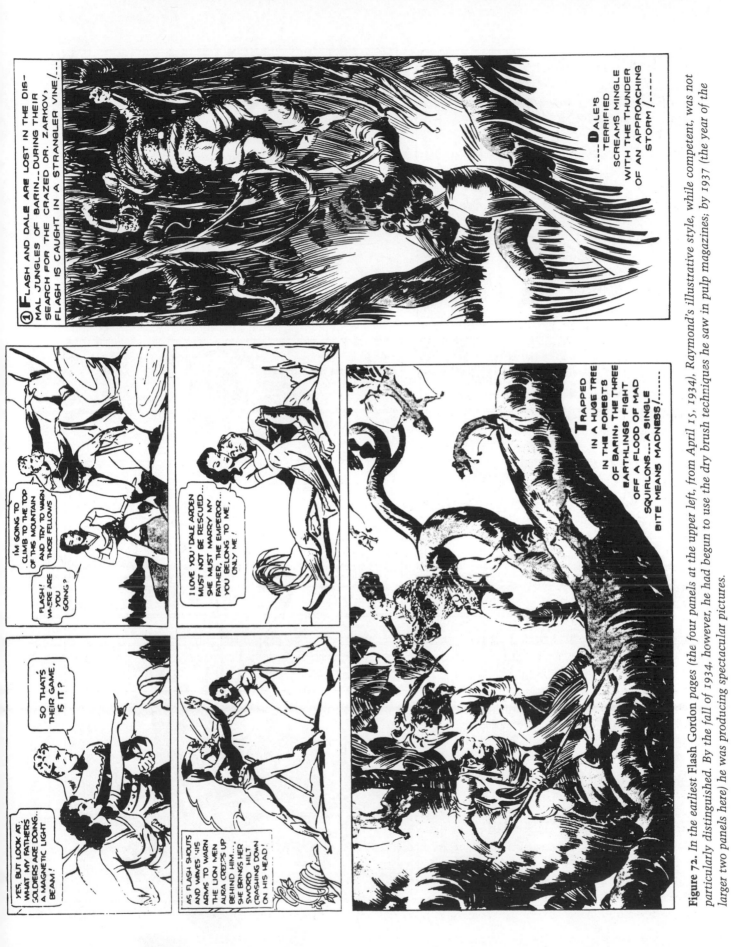

Figure 72. In the earliest Flash Gordon pages (the four panels at the upper left, from April 15, 1934). Raymond's illustrative style, while competent, was not particularly distinguished. By the fall of 1934, however, he had begun to use the dry brush techniques he saw in pulp magazines; by 1937 (the year of the larger two panels here) he was producing spectacular pictures.

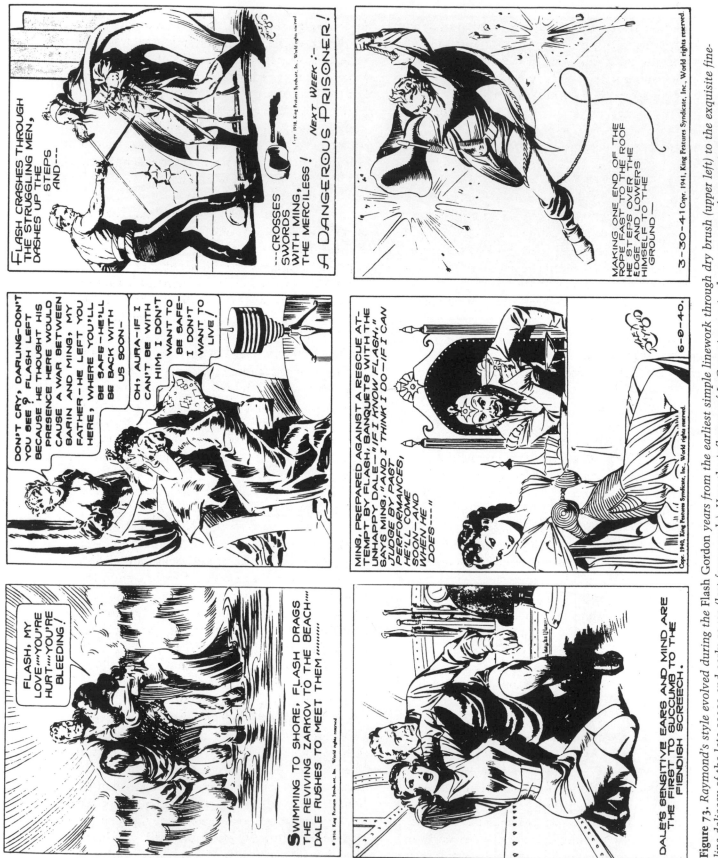

Figure 73. *Raymond's style evolved during the Flash Gordon years from the earliest simple linework through dry brush (upper left) to the exquisite fine-line delicacy of the late 1930s and early 1940s (last four panels). Here the influence of LaGatta is seen in the treatment of women's garments.*

ture that spanned vertically the space of two tiers on the four-tier grid—in order to capture more dramatically the atmosphere in which his hero lived. A Booth-like city in the sky is pictured in one such large panel, the increased vertical space giving the scene a dramatic impact it would not have had in a single-tier panel. Seeing the results, Raymond quickly abandoned the four-tier layout in favor of a three-tier arrangement that gave him room to develop all his pictures more extensively. With the larger panels, his backgrounds grew more lavish, and the strip's locale acquired an authentic ambiance. And in these spacious surroundings, the heroic posturing of his characters lent the entire enterprise a majestic air. The world of *Flash Gordon* was becoming manifestly real.

By 1936 the strip was being drawn on a two-tier grid, every panel at least twice as large as the panels had been when *Flash* began. Raymond had given up *Secret Agent X-9* by this time, focusing entirely on his weekly page of comics. But it was *Flash* not *Jungle Jim* that absorbed his creative energy. The pictures in *Flash* were luxuriant with telling atmosphere, whereas in *Jungle Jim*, as I've noted, they were scarcely furnished at all. By 1937 the drawings in *Flash* were heavily modeled, the figures given weight and shape by an intricate pattern of brush strokes, the backgrounds enhanced by an extravagant latticework of shading. And still Raymond continued to develop as an artist. Having reached a level of stylistic achievement unequaled elsewhere in the Sunday funnies, Raymond went on to evolve yet another impressive style in rendering *Flash Gordon*. By the end of 1938 the dry brush-like modeling and shading was giving way to a less sketchy style. Raymond's lines became thinner, more continuous and graceful; his pictures were defined more by linework and less by shading (figure 73). They became exquisite tableaux, delicately rendered in copious detail. In this period—from 1939 until 1944, when Raymond joined the marines for the rest of World War II—Raymond's work closely resembled Hal Foster's in *Prince Valiant*; it was the only time the work of these two great illustrators looked much alike.

Early in 1938 Raymond, perhaps following Foster's lead, had begun to eschew speech balloons in *Flash*, instead floating his characters' remarks in clusters of verbiage near their heads; a year later, he began burying speech within quotation marks in the caption blocks at the bottom of each panel. By this time, his storytelling technique was established. He simply illustrated bits of narrative prose, in one superbly rendered panel after another. But the beautiful pictures were sequentially related only insofar as they depicted successive moments in the narrative. *Flash Gordon* was an illustrated novel, not a comic strip. I don't mean by this to belittle Raymond's achievements—only to pinpoint them, to give him his due for what he actually did. And he did plenty.

That Flash Gordon, Dale Arden, Ming the Merciless, and all the rest have become a part of the American cultural heritage is, in itself, a testament to Raymond's accomplishment as well as to the power of the medium. Like Sherlock Holmes before him and James Bond afterwards, Flash Gordon leapt from the printed page into the hearts and minds of his readers, eventually emerging onto the motion picture screen. But even before his celluloid incarnation in the 1936 serial, Flash was already as real to his readers as it is possible for a literary creation to be. And that was due almost entirely to Raymond, whose consummate artistry stamped the strip, the characters, and the stories with an illusion of reality that was more than convincing: it was spectacular.

Although Raymond is no longer credited with single-handedly producing *Flash*, it is undeniable that it was his graphics that clothed Don Moore's stories in their most irresistible raiment. As Stephen Becker has observed: "What made *Flash Gordon* outstanding was not the story; along the unmarked trails of interstellar space any continuity was original. Nor were Flash and his lady friend radical departures from the traditional hero and heroine. But *Flash* was beautifully drawn."[5]

No one can deny Moore's contribution. His stories, built archetypally around Flash as godlike redeemer, a savior from another world, were suspenseful, fast-paced, and ingenious. But for all their ingenuity of incident, they were too fast moving to allow much time for character development. Flash, the polo player turned savior, is everything we expect in an adventurer—courageous, honest, nobly motivated, and above all resourceful. But he is nothing more. Apart from possessing the traditional, culturally prescribed traits of a hero, Flash has no personality. His love for Dale is perfunctory: he is the hero; she, the heroine; and the

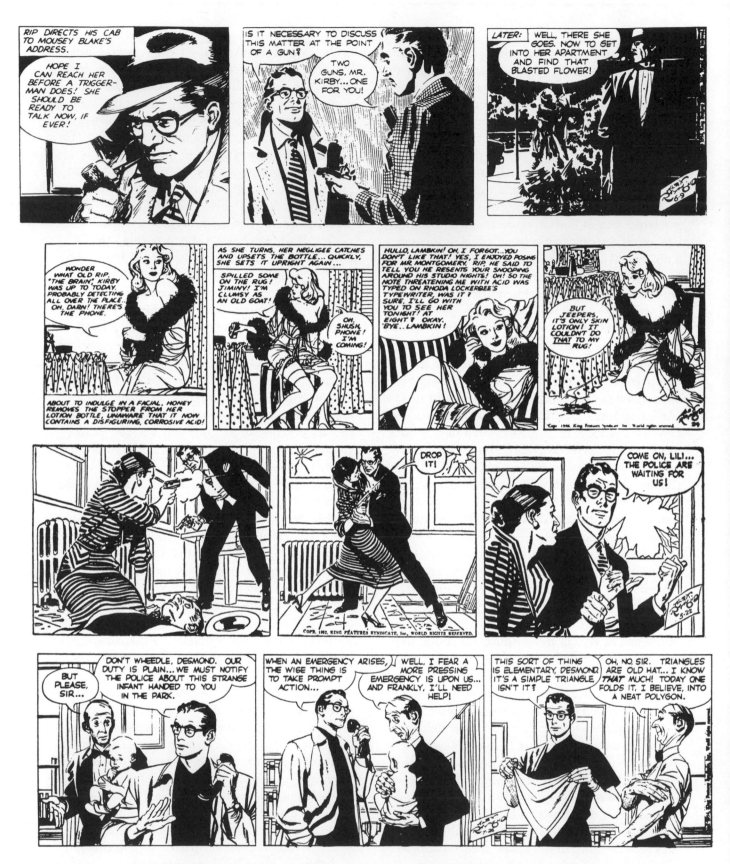

Figure 74. *Raymond's* Rip Kirby *was another stylistic tour de force. The top panels are from 1946 (the first month of the strip), 1950, and 1956. As these drawings and those in the strips (from 1946, 1952, and 1954) show, Raymond used a crisp fine line against which he deployed solid blacks in artful contrast. In this selection of strips, we also see the regular members of the cast—Kirby's man servant Desmond (bottom) and, in the second-tier strip, Kirby's beauteous paramour, Honey Doran. Although she appeared in the strip quite often at first, Honey eventually dropped from view, probably to permit Rip an occasional dalliance with the itinerant females he encountered in his adventures.*

customary relationship between such persons is love. In Dale's pettish flashes of jealousy (which spark with such routine predictability throughout the run of *Flash*), we see all the individuality that she is allowed. Said Coulton Waugh: "These lithe, sexy young people have an empty look—one feels that a cross-section would show little inside their hearts and heads."[6] But with Raymond's drawing, we seldom notice this flaw. His graphics give the strip's characters such lifelike appearance that we overlook the absence of individual personality in them. They are larger than life—or, at least, more beautiful, handsomer, more graceful. And the beauty of these visuals seduces us into believing in the characters, who look and move as we would like to look and move. "The total effect," Becker said, "—slick, imaginative drawing with literate narrative—was one of melodrama on a high level, which should not obscure the fact that Raymond's villains were throughly wicked or that his female characters were generally sexy. *Flash* rapidly became the premier space strip. It was wittier and moved faster than *Buck Rogers*; it was prettier and less boyish than William Ritt's and Clarence Gray's *Brick Bradford*."[7]

There is no question that it was Raymond's art that brought *Flash Gordon* alive, his art that made the characters live in the minds of their readers. But that art could not flourish, could not reach the luxuriance of its full growth, in the small daily panels of *Secret Agent X-9*. Despite the considerable merit of Raymond's work on *X-9*, neither the format nor the subject was amenable to the levitating magic that his art performed in *Flash*. And while the format of *Jungle Jim* was ample enough, the subject did not fire Raymond's imagination as did the mythology of the redeemer in Moore's tales of Flash Gordon on the planet Mongo. *Flash Gordon* is a clear instance of subject and artist locked in symbiotic embrace, the artist driven to achieve at ever higher levels by his subject, the subject elevated in turn by the artist's endeavors.

Raymond returned to comics after his stint with the marines, but since he had left *Flash Gordon* voluntarily to enlist, he could not return to the strip. Instead, he introduced yet another strip for King Features, becoming the only cartoonist except Mort Walker to inaugurate four successful comic strips. *Rip Kirby*, which started March 4, 1946, was a detective strip with a decidedly urbane hero. Kirby wore glasses (in the stereotypical world of the comics, a dead giveaway that he was an intellectual), dressed fashionably, moved in the best circles of society, employed a British man servant, and had a beautiful girlfriend who was a professional model. Illustrating the scripts of Fred Dickenson, Raymond developed a distinctive pen technique that set *Rip Kirby* apart from his earlier work (figure 74). Deploying solid blacks dramatically in contrast to fine-line penwork, Raymond produced another masterpiece of illustration, and this time his (or Dickenson's) command of the medium of the daily strip was equally masterful. This time, Raymond used speech balloons, and the breakdowns of the action and the visual variety of the panels, while not at all innovative, were entirely in step with the best traditions of the medium. Sadly, Raymond's tenure on the strip was brought to a tragic conclusion when he was killed in an auto acccident in 1956.

Foster and Raymond produced impressive works. But for all their undeniable skill as illustrators, neither Foster nor Raymond were cartoonists. The works that brought them fame and earned them their niches in the history of the medium were illustrated narratives, not comic strips. Word and picture did not blend in *Tarzan* or *Prince Valiant* or *Flash Gordon* in that uniquely reciprocating way that defines a comic strip. Foster and Raymond were certainly successful illustrators—spectacularly so on the pages of the Sunday funnies. But the real master of the comic strip form was Milton Caniff, who, as Foster labored in the African jungles of the Sunday *Tarzan* and Raymond started dashing from the jungles of southeast Asia to the drawing rooms of urban America to the alien tyranny of Ming's Mongo, was waiting in the wings, doing a warm-up with a comic strip about a boy who dreamed great adventures for himself.

CHAPTER 8
Redefining the Art
Milton Caniff and Terry and the Dragon Lady

"Heroism cannot thrive without rascality. Slinky, oily Malayans and sundry other Eastern types had been standard for years. Why not twist it a bit and make the Number One Menace a woman? One who combines all the best features of past mustache twirlers with the lure of a handsome wench. There was a woman pirate along the China coast at one time, so it wasn't beyond reality. She's fabulously wealthy. [Her name,] Lai Choi San, means Mountain of Wealth. That's too much for readers to remember. Call her that once to establish the atmosphere, but the Occidentals have nicknamed her the Dragon Lady."[1] With these words, written a few years after her introduction, Milton Caniff described the inspiration behind his most celebrated creation. But in the history of comic strips, he is revered for much more than creating one of the medium's most intriguing villains.

With *Terry and the Pirates*, the strip in which the Dragon Lady lurked, Caniff virtually redefined the continuity adventure strip. He perfected a technique of realistic rendering that revolutionized comic strip illustration. As a storyteller, he infused the most exotic of tales with palpable realism. And he enhanced the drama of the traditional adventure story formula by incorporating character development into the action-packed plots.

Caniff created scores of fascinating characters, including a dozen or so of the most memorable in literary fiction. When he started in 1934, though, he had only a single hook to hang stories on. Orphaned Terry Lee, some twelve to fourteen years old, is in China with his mentor, Pat Ryan. They are there to find a lost gold mine that appears on a map Terry's dying grandfather left him. That was all there was to start with. But it was enough for a master storyteller.

Some years after the strip's debut, Caniff attempted a novel about his characters, and in it he fleshed out the relationship between Terry and Pat: "Pat had found Terry on the docks of San Francisco, a lonely little orphan living as best he could from day to day, in an old piano box. [Pat was] an orphan himself with no family ties, [and] the boy's loneliness appealed to the older man: he forthwith 'adopted' Terry. The two have been together ever since."[2] The rest of their history, we find in the strip. Apart from his being an orphan, Terry is not much different than any teenager of his day. A little more self-reliant, perhaps (understandably so), and probably a little older in experience than his years. But otherwise, he's the putative typical American boy—eager for adventures, excitable, wide-eyed at the novelties of a foreign clime. Terry will grow to maturity in the strip over the next seven or eight years, and as he does, he will become more and more like Pat Ryan—maybe not quite so ruggedly handsome, but every bit as intel-

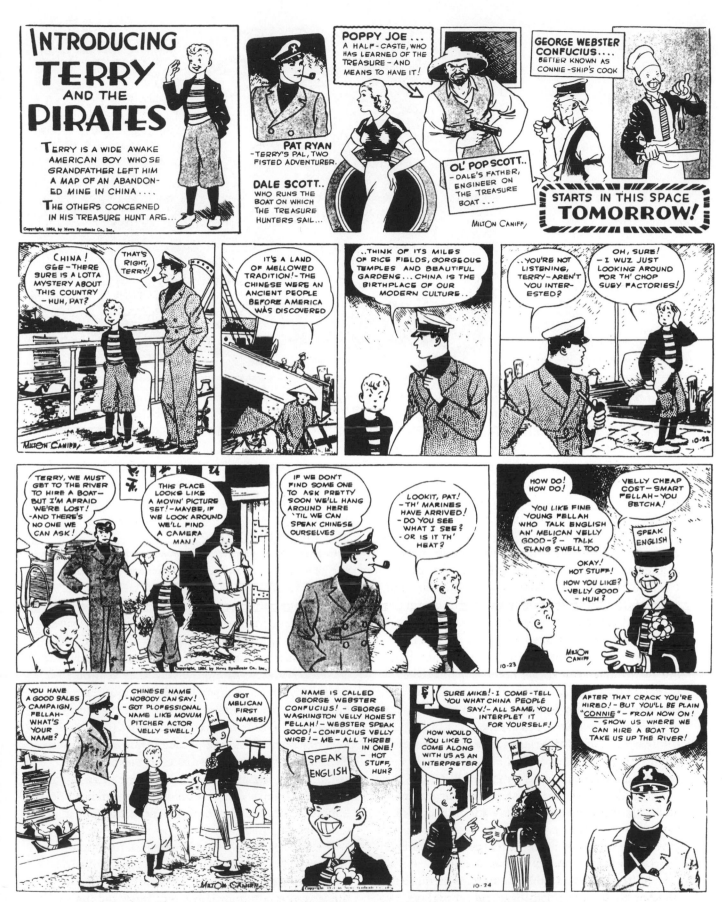

Figure 75. *The first Terry strips, rendered in a simple, albeit wholly competent, manner.*

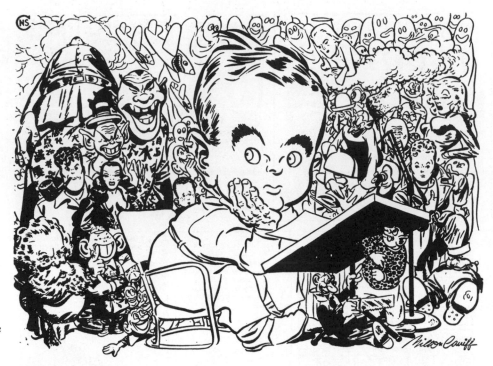

Figure 76. *Here's how Caniff drew himself in the early 1940s; the caricatures of his characters in the background were drawn by Ray Bailey, one of his assistants at the time.*

ligent, courteous, charming, occasionally witty, and gallant (not to mention resourceful and courageous). Ryan is a free-lance writer—a vagabond really, a soldier of fortune. And there is about him the air of a man with a past, a man who has knocked around the world a bit. Tall, dark, handsome—and mysterious—Ryan, in the strip's most pervasive cliché, is fated to be absolutely irresistible to women. But after the first adventure or two, he proves immune to their charms: early in the strip's run, he loses his heart to the unobtainable Normandie Drake, who, in the course of a misunderstanding, marries another. For Caniff, Normandie was Catherine to Ryan's Heathcliff.

To help them find their way around China, Pat and Terry hire a Chinese youth as a servant. Connie is introduced as comic relief, a distant and somewhat confused admirer of America. The comedy arises from his wild attempts to ape American ways, which he knows only imperfectly, filtered to him through such Americans as he has encountered in his native land. As a consequence, his speech (here adroitly aped by Coulton Waugh) is an antic muddle of American slang and pidgin English: "Is miriclement! Is hotsy-dandy! Comes Chinese goofer all spread-eagled between the ears; allee-time hot goggle talk, catch cash customers neatish in belly-chuckle section. Plenty wise head-clocker belong like Confuscius. . . . Job: number one boy to Terry and Pat. Ears and teeth: both

huge. Head: bald. Dress: Connie got aspilations for allee-time China-seas playboy, so dress him accordingly."[3] Caniff threw an Occidental-style tuxedo coat (with tails) over Connie's Oriental kimono, plopped a cook's hat on the boy's naked dome, and sent him, ears waving, into battle. Over the years, Connie would demonstrate courage and loyalty and no little sagacity, rising considerably above his initial function as buffoon.

In the twelve years Caniff produced the strip, his trio of starters would become ensnared by countless "pirates"—bandits, smugglers, thieves, and swindlers of all description, not to mention the traditional Chinese ogre, the local warlord, always a despot with a sadistic streak, or the unrepentant Tony Sandhurst, Normandie's husband, a study in craven cowardice. Along the way, they acquire another companion, a giant Mongolian mute named Big Stoop, who towers in the strip's background, a silent symbol of loyalty and an almost elemental force for retribution and justice. And they meet an incarnation of Sadie Thompson in Burma, a bad girl with a heart of gold, dancing alone in an island plantation house to the tune of W. C. Handy's "St. Louis Blues." As Terry matures, he betrays an interest in the opposite sex, and as soon as he does so, he's swept away by the shameless flirtation of a displaced American southern belle named April Kane, a teenage version of Scarlet O'Hara. When the Japanese bomb Pearl Harbor, Terry and his

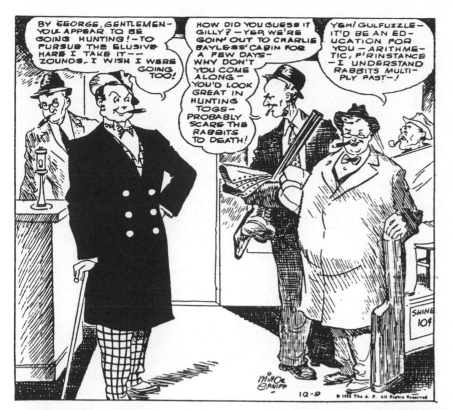

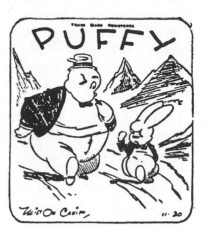

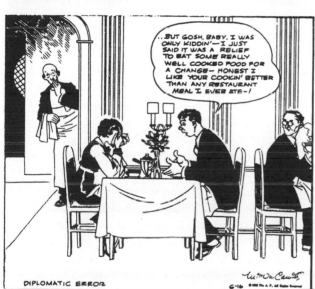

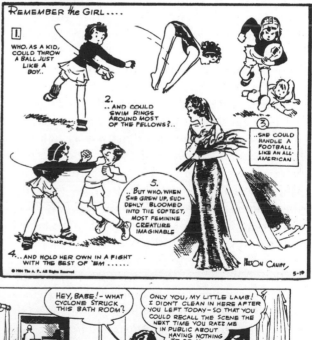

Figure 77. *Arriving at the Features Service bull pen of the Associated Press in the spring of 1932, Caniff did routine illustrative work until that fall, when he inherited Gilfeather (upper left), a tedious panel about a blowhard done in imitation of Gene Ahern's successful Major Hoople. Caniff's cartoon assumed more human dimensions when Caniff put into it likenesses of Hugh Fullerton and Billy Ireland (as above), who had worked on the Columbus Dispatch while he was there in the late 1920s. Caniff also did the jingle feature, Puffy, whose companion evoked Caniff's wife Esther (nicknamed "Bunny"). Mrs. Caniff and their married life in the big city also inspired cartoons when Caniff changed Gilfeather to The Gay Thirties, a panel cartoon of contemporary gags (above and right).*

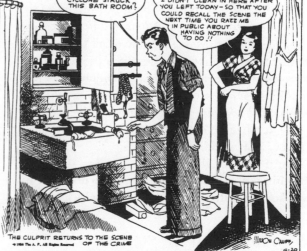

comrades, already on the scene, are immediately in the midst of the hostilities. Pat Ryan joins the U.S. Navy; Connie, the Chinese resistance; Terry, the U.S. Air Corps, where he is taught to fly by the picturesque Flip Corkin, a wise-cracking flyboy Caniff patterned after a college chum and real-life war hero, Philip Cochran. Later in the war, Terry acquires a sidekick in that irrepressible fugitive from Boston, "the little man with the big smile" and a nonstop gift of gab, Charles C. (for Charles) Charles—Hotshot Charlie for short. And through all these adventures, the enigmatic and irresistibly alluring Dragon Lady glides in and out like a recurring nightmare (or, as Caniff memorably put it, a wet dream).

With these characters and their adventures, Caniff advanced the art of the adventure strip by erecting new standards of excellence for most of the genre's basic ingredients. Once the "Caniff years" were fairly underway, nearly every new adventure strip would be measured (in one way or another) against Caniff's accomplishments.

For Caniff, the Caniff years began in 1907 in Hillsboro, Ohio, where he was born and raised, and in Dayton, where he apprenticed in the art department of the *Dayton Journal* while in high school. At Stivers High, he excelled in both the graphic and performing arts. He continued to indulge his thespian aptitude at Ohio State University (from 1925 to 1930), but he earned his way as an artist at the *Columbus Dispatch*, already fully aware of the practical wisdom in the advice given him by the paper's noted cartoonist, Billy Ireland: "Stick to your inkpots, kid; actors don't eat regularly." In April 1932 Caniff was offered a staff artist job with the Features Service of the Associated Press in New York. By September 12 he was already doing a panel gag cartoon, *Mister Gilfeather* (inherited when another young cartoonist, Al Capp, abandoned it to return to his wife in Boston). In March 1933 Caniff took over an illustrated jingle feature, *Puffy the Pig*; on May 4 he converted the panel about the pompous Gilfeather into the topical *Gay Thirties*; and on July 31 the AP launched his first nationally syndicated strip, *Dickie Dare*, which dramatized a young boy's dreams of adventures with such literary heroes as Robin Hood, Robinson Crusoe, and Aladdin.

Caniff was delighted to have his own strip (for one thing, it meant he could work at home on his own schedule instead of punching a clock at the AP office), but he soon perceived a flaw in the *Dickie Dare* formula. Since the youngster was dreaming himself into traditional juvenile literature, all the readers knew how the stories would end. His storyteller's instinct for tantalizing his audience frustrated, Caniff changed the formula. In May 1934 he brought a new character into the strip—a free-lance journalist named Dan Flynn. A friend of the Dare family, Flynn obtains the permission of Dickie's parents to take him on a trip abroad. Once overseas, the duo begin to have real adventures, not dreamed ones. Flynn handles the rough stuff, the really serious adventuring action; Dickie helps when he can, sometimes precipitating the action by getting in the way. The relationship between the older man and the youth resonated with influence, and in two directions: it would be reprised later with Pat Ryan and Terry, but in both relationships are more-than-faint echoes of another adventuring team, a rugged and experienced soldier of fortune teamed with an exuberant young companion. Captain Easy and Wash Tubbs. Caniff was at last doing an adventure strip, the genre that he was best suited for (although at the time, he perhaps didn't know it).

Adventure strips of the day traded chiefly in exotic situations and physical danger, as we've seen. Given the emphasis on incident—dangerous situations—most of these strips spent relatively little time on characterization, relying instead on danger to create suspense, and plunging their heroes headlong into one predicament after another. What character development there was arose largely as a by-product of demonstrating the hero's resourcefulness in extricating himself from his current dilemma or in solving the latest mystery. I don't mean by all this to deprecate these pioneering strips. They set out to offer their readers an exciting new world of adventure, and they did that—well. Until Caniff came along, an adventure strip didn't need to be much more than exciting.

Graphically, most of the early adventure strips were scarcely photographically accurate visual records. But they were drawn realistically enough to be easily distinguished from the funny comic strips. A few strips (Phil Davis's *Mandrake*, Hal Foster's *Tarzan*, Lyman Young's *Tim Tyler's Luck*, and all Alex Raymond's strips) were marked with illustrative rendering techniques, but most of the strips featured relatively uncomplicated linework by pen. And for the most part, the camera angle

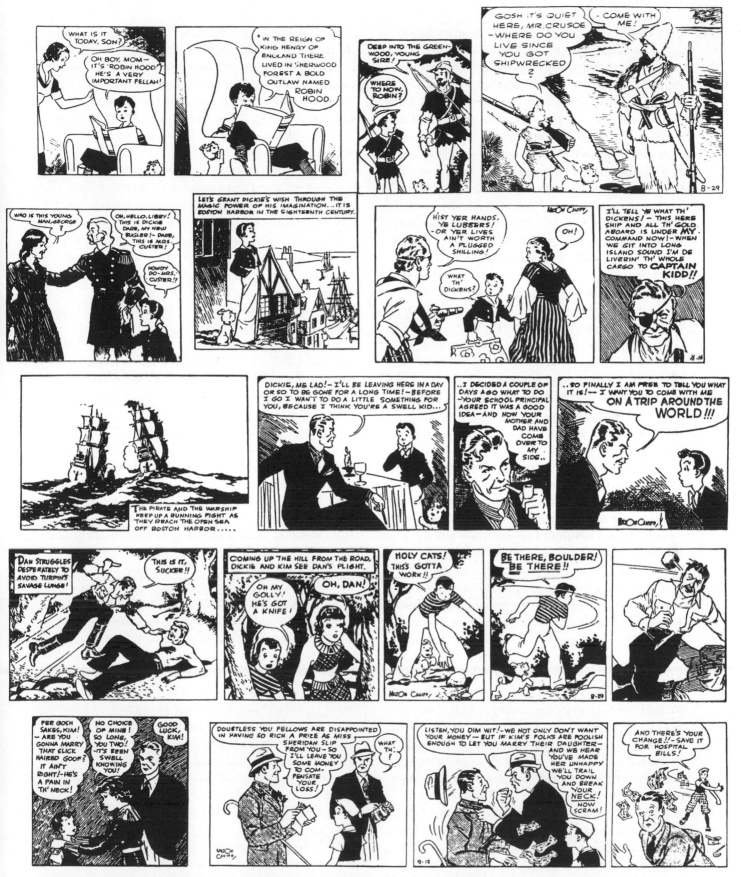

Figure 78. Dickie Dare, *the daily strip Caniff started doing for the Associated Press in July 1933, was drawn in a fairly simple style throughout his fifteen-month tenure on it, but he became more and more illustrative as time passed. Note the treatment of buildings (sixth panel) and seascape (ninth panel) and tree foliage (panels 14 and 15). The unrequited love affair between Dan Flynn and Kim Sheridan anticipated a similar relationship between Pat Ryan and Normandie Drake.*

didn't shift unless the nature of a panel required a distance shot instead of a medium-length shot. *Dickie Dare* was no different from its fellows: Caniff drew with a simple albeit discerning line (figure 78). But all the special effects for which he would gain renown were just over the horizon.

By 1934 Caniff was ready for something more than the Associated Press. The AP had been a good place to begin, but his sights had always been set on national distribution with a feature syndicate, not with a news service. The AP did not devote much energy to selling its features, for one thing; nor did it pay as well as a bona fide feature syndicate. With a letter of introduction from a Sigma Chi fraternity brother, the *Chicago Tribune's* front-page editorial cartoonist John T. McCutcheon, Caniff had visited the Tribune-News Syndicate offices on 42nd Street and had met Arthur Crawford and Mollie Slott. Nothing came of his visits, though, until late in the year, when Joseph Patterson summoned him to his office.

Both Walter Berndt and Mollie Slott had been watching Caniff's work and singing his praises to Patterson; now the Captain would give the young AP cartoonist a chance to prove them right. Or wrong. Patterson was unhappy with *The Teenie Weenies*: he had persuaded Donahey to adopt a strip format in the fall of 1933, but it wasn't working out. Besides, the buyers of the *Daily News* weren't likely to be fans of children's stories. They were followers of scandal and gossip. They liked action; they liked being titillated. Patterson knew what they wanted, and he quickly outlined his ideas to Caniff. The Captain specified an adventure strip with a young boy as hero (to appeal to young readers) but with plenty of pretty girls around, too (for the kids' fathers, those who bought the paper). The boy should have an adult sidekick, a rugged handsome fellow to handle the rough stuff and to romance the girls. Patterson urged Caniff to give his strip sex appeal but to confine the heartthrobs to daily strips—"Do the Sunday page for the kids," he said. The action should be set in the Orient, the Captain ordered. "Adventure can still happen out there," he said.[4] There were still pirates active along the China coast, he added, and, referring Caniff to a book on the subject, he suggested that a beautiful lady pirate might make a good villain.

Patterson did not give the young cartoonist much time to develop his concept. Within a week, he wanted to see some Sunday pages. (He needed a Sunday strip because he wanted to drop *The Teenie Weenies* as soon as possible.) According to legend (of which Caniff was chief author), Caniff researched the Orient (about which he knew next to nothing), developed characters (changing Dickie's black hair to blond for Terry; Flynn's blond hair to black for Ryan), and wrote and drew up a couple sample Sunday pages—all within a single week, while also producing the next week's set of *Dickie Dare* strips and a week's worth of *The Gay Thirties*. By way of research, Caniff consulted not only the book Patterson had recommended—*Vampires of the China Coast*, a lurid potboiler about a marauding pirate band—but several other works on the Far East that he found at the New York Public Library (including Somerset Maugham's *Ah King*, from which he later derived Connie). Following another of the Captain's recommendations, he also read *Wuthering Heights*, where he found fully developed the theme of passionate but thwarted and unconsummated love. He recognized immediately that such a circumstance was perfect for dealing with a footloose romantic lead who was to encounter an endless parade of toothsome ladies, becoming involved with each of them but entangled by none. And the frustration in an unrealized love affair would grip readers by building and sustaining suspense. Although Caniff always credited Patterson with suggesting the basic formula for *Terry*, it's clear that *Terry* was but another incarnation of *Dickie Dare*. And Caniff had even introduced the unrequited love theme in the AP strip at the conclusion of the first adventure with Dan Flynn.

At the end of a week, he submitted a strip called *Tommy Tucker*. Patterson liked everything he saw except the name, so he asked for a list of alternatives; from that list, he picked "Terry," adding "and the Pirates" to create the strip's title. He then put the Sunday pages into production and told Caniff to produce a week's worth of dailies. The first Sunday page wouldn't get into print for about two months (standard lead time for preparing a color strip), but Patterson wanted to start the daily strips immediately—the following Monday, October 22, if possible; so Caniff concocted another story line for the dailies, and *Terry* began that Monday.

The first daily adventure in *Terry* was not so very remarkable, except, perhaps, for the fact that the heroine's father was killed; as Patterson suggested, such a death would persuade readers that

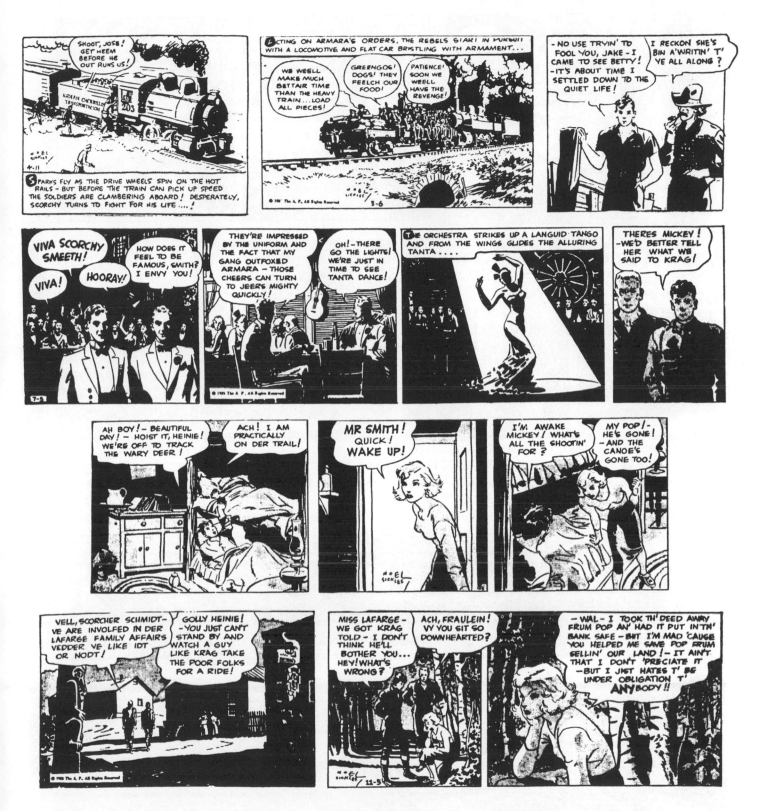

Figure 79. *A sampling of panels from Scorchy Smith, the strip being done by Caniff's studio-mate, Noel Sickles, at the same time as Caniff was launching Terry. Starting in the winter of 1935 (top tier), Sickles shadowed the strip profusely. And when the action took place at night or in the dark (second tier), the effect was particularly striking. Eventually, Sickles laid in the black shadows as copiously during supposed daylight hours (bottom tier, left; fall 1935) as during nighttime, his chiaroscuro technique creating the illusion of reality impressionistically.*

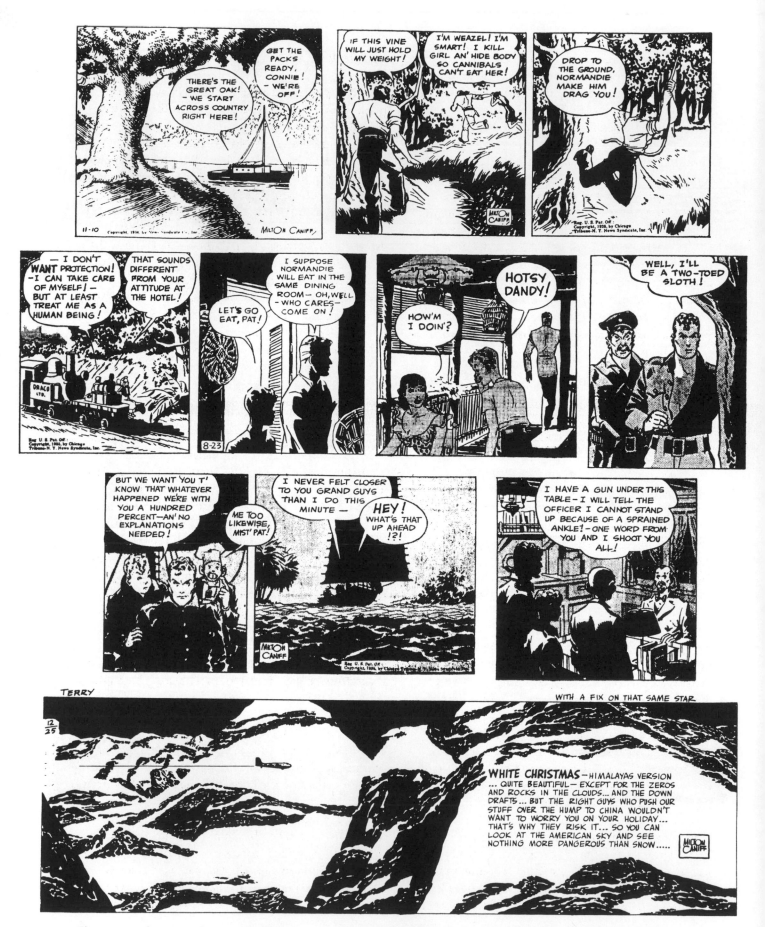

Figure 80. *When* Terry *began, Caniff drew it as he had Dickie Dare (upper right). But when he saw what Sickles was achieving in* Scorchy *during the winter of 1935, he applied the same treatment to his strip—slowly at first (note the tree foliage, upper right, spring of 1935; and the train and the nighttime scenes, second tier, summer and fall 1935), then more enthusiastically (third tier, 1936). Bottom tier: another deployment of contrasting black and white—a spectacular treatment of mountains that Caniff said he "stole" from Roy Crane.*

the dangers in the strip were serious. The story was a simple progression of events. The artwork was still done with a pen, the figures rendered in relatively simple outline (however flexible the line), and the blacks solid, filled-in shapes. But before the strip had finished its first year, both story development and graphic technique changed remarkably.

The principle of the new graphic technique was simple: in nature, there are no lines—the shapes, the edges, of things are determined by contrasting colors, textures, and, most important for this technique, shadows. Everything casts a shadow, and parts of most things are in shadow, in varying degrees of darkness. In a daily comic strip, there are only two "colors"—black and white. Caniff began using black for shadows. Until then, black was treated by most comic strip artists as a "color": a character would have black trousers or a black sweater. In Caniff's work, too, black was sometimes a "color," but more often his strips seemed to contain no such "colors"—only light and shadow. Imagine a character standing in a room with a single source of light; half the character's form would be in shadow. Take, for example, a man's face: the features on the "light-source side" are drawn in fine lines with a pen; the features on the "shadow side" are lost in black shadow. Only the high points—a cheekbone, the top of an ear—catch the light, and thus they remain tiny flecks of white in a sheen of black.

That's the principle. In practice, most of the faces of Caniff's characters were in the light, but their figures were half bathed in shadow. Everything—furniture, airplanes, automobiles, houses, people—had a side away from the light source, so part of the shape was suggested with a deft stroke of a black-inked brush, and unimportant props were all but lost in shadow. Caniff sculpted shapes with nicks of black, the shadows etching the forms. Shadowy folds on a figure's clothing, well done, define the shape of the figure; badly done, everything is reduced to blots of black ink. Caniff's were well done. From Caniff's point of view, though, the most important advantage in deploying this impressionistic chiaroscuro technique was in the time it saved him. Instead of having to spend hours drawing every wrinkle and every background detail, Caniff could render his cast and settings with strategically placed shapes and shadows, sacrificing none of the illusion of reality.

Although the technique is always associated with Caniff, it had appeared first in the AP strip called *Scorchy Smith*. In 1934 *Scorchy* was being written and drawn by Noel Sickles, a friend of Caniff's from his college days. The two cartoonists shared a studio during this period and sometimes took turns at each other's strips—Sickles doing backgrounds on *Terry* while Caniff worked out dialogue for *Scorchy*. Caniff has always acknowledged his debt to Sickles: "I shall always be grateful that Noel allowed me to pick his brain those formative years. Today in *Steve Canyon* I continue to use Sickle's formula and it has lost none of its original effectiveness."[5] But even though Caniff did not invent the technique, he made it his own—and once perfected, it was widely imitated. Those who followed in Caniff's footsteps constituted the second major "school" of art about realistic comic strip illustration (the other school being composed of the followers of Foster and Raymond).

To the realism of his graphic technique, Caniff added realism of detail. He sought absolute authenticity in rendering the Eastern setting for *Terry*, building up a vast file of reference material on the Orient and, later, on military equipment and lore. He researched thoroughly. Once when Pat Ryan was involved in an amphibious operation, Caniff felt obliged to read or consult at least thirty-eight books, many of which were in his own library. "There is no half-way in doing a realistic feature that will hold readers," Caniff once said. "Every detail must be accurate because there is always a man or woman who has been to the place you are portraying. If the locale is the Algiers waterfront, I look in my file and select the photographs of that region showing costumes and atmosphere which I have carefully saved from magazines and newspapers. I might add at this point that I never save drawings by other artists. Photographs are accurate in detail; an artist may have made some major error which I would simply repeat."[6]

Caniff's readers told him when he made a mistake—and when he didn't. One reader (Roy Chapman Andrews, zoologist, explorer, and author of scientific books on China) once wrote to say that he had picnicked in exactly the same spot in which Terry, Pat, Connie, Big Stoop, and Burma were shown on a picnic. (That, Caniff told me, was quite understandable: "He recognized the spot because he took the photograph from which I stole the background," he explained with a chuckle.[7] Chapman's books were among Caniff's most commonly used resources then.) "I was forced into realism," Caniff said, perhaps tongue-in-cheek, as a consequence of such reader response. "I didn't sell comic strip realism to my readers. My readers sold realism to me."[8]

The first adventure in the *Terry* dailies is fast-paced: event follows event in rapid succession as the plot unfolds, and physical activity is plentiful. For the most part, the dialogue is spare and serves chiefly its utilitarian purpose: to advance the story. Under these circumstances, visual-verbal blend is achieved almost as a matter of course: the words depend on the pictures in order to make sense, and vice versa. With the second weekday adventure, however, the plot gets more complicated, requiring more "explanation" in the strip's dialogue. As the strip rapidly became more and more verbal, Caniff's initial reaction seems to have been to make the words themselves more interesting. The speech becomes snappy and slangy, developing a tendency already underway in Terry's conversation in the first adventure. Caniff continued to polish his prose throughout *Terry's* life, and eventually his characters spoke a sophisticated and crackling patois, suggesting with its slangy (albeit often grim) humor the nonchalance with which his heroes accept their dangerous lives. The increasingly high verbal content of the strip did not, however, immediately threaten verbal-graphic balance. The story still relied heavily upon pictures for its sense, and plots continued to develop rapidly, offsetting potential verbal monotony with action scenes.

Meanwhile, two other aspects of Caniff's cartooning artistry kept the words and pictures in balance. The first was the ever-present element of humor. Patterson had insisted that the strip have a humorous as well as an adventurous vein, and Caniff was glad to oblige. (Another bow here to Roy Crane: the humor in *Wash Tubbs* was always as much an integral part of the strip's appeal as the exotic adventures were.) Eventually, the comic relief provided (most steadily) by such characters as Connie (and, later, Hotshot Charlie) became a Caniff trademark. His storytelling sense told him when comedy would provide valuable respite from the high drama of straight adventure, and his instinct as a cartoonist often led him to use sight gags for that relief. Relying heavily upon a picture to make their comic point, sight gags also functioned to restore verbal-graphic balance in the strip. In the strip for January 31, 1935, for instance, Connie's luggage clearly consists entirely of the tails of his coat (figure 81). Words work in tandem with pictures—either setting us up for the visual punch line or blending with the pictures to create the humor. On the previous day, Terry picks up a word of a snooty doorman and rubs his nose in it, the picture and the words of the last panel combining to create a chorus of comic revenge.

On June 4, 1935, the picture in panel three gives humorous meaning to Connie's words (figure 82). The next day's strip is a gem, a minor masterpiece of verbal-visual blending. Normandie Drake is searching for Pat in Singapore just after he has abandoned all hope of a romance with her. Here neither words nor pictures make complete sense alone. The pictures tell us who it is in the rickshaw that splashes mud on Connie; without them, the scene loses its poignancy and its point. Meanwhile, the verbal byplay about the cleanliness of the city provides the incident with a humorous gloss, the comic implication of Terry's remark depending entirely upon the event being pictured. The humor is gentle, but as a counterpoint to Normandie's dilemma, it enhances the irony of the moment. Typically, the humor in *Terry* depended upon a perfect blending of word and picture in the best tradition of comic strip art. Thus, the characteristic Caniff humor helped maintain the verbal-graphic balance of his strip even as his increasingly complex plots forced him to labor over words.

As the speech balloons grew larger and larger, Caniff sought other ways to forestall graphic monotony in his panels. More and more, he turned to techniques he saw in films. Before *Terry* was a year old, the parade of static panels depicting two persons in conversation was seen less and less frequently. One panel, yes; but the second and third saw the "camera" shifting—the scene was portrayed from different angles and varying distances, as in the first three panels of the strip for June 4 (figure 82). And the resultant visual variety restored the verbal-graphic balance that the heavily laden speech balloons threatened. Caniff did not invent the roving camera technique of varying otherwise static scenes. But the growing complexity

TALE OF A STUFFED SHIRT

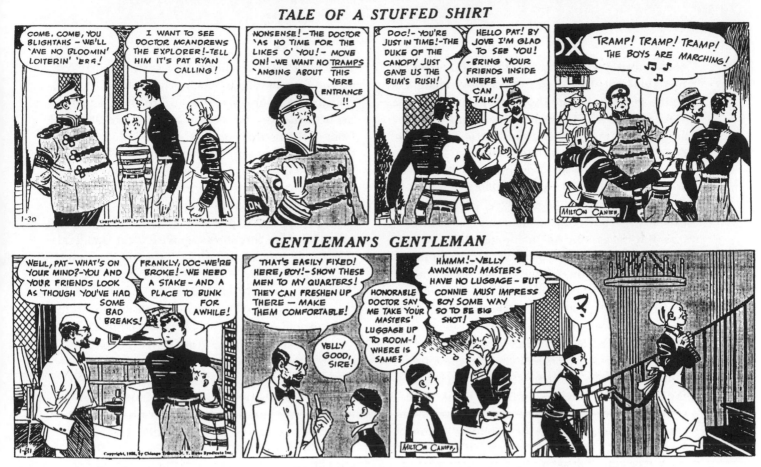

GENTLEMAN'S GENTLEMAN

Figure 81. Caniff's characteristic use of humor usually blended word and picture to produce the punch line as in the two strips above.

I GET A KICK OUT OF YOU

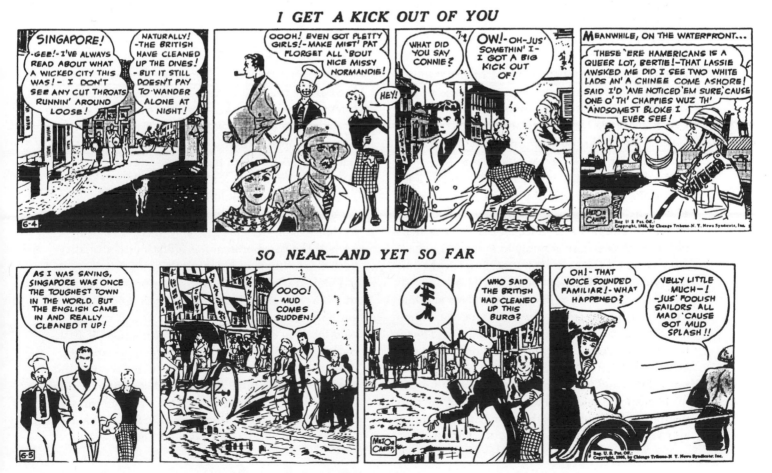

SO NEAR—AND YET SO FAR

Figure 82. In these two strips, more verbal-visual blending for comic effect.

of his stories, with the attendant requirement for more dialogue, forced him to use the technique and to develop it more thoroughly than others had.

An impressionistic graphic technique of light and shadow, the realism of authenticity in every detail of the strip, sparkling sophisticated dialogue, and cinematic variety in the composition of the strip's panels—in each of these departments, Caniff set a new standard of excellence for adventure strips, thereby inspiring a number of imitators. But his greatness—his uniqueness—derives also from his ability as a storyteller. And this aspect of his art, although widely admired, cannot be as readily imitated as his other innovations.

Caniff's *Terry*, like most adventure strips at the time, was both exotic and realistic: it engaged its characters in extraordinary events, threatened them with physical dangers, and did these things in realistic terms, creating suspense by dribbling the story out a little at a time, day by day. The continued success of adventure strips over the next couple decades attests to the durability of this basic formula. Caniff's early interest in the theater doubtless helped develop the keen sense of the dramatic (in staging as well as in story line) that is found in his mature work. But his signal accomplishment as a storyteller stems from the fact that he enriched the adventure story formula in a way that enhanced the realism of his strip and thereby pitched the resulting suspense at higher levels: Caniff made character development integral to his stories. To illustrate how character functions in Caniff's stories, let me rehearse the first *Terry* adventures, which reveal not only how Caniff used character but how he grew as a storyteller.

The first adventure in the daily strips has a fairly simple, straightforward plot. To go up the river to the site of the gold mine marked on their treasure map, Pat and Terry hire a boat from a crusty old American expatriate named Pop Scott, who goes along on the expedition, accompanied by his pretty daughter Dale. A local river pirate named Poppy Joe gets wind of the group's plans and follows them upstream, and when Terry, Pat, Connie, and Dale go ashore in search of the mine, Poppy Joe captures Pop Scott, who blows up his boat and escapes. Undaunted, Poppy Joe and his gang come upon Terry and his friends as they search for the mine entrance in an old temple. Pat and the boys overpower Poppy Joe and his toughs, but Dale disappears, spirited away by the mysterious inhabi-

tants of the temple. Terry and Pat are then captured by the same bunch, led by a sinister Fu Manchu megalomaniac who makes the old temple his headquarters. Pat is knocked out, but Terry and Connie escape their cell and rescue Dale from the temple chieftain's amorous intentions. Reviving Pat, they all flee through the mine tunnel, where they discover a treasure room of gold. The temple chieftain catches up to them and threatens to blow them all up with explosives. At this unhappy juncture, Old Pop Scott shows up with a gun and holds the temple gang at bay while Terry and his friends escape. In a scuffle with the temple chief, Pop accidentally sets off the explosives. As Patterson had specified, Old Pop dies—buried with the hoodlums and the gold under the rubble of the temple.

The treasure-hunt motivation that initiates the action was a fairly hackneyed device in the adventure story genre even then. It was another of Patterson's contributions, and while Caniff would not resort to anything so threadbare again, he was probably glad to have the suggestion, considering the short production time Patterson had allowed for delivering a week's strips. The story itself is pure formula. While the people react to events and to each other, there is relatively little effort devoted to developing the characters (apart from the principals), to defining and shaping individual personalities. For the most part, all the characters—even, to a great extent, Caniff's heroes—do very little more than fill admirably the stereotypical roles dictated for them by an adventure story. Events alone conspire to show us Terry's spunk, Pat's unflappable resourcefulness and stalwart reliability (except when his otherwise good judgment is overwhelmed by a too rapidly flaring Irish temper, a trait Caniff would later abandon), and Connie's fidelity even while in the grip of irrepressible hysteria—and the courage of all three. Even so, each of the three emerges as a distinct personality with the promise of some depth.

The rest of the cast had distinct personalities, too, but without a hint of any depth. Old Pop is suitably cranky and gutsy but not much more. And Dale, in spite of her apparent courage, is little more than a decorative walk-on. She was another of Patterson's inventions and, as such, failed to fire Caniff's imagination. (So little did she interest him that he made no effort to strike romantic sparks between her and Pat, thereby neglecting a ploy for interesting readers that he would never overlook again.) And the villains—Poppy Joe and the Fu Manchu look-alike—are cutouts from the most dog-eared pasteboard in the adventure storyteller's deck. In short, the story is almost all incident, a succession of events and hazards—albeit a rapid succession. The action is fast and furious, and we lose ourselves in the tale, proving that the adventure story formula works, that it has holding power, even if it involves people many of whom are no more than stereotypes.

In the separate continuity on the Sunday pages, however, Caniff was already telling a more complex tale than this. On Sundays, in the first story Caniff invented about them, Pat and Terry are captured by the Dragon Lady, and her interest in Pat—an undisguised romantic interest coupled to an offer that he join her pirate band as her first lieutenant—has us wondering whether lust or larceny will shape events. Will she murder the two Americans because they are in her way? Or will her interest in Pat result in a stay of execution? All at once in this tale, personality is as important as incident. But before these questions can be resolved, the pirate queen's ship is attacked by a rival buccaneer, who takes the Dragon Lady prisoner in order to torture her into revealing the secret location of her storied treasure trove. He throws Terry and Pat into the brig, too, planning to use them as decoys in his next ambush of merchant shipping. Finding themselves fellow prisoners, our heroes and the Dragon Lady join forces to escape. In the midst of the ensuing swordplay on deck, the marines land: using the Dragon Lady's compact mirror, Pat had signaled a passing ship, which, in turn, contacted the U.S. Marines, who now board the ship and rescue our heroes and their erstwhile captor. But when the marine officer questions Pat and Terry about the Dragon Lady, the two offer only evasive responses and do not reveal that the woman is the infamous Dragon Lady who has so long terrorized the coast. Something has happened among these three. The Dragon Lady is allowed to go her own way, promising as she leaves not to forget that she is indebted to them. It's clear that the character had piqued Caniff's interest. He would return to mine this vein of personality more thoroughly.

Even in the simpler story in the daily strips, Caniff's storytelling instinct for complicating matters to make them more interesting found expression. He enlivened Patterson's trite plot by investing it with more than one story line. To the threat posed by Poppy Joe and his band, he added the mysterious menace of a second string of villains in the old temple. While Poppy Joe and his thugs cast a glowering cloud over the first part of the story, the antique shrine with its Fu Manchu landlord reeks with Oriental intrigue throughout the second part. Caniff further convoluted the proceedings by splitting up his band of good guys and letting them fall by turns into the hands of one bunch of baddies and then the other. At one point, he held the reins for three subplots at once—Old Pop in Poppy Joe's clutches, Terry and Pat in a dungeon cell, and Dale trying to avert the embrace of Fu Manchu. These complications permitted unexpected twists in the overall story, and Caniff increased the torque with numerous action scenes of fisticuffs and gunplay. At the end, he pulled his story lines together in a finale that destroys all the villains (as well as any prospect of unwholesome wealth for his protagonists). Still, the intricacy is mostly razzle-dazzle compared to the kind of story Caniff would soon produce.

The second adventure in the daily strips is so different that we might suspect it to be written by a different author (except that we know better). It begins simply enough. One day while wandering the streets of an unnamed coastal city, Terry sees a purse snatcher making off with a young woman's purse. He knocks the thief down, retrieves the purse, and returns it to the woman. She's Normandie Drake, the beautiful but spoiled niece of Chauncey Drake, a rough-cut tycoon, who, it develops, longs for the days of his freewheeling youth. When he meets Pat Ryan, he sees something of himself in the adventurer, and he invites Pat, Terry, and Connie to go with him "for company" on a yacht cruise with Normandie and her friends. Once aboard, Pat is snubbed as an uncouth soldier of fortune by Normandie, who is accompanied by Dmitri Phoneeski, a fake count with an eye on her money. While our heroes settle into their accommodations, we meet two crew members, Weazel and Limey, who plan to sabotage the cruise—to sink the ship and kill Drake—in order to create a stock market scare with the death of the millionaire. Learning that Dmitri is a fraud, they blackmail him into joining their scheme as the murderer of Drake. When a storm comes up, the trio scuttles the ship, and Pat, the boys, and the Drakes are locked up on board to sink to their deaths. But they break free and are washed up on a desert island.

Unaccustomed to such survival hardships as they now all face, Normandie flounces into the jungle in a fit of arrogance rather than do her share in making camp. She falls into the hands of Weazel, Limey, and Dmitri; also stranded on the island, they hold her for possible ransom. Her eyes opened at last about Dmitri, Normandie realizes that she was probably wrong about Pat, too. During the night while her captors sleep, she improvises smoke signals, which catch Pat's attention. Pat and his cohorts resolve to rescue her, but since they are without weapons, they can't attack the armed kidnappers, so they devise a scheme to demoralize and weaken the hoodlums until they are unable to put up a fight. They contaminate the kidnappers' water supply, a spring near their camp. And then, all night, every night, they beat jungle drums like marauding cannibals. After several sleepless nights of drums and thirsty days without water (and with Normandie egging them on against each other), the outlaws crack under the strain and fight among themselves. When Weazel is the only one left standing, Pat moves in to rescue Normandie. Weazel escapes during the fight, but Normandie is now safe. Shortly, they are all picked up by a passing ocean liner. During their adventure, Pat and Normandie have fallen in love, but Pat jumps ship with the boys at Singapore rather than endure the prospect of being a penniless vagabond adventurer living off a wealthy woman.

Instead of a single plot—a single series of events, calling for a single resolution—there are two plot lines or strands. The first involves the shady machinations of Weazel and Limey; the second, Normandie Drake and her relationship with Pat. It is in developing his second plot strand that Caniff began to make his mark on adventure strip storytelling. The success of his story depends upon his building and maintaining suspense in both plot strands at once—and then, eventually, knitting both strands together to produce a satisfactory resolution. In turn, the success of this effort, particularly with the second plot strand, depends greatly upon his ability to portray accurately the characters—the personalities—of his chief actor and actress.

At her first meeting with Pat, Normandie's spoiled and pertinacious nature emerges at once,

fully and deftly drawn with an impudent speech (and an uptilted nose): "I am happy to hear that these two persons [Terry and Pat] are servants and not guests—after all, one must draw the line somewhere. . . . See that they remain below decks when off duty." But Caniff's portrait is not entirely one dimensional: a headstrong personality can grow into a courageous one, and Normandie's first remarks in the strip (several days before her encounter with Pat) show that she has normal, decent feelings. To her escort, who has just insulted Terry after Terry recovered Normandie's stolen purse, she says: "Dmitri, you were rather unkind to that boy who recovered my purse. I thought he was very nice about it."

Clearly, Normandie's snobbery is not wholly second nature to her. It's partly "learned"—or, rather, imposed upon her by her situation. And Dmitri's reply bears out this assessment: "Come, come, my dear. He probably recognized you and hoped to put you in his debt. But I dismissed him, didn't I? Ah, indeed yes. Quite!" Dmitri's remarks, particularly their tone, "teach" Normandie what her role should be. But his remarks tell us as much about Dmitri as they do about Normandie, showing Caniff's expert economy in characterization as well as his acutely realistic assessment of human psychology. People often tend to suspect others of motives that are actually their own, particularly people who are fundamentally insecure or who feel guilty about their intentions. A few days later, Dmitri accuses Ryan of harboring a mercenary interest in Normandie—the sort of interest that, as it turns out, is precisely Dmitri's. That Dmitri is insecure is also demonstrated later when his insecurity emerges in its most repellent form, cowardice.

Normandie's potential as a fit heroine for Pat is borne out in the course of this first adventure—and our expectations for her form the basis for the suspense that attends this plot strand. Meanwhile, the threat posed by the sinister plans of Weazel and Limey keeps us equally edgy: what will happen to Terry and Pat, and how will they escape their fate? Both plot strands come together on the desert island after Drake's ship is wrecked. The treachery of the villains is revealed, and when Normandie falls into their clutches, she proves to be of the stuff of which heroines are made: divining what Pat is up to with his jungle drums, she invents ways of accelerating the deterioration of the kidnappers' morale. What's more, as Pat routs the baddies, Normandie reveals her affection for him—and he for her. All in all, a tidy resolution to a relatively complicated plot.

One could fault Caniff's characterization of Normandie: her conversion from snooty heiress to resourceful heroine is, perhaps, too sudden—despite the fact that such a personality might very well, given the right combination of circumstances, turn out that way. But the point of this discussion is not that Caniff's first significant effort in *Terry* at character drawing was faultless but that he made character a vital ingredient in his story, interacting with events and developing as events unfold. Henceforth, characterization would become a major element in Caniff's work. And by his attention to this element, Caniff raised the realistic standards of his strip—and set new goals for adventure strips in general.

Caniff's strip enhanced the exoticism of the adventure strip genre with realistic people, who in turn lent the authenticity of their personalities to the events of the story. Characterization here does not exist in isolation: events and people interact, one feeding off the other in a reciprocating cause-and-effect relationship. Not only is the result a realistic story: it is also a suspenseful one. As a storyteller, Caniff wove personalities and events together into an intricately patterned fabric that closely resembled the whole cloth of real life by reason of its very complexity of design. His stories thus invariably create suspense on at least two levels at once: we want to know what will happen, and we want to know how the people involved will react, develop, change, and/or grow. Simply stated, Caniff's accomplishment was to make us avidly interested in his people as well as their adventures. And that, perhaps, is the secret of the storytelling art.

Caniff's characterizations in *Terry* eventually became so acute that some of his characters were very nearly portraits of psychological types. Tony Sandhurst, for example, is the consummate coward. How he induced Normandie Drake to marry him is a mystery, but he did. He then took a "son's" share in her uncle's business, using the power he found in his position to shore up his feelings of inadequacy. A coward feels constantly threatened, and any event that touches him is often imagined as a deliberate slight, an attack on his manliness. A coward in a position of power

will use that power, often arbitrarily and seemingly without reason, to lash back at those who he imagines have injured him—or who might be planning to injure him. In the exercise of that power, the coward thinks of nothing save himself. The consequences for others are unimportant, so long as he can preserve and maintain the aura of power about him that disguises his basic weakness, his cowardice. Sandhurst is exactly true to this form. Later, in *Steve Canyon*, Caniff would give us Dean Wilderness, whose martyr compulsion drove her to disaster; Colonel Index, a study in paranoia; and the Duchess of Denver and her beau, Fungo, the perfect couple—masochist and sadist. To name a few. But his most enchanting creation was achieved in *Terry*, and she was far from being a canned psychological type.

The Dragon Lady is a unique bit of characterization in the history of comic strips. She is, of course, beautiful. And she is the first of a long line of Caniff femme fatales about whom the air of mystery swirls like early morning mist. There is nothing unusual about beauty and mystery in comic strip women. But Caniff gave to his characterization of this stock character a profound twist: the Dragon Lady is hard and seemingly unscrupulous, a princess of sorts, who fills a hereditary masculine role so thoroughly that her minions ignore her obvious feminine attractions and call her always "Master." To this already formidable creation, Caniff added two final and masterfully delicate touches: a note of doubt about her unscrupulousness and the poignant suggestion (ever so slight) that perhaps the Dragon Lady would rather be loved by men than lead them.

The doubt about her ruthlessness is especially evident in the Dragon Lady's later appearances in the strip. Although the Dragon Lady claims for her deeds only the most self-serving of motives, the effect of many of her intrigues is to do a good turn for the cause of humanity. What's more, we actually see her occasionally performing some act of kindness (which she is likely to do covertly, as if almost ashamed of it). Is she really humane beneath that snarling, albeit beautiful, exterior? Should we believe her claims to unscrupulous self-seeking? Or are those claims only a mask, covering her real humanity in order to preserve her necessarily unyielding image as a leader of men? And does she love Pat Ryan? Or, later, Terry? Or is she, in those scenes in which she seems to reveal to

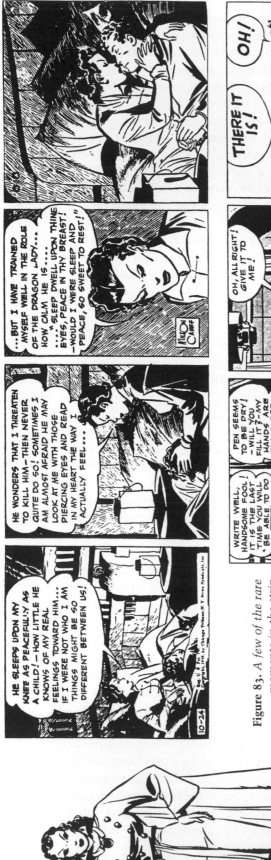

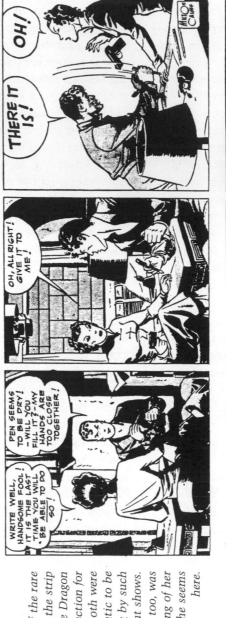

Figure 83: *A few of the rare moments in the strip during which the Dragon Lady reveals affection for Pat Ryan. But both were too pragmatic to be captivated long by such emotions—as Pat shows. The Dragon Lady, too, was usually less revealing of her emotions than she seems here.*

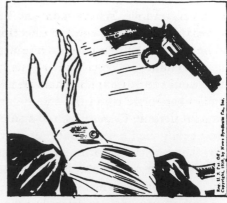

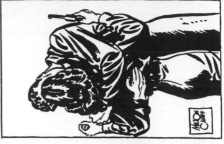

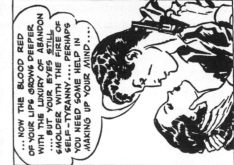

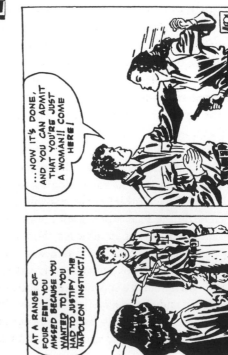

them a secret love, merely indulging herself during an idle moment in yet another exercise of her power? Having proved her power as a leader of men, is she now just trying to prove her equally potent strength in the more traditional role of a woman? Or does she really regret the role she must play and secretly long to be enfolded in some strong hero's arms?

Only about seemingly real people can we ask such questions. Perhaps we'll never learn the answers, just as we can never know for sure about many people we meet in our own lives. But we'll believe what we choose to believe. This sort of ambiguity about a character is possible only when the personality drawn is complex—as well as fully and realistically rounded with many subtle strokes. With such strokes, Caniff did more than make the Dragon Lady live. He gave to his woman of mystery a psychological depth that underscores the mysteriousness of her circumstances with the puzzle of her personality. And in the ambivalence of our judgment about her (a necessarily male judgment with yours truly) are the outlines of archetypal male fears and longings about women in general. Despite our ambivalence (or, indeed, perhaps because of it), the Dragon Lady is profoundly real. Indeed, she was real enough that John Steinbeck once wrote: "When my grandchildren speak of their sugarplum eroticisms, I can say, 'You see? This is how it was in my day. This Dragon Lady, with the figure of a debutante (if debutantes have figures) was one of your old man's girl friends.'"[9]

For Caniff, the Dragon Lady was more than a unique creation: she was the philosophers' stone of his transformation into master storyteller, the lodestar that guided him to a new undertaking, the reagent that stimulated his creative prowess. He told me that he knew he had "a good thing" with the Dragon Lady as soon as he was into that first Sunday continuity. "I was lucky," he said, "to find that kind of a person, the kind that gave you license to be strong—to have people's heads cut off and that sort of thing. Out in that far place, you could do things like that. Wouldn't be credible to have things like that in Chicago. You'd never get away with it. But in China, there were women pirates, who were probably miserable little frumps, but the thing is having a beautiful dame like that doing those things. Makes you shudder."[10]

The Dragon Lady's personality intrigued him, and to explore it he brought her back into his story again and again. She appeared in all the Sunday stories except one from December 1934 until August 1936, when the Sunday and daily stories were at last integrated into a single story line; and she appeared in the first unified story, which ran until February 1937. In shaping her personality over those twenty-seven months, Caniff dipped into a wellspring of his imagination, and from the resultant success with her—the attention and acclaim of his readers as well as in his own satisfaction and delight in the character—much of the entire saga of *Terry* and of Caniff's subsequent career flowed. Once Caniff had discovered the riches that lay waiting to be mined in a complex personality, he devoted similar energy to developing the personalities of all his characters. Strong, individualized characterization of those in secondary roles, particularly, thus became a hallmark of his work.

Burma, another masterpiece of characterization in many ways reminiscent of the Dragon Lady, poses no similarly ambiguous problem. In spite of her alleged crimes, she does have a heart of gold. And she does love Ryan. On the archetypal level, she is the counterpoint to the Dragon Lady: our certainty about Burma's character relieves the tension wrought by our doubts about the Dragon Lady. Although we are confident of Burma's feelings, we are uncertain about her criminality. And with that uncertainty, Burma reclaims her status as a woman of mystery. But Burma, too, is real. Pat Ryan is exactly the sort of man—strong, resourceful, adventurous, courageous, a sort of law unto himself in a lawless land—who would capture the affections of a woman like Burma. Her snappy patter notwithstanding, she has feelings for Pat that enlist our support and sympathy—and along with that, our conviction that she lives and breathes like all of us.

The interplay of the personalities of these two women with those of Pat Ryan and Terry creates and maintains its own kind of suspense in the strip. We look for some sort of final and satisfying resolution of the relationship among the characters as well as for a satisfying conclusion to their current adventure. And Caniff brings them back on stage again and again to tantalize us (initiating in these repeat performances yet another aspect of his storytelling art that is distinctly his own). The suspense is never completely eased.

To weave into the tapestry of Terry's history two such intriguing characters as the Dragon Lady and

Burma (to mention only these two) is to add to the strip's exotic locale a powerful attraction. The characterizations of the Dragon Lady and of Burma complement the mysteriousness of the Orient with the mystery of their personalities. In our fanciful dreams, such an interlocking relationship of person and place is hardly unexpected, so in Caniff's story, character and locale act together to reinforce the aura of reality in the strip. What we expect (or want), we find; and that makes us believe in it. At the same time, the characterization of each woman seems so true to life that it lends the authority of its authenticity to the strip's stories, making the most improbable adventures real. This complex combination of realism and exoticism, character and event raises the appeal of the strip to the level of mystique. Our longing for exotic adventure is satisfied in terms so real as to convince us that such adventures are possible, that they have (even) actually happened. Where such dreams are so ably fulfilled, we cannot help but return again and again.

Caniff reached the pinnacle of his fame during World War II. In the strip, Terry joined the Air Force, and Caniff's realistic and sympathetic treatment of military life championed the achievements of ordinary men and women in uniform. The cartoonist became an American Kipling. *Terry's* trenchant, pragmatic patriotism warmed hearts and steeled nerves on the home front as well as at the battlefront. The Sunday page for October 17, 1943, so incisively captured the wartime spirit of the times that it was read into the *Congressional Record* to become a part of the national archive. One of Caniff's most famous creations came about through one of his numerous contributions to the war effort: Miss Lace, a curvaceous bundle of camaraderie, was the central figure (so to speak) of *Male Call*, a mildly risqué weekly strip he drew without remuneration for distribution as a morale booster to camp and unit newspapers (from March 1943 to March 1946). Immensely popular, the strip was published regularly in more than three thousand papers, the greatest circulation in number of individual publications ever attained by a comic strip. After the war, Caniff caused yet another sensation: he abandoned *Terry*, which was owned by the Chicago Tribune–New York Daily News Syndicate, to create for Field Enterprises a new strip, which he would own himself.

Steve Canyon hove into public view on the crest of a wave of unequaled ballyhoo, the culmination of a promotional campaign unique in both its length and content. Caniff's popularity was such that his name alone sold the feature: on January 13, 1947, *Canyon* began in 234 newspapers, 162 of which had bought the feature before seeing even the earliest promotional drawings of the characters (which had appeared only seven weeks previously). In personality, Caniff's new hero was an older, more mature Terry, but Caniff had taken pains to make him look markedly different, giving him a theatrical dark streak in his blond hair—a feature of his appearance that excited great comment in the promotional materials. Deliberately contrived to appeal to a postwar audience of former GI's, Canyon was an ex–Army Transport Command pilot, and, like thousands of other veterans, he had set himself up in business, operating his own cargo airline. His vocation gave him a plausible excuse for going anywhere and doing anything, and Caniff gave the airline a name to match that promise— Horizons Unlimited.

Steve Canyon was conceived as a modern, sophisticated incarnation of the plainsman of the American West ("airplanesman," the publicity punned), and Caniff completed the equation by giving him a sidekick reminiscent of the stock character that Gabby Hayes had virtually invented in Western movies. With the grizzled old 7th Cavalry trooper Happy Easter at his side, Canyon spent the next four years barnstorming around the globe in an epic-length string of adventures. One story grew into the next almost imperceptibly. Instead of an episodic structure, the strip had the loping ease of an unending saga; in that, *Canyon* was, for a time, an evocation of the spirit and feeling of the prewar *Terry*. But when the Korean War broke out, Canyon reenlisted in the Air Force, and from then on *Steve Canyon* was a military strip; henceforth, Canyon's adventures took place in military settings and with such an authentic representation of the military point of view that he became an unofficial spokesman for the Air Force. Caniff's propagandizing was entirely unforced. Military life was amicable to the themes of courage, resourcefulness, and (above all) loyalty that had predominated in Caniff's work all his life: in the military context, dramatic expression of these values was achieved naturally in patriotic as well as personal forms.

Maintaining the high standards of craftsmanship

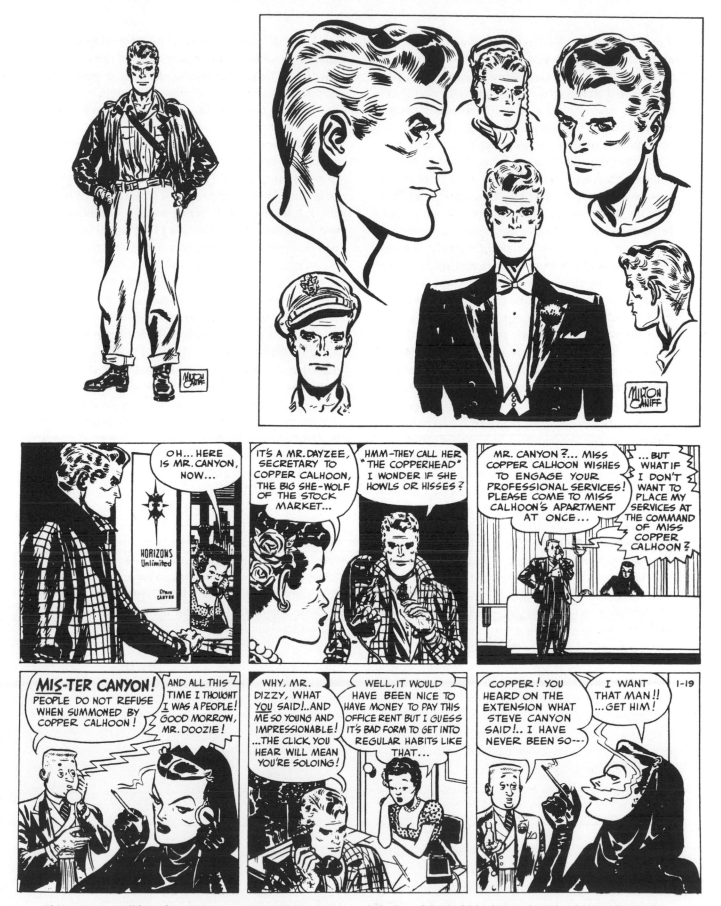

Figure 84. *Caniff kept his postwar creation, Steve Canyon (with the celebrated black streak in his hair), offstage for the entire first week of the strip, introducing him at last on Sunday (bottom two tiers), at which time we also meet Copper Calhoon, the "Copperhead," Caniff's new serpentine villainess.*

that he had raised in *Terry*, Caniff also continued to explore the medium's potential. He introduced the repertory concept, rotating stories among several leading players. It was a extremely useful innovation: the one-man show formula employed by most of Caniff's colleagues limited adventure story possibilities to those appropriate to the hero, but Caniff could pursue a great range of subjects, depending upon the character he picked to be the protagonist. By such devices, he sustained his adventure strip through the postwar decades as the daily gag strip emerged as the dominant genre on the funny pages. But his luck didn't hold: during the Vietnam War, he underestimated momentarily the extent of antiwar sentiment in the country. When readers protested the hawkish tone in the strip, Caniff quickly regrouped, taking Canyon out of uniform to serve the Air Force as a special agent in mufti. But the strip's circulation was irreparably damaged: it never again approached the number of papers it had enjoyed at its peak in the late fifties when, with a *Steve Canyon* television series boosting the strip's popularity, it ran in over six hundred papers. During the last decade of the strip's run, Caniff, in a manner of speaking, returned to *Dickie Dare*: he experimented with fantasy by letting his characters occasionally dream themselves into adventures in other times and places.

The golden age of American newspaper comic strips passed with the coming of television, and in the jaded postwar ambiance, Caniff had been unable to recreate in *Steve Canyon* the exotic *Terry* mystique. But responding as he always had to the needs he felt in the audience of the times, he had created a different mythos, a multifaceted one perhaps more appropriate to the third quarter of the century. Still, *Steve Canyon* could not survive Caniff's passing; it ended June 5, 1988. By then, something Caniff had drawn had been in print every weekday continually for nearly fifty-five years, every Sunday for fifty-three years—a publication record without equal.

Caniff's work and the achievement it represents in so many departments of creating an adventure strip is monumental. He touched every aspect of the art of the adventure strip, and every place he touched, he improved. Yet he remained a modest, even self-effacing, man all his life. Pressed in a 1978 interview by Canadian cartoonist Arn Saba, however, he confessed this much: "I think I have taken as great an advantage as I could out of everything that was within my range. I'm not the best artist in the business. I'm not the best—whatever. But I know how to put [what skills I have] together in such a way that they will sell. I'm fortunate in that when I fell into a slot, it was the kind of thing that I did best."[11]

True. *Terry and the Pirates* was his catapult to success. And in giving Caniff the assignment and the strip's provocative locale in the Orient where anything could happen, Joseph Patterson had unknowingly given the ambitious young cartoonist the very material most congenial to his talent. More than congenial: it was to prove a uniquely prolific union, a conjunction of talent with material that continually stimulated it. Patterson had given Caniff just the right slot to fall into. But Caniff did not drop naked into this groove of luck: he already had the talent that Terry and the rest would so inspirit. He had brought that talent with him into Patterson's office that day in the fall of 1934.

CHAPTER 9
What This Country Needed Was a Good Segar
Popeye and the Great Depression

Before crossing the threshold into *Thimble Theatre*, let us pause here under the marquee to salute the signal accomplishments of that strip's creator, Elzie Crisler Segar. Segar did not shape the medium of comic strip art as Roy Crane did in *Wash Tubbs* or Harold Foster in *Tarzan* or Alex Raymond in *Flash Gordon* or Milton Caniff in *Terry and the Pirates*. But that is not surprising: Segar's work was—and is—inimitable. He did not therefore set a pattern that others could follow. Segar was an exemplar of a different sort: in his strip, he conducted a persuasive demonstration of the sorts of things this narrative art could do. He exploited the possibilities of the form, plumbing its unique capabilities. And in the process, he created one of the most unforgettable characters in twentieth-century fiction, and he constructed a morality play of profound and lasting import.

Popeye was born at the brink of that economic and social watershed that divided the prosperous Roaring Twenties from the hardscrabble Depression thirties. And the time of his birth and the period of his development have as much to do with his greatness as does the excellence of the strip and the genius of its execution. The Depression years were terrible for many of those reading the funny pages in the nation's newspapers, but those years were the golden years in the history of the comic strip. The times and their technology con-spired to enable the medium to flourish as it never had before (and never would again). As might be expected, some of the distinctive character of the 1930s emerged as a direct consequence of what happened in the 1920s.

The 1920s in America roared with the exuberance of a nation shaking off the fetters of the Victorian era, it roared with the defiance of the young rebelling against outmoded conventions and mores, it roared with the outrage of the older generation at the audacious behavior of their offspring, and it roared with the sound of cash registers ringing up sales in celebration of the country's unprecedented prosperity. Underlying all the roaring was another sound—a hum. A quiet hum at first, quiet but persistent. A hum that grew in volume until it became a steady drone and then, finally, a thunderous rumble. It was the sound of business enterprise, of manufacturing and commerce. It was the sound of twentieth-century America.

In the wake of World War I production efficiencies and the modern manufacturing developments that made them possible, America was converting to a mass production, mass consumption economy. In this new economy, the congenial itinerant peddler of yore quickly disappeared from the national scene, elbowed out of the way by the more aggressive *salesman*, that predator of the marketplace who cajoled or seduced the consumer into consuming. His role was to make people want more than they had so that the surpluses of the assembly lines could be turned into profits. The salesman replaced the frontiersman as a culture hero, and George Babbitts by the thousand sprang up across the land to pay him homage. And so during the twenties, Americans worshiped at the altar of business enterprise with the "go-getter" as their patron saint. The religion of business spurred the traditional American values of striving for success, of self-reliance, of competition, of acquisitive individualism. One's own interest was the guiding light, and material gain was the chief measure of individual success.

The crash of the stock market at the end of the twenties stilled both hum and roar. The crash also brought into serious question a basic creed of capitalist society. The collapse of the financial edifice in 1929 could be seen as a sign: it signaled that a social structure built upon acquisitive individualism alone could not stand.

But this realization did not bankrupt an entire ethical inheritance. The drive to succeed in material terms was only a single aspect of the traditional American ethos based upon the rights and aspirations of the individual. The same value system also held that selfishness was bad and that personal advancement should not be achieved at the expense of others. During the 1930s these traditional values were reaffirmed. The cumulative psychic impact of the Depression years was to discredit the self-centered, success-oriented ethic of the twenties and to replace it with communal values founded upon notions of a moral economy in which compassion, loyalty, equity, cooperation, and human reciprocity were stressed. And so great numbers of Americans turned their backs on what now seemed the amoral competitive individualism of the twenties and embraced the partly mythical values of an older America, the cooperative barn-raising spirit of the frontier where people had worked together to help their neighbors achieve independence. And these were values that Popeye would embody.

The medium in which Segar's hero appeared entered its gilded age just as Popeye stepped onto the stage. The daily newspaper had peaked and was beginning to decline in power and influence, but the comic strip was just coming into its own. Although by the 1930s radio had displaced the daily newspaper somewhat as the nation's anodyne (al-

beit not as thoroughly as television would replace radio a generation later), the newspaper was still a major presence in American households.[1] Indicative of the entertainment function that newspapers continued to perform is the fact that syndication of non-news entertainment features reached its highest point in the mid-thirties.[2] And comic strips were among the most popular of those features.

Comic strips, as we've observed, were no longer merely humorous. By the mid-thirties, the comics pages were bustling with a great variety of strip genres—joke-telling strips and storytelling strips, family situations and detective situations, kid strips and girl strips, space opera and soap opera, realism and fantasy, mundane domestic drama and exotic high-risk adventure. With canny genius, Segar combined several of these genres into one. His strip told stories but told them humorously; his characters were broadly comic but the dangers they faced seemed nonetheless real. Comedy, adventure, satire, fantasy, and suspenseful continuity—*Thimble Theatre* had them all.

During the Depression years of Segar's tenure on the strip, the entertainment media of the nation were more important than ever. The nation sought solace in its entertainments from the anxieties of its economic life. Radio flourished, regaling its listeners with soap operas and music and comedy shows—particularly comedy shows. In the country's movie houses, Hollywood cheered the nation with the brightest of its new film forms, the musical. With rousing songs and high-kicking chorus lines, musicals inspired people newly stirred by Franklin Roosevelt's confidence and his action-oriented administration. In the same spirit, Walt Disney urged the country to scoff at fear by teaching everyone to sing "Who's Afraid of the Big Bad Wolf," the hit song of his 1933 production *The Three Little Pigs.*

Audiences came away from movies with their attitudes reinforced: these productions emphasized the values of the day. In musical after musical—in movie after movie—rich businessmen are portrayed as greedy and self-serving villains, who are redeemed only when they give up their wicked ways and adopt the homey values of ordinary people. In comedies of the period—like Frank Capra's *Mr. Deeds Goes to Town* (1936) and *Mr. Smith Goes to Washington* (1939)—the common man is the hero, and in achieving his triumph, he overcomes cynical, selfish urban businessmen and other similarly caricatured power figures. Reflecting the values of the ticket-buying public, Hollywood consistently undercut the ethos of the previous decade by associating the unsavory traits of selfishness and greed with wealthy ambitious characters. At the same time, the more communal values of the thirties—loyalty and compassion—were assigned to the films' protagonists, idealists of modest means and station, who, if they became wealthy and powerful in the end, did so incidentally, as it were, while otherwise occupied in pursuing the nobler goals of their idealism rather than as a consequence of purposeful devotion to the acquisition of material things.[3]

Newspaper readers found similar entertainment on the pages of their daily papers, particularly on the comics pages. There, in the increasing variety of types of strips offered, readers now found a great array of amusements that could momentarily divert them from the cares of life in the Depression. It was a propitious time for comic strip cartoonists. The diversity of strip genre fostered creativity, stimulating the genius of people like Segar, not to mention Milton Caniff and Chester Gould and Ham Fisher and Harold Gray and Al Capp and V. T. Hamlin and Roy Crane and a host of other distinctively individual talents. And comic strip readers likewise stimulated cartoonists. Readers were relentlessly faithful in those days: the newspaper was still a fixture, a necessity, of their daily lives, and the readers of comic strips were passionate fans, devoted followers of the installment appearances of their favorite strip heroes and heroines. Such readers reacted emotionally to the adventures unfolding before them daily on the comics page, and they regularly wrote letters to cartoonists to criticize or applaud their work. When Segar brought Popeye into this stimulating and supportive milieu, a minor miracle occurred.

Popeye turned out to be the perfect vehicle for expressing Segar's narrative and comedic talents. With a character so congenial to his genius, Segar converted what had been an adequate but undistinguished comic strip into a classic, a masterpiece of the art form. It was one of those happy conjunctions in history when the right person is in the right place at exactly the right time: Segar's inspiration came to him just as the Depression began, and the temper of the times would prove wonderfully receptive to the notions embodied in Popeye

and the strip he starred in. But it hadn't always been like that for Segar. He had served a long apprenticeship learning his craft—how to draw, how to deploy the resources of his medium, and, most important, how to appeal to readers and to manipulate their interest.

Born and raised in the Mississippi river town of Chester, Illinois, Segar began his apprenticeship in the entertainment industry at the age of twelve, working in the Chester Opera House, which offered both movies and live performances on stage. He drew ads for slide projection and posters for the entrance of the building, he played a drum to accompany the movies and changed the reels, and sometimes, when the show inside was over, he recreated the performances outside on the sidewalk in chalk. He took the eighteen-month W. L. Evans Correspondence Course in cartooning, and when he was certified as a cartoonist in the spring of 1916, he went to Chicago, where he found a cartooning job on the *Chicago Herald*. On March 12, 1916, his first comic strip work appeared on the Sunday pages when he took over a pen-and-ink incarnation of the country's most popular movie comedian called *Charlie Chaplin's Comic Capers*. His drawings made a crude attempt at realistic (albeit comic) rendering, and although the strip perished a year later, Segar continued in the same style on April 23, 1917, with another strip, *Barry the Boob*, about a nutty soldier in the European war.

When the *Herald* was absorbed by the Hearst empire the next year, Segar went to the *Chicago American*, and beginning on June 1, 1918, he employed a simple, big-foot cartooning style to do *Looping the Loop*, a vertical strip that made comic commentary on movies, plays, exhibitions, and other newsy doings in downtown Chicago. Late in 1919 Segar was sent to Hearst's *New York Journal*, presumably to do another vertical format feature. Ed Wheelan had been producing a motion picture parody strip, *Midget Movies*, in which Wheelan's repertory cast of actors and actresses "starred" in stories that spoofed popular movies of the day. Wheelan left Hearst in 1919 to resurrect his strip as *Minute Movies* for the George Matthew Adams Service, and Segar arrived at the Hearst works to take Wheelan's place. Following the now-established custom of naming comic strips of this kind as if they were miniature motion picture houses, Hearst christened Segar's endeavor *Thimble The-*

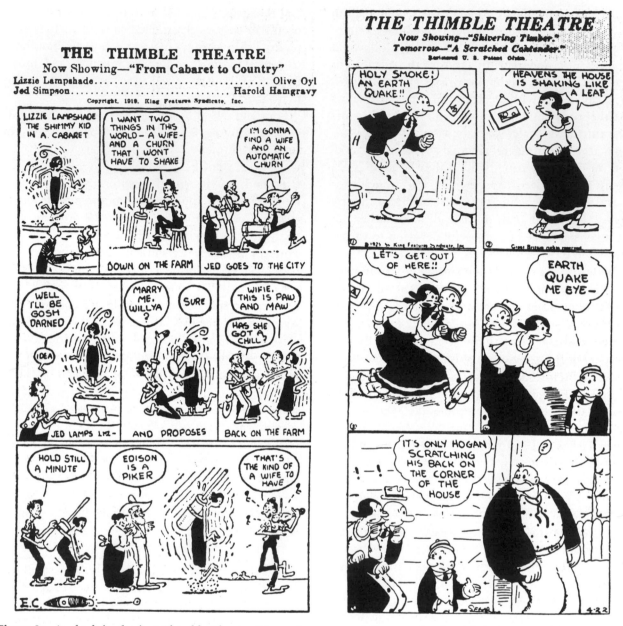

Figure 85. *At the left, the first* Thimble Theatre *(December 19, 1919). By 1925 (at the right), Castor Oyl has joined the cast (whose members have changed in appearance a little since their debut).*

atre, and the curtain went up December 19, 1919. But the show went on without Popeye.

Thimble Theatre was supposed to parody movies and stage plays, and so Segar cast the strip with "actors" who would take parts in the lampoon productions: Willy Wormwood, a moustache-twirling villain akin to Desperate Desmond; the pure and simple heroine, Olive Oyl; and her boyfriend, Harold Hamgravy (who would soon lose his first name and become Ham Gravy). But after a few short weeks of daily or weekly productions along the intended line, Segar abandoned the original

plan to focus instead on his actors and their real (as opposed to "reel") adventures. And with the introduction shortly thereafter of Olive's brother, the pint-sized Castor Oyl, the strip found its footing.

Castor Oyl was, in Segar's words, "Olive's foolish brother, not exactly half-witted but exceedingly dumb. Just this dumb: when Olive's pet duck fell into a deep hole and no one could extricate it, Castor came by with a water hose and floated the duck to the top. He was clever in his own inimitable way. He even invented coal that would last forever, and he fireproofed safety dynamite so it

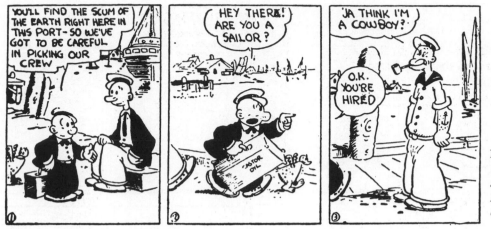

Figure 86. *On January 17, 1929, Castor Oyl hires a sailor—another of those historic occasions for the comic strip medium.*

couldn't explode."[4] But Castor wasn't merely kooky. He was maniacally ambitious. He wanted money and success, women and power. Having almost no special abilities that would enable him to achieve these ends, he pursued his aims with no more than single-minded, dogged determination. As an obsessive seeker after wealth and power, Castor was the perfect 1920s protagonist—a caricature of the materialistic go-getter, the icon of the age. He soon emerged as the star of the strip.

Castor's greedy ambitions motivated the strip throughout the decade. One get-rich-quick scheme followed another, and the strip developed continuity. Daily installments ended with comic punch lines, but the story of one day's installment did not end with the last panel's laugh: Segar strung the dailies together, stretching stories out for a week or more. Soon the stories began roaming on for months, but such was Segar's comic inventiveness that people enjoyed the ramble. One of Segar's devices for creating suspense and maintaining intriguing comic continuity was to introduce wildly eccentric characters into his stories. The strip would focus for days—even weeks—on the Dickensian quirks and foibles of some minor character. As this character kept us entertained, Segar could, at the same time, inch his story along, day by day.

Popeye was one of these characters.

In one of his get-rich-quick plans, Castor turns gambler. But not before he has a surefire system: his uncle has given him a Whiffle Hen, a good luck bird that guarantees winning at games of chance for anyone who rubs the three hairs on the bird's head. Castor decides to take the Whiffle Hen to an offshore gambling hell called Dice Island and

use the bird to fleece the gamblers. Castor buys a boat, but the boat has no crew, so Castor goes in search of one. And that's what he hires: a crew of one—namely, Popeye. On January 17, 1929 (just ten days after *Tarzan* and *Buck Rogers* debuted), Castor approaches a one-eyed sailor with a corncob pipe standing on the dock and hires him (figure 86).

Popeye is clearly no fool: when he sees that he must do the work of a twelve-man crew, he demands the pay of twelve men. And so off they sail for Dice Island. The upshot of the adventure is that, with the help of Popeye, Castor and company clean up the gambling hell—and Popeye moves onto center stage in *Thimble Theatre*. As Coulton Waugh tells it:

> It was on this voyage to Dice Island that Popeye revealed the great quality that endeared him to *Thimble Theatre* readers. His mean employers had been depriving him of his slender wages through the use of the Whiffle Hen. Discovering the trick, Popeye very justly got to the Whiffle Hen first. Result: two "broke" employers. Cap'n Oyl ordered Ham Gravy to thrash the offending one-man crew. Ham Gravy sought a solo audience.
>
> "I'm gonna wipe up the deck with you and step on your face. I'm like that."
>
> Crack!
>
> But it wasn't Ham Gravy's fist that set off the explosion; it was Popeye's.
>
> Ham Gravy, angrily, with black eyes: "You're just what I thought you was—a low-down roughneck. I *won't* fight with you."[5]

Popeye was ready with his fists from almost the moment of his introduction. Rather than redress

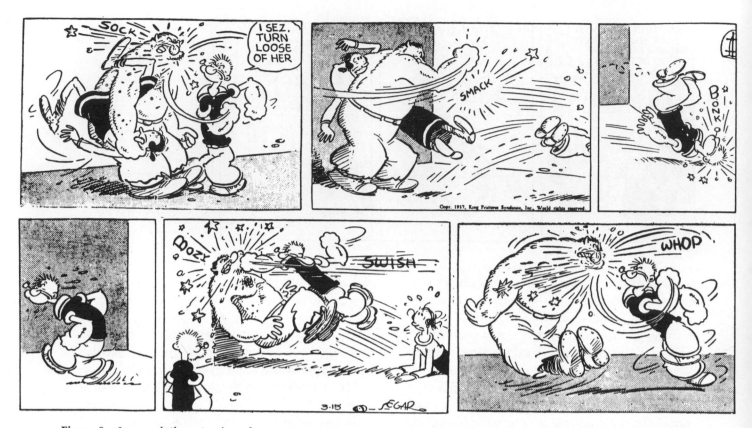

Figure 87. *In two daily strips from late in Segar's tenure on* Thimble Theatre, *a typical Popeye fight scene exploits the visual character of the medium. The brutish villain's hulking size contrasts ridiculously with the sailor's puny build, making Popeye's eventual triumph comic because it's so unlikely. Segar lends credence to the improbable, however: with exaggerative comic logic, he concentrates all of Popeye's muscle and fighting weight in his bulging forearms and fists—right there, at the end of a swinging arm is the very instrument of pugilism, at the point of impact with the villain's jaw. When Popeye throws everything he's got (as in panel 5 here), the weight and centrifugal force of his punch bring the rest of his body along with it, adding to the impact of his blow. With comic visual exaggeration, Segar mocks the fine art of fisticuffs, but he also evens the odds for his hero, heightening suspense and making impossible victory credible.*

injustice with words and sweet reasonableness, Popeye simply bopped it on the nose. Waugh concludes: "The readers liked this. Here was someone who did what, ideally, they would have done. Letters began to pour in to Segar, praising the new character. Segar took the hint. If they wanted a fight, they'd get it."

Before the fighting got too fierce, though, Segar made his fighter a gladiator who could last through any series of battles. Since he reacted with his fists instead of his feet or his mouth (like the other, less violence-prone characters in the strip), Popeye seemed, in comparison, more than ordinarily strong. What began as a simple comic comparison between a roughneck sailor and a pint-sized schemer became, as Segar fine-tuned the focus of his comedy, an exaggerated comic contrast.

Popeye's ordinary (probably) prowess at waterfront tavern brawling was elevated over the years to superhuman strength as he proved himself again and again superior to a series of successively more intimidating foes. Before too long, his reputation as a superman was well established.

The process began almost immediately, when Segar enabled Popeye to survive otherwise mortal gunshot wounds. Shot sixteen times during the escape from Dice Island, Popeye recuperates in the ship's hold—cradling the Whiffle Hen, rubbing the hairs on its head, and hoping he'd have the "luck" to survive. He does, of course—and thereby establishes himself as indestructible. A brawler of superhuman strength who is also indestructible, Popeye is a formidable fighter indeed.

Segar's finishing touch was a stroke of visual

comic genius. Popeye's bulging forearms, those watermelons attached to his body with pipe cleaners, give "ham-fisted" a visual metaphor. Although the graphic device defies anatomy and affronts common sense, it succeeds remarkably in suggesting pugilistic power. Popeye's arms evoke the velocity of his swing: it's as if the centrifugal force of repeated roundhouse punches have shoved all the sailor's muscles into his extremities. His arms suggest the enormous impact of his blows: ballooning around his hands, his arms convert his fists to sledgehammers that gain more striking force by being at the ends of long handles. In comparison, the bulging biceps of conventionally constructed comic book superheroes seem scarcely sufficient to their tasks—as if too far removed from the point of the impact, the striking fist. But all Popeye's muscles—and most of his weight—are bunched just where they'll be felt the most: right behind his knuckles. Conceptually and visually, Popeye is the comic epitome of the perfect fighter.

Segar made canny use of his hero's abilities. He was inventive enough that he didn't need to rely on Popeye's amazing capabilities for his stories. The *Thimble Theatre* tales continued to roll on, introducing more minor characters with comic eccentricities and involving them in fantastic plots—sometimes ignoring for weeks on end the spectacular abilities of the strip's star performer. Still, Segar knew better than to deny his readers indefinitely the pleasure of seeing Popeye in vivid action. Eventually, the cartoonist would unleash his hero, and Popeye would proceed with businesslike dispatch and no fanfare at all to settle the hash of the bad guys with a few unequivocal punches.

Our immense satisfaction at this turn of events in every story derives from two aspects of the strip: the nature of the bad guys and the nature of the avenging hero. Elementary: the bad guys deserve what they get. They are invariably self-seeking and heartless. Brutal and inhuman, their very excesses are exaggerated to the point of comic caricature (hence, our enjoyment of the strip even while we wait for Popeye to set things right). In contrast to this extreme (and therefore humorous) villainy stands the strip's hero. Popeye burns with moral fervor. There are few "grays" for Popeye: he knows what's good and what's evil, and he has no doubts about which he should choose. He is none-

theless kindly and charitable, willing to forgive most human foibles. But if a supposed foible is revealed as fully-fledged villainy, Popeye moves inexorably to redress the wrong. In this, as Waugh observes, Segar captured the essential aspect of the American character—the impulse to act with pragmatic decisiveness: "Popeye is action incarnate. He wastes energy; his temperament is ardent; even his good deeds are done with intensity, with fierce face and furious tempo. . . . He proceeds always under full steam, with fluttering flags and bands playing. God bless him, he is America."[6]

He is indeed. As stirring as a Sousa march, Popeye is the American propensity for action incarnate. And he has the philosophical stance to match. As he himself says: "No matter what you says I yam—I yam what I yam an' tha's all I yam!" With these words, Popeye completes his own portrait. Says Waugh: "Here he emerges in full splendor. One 'I yam' and he would have been esoteric; two 'I yams' would have made him a fascist, caring nothing for other men's fate; three 'I yams' define him as a democrat, and an inheritor of common weaknesses, whose fruition must be found in union and understanding with others."[7]

Popeye's last words—"tha's all I yam!"—mark him as conscious of his own failings, and that awareness makes him one of us. He recognizes his mistakes and is as fiercely humble about them as he is fiercely indignant about evildoers.

Although there are few moral grays for Popeye, Segar realized that the world is not easily divided into the clear-cut moral blacks and whites that animate his hero. Most of us see mostly shades of gray. Popeye, while not morally myopic in this way, has traits that are equally inhibiting, traits that make him in moral matters somewhat like most of us—indecisive.

One I've mentioned: he is charitable. He therefore bends over backwards to excuse the evils he encounters as being foibles not felonies. But he is also sometimes incapacitated by plain ignorance. Not that Popeye is stupid: ignorance is not stupidity. Ignorance is the absence of knowledge, and in Popeye's case it stems from his simplemindedness, his black-and-white vision of the world, and from his impulse to be kind. Often Popeye simply can't believe (or refuses to believe) the evils that surround him. He chooses to believe that everyone is motivated instead by impulses similar to his own. When he gives a poor woman the clothes off his back, she wonders aloud: "I'm not accustomed to such kindness. I can't understand all of this unless you are crazy." But to Popeye such behavior is supposed to be normal. "When people think that a kindhearted person is crazy," he says, "it ain't saying much for the world which is supposed to be civilized." Popeye chooses to believe that everyone is as civilized as he is. And that is the chief manifestation of his ignorance.

All of this works to build suspense in the strip. We know Popeye is indestructible and that his superhuman strength makes him well-nigh invincible. What we don't know is how he'll extricate himself from a given predicament—how and when. When will he finally lay the bad guys among the swee'peas? Segar pushes his stories as far as he can before he gives us answers. And with each little push, the villainies become more exaggerated, more ridiculous—more the stuff of comedy and less the stuff of tragedy. And so we are kept amused as well as teased: we laugh at each passing day's events even while wondering what will happen next. But Segar's strip did more than simply bring newspaper readers back the next day to buy the paper. The strip spoke to the souls of those readers. It comforted them. And to discern how Segar achieved this modest miracle, we must examine once again the nature of his hero.

We know Popeye can't be destroyed. He'll cough up a clip of bullets, ignoring the holes in his hide, and go about his business. For most of his career, the reason for his indestructibility (the magical endowment of the Whiffle Hen) is forgotten, and we are kept in suspense not by doubt about his survival but by the question of why he survives. The answer is the strip's ultimate joke—and its moral. He survives because he doesn't know any better: he seems completely ignorant of any understanding of the human body that would link bullet holes to mortality. Once, complaining that a bullet embedded next to his heart was "tickling" him, Popeye simply shrugs it off, saying, "Aw, what th' heck! Sittin' here beefin' ain't helpin' none—if me ticker's busted, I'll have it took out like a tonsil."

The "joke" in this circumstance—which runs like a refrain through the strip—is sustained by Segar's exploitation of the visual-verbal nature of the medium. Although the words present us with "facts" that are patently impossible, the pictures persuade us to suspend disbelief. Here Segar reaps

benefit from his seemingly crude and wholly non-illustrative drawing style. His big-foot cartoony style divorces his story visually from reality as we know it, and once we have accepted the cartoony conventions of his manner of drawing as a way of representing seeming people in seeming predicaments, we have left the door open for fantasy to creep in. And we therefore accept the impossible "realities" with which Segar's words confront us because they seem of a piece with the pictures. And with the stage thus set, Segar can bring up the curtain on his morality play.

In this regard, Segar's signal achievement was to give to his sailor the mysterious power of an elemental force. Popeye is a force for good that is invincible. Segar's own faith becomes ours. We do not doubt that good exists. We ask about elemental forces not whether they can survive but when will they come into play. That this plaintive question echoes across human history is itself testimony to the inherent goodness of man that validates Segar's belief.

And in those Depression years, Segar's faith acted to renew that of his readers. Their faith in the institutions of their nation severely shaken by the economic disasters of the decade, Segar's readers doubtless took heart from Popeye's adventures, seeing in Popeye a force for good that could not be defeated. And because he represented many of the country's traditional values, his triumph in every encounter with evil reassured readers: if Popeye could win, those values were not bankrupt. However battered the economic and social institutions of the nation, the fundamental values of its people remained viable. Thus, in this pragmatic comic sailor's victories, Americans found an immediate comfort and, perhaps, a prophecy: surely his successes foreshadowed the eventual return to happiness and prosperity of the society that subscribed to the time-tested values of small-town America.

Segar showed masterful skill in keeping his readership engaged with this concoction of comedy and morality, but it is likely that he enjoyed assistance from an unexpected quarter in initially enlisting the attention of much of his audience. According to Bill Blackbeard, curator (and founder) of the San Francisco Academy of Comic Art, *Thimble Theatre* was not a widely published comic strip until the mid-thirties. Until then, Blackbeard says, it ran almost exclusively in Hearst papers.[8] Yet by the end of the decade, Popeye was as widely celebrated a popular icon as Mickey Mouse. The circulation of the strip clearly increased dramatically during the latter part of the thirties. Much of the credit for that growth can be assigned to Segar's genius in the practice of his craft, but some of the impetus to increase may be found in another medium altogether—the animated cartoon.

The first Popeye cartoon from the Fleischer Studios appeared in the summer of 1933. If Blackbeard is correct about the limited circulation of the strip at the time (and his experience in searching out comic strips in thousands of old newspapers suggests strenuously that he is), then it is probable that it was the Fleischer Popeye who introduced the character to much of the American public. And Americans liked what they saw on the screen. Popeye was an immediate hit, and the Fleischer brothers knew what to do with a hit: they produced more Popeye cartoons as fast as they could. Beginning in 1934, Fleischer Studios cranked out a Popeye cartoon every month for the next nine years. In fact, cartoons starring either Popeye or Betty Boop comprised virtually the entire output of the studio for the rest of the decade.

The comic strip had surely been growing in circulation before the Fleischers started producing their Popeye cartoons: the Fleischers would not have been interested in such a property had it not demonstrated some kind of appeal. At the same time, the animated cartoons must have accelerated the dissemination of the strip. Immensely popular, they catapulted Popeye smack into the public eye all across the nation—even in places where he didn't appear in the newspaper—thereby creating a demand for more Popeye. Salesmen from King Features undoubtedly moved with alacrity to supply that demand, and the client list of newspapers running Segar's strip increased apace. After that, it was up to Segar. And he proved equal to the challenge: once before the reading public on the funny pages of the nation's newspapers, Segar captured and held the interest and loyalty of his readers. Popeye's popularity was scarcely due entirely to the Fleischers. The Popeye on the screen attracted public notice, but it was the Popeye in the papers that sustained it.

Segar's Popeye and Fleischer's are not exactly the same character. But they are so similar that the differences are complementary rather than contradictory. For one thing, the animated cartoons

champion spinach as the source of Popeye's strength. Although Segar had introduced the idea in the strip, he didn't make much of it. (On Sunday, February 28, 1932, Popeye consumes a heaping bowl of the leafy stuff, and it gives him the strength to knock out an iron-jawed braggart. The day's episode concludes with a note from Popeye to mothers everywhere, which may have been the origin of the spinach mythology: "Please tell yer youngstirs I said they should eat spinach an' vegebles on account of I wants 'em to be strong and helthy.") Spinach figured more often in the strip's stories after the appearance of the animated Popeye, but the invigorating vegetable was seldom as integral to Popeye's success in the strip as it was in the Fleischer cartoons. And then there is Bluto. Popeye's constant nemesis in the cartoons, Bluto appeared only once in the comic strip—in the summer of 1932—and only long enough to fight Popeye and be defeated by him. (But the fight was an epic contest, lasting eleven days.)

Curiously enough, Popeye fights less often in the strip after the advent of his animated incarnation than before. Speculation has it that Hearst told Segar to tone down the violence of the strip. Judging from the strip itself, this advice was probably handed down to the cartoonist in early 1933. Certainly by, say, 1935, Popeye is a relatively docile character. In the summer of that year, Popeye builds an ark and voyages to a remote island where he establishes his own private nation, Spinachova. Come December, Popeye is at war with a neighboring country, Brutia. It's a comic war, with not much bloodshed. For Segar, it's an oddly nonviolent affair. Popeye bops a few of the Brutian soldiers, but there's something almost perfunctory about these brief encounters when compared to the marathon one-on-one scraps that Segar had once staged in the strip—brutal, bloody, sweaty, grunting struggles that went on for days and days and left the combatants ragged and bruised. In contrast, here Popeye wins Spinachova's war with Brutia by using his wits rather than his fists. Ironically, just as Segar had phased out much of the violence in the strip, the Fleischers started cashing in on precisely that aspect of Popeye's character—and that aspect alone. Meanwhile, in the comic strip, Segar was proving that his Popeye was the more complex and durable character, capable of provoking pathos as well as high comedy, of creating suspense without constant violence.

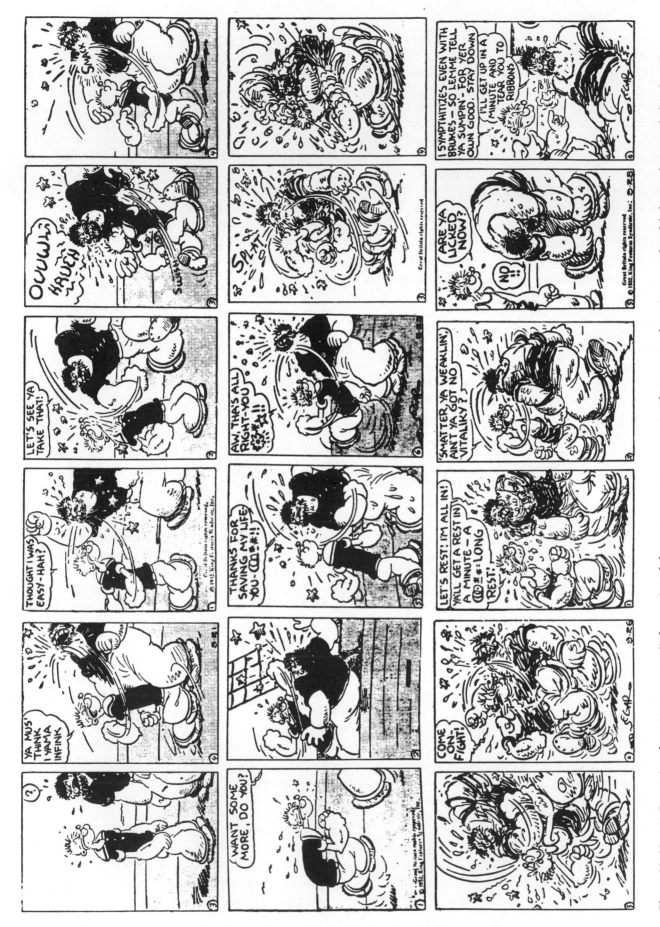

Figure 88. *Here in Popeye's only strip encounter (July 1932) with his motion picture nemesis, Bluto, we see how Segar rendered fights in the years before he was told to tone down the violence. This battle, however, was more spectacular than most. It lasted eleven days, for one thing—and with inexorable graphic logic, Segar's line steadily disintegrates as his fighters become tired and scarred by the scrap.*

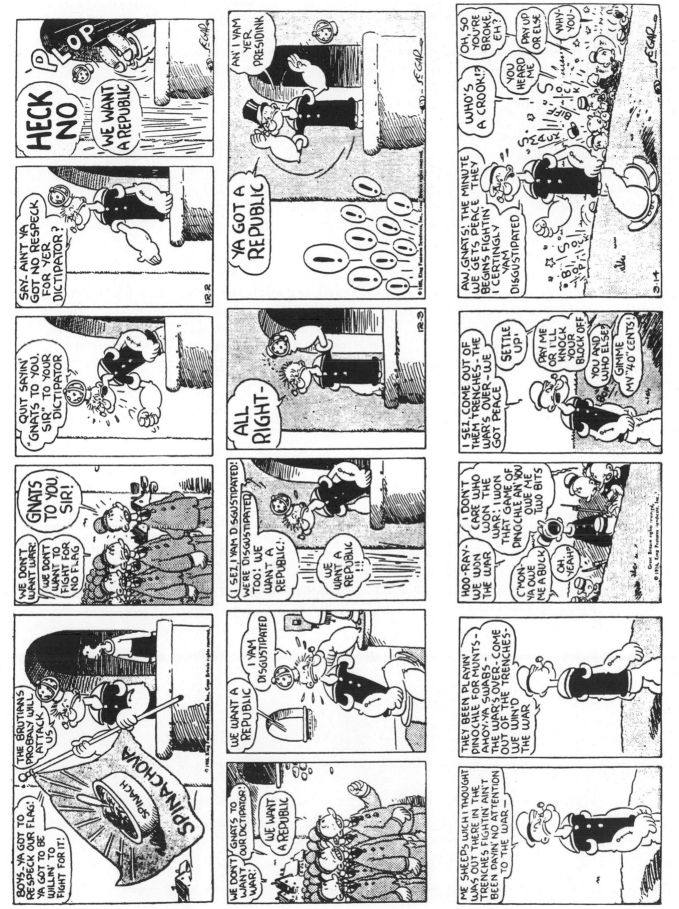

Figure 89. *Segar was more comfortable with social satire (bottom strip) than with outright political satire. While Popeye was ruler of his own country, though, Segar scored a point or two in the direction of FDR's regime (top two strips).*

The greatest differences between the screen and strip Popeyes, however, were in tone rather than substance. On the screen, Popeye was all action, and the visual excitement moved to the beat of the catchy theme song, "Popeye the Sailor Man," a happy little ditty the lyrics of which were punctuated by spritely tugboat whistles and toots. All this cheerful energy was well received by the Depression audience, but, as Leonard Maltin observes in his history of animated cartooning, "the Fleischer cartoons were out for one thing only—laughter."[9] And action, continual purposeful motion, was the means to this end, virtually the sole means. Segar, on the other hand, was a storyteller. He was interested in the twistings of plot and the nuances of character. He had a flair for the melodramatic, for the comedy of personality, and, on occasion, for satirical commentary of the gentle, jabbing sort. In the Spinachova sequence, for instance, Popeye converts his dictatorship to a republic by simply changing hats—and nothing else (figure 89). We must see this legerdemain as indicative of Segar's opinion of government in general, if not FDR's New Deal in particular. And all of this, as we have seen, Segar infused with a moral vision.

That vision embraces J. Wellington Wimpy as well as Popeye. Segar introduced Wimpy on March 31, 1931, as one of his Dickensian one-note characters, another of those obsessive personalities whose fixations he was able to parlay into a comic refrain of indefinite length. Wimpy is the perfect antithesis of heroism. In contrast to Popeye the selfless hero, Wimpy is self-interest personified; in him, selfishness transcends even the commonest

humanity. He is a craven coward, a traitorous friend to Popeye, a shiftless moocher whose placid determination is as elemental as Popeye's fundamental goodness. Segar etched Wimpy's shallow character in a series of unforgettably self-serving but comic one-liners that Wimpy delivered repeatedly: "I'll gladly pay you Tuesday for a hamburger today," "Come up to my place for a duck dinner; you bring the ducks," "Let's you and him fight," and so on. Wimpy is every bit as memorable a conception as Popeye, and as complementary fragments of Segar's caricature of man as hero, the comic duo completes the cartoonist's vision of the human condition.

To this vision, Segar added a lyric quality both comic and profound. We laugh at Popeye's mutilation of the language, at his hilarious mispronunciation of words. But in his unending struggle with this uniquely human attribute, language, we can see more than comedy. It is as if that elemental moral force were trying to come into being, to become articulate, to become human—to become, at last, effective. But Segar did more than embody in his sailor a fundamental truth about man's moral striving. He also made us laugh—at Popeye and at ourselves—as we kept the faith. (Indeed, laughter may be the best antidote against losing that faith.) We laugh at ourselves while laughing at Popeye for the simple reason that he represents so much in the American character. Strangely, the laughter does not belittle that which inspires it. Segar's comic genius resided, finally, in his ability to caricature the human condition without destroying our moral faith in humanity—our optimism about our own essential morality.

CHAPTER 10
Peddlers and Poets
The Lyric Clowns Who Captivated the Intelligentsia

Unabashedly commercial, comic strips have traditionally been a mass medium of the crassest sort. Introduced as circulation-building devices, comic strips were designed to appeal to the largest possible audience. They had to sell; therefore, they had to be popular. This coupling of imperatives is perhaps what makes comic strips so decidedly American. The comic strip was not invented in America, but the American way fostered the medium's rapid growth and development to an extent not achieved elsewhere. Propelled by the capitalistic impulses of the marketplace in free enterprise competition, the comic strip bloomed and flourished in a great variety of genres and styles. And despite its catchpenny function as commodity, the medium was capable of artistic achievements of a very high order. *Popeye*, as we've just seen, was such a creation—a complex expression of one man's artistic and moral sensibility. But *Popeye* was scarcely the only comic strip to qualify as high art.

That the crucible of commercial competition produced artistic as well as materialistic successes is beyond question. But it is the medium rather than the marketplace that is responsible. Comic strips are extraordinarily susceptible to individual creative impulse. A cartoonist is a kind of one-man band. Or, to employ a cinematic metaphor, a cartoonist is scriptwriter and story editor, casting director and camera operator, prop man and make-up artist, not to mention producer and director and actor and actress. Not all comics are produced by a single creative intelligence, but the medium readily permits such individual productions. And most of the greatest strips have been the expressions of a single creative vision, as unique with their creators as *Popeye* is with E. C. Segar. Among the most individual comic strip creations are the achievements of George Herriman and Walt Kelly.

These cartoonists are the lyric clowns of the medium. Their creations were bursts of poetry. Poetry in the literary tradition is a kind of word game: its great appeal lies in the sound and rhythm of the language and in the nuance and interplay of metaphor and meaning. Poetry is a game for the mind, an intellectual sport. And the creations of Herriman and Kelly—*Krazy Kat* and *Pogo*—are likewise divertissements for the mind. Their humor is intellectual rather than intestinal: we laugh in our heads not in our bellies.

In his 1924 book, *The Seven Lively Arts*, art critic Gilbert Seldes called Herriman's comic strip about an allegedly lunatic cat "the most amusing and fantastic and satisfying work of art produced in America today."[1] This accolade and the accompanying lengthy analysis of the strip by one of the foremost critics of the day gave social and artistic respectability for the first time to the erstwhile

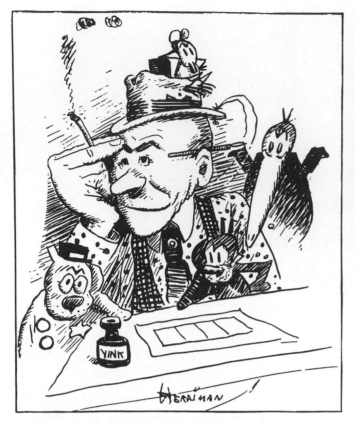

Figure 90. *George Herriman's self-portrait, done for* Judge *magazine, October 1922.*

"despised medium" of cartooning. It was Seldes who first analyzed the strip's plot and articulated Herriman's theme. Like any great work of art, *Krazy Kat*'s thematic complexity is masked by its seeming simplicity. The plot involves only three characters—a cat (Krazy), a mouse (Ignatz), and a dog (Offissa Pupp)—but each is doing something profoundly contrary to its nature. Instead of stalking the mouse, Krazy loves him and waits for him to assault her; instead of fearing the Kat, Ignatz scorns her (or him—Krazy is without sex, Herriman explained, like a sprite or elf)[2] and attacks her repeatedly; instead of chasing the Kat, the dog protects her out of love for her. This is Herriman's eternal triangle; and each of its participants is ignorant of the others' passions.

Into this equation, Herriman introduced a symbol: a brick. Ignatz despises Krazy and expresses his cynical disdain by throwing a brick at the androgynous Kat's head. Krazy, blind with love, awaits the arrival of the brick (indeed, pines for its advent) with joy because he/she considers the brick "a missil of affection." Meanwhile, the dog, motivated by inclination (his love for Krazy) as

well as occupation (he's an enforcer of law and order) tries to prevent the disorders that Ignatz attempts to perpetrate on Krazy's bean. Ironically, in seeking to protect the object of his affection from the assaults of the mouse, Offissa Pupp succeeds in making his beloved Krazy happy only when he fails to frustrate Ignatz's attack. Luckily, Offissa Pupp frequently fails in his mission; and Ignatz, perforce, succeeds. But it is Krazy who triumphs. As Seldes said: "The incurable romanticist, Krazy faints daily in full possession of his illusion, and Ignatz, stupidly hurling his brick, thinking to injure, fosters the illusion and keeps Krazy 'heppy.'" Hence, Herriman's theme: love always triumphs. And most of the time, it does so in the strip more by accident than by design.

Over the years, Herriman played out his theme in hundreds of variations, but there was always the Kat, the mouse, and the brick. And the brick usually found its way to Krazy's skull—much to the Kat's content (and often to Offissa Pupp's chagrin). The acclaimed lyricism of Herriman's strip arises partly from the seemingly endless reprise of this theme as Seldes first outlined it. But it arises, too, from the theme itself and Herriman's unique treatment of it.

For we are all of us lovers, seeking someone to love and to love us back—and fearing an unrequited outcome. That we should find humor in a comic strip about love that is requited more by accident than by intention is something of a wonder. True, there is some reassurance in the endless victories of love in *Krazy Kat*. But the accidental nature of so many of those triumphs cannot but undermine a little an overall impulse toward confidence. And hope. And yet we laugh. Perhaps because we are all of us lovers, and just a little krazy in konsequence. And so like Herriman's sprite, we persist in seeing only what we want to see.

By this circuitous route, Seldes's interpretation of Herriman's theme is embellished. *Krazy Kat* is not so much about the triumph of love as it is about the unquenchable will to love and to be loved. Love may not, in fact, always triumph; but we will always wish it would.

Herriman's paean to love began as a simple cat-and-mouse game in the basement of a strip called *The Family Upstairs*, which first appeared August 1, 1910. The strip had debuted under the title *The Dingbat Family* on June 20, 1910, but when the apartment-dwelling Dingbats developed an obses-

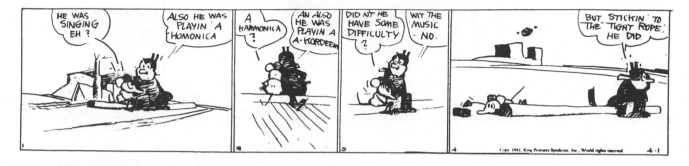

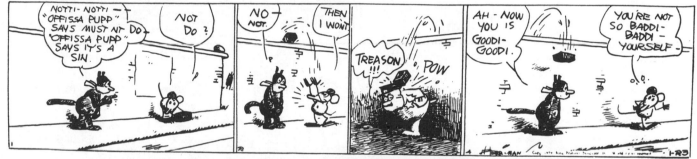

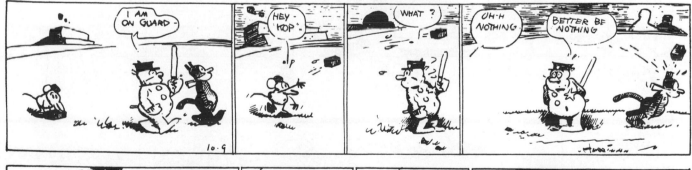

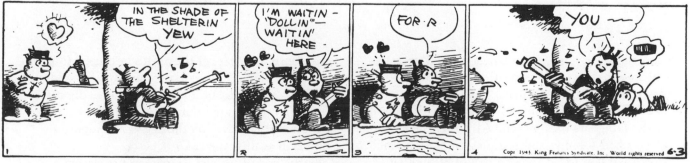

Figure 91. *Herriman's eternal triangle—Kat, mouse, dog. And the brick, which may have been used, after its initial introduction, as Ignatz's vaudevillian expression of exasperation at the Kat's latest foolishness, as in the top strip here, but which eventually came to symbolize love (to Krazy at least).*

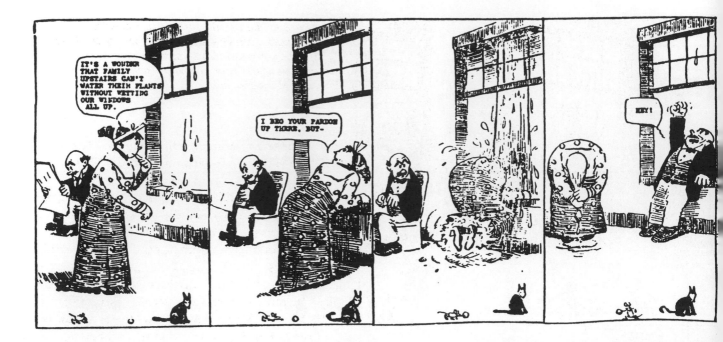

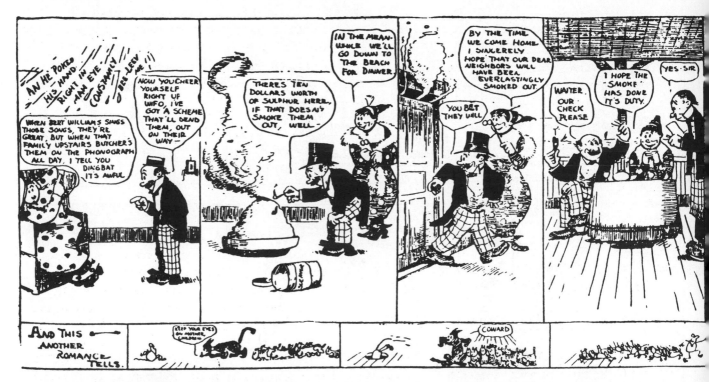

sion about the disruptive doings of their upstairs neighbors, the strip was retitled accordingly. Krazy first appeared as the Dingbat's cat. The spacious panels in which Herriman recorded the daily trials of the Dingbats in their feud with their neighbors always had some vacant space at the bottom, and Herriman developed the practice of filling that space with drawings of the antics of the cat (not yet Kat). Then, on July 26, a mouse appears and throws what might be a piece of brick at the cat. Thereafter, the drama that unfolds at the feet of the Dingbats focuses on the aggressive mouse's campaign against the cat.

By the end of August, Herriman had drawn a

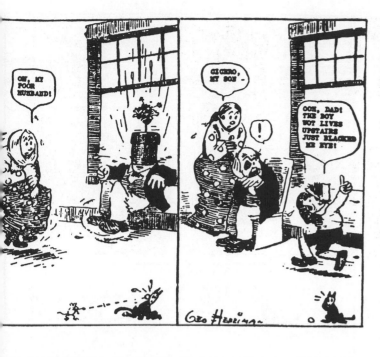

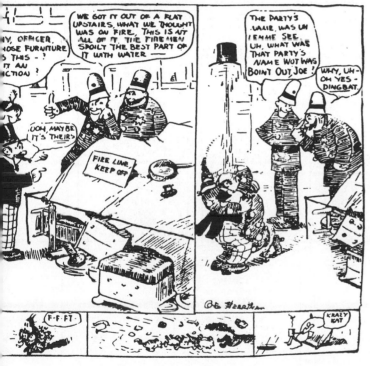

day's antics by christening his nemesis: "Krazy Kat," he growls, somewhat disgustedly. This exasperated utterance would become the strip's concluding refrain and, eventually, its title. But for the next two-and-a-half years, the Kat and the mouse carried on in their minuscule substrip without a title, and the mouse didn't acquire his name until the first days of 1911. On rare occasions, Ignatz and Krazy invaded the Dingbats' premises, taking over the more commodious panels upstairs for their daily turn while the baffled Dingbats looked on from below. But it wasn't until October 28, 1913, that they had a strip of their own.

The machinations of his eternal triangle (and the brick) preoccupied Herriman throughout *Krazy Kat*'s run. Most of the strips, whether daily or weekend installments, are stand-alone, gag-a-day productions. But on occasion, Herriman told continuing stories. Once Krazy was captivated by a visiting French poodle named Kisidee Kuku. And in 1936 Herriman conducted one of his longest continuities—a narrative opus chronicling the havoc wrought by Krazy's involvement with the world's most powerful catnip, "Tiger Tea." Mostly, however, the strip was a daily dose of Herriman's lyric comedy about love.

Herriman's graphic style—homely, scratchy penwork—remained unchanged through *Krazy Kat*'s run, but the cartoonist explored and exploited the format of his medium, exercising to its fullest his increasingly fanciful sense of design—particularly when drawing the Sunday *Krazy*. The first "Sunday" page appeared on Saturday, April 23, 1916, running in black and white in the weekend arts and drama section of Hearst's *New York Journal*; the full-page *Krazy* would not be printed in color until June 1, 1935. But with or without color, the full-page format stimulated Herriman's imagination, and for it he produced his most inventive strips—in both layout and theme, the latter often playfully determined by the former, as we shall see anon.

While the brick is the pivot in most of Herri-

line completely across the bottom of his strip, separating the cat and mouse game into a miniature strip of its own, a footnote feud paralleling the combat going on above. This tiny strip Herriman introduced with the prophetic caption: "And this," with an arrow pointing to the strip at the right, "another romance tells." The mouse ends that

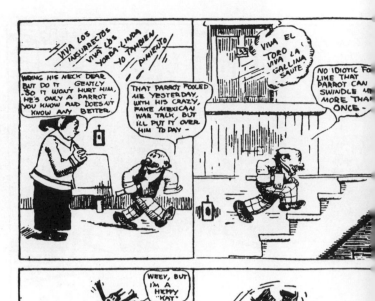

Figure 93. *By April of 1911 (top), Krazy and Ignatz were well established in the basement of* The Family Upstairs, *and the Kat's passion for the mouse (and the mouse's seeming detestation of the Kat) is likewise a fixture. This gave Herriman the theme around which he built another strip, Krazy Kat (here, two examples from 1918).*

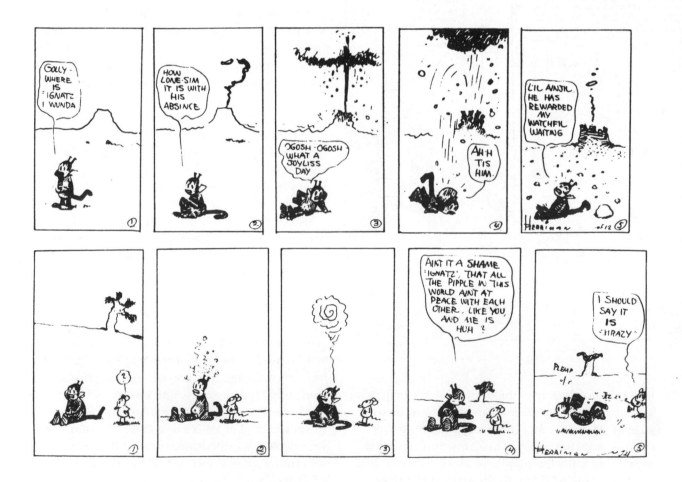

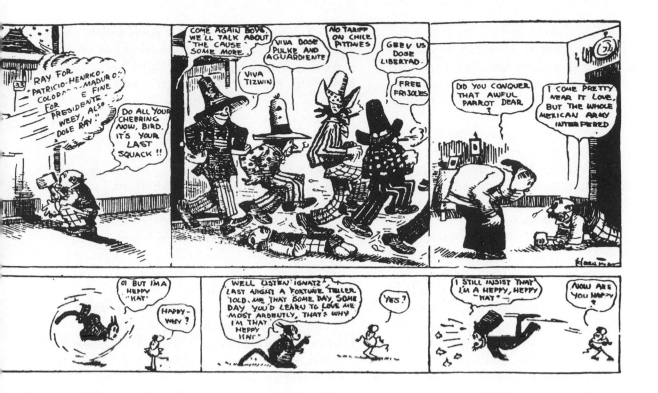

man's strips, the daily strips also reveal him playing with language and being self-conscious about
the nature of his medium. When Ignatz casually
observes that "the bird is on the wing," Krazy in-
vestigates and reports (in characteristic patois):
"From rissint obserwation, I should say that the
wing is on the bird." Another time, he is aston-
ished at bird seed—having believed all along that
birds came from eggs. In Krazy's literal interpretation of language there is an innocence at one with
his romantic illusion. When Ignatz is impressed by
a falling star, Krazy allows that "them that don't
fall" are more miraculous. Krazy's puns and wordplay were the initial excuse for Ignatz's assault by
brick: the mouse stoned the Kat to punish him/
her for what he considered a bad joke. From this
simple daily ritual, Herriman vaulted his strip into
metaphysical realms and immortality. More evidence of Herriman's playfulness resides in his characters' self-consciousness. They are frequently
fully aware of being in a comic strip. They often
take up pencils and draw parts of it, and then the
joke arises from blurring illusion and reality. More
metaphysics.

Appropriately enough, illusion and reality meet
in a dreamscape where the distinction between
them becomes forever lost, the perfect denouement for the topsy-turvy relationship among Herriman's trio of protagonists. Seldes drew attention to
the "shifting backgrounds" in *Krazy Kat*—to scenery that changes from mountain to forest to sea at
will, to suit Herriman's whim for varying his designs. Very early, in both daily and weekend editions, Herriman invested his strip with a dreamlike ambiance: evoking his favorite retreat, Monument Valley in the desert of southeastern Utah, he
created a surreal landscape of whimsical buttes
and cavorting cactuses that changed their shapes
and moved around from panel to panel as his characters capered before it, entirely oblivious to the
metamorphosis of their background. In the radiant
absurdity of this symbolic site, Herriman's lyricism was complete: setting and content were a
seamless whole, locale and refrain united in thematic reprise. Here, Herriman's dream becomes an
amiable reality.

No one can properly understand Herriman or
Krazy Kat, according to the authors of *Krazy Kat:
The Comic Art of George Herriman*, without
knowing something about Monument Valley with
its wind- and water-carved buttes of sculpted sand-
stone. Herriman's landscapes may seem irrational,
improbable, "but most of the backgrounds are realistic depictions of the rocky outcroppings and veg-
etation of the Valley. The perpetual metamorphosis
of Herriman's settings can, in part, be attributed to

the changing light playing over the huge rock formations. These sculptures, though unchanged for millennia, appear to alter in color and shape with each blink of the eye as they pick up every gradation of the rays of the sun, passing across the heavens from dawn to dusk."[3]

I'm not sure that familiarity with the actualities of Monument Valley is essential to an appreciation of *Krazy Kat*, but recognizing Herriman's fondness for the locale doubtless tells us something about the man. In addition to being a conglomeration of geological oddities, Monument Valley is a desert. Its landscape is parched and vast; its human population, sparse. Here, dwarfed by craggy monuments and isolated from the normal bustle of social enterprise, the solitude and insignificance of individual existence becomes a palpable thing. Baking in the desert sun, soaking up the peace and majesty of the place, and finding withal a kind of serenity, one can come to a great appreciation of the fellowship of humankind—perhaps to an understanding of the role of love in that fellowship.

Whether Herriman experienced precisely these feelings we cannot say, but he was clearly moved by the beauty of the area: "Those mesas and sunsets out in that ole pais pintado," he once wrote, "a taste of that stuff sinks you . . . deep too."[4] For twenty years he made an annual summer pilgrimage to Monument Valley, where he stayed in Kayenta with John and Louisa Wetherill, who had started a Navajo trading post there in 1910. Cartoonists James Swinnerton and Rudolph Dirks sometimes accompanied him. And they all painted landscapes a little (Herriman less than the other two). Perhaps it was, for Herriman, the idyllic end of a long odyssey that began in Louisiana.

Herriman was born in New Orleans in 1880, but he grew up in Los Angeles, where his family moved when he was about six years old. At seventeen he had his first drawing published in the *Los Angeles Herald*, and he subsequently was hired to work in the paper's engraving department. Drawing occasional cartoons for the paper whetted his appetite, and in 1900 he hopped a freight train to New York—then, as now, the Mecca for those who would be cartoonists. Unsuccessful at crashing into the big time upon his arrival, he found work as a barker for a Coney Island sideshow. And in his spare time, he drew and peddled cartoons to *Judge* and *Life*. He also sold "one shot" comic strips to various upstart syndicates—McClure, Philadelphia

North American, and Pulitzer's World Color Printing. In July 1902 Herriman returned to Los Angeles long enough to marry his childhood sweetheart, Mabel Lillian Bridge. In June 1903 he was hired as a staff artist by the *New York World*. The next year he left to work briefly for the *New York Daily News* before joining the art staff of Hearst's *New York American*.

In 1905 Herriman went back to Los Angeles again, where he created several short-lived features for the World Color Printing Company. Then in 1906 he began working for Hearst's *Los Angeles Examiner*. From there, Hearst beckoned him in 1910 back to New York and the comic art department of the *New York Journal*. For the next twelve years he worked in the paper's cartoon bull pen, where he rubbed shoulders and drawing boards with the comic art luminaries of the day—Tad Dorgan, Gus Mager, Harry Hershfield, Tom MacNamara, Winsor McCay, and George McManus, to name a few.

Like other cartoonists of the time, Herriman created numerous cartoon features, and, typically, most of them ran only a few weeks or months before their thematic possibilities were exhausted. For the Pulitzer papers he created *Musical Mose*, *Professor Otto and His Auto*, and *Acrobatic Archie* in 1902; *Two Jolly Jackies* in 1903; *Major Ozone's Fresh Air Crusade* in 1904; *Rosy Posy—Mama's Girl*, which ran from May 19 to September 15, 1906; *Alexander the Cat* (November 7, 1909–January 9, 1910); and *Daniel and Pansy* (November 21–28, 1910). For various papers he did *Home Sweet Home* (February and March 1904), *Bud Smith* (October and November 1905), *Grandma's Girl—Likewise Bud Smith* (November 26, 1905–May 12, 1906), *Mr. Proones the Plunger* (December 10–26, 1907, in the *Los Angeles Examiner* just about the time Bud Fisher took *A. Mutt* to Hearst's *San Francisco Examiner*), *Baron Mooch* (October 12–December 19, 1909), *Mary's Home from College* (December 1909), and *Gooseberry Sprigg* (December 23, 1909–January 24, 1910). Even after *Krazy Kat* was safely launched, Herriman kept coming up with other ideas. For twenty-two of the thirty-four years he drew *Krazy Kat*, Herriman was also producing another strip of one sort or another. *The Family Upstairs* (née *The Dingbat Family*) ran until January 1916. It was followed by *Baron Bean* (January 1916–January 1919), *Now Listen Mabel* (April–December 1919), *Stumble Inn*

(October 1922–January 1926, a Sunday strip for most of its run), *Us Husbands* (January–December 1926), and then *Embarrassing Moments* (or *Bernie Burns*), a panel (c. 1928–1932). Krazy claimed Herriman's exclusive attention only from 1932 on.

In 1922 Herriman moved his young family (wife and two daughters) back to Los Angeles for good. Several of his East Coast friends had moved to California by this time, and he enjoyed their company as well as that of the friends of his youth. He also liked the fellowship of people in the burgeoning motion picture industry. Two of his oldest friends—Tom MacNamara and Beanie Walker—were working for movie studios, and Herriman spent considerable time with Walker at the Hal Roach Studio, even occasionally drawing *Krazy Kat* strips while on the lot.

A mulatto, Herriman is the first person of color to achieve prominence in cartooning. (Although recognized for his talent by his peers and by the press and the public in a general way, his stature is largely a posthumous distinction. During his lifetime, Herriman's work was esteemed by intellectuals, but their high opinion of *Krazy Kat* did not translate into circulation: *Krazy Kat* appeared in very few newspapers, relatively speaking. Ron Goulart, in his *Encyclopedia of Comics*, says the strip never ran in more than forty-eight papers in this country. Half of them were doubtless in the Hearst chain, which numbered about two dozen at its peak. Hearst loved the strip and insisted that he would keep running it as long as Herriman wanted to do it, circulation notwithstanding.) Herriman is reported to have said he was Creole but of mixed blood. He was probably one of the "colored" Creoles who lived in New Orleans at the end of the nineteenth century—descendants of "free persons of color" who had intermarried with people of French, Spanish, and West Indian stock.

Herriman was clearly sensitive about his racial origins. He had kinky black hair and always wore a hat—indoors and out—probably to conceal the fact. By all accounts, he was self-effacing, shy, and extremely private. After the death of one of his daughters in 1939 (a mere five years after his wife of thirty-two years had died), Herriman became a virtual recluse, confining himself to the living room of his Spanish-style mansion in Hollywood, where he slept on a couch near his drawing board. He went out only to take his strips to the post office.

Herriman's race would be of no particular interest were it not for the peculiar manifestation he created for love in his strip: Krazy chooses to take an injury (a brick to the head) as symbolic of Ignatz's love for him/her, and Krazy is a black cat. While I would hate to see *Krazy Kat* converted by well-meaning critics and scholars into an allegory about race relations (it would then seem somehow less universal in its message, and we all need its reassurances, regardless of race), Herriman's sensitivity on the matter suggests an unconscious emotional source for his inspiration. He may not have been fully conscious of the kind of self-hatred that racial prejudice induces in persecuted minorities, but his subconscious knew. And on the murkier levels of the subconscious, self-hatred is associated with guilt, and guilt requires punishment. And thus the brick, erstwhile emblem of love, becomes the instrument of punishment. But not altogether: perhaps to Ralph Ellison's invisible man, even abuse is a form of acknowledgment and is therefore to be desired if all other forms fail to materialize.

African American scholars see other artifacts of life in black America in the strip. William W. Cook of Dartmouth College told me about the comedy of reversal that *Krazy Kat* seems to embody.[5] Among the characters that populated the vaudeville stage were comic racial stereotypes left over from the days of minstrelsy. A large imposing black woman and her diminutive no-good lazy husband comprised a traditional stage pair, the comedy arising from the woman's endless beratings of her husband and his ingenuity in evading the obligations she urges upon him. Noting Krazy's color and size relative to Ignatz, Cook sees the large black woman of the vaudeville stage in the Kat; and in the mouse, the wizened husband. In Herriman's vision, however, their vaudeville roles have been reversed: with every brick that reaches Krazy's skull, the browbeaten "husband" avenges himself for the years of abuse he suffered on stage. And Offissa Pupp is another vestige of the same vaudeville act: driven to distraction by her husband's derelictions, the scolding stage wife often concluded her rantings with the threat, "I'm gonna get the law on you."

But the strip's central ritual has a more obvious origin in another vaudeville routine. We saw it first in Bud Fisher's *Mutt and Jeff*. The pie-in-the-face punch line. Ignatz's brick-throwing belongs in

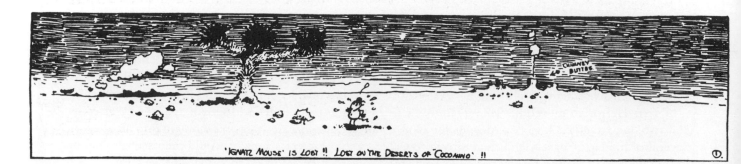

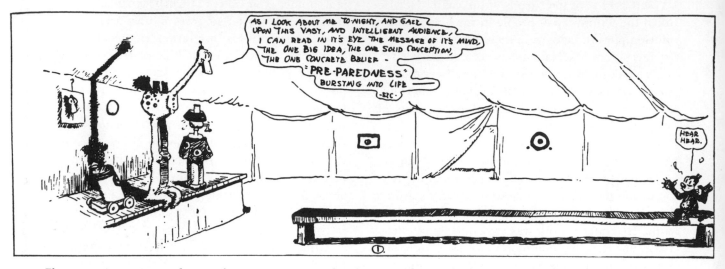

Figure 94. *Appearing at the top of two successive weekend pages (July 9 and July 16, 1916), these page-wide panels emphasize spaciousness.*

the same tradition. Krazy would say or do something silly or idiotically insightful, and Ignatz would react by braining him with a brick. It was a commonplace of comedy in those years (and to a large extent, it still is). But Herriman, as we've seen, gave the slapstick routine a metaphysical significance it never had on stage. This lyric lesson came about, I believe, through the cartoonist's impulse for visual comedy.

The Sunday or weekend full-page *Krazy Kat* is the flywheel of the strip's lyric dynamic. And it was on these pages that Herriman developed and embroidered the strip's overarching theme. By the time the weekend strip was launched, *Krazy* was five years old. In its daily version, the strip reprised its familiar vaudeville routine with an almost endless variety of nuance. The love that this routine obscurely symbolized had started to blossom in these daily strips, but when Herriman gained the expanded vistas of a full page upon which to work his magic, his grand but simple theme began to emerge in full flower. And before too long, the weekend strip was a page-long paean

to love—to its power, to our passionate and unwavering desire for its power to triumph over all.

I suspect that the gentle theme of love overran the weekend pages almost accidentally. Judging from the earliest pages themselves, Herriman's driving preoccupation was a playful desire to fill the comparatively vast space by humorously redesigning it—and while he was about it, he redesigned the form and function of comic strip art as well. Beginning with the first weekend page in 1916, we can watch Herriman as he started to experiment with the form of the medium. Antic layouts were not long in surfacing. On the very first page for April 23 he used irregularly shaped panels, and by June some panels were a page wide. In July he sometimes dropped panel borders and sometimes used circular panels instead of rectangles; by August he was mixing all these devices. And by the end of October his graphic imagination was shaping the gags: layout sometimes determined punch line or vice versa, as page design became functional as well as fanciful.

On the page for July 9, 1916, page-wide panels

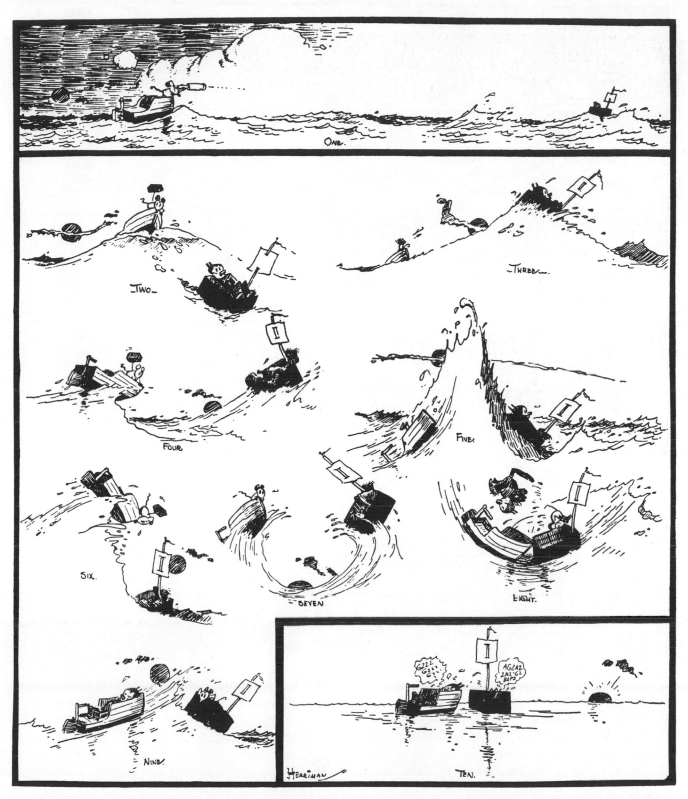

Figure 95. *Herriman discarded conventional panel borders if he thought he could improve his story by doing so.*

emphasize the vastness of the desert setting (figure 94). The opening panel the next week likewise runs across a whole page by way of dramatizing a gag: a fatuous ostrich performer on stage addresses his "vast and intelligent audience," which consists solely of Krazy, whose solitude and inconsequence, in comic contrast to the ostrich's remarks, is made hilariously plain by the emptiness that stretches all around him. On September 3 Herriman sets the scene for an adventure at sea with a page-wide

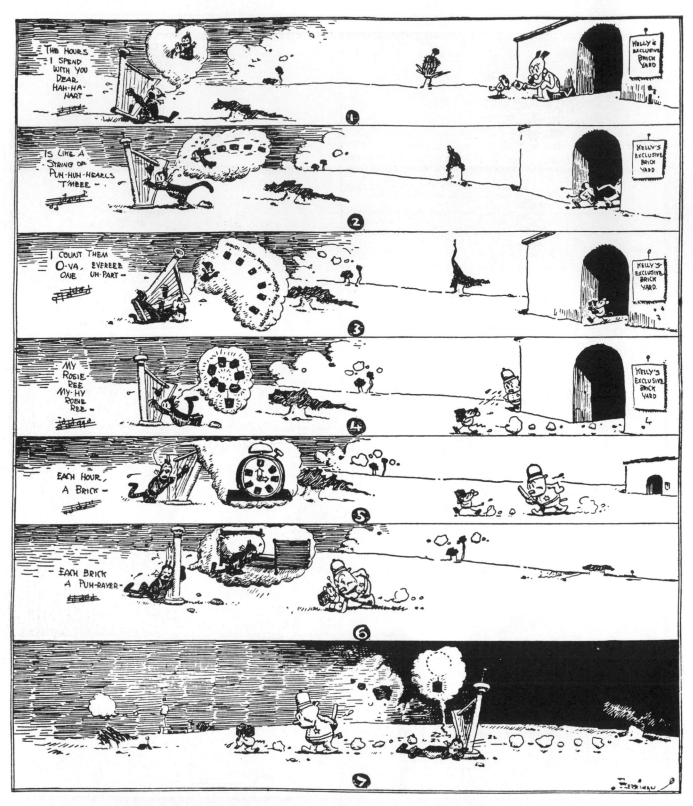

Figure 96. *Page-wide panels here permit Herriman to relate two "stories," the one at the right in ironic counterpoint to the one at the left.*

panel suggesting the vast and vacant reaches of an ocean. Panel borders disappear for much of the page in order to give emphasis to the unruly waves that toss Krazy and Ignatz about; then, for the conclusion, the panel borders frame a scene in which the sea has grown calm (figure 95). On October 15 the entire strip consists of page-wide panels (figure 96), a maneuver that permits Herriman

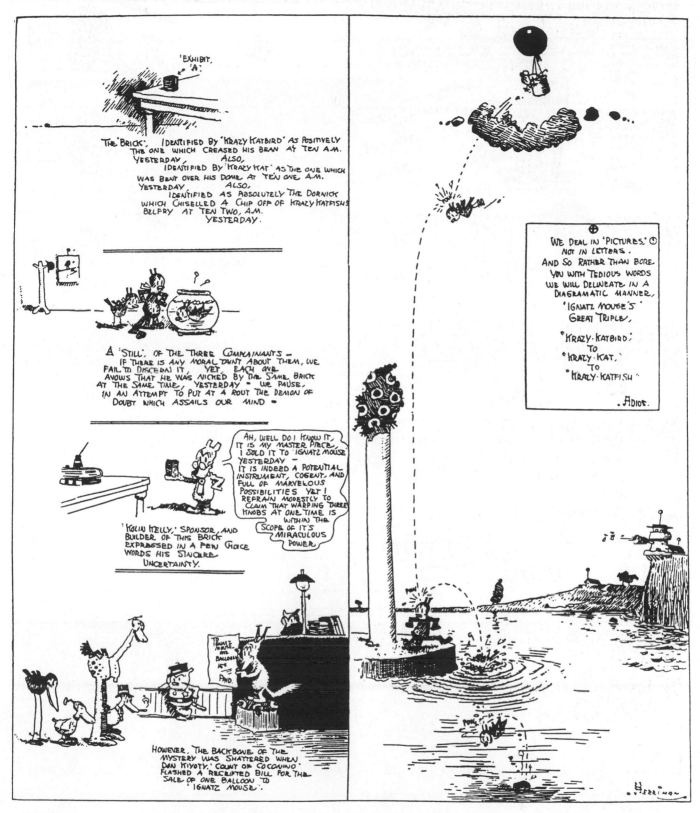

Figure 97. *How can a single brick bean a katbird, Krazy, and a katfish? The panel at the right shows how.*

to tell one story about Krazy at the left of each panel while unfolding an ironic comedy in counterpoint at the right. The humor arises from the simultaneity of the actions, the depiction of which is made possible solely by the layout of page-wide panels.

On May 6, 1917, a top-to-bottom vertical panel on the right-hand side of the page gives the comic

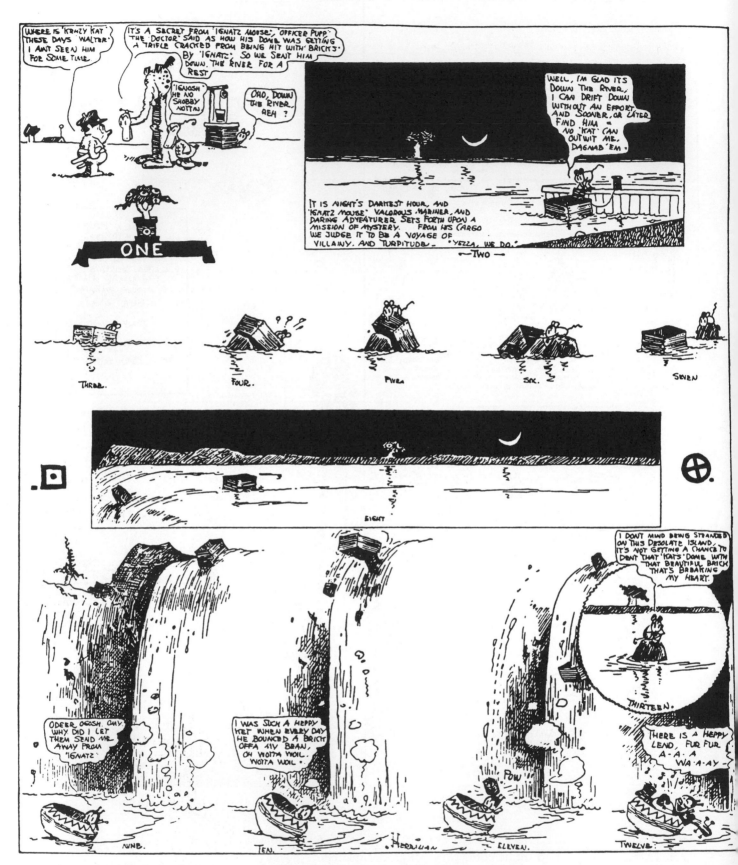

Figure 98. *Once again, Herriman uses the layout of his page to tell the joke.*

explanation for the "mystery" outlined in the panels on the left: how could a single brick from Ignatz bean a katbird, Krazy, and a katfish? The vertical panel allows Herriman to explain (figure 97). The next week, layout also contributes to the comedy. The bottom third of the page is a series of images large enough to show Krazy bemoaning his banishment from Ignatz at the bottom of the drawings while simultaneously, at the top of each drawing, the usual symbol of the mouse's regard is being launched in the Kat's direction by forces over which neither Kat nor mouse has any control (figure 98).

That the stories Herriman told on Sundays focused on love is largely incidental. Love is the storyteller's stock-in-trade. Love insinuates itself into most human dramas: in many ways, all stories are love stories. Love stories find their way into virtually every other kind of tale. They fit readily into any narrative setting. War stories have love stories as subplots; so do Westerns and whodunits and every other kind of narrative. The theme of love is universal enough to furnish a focus for any story. Herriman's sense of graphic play needed a narrative focal point; love was the most easily understood and adaptable organizing device at hand. Herriman seized it, and, by making it central to an endless comic refrain, he made poetry.

On the weekend pages, Herriman found room to indulge and develop his fantasy—his visual playfulness, his inventiveness. His poetry. Here, then, the quintessential *Krazy Kat* bloomed and ran riot.

And because the daily strips echoed the refrain, the lyricism of the theme permeated Herriman's week, giving us one of the masterworks of the medium.

But these are the maunderings of the critical faculty. For the readers (and lovers) we all are, it is probably enough to know that regardless of the source of Herriman's inspiration, his Kat, the embodiment of love willed into being, is a comfort to us all—a balm of wisdom wrapped in laughter. Herriman was not only shy: he was, according to those who knew him, also saintly. And so was his strip. Herriman died on April 25, 1944, and his strip, too idiosyncratic for another to continue, ceased with the Sunday page for June 25. But in soaring into metaphysical realms, *Krazy Kat* had long since achieved immortality.

Krazy Kat was comic strip art at its most profoundly poetic. But in Walt Kelly's great *Pogo*, the comic strip achieved the maximum of which the medium is capable, a zenith of high art. If we accept the definition of comic strip art as a narrative of words and pictures, both verbal and visual, in which neither words nor pictures are quite satisfactory alone without the other, then we must say that Kelly welded the verbal and visual elements together into a comic chorus so unified, so mutually dependent, that it crystalized forever the very essence of the art.

For those who aren't acquainted with *Pogo*, it's scarcely enough to describe the strip as an "animal strip" set in a southern swamp. In Kelly's hands,

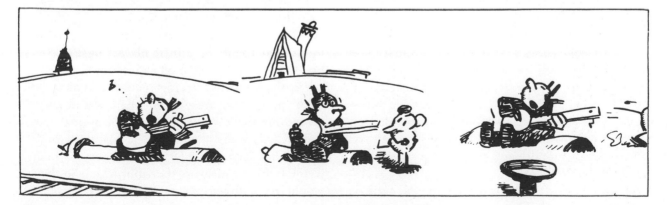

Figure 99. *Herriman's last strip, left unfinished on his drawing board, April 1944. Or is it unfinished? Even without words, the pictures convey a message: Krazy's song (the strip's poetry) seems destined to continue regardless of the comings and goings of Ignatz (and even, perhaps, Herriman). Herriman's parting behest? With metaphysical poets, you never can tell.*

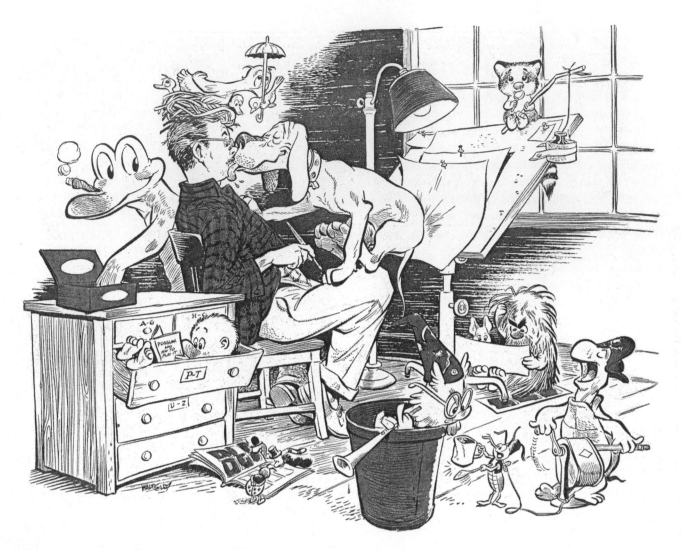

Figure 100. *An early (1950) self-portrait by Walt Kelly in which he depicts himself surrounded by the six principals of his strip (clockwise, beginning with the bureau drawer): Pogo, Albert, Kelly himself, Houn'dog, Porkypine, Churchy Lafemme, and Howland Owl.*

the strip reached above and beyond the animal strip tradition (as continued in such strips as *Bugs Bunny* and *Donald Duck*—even in *Animal Crackers*). At its core, Kelly's strip was a reincarnation of vaudeville, its routines often laced with humor that derived from pure slapstick. To that, Kelly added the remarkably fanciful and inventive language of his characters—a "southern fried" dialect that lent itself readily to his characters' propensity to take things literally and permitted a shameless delight in puns.

An animal strip, yes, but Kelly's animals were more than animals. They were perfectly content being animals, you understand, but sometimes on an otherwise idle summer's afternoon they would (for their own amusement) try out for roles as hu-

man beings. They'd wander backstage at the human drama, picking up a script here, a bit of costume there, and then assemble after hours before the footlights for a little playacting. But somehow it never quite came off as intended.

We, the human spectators, could recognize some of the parts being assayed, but there was always something vaguely out of kilter. The animal actors had picked up the jargon and the costumes, but they didn't seem to understand the purpose in any of the human endeavors they mimicked. So they would make up reasons, rationales, as they went along—discarding perfectly sound, human reasons for everything they did in favor of those of their own invention. Sometimes, to derive purposes that made sense to them, they attached meaning and

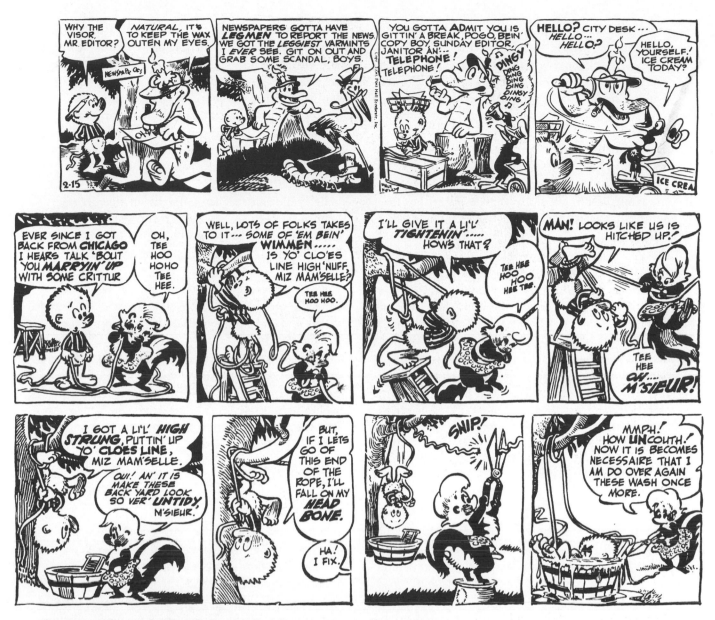

Figure 101. *The vaudevillian bent of Kelly's humor is amply displayed here.*

significance to words taken literally, rather than to the ideas the words represented. Adrift in misunderstood figures of speech, mistaken identities, and double entendres going off in all directions at once, Kelly's creatures wandered further and further from what appeared to have been their original intentions.

One thing led to another by free association leapfrog: it made a wonderful kind of logic all its own, but it left motivation in tatters somewhere along the way. An episode in the fall of 1950 began with the swamp's wholesale courtship of a skunk that turned into a brief panic about sea serpents

that became a migration west that subjected everyone momentarily to the ministrations of the resident con man that resulted, finally, in a cow taking work as a cat.

But you had to be there: it loses a lot in the telling.

Easily distracted (even from the scripts they'd apparently undertaken), the residents of Kelly's swamp needed almost no encouragement to abandon the human roles they'd taken up so lightly in order to bask in the friendly glow of a fish fry and perloo. In the fellowship of the feasting, the animals regained their good and common sense:

concentrating upon the meat-and-potatoes of existence presumably regenerated them, after the strain of behaving nonsensically like humans. And that was the trick of Kelly's social satire: we couldn't help but glimpse ourselves in his menage—looking just as silly as we often are. But if the animals knew we were silly, they didn't often let on. They, after all, didn't take life as seriously as we: "It ain't nohow permanent," as Kelly—or was it Porkypine?—used to say. All of this is funny enough in itself, but Kelly went even further in honing the satirical cutting edge of his humor.

In 1952, three years after the national syndication of *Pogo* began, Kelly ran Pogo for president against Dwight Eisenhower and Adlai Stevenson. Pogo lost (as you may have noticed), but the popularity of his campaign showed Kelly that the time was ripe to enter a whole new field of comedy. "It was the sort of period," Kelly wrote, "in which the naive boy cartoonist began to examine the gift horse's feet. He looked to see if they were straw or clay. . . . Crime investigations, a political campaign directed by PR men, real and fancied traitors in government . . . made the believer count all his beads to see if a few had stuck to the pot. I finally came to understand that if I were looking for comic material, I would not ever have to look long. We people manufacture it every day in a hundred ways. The news of the day would be good enough. Perhaps the complexion of the strip changed a little in that direction after 1951. After all, it is pretty hard to walk past an unguarded gold mine and remain empty-handed."[6]

Before long, the double meaning of the puns in the strip took on political as well as social implications, and the vaudeville routines frequently looked suspiciously like animals imitating people high in government. Just so we wouldn't miss the point, Kelly underscored his satirical intent with caricature: his animals had plastic features that seemed to change before our very eyes until they resembled those at whom the satire was directed. And the species suggested something about Kelly's opinions of his targets. Khrushchev showed up one time as a pig; Castro, as a goat. And Spiro Agnew appeared as a uniformed hyena; J. Edgar Hoover, as a bulldog. One consequence of this technique was that the verbal and the visual, the words and the pictures, were perfectly, inseparably, wedded—a supreme achievement in the art of the comic strip.

"No cartoonist had more gifts than Walt Kelly," Jules Feiffer once wrote. "He drew like a dream and wrote better. And imagined even better than he wrote. *Pogo's* swamp was less a metaphor for our world than our world was a metaphor for *Pogo's* swamp; our reality, our attitudes, our excesses humanized, made tolerable by Kelly's poking fun at them. Kelly, among the most angry of satirists, was also the most benign, the most jovial, the most affectionate."[7]

Kelly did not reach the heights of this artistic achievement overnight. He grew up to it, leafing into full foliage in the midst of that long summer afternoon that was the Eisenhower fifties. The seeds were sown in Kelly's youthful enterprises in the newspapering game while in high school, in his apprenticeship at the Walt Disney Studios, and in his journeyman labors for the burgeoning comic book industry.

Kelly grew up in Bridgeport, Connecticut, and shortly after graduating from high school in 1930 he worked for a year or so at the *Bridgeport Post*, where he did reporting as well as some artwork. (Kelly was always proud of his experience as a newspaperman, and throughout his life his closest friends were journalists: he sought and enjoyed the fellowship of newspapermen and spent most of his recreational hours in their company.) By the mid-thirties he had held a few other nondescript jobs, and he had fallen in love with Helen DeLacy, who worked for the Girl Scout Council in Bridgeport. Perhaps desperate to give himself one more crack at an artistic career before settling down to the sort of steady employment that would support a wife and family, Kelly went to New York, where, he said, he "starved quietly" for several months. He also did some drawing for various comic books. But in late 1935 Helen was transferred to Los Angeles, and Kelly packed up and followed her.

If you were a cartoonist on the West Coast in the Great Depression, chances are you worked for the Mouse Factory. On January 6, 1936, Kelly joined the growing staff at the Disney Studios, working in the story department at first, then in animation. Although his later work carries none of the earmarks of the Disney style, he couldn't help but pick up valuable skills and concepts by going through the rigorous and exacting Disney training program. Disney animators learned their craft through a technique called "action analysis." De-

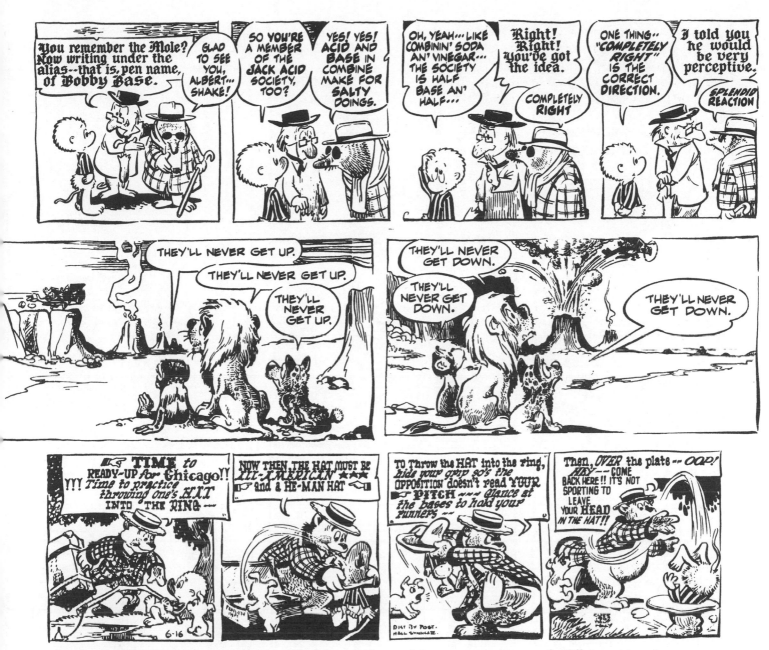

Figure 102. *Kelly littered* Pogo *with puns and other word play. And the puns sometimes made Kelly's satiric points, as in the top strip here—from the sequence about the Jack Acid Society (a group of "America firsters" whose very name tipped Kelly's hand). And when the characters weren't punning, they were taking language literally, as when the political bear, P. T. Bridgeport, runs Pogo for president.*

veloped by Don Graham, an instructor at the Chouinard Art School in Los Angeles, action analysis required animators to observe a model executing a complete movement and then to sketch from memory, creating an *impression* of the movement rather than duplicating the movement in photographic detail.[8] The technique suited exactly Disney's own notions about what animation should be. Exaggeration was important in animation, he believed, and in capturing the impression of movement, animators were dealing in a species of exaggeration. Under the Disney tutelage, animators also learned the importance of balance to a body in motion, the ways that folds in clothing are formed by anatomical stretch points, and how to give weight—physical presence—to their characters. Hank Ketcham, who was at Disney when Kelly was there and worked with him, gives the "Univer-

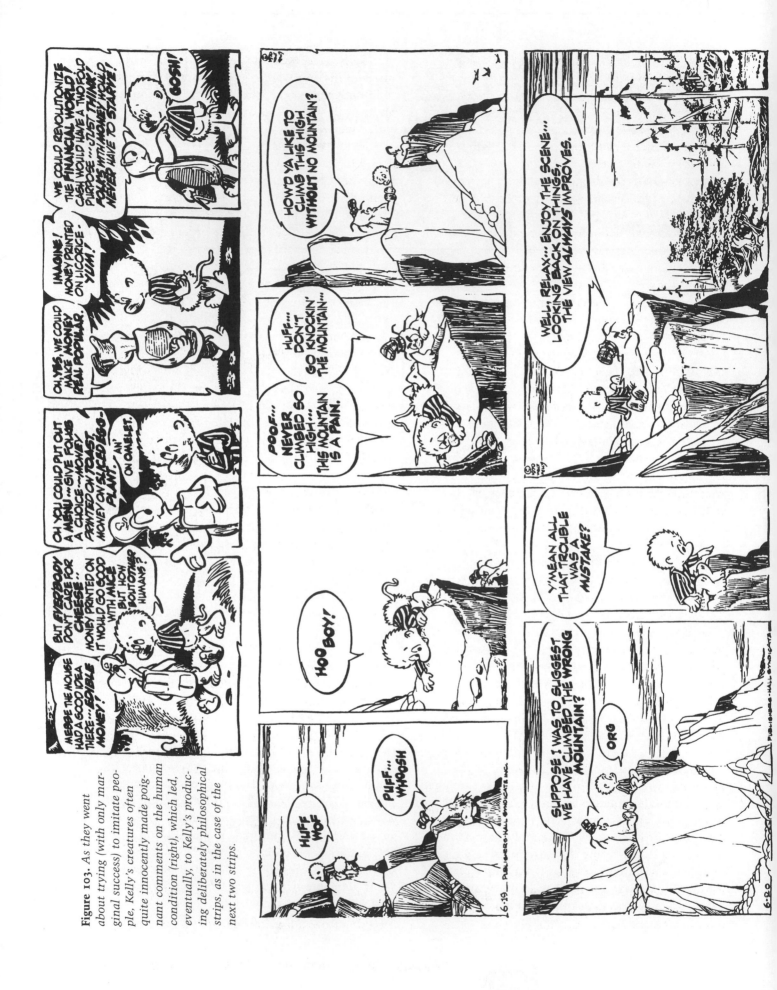

Figure 103. As they went about trying (with only marginal success) to imitate people, Kelly's creatures often quite innocently made poignant comments on the human condition (right), which led, eventually, to Kelly's producing deliberately philosophical strips, as in the case of the next two strips.

sity of Walt Disney" as his alma mater.[9] Kelly could say the same.

Despite the fellowship of cartoonists and the challenges of the work, Kelly was not happy at Disney. Animated cartooning is assembly-line work: the final product is the result of hundreds of contributions by others. Cartoonists who work in animation suppress their personalities and styles in order to produce the standard product. And this was not the sort of work Kelly was suited for. He was undoubtedly looking for some excuse to escape when the notorious labor dispute erupted in the spring of 1941. Kelly, who had friends on both sides of the picket line, took a leave of absence to attend to "family problems" (his sister was ill) and was back east in a few days. Helen followed, and Kelly never returned to Disney.

After moving frequently into various homes in the vicinity of Bridgeport, the Kellys settled in Darien, from whence Walt made forays into New York City to find work. Not much identifiable Kelly artwork has surfaced from this period. Eventually, according to Helen, Walt Disney helped Kelly find work at the Western Printing and Lithographing Company, where Disney and Dell comic books were produced. But the first comic book work that's clearly Kelly's didn't get into print until late 1942, so it's likely he foraged on his own for some ten to twelve months before he landed with Oskar Lebeck, drawing for the first issue of *Animal Comics*. For historians of cartooning, it was a historic moment: on the pages of this comic book Kelly limned Pogo Possum for the first time.

But Pogo was not yet a star player. He appeared first in a story starring a voracious alligator named Albert; Pogo was, Kelly said, "a sort of Jeff to Albert's Mutt." Not even that. Albert has the title role and plays a pivotal part in the story, but his principal second is a black kid named Bumbazine. Although Bumbazine is billed as Albert's costar in the next three stories, it is clear that Kelly's imagination was on the side of the animals in his cast: he gave them all the best lines. Bumbazine is less and less a presence in the stories, and by early 1945 he has faded away entirely. Kelly said he dropped the character "because, being human, he was not as believable as the animals."[10] Some historians have speculated about possible racial causes for Bumbazine's disappearance. While it would be foolish to discount this reasoning, it is more likely that Bumbazine simply failed to en-

gage Kelly's creative energies. Fascinated by the antics of his animals, Kelly concentrated on them, and Bumbazine was gradually nudged off the stage. And by mid-1945 Pogo was given equal billing with Albert.

Most of the regulars in the Pogo cast first appeared in the pages of *Animal Comics*, although frequently they are not called by the names they would later make famous in the newspaper funnies. The comic book was aimed at children, and so are Kelly's stories, but he nonetheless sometimes touched chords that could resonate only in adult readers (presumably reading to their offspring). And many of the themes that Kelly introduced in the comic book he would return to in the strip.

Kelly worked in comic books for most of the decade, creating material for several Dell titles, including *Walt Disney's Comics and Stories*. He also renewed his friendship with an old *Bridgeport Post* chum, Niles White von Wettberg, who introduced him to John Horn, a fellow *Newsweek* staffer. Childhood illnesses had rendered all three men ineligible for military service, and they had much else in common: they shared a passion for newspapering, and they loved to talk politics in bars. For the next twenty years, the three of them had lunch together at least once a week in one or another of Manhattan's most convivial saloons. Through his friendship with Horn, Kelly met the editor of the fledgling *New York Star*, George Wells, who invited the cartoonist to be art director of the paper when it began publication in the summer of 1948.

The *New York Star* was what was left of a journalist's beatific dream, a reincarnation of *PM*, a newspaper founded to publish the truth as its staff saw it (not as it was seen by advertisers). When the *Star* folded after a meteoric seven-month run, the *New Yorker* said of it that it had been the "semi-official outlet of advanced liberal thought" put out by "a staff of indefatigable crusaders." Kelly was at home at the *Star*. And he was an inexhaustible worker. He did all the artwork for the paper—all the column headings and decorations and the political cartoons. And in late September, having decided the paper needed a comic strip, he resurrected the swampland characters he'd been doing for *Animal Comics*. Pogo made his newspaper debut on October 4, 1948.

By this time the feature's cast had taken fairly

definite shape in Kelly's mind. Pogo was now the uncontested title character. According to Selby Kelly (Walt's third and last wife) and Steve Thompson, Pogo is "the friendly ideal we like to imagine ourselves to be." They go on to describe Pogo as "gentle, unassuming, level-headed, intelligent but not brainy, honest, forthright . . . the touchstone that keeps the swamp on an even keel. He can always be counted on to straighten out confusions, solve misunderstandings, organize the fish fry and keep a full pantry for everyone to borrow from."[11] A rather bland personality, he is the neutral center around which the other characters revolve.

Albert, no longer the titular star, frequently assumes that role by virtue of a transcendent ego. He thinks he's Pogo's best friend and, as Kelly and Thompson say, "will do Pogo good whether Pogo wants it or not." Because Albert sees himself in a heroic mold, he takes the center of the stage whenever the opportunity arises. His great redeeming trait is that he sometimes deserves that spotlight. Porky the porcupine is a suitably prickly personality—a sourpuss and a cynic, as Kelly and Thompson observe; but his show of cynicism masks a compassionate heart. Howland Owl is the ostensible brains of the strip; clever in a cunning, self-serving way, he foments plans and plots, and he therefore initiates many of the characters' activities. The turtle, Churchy Lafemme, plays the good-natured dupe in many of Owl's schemes. And Beauregard Bugleboy the Bloodhound is full of himself and his tradition—"the noble dog," he often intones, referring, naturally, to himself. Over the years, Kelly would increase his cast by hundreds (not counting a host of unnamed bugs and birds and bunny rabbits), but these six were his principal players.

The strip accompanied the *Star* through the remaining weeks of its fated life, ceasing with the paper's last issue on January 28, 1949. But the brief four-month run had convinced Kelly that what he wanted to do was to draw a comic strip. For the next several weeks he made the rounds of the syndicate offices in New York, finally selling *Pogo* to Post-Hall, which launched the strip anew on May 16.

At first, the strip was much the same as it had been in *Animal Comics* and in the *Star*, a slapstick comedy with animals imitating humans in their various enterprises. The satire was on broad societal matters rather than specific political issues. But after a year or so, Kelly could no longer restrain himself. That gold mine of political foibles beckoned irresistibly.

For Kelly's first foray into the jungle of politics with caricature as his machete, the prey was Senator Joseph R. McCarthy. McCarthy, as every schoolboy knows, gained notoriety by attempting to ferret out Communists in high places between 1950 and 1955. It was the age of the "Red Menace," when many Americans feared that our institutions would crumble and fall owing to the secret maneuverings of Soviet agents working within the United States. McCarthy, a graceless freebooter with a gift for self-promotion, saw the issue as the means by which he could gain reputation enough to be reelected when he ran again in 1952. He began by waving sheets of paper that, he alleged, were lists of card-carrying Communists working in the State Department. When officials questioned his allegations, McCarthy countered by questioning their loyalty: they were either Communists themselves, he would insinuate, or unwitting tools of Communists.

To purge the government of Reds, Congress launched a series of investigations, and McCarthy put himself conspicuously at the head of the probe. "McCarthyism" was the name given to the Senator's mode of operation, a method founded on a basic disregard for the truth. He determined guilt by association, half-truth, and innuendo, and deployed reckless accusation, equivocation, and outright lying, not to mention smearing, character assassination, and—once he was thoroughly launched on his course—intimidation. It was name-calling raised to the *n*th degree. McCarthy didn't invent McCarthyism (which, as you may have noticed, is still being practiced today): he merely personified it. Much of the information upon which McCarthy based his charges eventually proved to be faulty, but "eventually" was a long time in coming, and in the interim McCarthy achieved his objective: he became a national figure. He proved a master at manipulating the news media: he'd call a press conference to announce that he planned a press conference for the next day, and the newspaper headlines would obligingly scream, "McCarthy Calls Press Conference Tomorrow."

To many, McCarthy was a hero. He inspired a vociferous following of millions. And as others took up his cause and techniques, reputations and livelihoods were destroyed with little or no regard for feelings or facts. McCarthyism infected the nation. The senator was so popular that other politicians, however much they disapproved of the man's methods, were reluctant to voice their disapproval because that might make them appear "soft on Communism," and they might in consequence lose their next contest at the polls. And McCarthy was a power to be feared in every walk of life, whether political or not: many of his nonpolitical critics didn't speak out—didn't label him as the posturing publicity hound and fraud that he was—for fear he'd name them on his next list of Communist conspirators.

Many newspapers attacked McCarthy on their editorial pages (while awarding him space on their front pages), but nationally prominent figures (for instance, President Eisenhower) were slow in rising to the challenge. Washington's celebrated muckraker, Drew Pearson, fired a shot or two, whereupon McCarthy rounded on him, insinuating that Pearson was a tool of Moscow and advising people not to buy the hats manufactured by the sponsor of Pearson's radio program, the Adam Hat Company. Pearson wasn't silenced, but he lost his sponsor, who chose not to risk a boycott led by the powerful senator.

Television journalists were curiously silent. Although television was still in its infancy in those days, it was already regarded as a powerful medium. Its audiovisual impact was immediate and persuasive, but its ability to air complex issues thoroughly and fairly was (and still is) suspect. So broadcasters were inclined to stick to the barest of facts—and the evil McCarthy's critics saw in his method did not lend itself readily to the kind of objective treatment that TV newsmen aspired to. Finally, Edward R. Murrow, the patron saint of CBS News and one of the most prestigious journalists in the world, attacked McCarthy early in 1954 on his highly regarded "See It Now" program. Murrow's exposé consisted of film clips of McCarthy, carefully selected to show the man condemning himself in his own words and actions. Some said it was as artfully constructed of half-truths as anything McCarthy did. But, given McCarthy's power, there's no denying that Murrow showed moral courage, thereby securing his honorable spot in the history of American journalism.

The purpose of this digression is to put Kelly's assault on McCarthy in its proper historical context: Kelly did his number on McCarthy almost a year before Murrow's acclaimed broadcast.

Editorial cartoonists (led by Herblock) had skewered McCarthy regularly once the senator became well known. But syndicated comic strips in those days were still relatively free of political satire. Al Capp made fun of the rigid right, but no one named names. Kelly changed that. And as a cartoonist satirizing a national figure of McCarthy's power in a syndicated strip at the height of the senator's popularity, Kelly ran a greater risk than Murrow (who, taking the public pulse before taking on McCarthy, waited until McCarthy had almost hung himself before coming in to help with the noose). Newspaper editors are notoriously fickle about the features in their papers. They listen to their readers with fear and trembling. Keeping readers happy keeps circulation steady; ditto editors' incomes. And it doesn't take many readers objecting to a syndicated feature to convince an editor that he risks losing circulation by continuing to run anything controversial. Syndicated features, aiming assiduously for well-nigh universal acceptance—the greatest possible appeal—are consequently inclined to be studies in the most unobjectionable social fodder imaginable. And McCarthy was still a national hero to huge segments of the populace in the summer of 1953 when Kelly launched his attack. Substantial numbers of readers could have objected to Kelly's satire; scores doubtless did. The cartoonist, scarcely Murrow's equal yet as a mover and shaker, was thus risking his very livelihood. To their everlasting credit, most editors stuck with him. But Kelly could not have known they would when he started; in fact, all the evidence of newspaper history would presumably have convinced him that they would desert him in droves. The McCarthy sequence in *Pogo* is therefore a ringing testament to the cartoonist's courage.

To create a narrative metaphor for McCarthy's commie hunt, Kelly turned to the swamp's Bird Watchers Club under the leadership of Deacon Mushrat. The Deacon is first joined by Mole MacCarony, who, despite his handicap (he can barely see), begins a program to purify the swamp of all germs. He then moves to rid the swamp of all "impurities," all "migratory birds"—that is, foreigners—but because he can't see well enough to identify his victims, it isn't long before every-

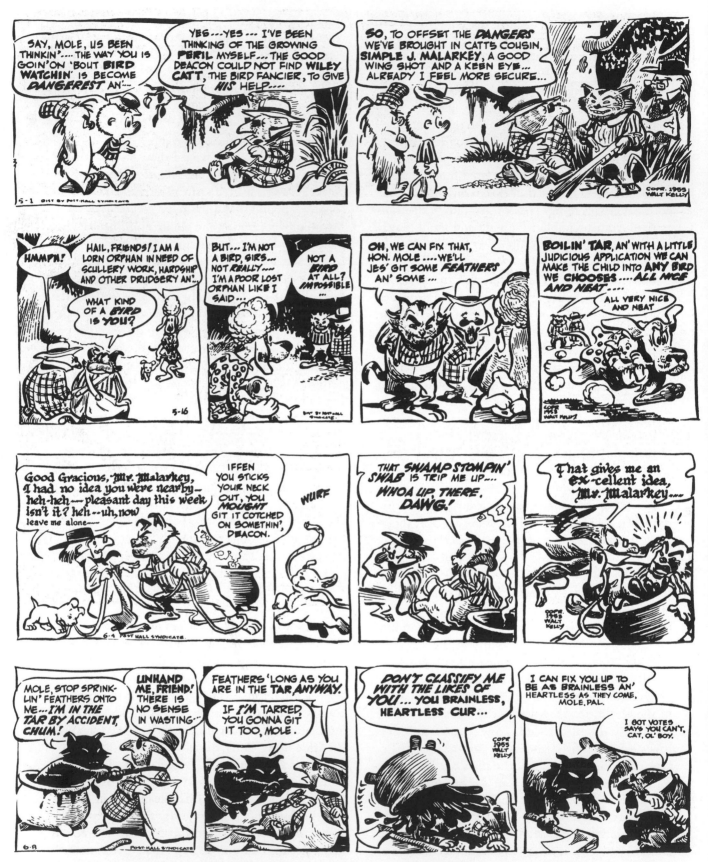

Figure 104. *In introducing his Joseph McCarthy character in 1953, Kelly made the senator's stand-in, Simple J. Malarkey, a genuinely threatening individual, whose ominous presence endangered life, limb, and the integrity of the republic. The satiric resolution of the sequence (bottom two strips) demonstrates that those who seek to smear others are likely to be tarred with their own brush, as adroit a coupling of visual and verbal messages as the comics have ever seen.*

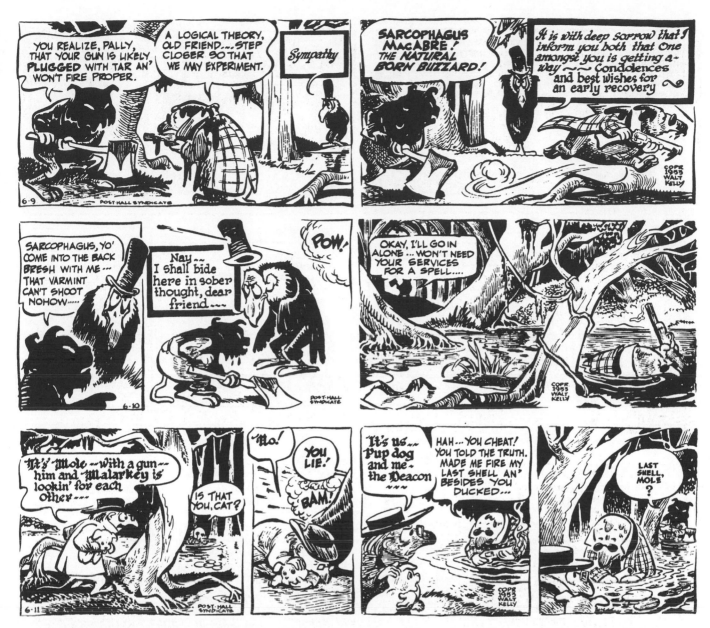

Figure 105. *As Malarkey goes after Mole for the three days following the tarring, Kelly successfully converts his erst-while friendly swamp into a gloomy, menacing place, a genuinely frightening venue—a trick as accomplished as his satire earlier in the week.*

one is under suspicion.

"What kind of an owl are you?" Mole asks Turtle.

"I ain't no owl," says Turtle. "I ain't even a bird."

"Were you ever a bird," asks Mole, "or are you thinking of becoming one?"

To assist in his work, Mole brings in a wildcat named Simple J. Malarkey, "a good wing shot and a keen eye." Malarkey gets himself elected president of the Bird Watchers Club by waving his shotgun under Deacon's nose: "Betsey, here," says the leering cat, "got six or seven votes in her alone." The reign of terror and intimidation begins. Malarkey, in case you haven't guessed, looks remarkably like Joseph McCarthy, and the echo of McCarthy's technique is clear.

Faced with a number of swamp creatures who claim they aren't birds, Malarkey undertakes corrective action: "We'll jes' get some feathers an' some boilin' tar," says Malarkey, "an' with a little judicious application we can make the creature into any bird we chooses—all nice and neat."

At one satiric stroke, Kelly equated McCarthy-

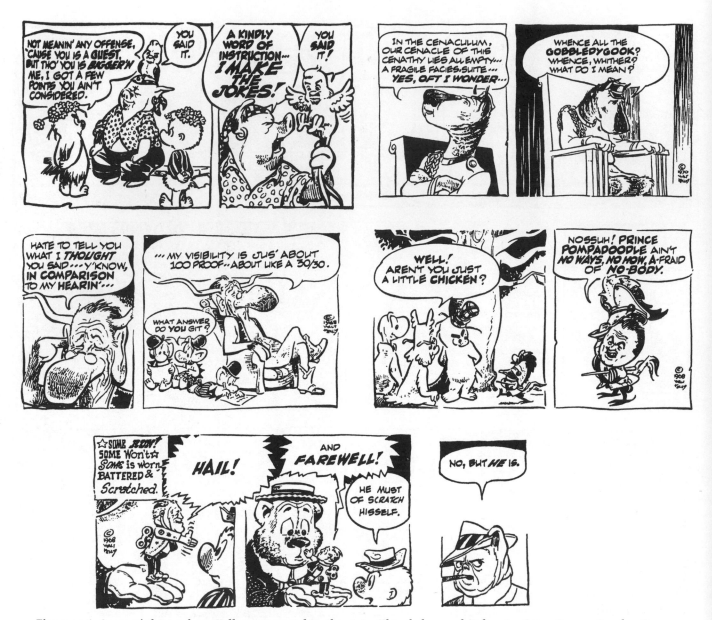

Figure 106. *Some of those whom Kelly caricatured in the strip: Khrushchev and Bulganin, Spiro Agnew, Lyndon B. Johnson (the Texas longhorn steer), George Wallace (who, in a takeoff on Chicken Little, became convinced that the sky was falling), George Romney (a presidential candidate who withdrew from the race), and J. Edgar Hoover.*

ism with an appropriately belittling analogue, tar-and-feathering—a primitive method of ostracizing that is universally held in low repute. In the delicious finale, Deacon, horrified by what he sees the Bird Watchers Club becoming, shoves Malarkey into the kettle of tar. Satirical translation: those who seek to smear others are likely to be tarred with their own brush (figure 104).

It was as neat a piece of satire as had ever been attempted on the comics pages, or anywhere. And the success of it depended upon Kelly's plumbing the potential of his medium to its utmost. Word

and picture worked in perfect concert: neither meant much when taken by itself, but when blended the verbal and the visual achieved allegorical impact and a powerful satiric thrust.

Kelly was to deploy these weapons again and again during the next twenty years. And all of the satiric action took place seemingly without the characters themselves being aware of it: the graphic portrayal of these denizens of the swamp as soft, plastic, and harmless joined the vaudevillian strain of the strip to proclaim the essential innocence of the characters, who went about their business,

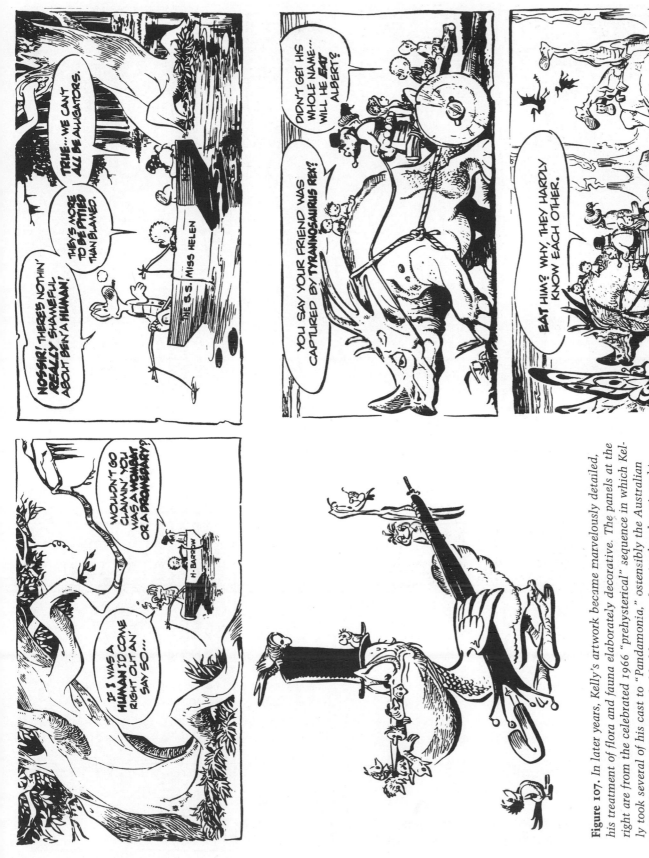

Figure 107. In later years, Kelly's artwork became marvelously detailed, his treatment of flora and fauna elaborately decorative. The panels at the right are from the celebrated 1966 "prehysterical" sequence in which Kelly took several of his cast to "Pandamonia," ostensibly the Australian outback but looking remarkably like some place in the planet's prehistorical ages.

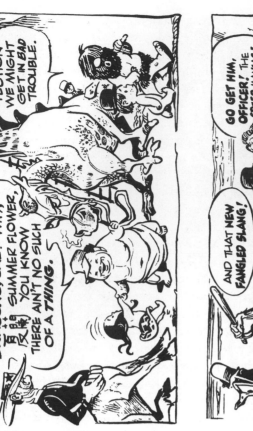

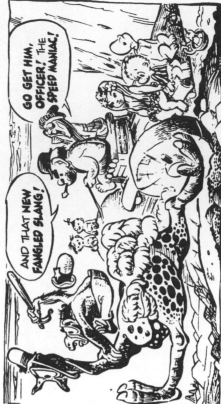

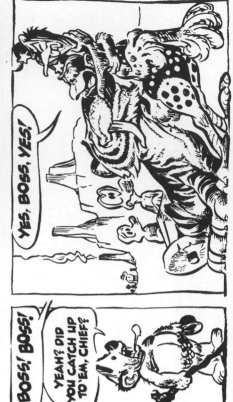

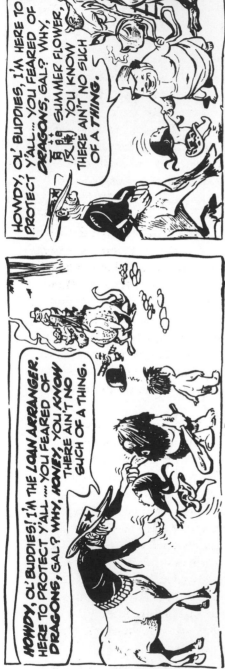

Figure 108. *In* Pandamonia, *Kelly introduces human beings into the strip for the first time since the prewar comic book days when Bumbazine was a cast member. The LBJ character (top) was only halfhuman (a centaur), but the Buddha figure (Mao Tse-Tung) and all the cave men and women were clearly full-fledged people—as was the comically mysterious curmudgeon, Doctor Noah. The entire sequence evokes memories of the work of T. S. Sullivant, a cartoonist of whose work Kelly was especially fond. Sullivant drew cave men and animals in his cartoons for the old* Life *and* Judge *humor magazines from about 1890 until his death in the mid-1920s.*

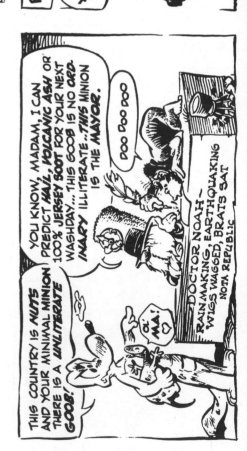

playing at being people, without being conscious of the larger satiric implications of the acts. The result was a tour de force: humor at each of two levels—one vaudevillian, the other satirical. At times, the stories took on an allegorical cast; at times, the whimsical innocence of the creatures emerged in poignant commentary on the human condition. *Pogo* thus opened to a greater extent than ever before the possibilities for political and social satire in comic strips. Many strips since *Pogo's* first decade (*Li'l Abner*, for example) have made their satirical barbs a little sharper. And without *Pogo*, we'd surely have no *Doonesbury*.

In later years, Kelly, in consideration of the sensitivities of the editors of his client newspapers, sometimes produced sequences of alternative strips that could be run in place of the regular *Pogo* whenever his satire became too pointed for the delicate stomachs of a paper's readers. Called "bunny rabbit strips," these featured innocuous comic exchanges between anonymous bunny rabbits. In the last decade or so of *Pogo's* initial run, Kelly's satire seemed a little strained. It was as if he felt compelled to continue the political commentary of the strip, to equal his past performances, in order to avoid breaking faith with his readers. But the satire was often directed at such minor peccadilloes of politicians that it could be appreciated only by those who followed the daily news with avid concentration. And the pointed topicality of such humor is all but lost on readers of another time.

No matter. If the master faltered, he did so only rarely in nearly a quarter of a century. And the body of his work remains a monument to the potential of comic strip art.

Although renowned for its political satire, *Pogo* is much more than a political strip. Much of its humor is driven by the personalities of its characters, and Kelly often gave them their heads, letting them take the action wherever they inclined. Kelly always delighted in vaudevillian routines, sight gags, slapstick, and wordplay. One of his earliest forays into the latter occurred around Christmas 1948 in the *Star*. The characters have all gathered around to sing carols, but because, as usual, they only half understand what they hear humans saying (or maybe only half hear what they think they understand), their version of "Deck the Halls with Boughs of Holly" comes out "Deck the Halls with

Boston Charlie." That's the way they heard it; that's the way they sang it. "This caught on with a number of elderly child minds," Kelly later wrote, "and finally children themselves. There was relief in it, and few feelings were bruised. Those that protested against this violation of all that was holy were told as gently as possible that the carol in question was one that was left over from the midwinter pre-Christian pagan rites celebrating the return of the long day in ancient Britain."[12] Over the years, Kelly would write six verses for his parody. And Pogo fans took them to heart (which is to say, they memorized them all).

Pogo was also responsible for the spread of a couple of catchphrases. The first arose from Churchy Lafemme's paranoia about Friday the Thirteenth, which for him could spring out of the bushes at him any day of the week: "Friday the Thirteenth comes on Wednesday this month," he'd shriek. The other phrase has been adopted by almost every pressure group in the country at one time or another to support its cause: "We have met the enemy, and he is us," Pogo said on several occasions, in support, usually, of ecological campaigns. Kelly's first use of the expression, however, was not in the strip but in the introduction he wrote to a reprint book, *The Pogo Papers*: "There is no need to sally forth, for it remains true that those things which make us humans are, curiously enough, always close at hand. Resolve, then, that on this very ground, with small flags waving and tinny blasts on tiny trumpets, we shall meet the enemy, and not only may he be ours, he may be us. Forward!"

On Sundays, Kelly avoided politics altogether in favor of purely comic nonsense. On Sundays, he celebrated the World Series every year. And the Easter Bunny. And fairy tales. And he produced parodies, continuities, that often ran for weeks. The parodies are plays within a play: the Pogo ensemble decides to enact the story of Goldilocks and the three bears, for instance, and Pogo puts on a wig of blond curls and takes the part of the heroine. Albert, a little muddled as usual about details, takes the heroic part of the woodsman, having confused Goldilocks with Little Red Riding Hood.

Pogo is not only high art: it is downright therapeutic. It is uproariously funny.

More than a boon to the risibilities, the Sunday pages were also a delight for the eye. In the last

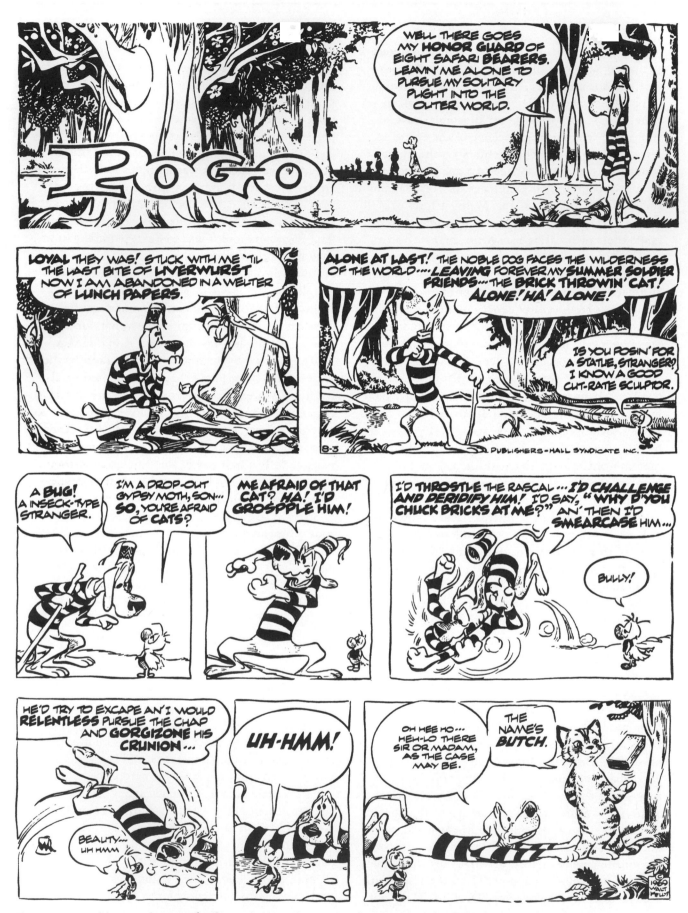

Figure 109. *And here, to bring us back to where we began this chapter, part of Kelly's seventeen-page homage to Herriman and Krazy Kat.*

few years, particularly, they all began with wonderfully detailed renderings of swamp scenes in the splash panels—great gnarly cypress trees festooned with Spanish moss and, in the distance, waterfowl aloft, cranes gliding gracefully through the air over the placid surfaces of the swamp's waterways. And (by way of bringing this chapter full circle) one of these beautifully drawn sequences is Kelly's seventeen-week homage to *Krazy Kat*.

A strange cat shows up one Sunday in June 1969 and, without preamble, heaves a brick in the direction of Beauregard Bugleboy's head. This performance is repeated for several Sundays, leaving the poor dog baffled about why the cat is doing it.

"The cat's *crazy* about you," says Howland Owl, providing a clue to alert (and comic strip history–minded) readers.

And when the cat tosses another brick and misses, Howland shouts: "See! Missed you again! That proves it: the cat's in love of you!"

Later Beauregard meets his nemesis and puts the question point-blank:

"Why do you chunk bricks at me? Some said it was hate . . . some said love."

"The latter is correct," says the cat.

"Love!?" says the dog, aghast.

"Yeh," says the cat. "Love of brick chunking. I love to throw 'em."

And that's Walt Kelly for you. He loved to deflate pretension, to reduce the grandiose and pompous to an appropriately human dimension, where we are all equals—all a little imperfect and often a little silly in our delusions about ourselves and our importance. Kelly showed us that better than George Herriman ever did. But he did it by appealing to the same faculty in his readers that Herriman appealed to: their intellects. These two great cartoonists proved beyond question that comics can be intelligent and adult. And Kelly proved that they can be high art, too.

Kelly loomed large on the comics pages while he was among us. But when he left—too soon, too young at merely sixty, dying of complications from diabetes in the fall of 1973—he didn't leave a void behind: he left a body of work, a cathedral of accomplishment. A swamp. A swamp, moist and warm, brooding in the soft accents of the South. And in that swamp, we ponder not Kelly's untimely death but life itself. There, in Kelly's swamp, we can learn to laugh at ourselves a little and lose our fear of life, and so, live more fully. Porkypine once observed about death that he "could live without it." And we can live without Walt Kelly's death, too: he lives on in the swamp he left behind.

Chapter 11

Of Infinite Jest
The Dawn of the Modern Comic Strip

In the world of cartooning in the fall of 1950, two watershed events began a trickle-down of consequences that would one day divide all that went before from what was yet to come. The first of these events that history and hindsight have invested with portent occurred on September 4: on that date, a comic strip by Mort Walker called *Beetle Bailey* began its run. It appeared in only twelve papers, a painfully inauspicious beginning. And its circulation didn't improve much over the next six months: by the end of February 1951 it claimed only twenty-five subscribing papers. But in the fullness of time, *Beetle Bailey* would become the third most widely distributed comic strip in history. The perennial *Blondie* would rank second, and first place would go to the other strip the debut of which marked the fall of 1950 as a turning point in the history of the medium—*Peanuts.*[1]

Charles Schulz's colossally successfully strip about introspective "li'l folks" (his original title for the strip) had an even more unspectacular start than *Beetle Bailey*: only seven papers ran the earliest strips, beginning October 2, and its circulation was still well under a hundred papers a year later. But within the decade, it would become one of the nation's most popular comics. Schulz's strip would also revolutionize comic strip art: his deceptively simple graphic style set a new fashion for newspaper cartoonists. And Walker's equally simple but geometrically distinctive style gave cartoonists another model on the funny pages of the coming decades. But the milestone marked by the launching of these two strips had more to do with content than with style.

Both strips told jokes, not stories, ending each installment with a punch line. Although a week's run of strips might have a common theme, there was no story line. With the success of Walker and Schulz and their imitators (and of others like Hank Ketcham, whose gag panel cartoon *Dennis the Menace* began March 12, 1951, and was immediately a smash hit), the humorous function of cartooning would emerge during the fifties into pacesetting popularity once again, after a quarter of a century hiatus throughout which story strips had held nearly absolute sway. In the autumn of 1950, though, continuity strips still reigned supreme. Four of the top five strips (according to *Time*) were story strips—*Little Orphan Annie*, *Dick Tracy*, *Joe Palooka*, and *Li'l Abner.*[2] Only *Blondie* relentlessly told a joke every day. And six of the ten strips that ranked highest with the readers of the *Saturday Review of Literature* were continuities—*Li'l Abner*, *Gasoline Alley*, *Dick Tracy*, *Steve Canyon*, *Pogo*, and *Terry and the Pirates.*[3] *Li'l Abner* and *Pogo* were humorous continuities, to be sure, but the fullest understanding of their humor depended upon following the strips day by day. The only strictly humorous strips to finish in the *Review's* top ten were *Blondie* (heading the list), *Penny*, *Gordo*, and *Moon Mullins*. But that would change.

By the end of the decade story strips had been virtually swept off the comics pages by a deluge of their chortling brethren. But it wasn't fratricide: story strips weren't done in by gag strips. The culprit was that box in the living room. Television, which could be seen coast-to-coast by the mid-fifties, displaced radio and the daily newspaper as the nation's source of entertainment in the home. Newspaper editors were understandably desperate to preserve some remnant of their former hold upon the American public. First they fought television, refusing to give up space for any coverage beyond the most cryptic program listings. But when they saw that stories about television increased their readership and circulation, they devoted more space to TV news. Elsewhere in the paper, they sought to provide features and services that readers could not find on their TV sets. And when it came to the funnies page, the continuity strips were immediately singled out. Why would people read a story strip that takes two or three months to tell its tale when they can see an entire adventure in a hour on television? Editors stopped buying story strips; syndicates stopped buying them. They all bought gag strips instead. In doing so, they conveniently ignored an obvious argument against such strips: you can get more laughs in half an hour of watching TV than you are likely to get in the ten minutes it takes to read the funnies every day. Nonetheless, gag strips were the de facto beneficiaries of the television age, inheriting the newspaper space once occupied by epic continuities. It was the immense success of *Beetle Bailey* and *Peanuts* that showed cartoonists how to survive the advent of television. At the same time, the arrival of these strips in the fall of 1950 signaled the beginning of the end for story strips, although no one realized it at the time. At the time, as we've observed, these new strips slipped into public view virtually unheralded.

When Mort Walker submitted his comic strip to King Features, he was editing a couple of anthology magazines of gag cartoons for Dell (*1,000 Jokes*, for instance), and he had been proclaimed

the top-selling gag cartoonist in the country. According to a survey "someone" had conducted, he sold more gag cartoons than any of his fellows in 1949. It was, Walker realized, an empty triumph: he made only $7,500 that year. As his wife put it, "If you're the top seller and that's all you're making, then it must be a bad business."[4] Knowing there was more real money to be made in syndication to newspapers than in gag cartoons for magazines, Walker decided to try to sell a comic strip to a feature syndicate. He had tried once before without luck, but this time, following the advice of John Bailey, cartoon editor for the *Saturday Evening Post*, he focused on something he knew well—college life.

Bailey had liked a funny-looking character Walker had penciled into several of his cartoons—a lazy, lanky college kid who wore his hat down over his eyes—and Walker had done several cartoons featuring the kid, whom they called "Spider." Now Walker picked Spider to star in his comic strip. For situations and gags, he drew upon his experiences at the University of Missouri, where he was a journalism student after getting out of the army at the end of World War II. He surrounded Spider with eccentric professors and even odder classmates. And he gave Spider a mission: the kid became a champion goof-off, forever fleeing work and responsibility. King Features bought the strip, but since another feature bore the name "Spider," they renamed Walker's protagonist "Beetle" (and for the sake of euphony, Walker gave him a last name by which he thanked John Bailey for his good advice). The feature was forthwith launched into the world of newspaper comics. But nobody heard a splash.

After about six months, the silence was deafening. Walker didn't know it at the time, but King was thinking of dropping the strip. Then inspiration struck. The Korean War was going on at the time, and since men of Beetle's vintage were being called up left and right, it seemed logical to take the kid out of college and put him in uniform. So Walker did just that—on March 13, 1951. And a hundred papers picked up the strip.

The potential readership for a strip about army life was enormous. Every able-bodied American male had been in miliary service or was in military service—or would be in military service. Military experience was the great common bond. And again, Walker drew upon his own experience.

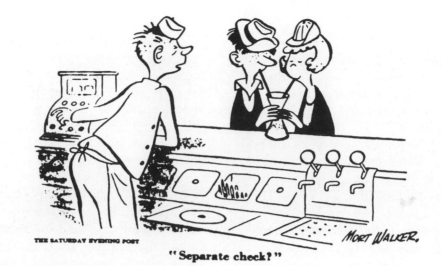

THE SATURDAY EVENING POST

MORT WALKER.

"Separate check?"

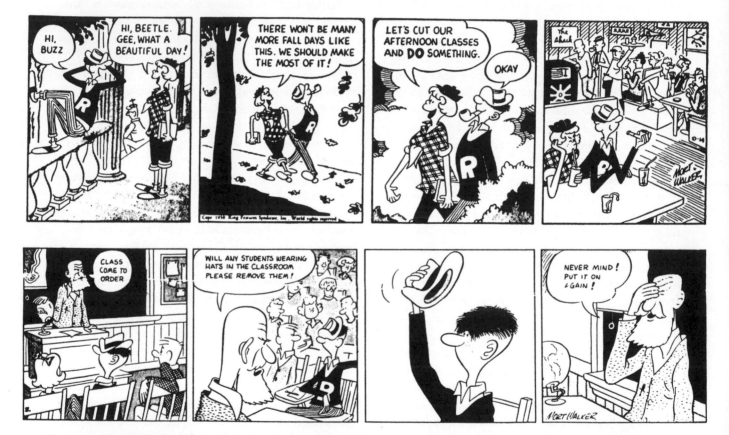

Figure 110. *Beetle Bailey first appeared as a character called "Spider" in* Saturday Evening Post *cartoons (top). In the middle, the first* Beetle Bailey *strip Walker drew (although it was published ten days after the strip's debut). And at the bottom, a strip that was never published as part of the strip's run—the only time Beetle ever took his hat off.*

While working at Hallmark and attending classes at a local college in Kansas City in 1943, Walker had been drafted. The army shuttled him around to an assortment of military training schools before finally settling him at Washington University in St. Louis, where he earned a two-year diploma in basic engineering. Then, with the sort of logic for which the military mind is duly celebrated across the breadth of the known universe, the army assigned Walker to the infantry and sent him overseas, where he was put in charge of disposing of the inventory of a supply depot in postwar Italy.

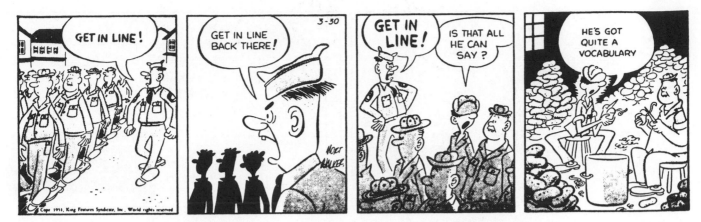

Figure 111. *At first, Sergeant Snorkel was not so rotund and cuddly as he eventually became.*

The army was clearly lining itself up as a target for the would-be cartoonist's shafts. And when Beetle enlisted, Walker opened fire.

Beetle would never see action on the battlefield. There was nothing funny about battle. But at the training command of Camp Swampy, there was plenty to laugh at. And an entire nation joined Walker in the laughter.

The strip's next growth spurt occurred when the Far East edition of *The Stars and Stripes* "banned" *Beetle* in January 1954. The army brass said the strip was bad for morale, on top of which it gave the public an unfavorable impression of the army because it made fun of officers. The ban lasted for ten years, but the rumpus it raised (egged on by syndicate publicity manufactured at Walker's urging) inspired another hundred newspapers to buy the strip, bringing *Beetle's* circulation to around three hundred. The strip hit five hundred in 1956, going on to become the second strip in history to pass the thousand mark, which it did in 1965. (Until then, only *Blondie* appeared in more than one thousand papers.) Five years later, Beetle was in nearly 1,400 papers. And by the mid-1980s, according to *Editor & Publisher*, the strip was in 1,660 papers (ranking third behind *Peanuts*, with 1,941, and *Blondie*, with 1,900).[5]

Although the military setting provided the initial attraction by which readers were lured into Walker's clutches, *Beetle Bailey* is a strip driven by the personalities of its characters rather than its situation. Writing in *The Best of Beetle Bailey* in 1984, Walker observed that *Beetle's* cast is larger than that of any other strip (with the exception of *Pogo*). As he reviewed thirty years of the strip, Walker paused to comment about his principals.

About Sergeant Orville P. Snorkel, Walker wrote:

"Sarge is probably my favorite character to draw. Not only does he look funny in all positions, but he takes up a lot of space which saves me from drawing a lot of backgrounds. He's garrulous, profane, ecstatic, rough, sentimental, voracious. . . . He does everything to the extremes. . . . Top sergeants have been called the backbone of the Army. Most GI's refer to them as a lower part of the anatomy. . . . Most of them are career Army types who are so immersed in military life, they think a civilian is a soldier in drag. Sgt. Snorkel is the epitome of that breed."[6] About Zero: "We all know someone like Zero who isn't quite with it. His name is a clue to his IQ. But he's not really as mentally deficient as he is uninformed. . . . Zero couldn't be in the Army if he were retarded. He's just an innocent young farm boy as sweet, honest and unsophisticated as an ear of corn." And about General Amos T. Halftrack: "Halftrack is what every GI knows a general is: he's lousy at running the camp and when he gets home his wife runs him. . . . As a leader, General Halftrack couldn't lead a cub scout to a candy store, but he's one of my favorite characters."

Apart from the voluptuous Miss Buxley (who inspired charges of sexism), Lt. Flap was the most controversial of Walker's characters. Walker had wanted to bring a black into the strip for years. "Trouble was, if I made him a lazy goof-off like the regular cast, I'd get complaints." All the *Beetle* characters were objects of laughter, and a black as fall guy might be offensive. Walker put the idea on a back burner. And then in the middle of the night one night, Flap came to him—"with his Afro, goatee, and jaunty manner. It was as though he'd always been there."

Walker's assistants were divided about introduc-

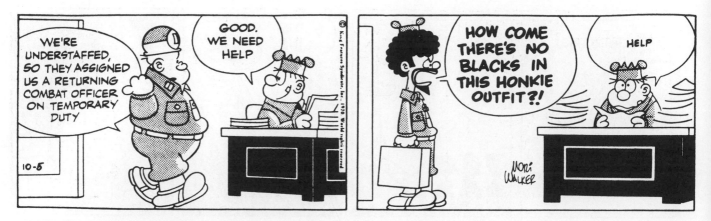

Figure 112. *Lt. Flap, the strip's first black character, walked onstage October 5, 1970.*

ing Flap. Half of them thought he was a good character. The other half wondered why the circulation of the strip should be risked: "Why do it? You don't need to."

"I felt I had to do it for the sake of honesty, if nothing else," Walker explained. "The Army had been integrated for years. Blacks exist. Beetle Bailey's army was a phony. I was a coward if I didn't try it. The trick was to do an honest job of it, come up with a character that was not offensive yet was as funny as the rest of my characters. Making Flap a lieutenant gave him some status and power, and I would base his humor on his firm stand of being accepted as a man."[7]

The syndicate hesitated but finally gave approval, and Lt. Flap debuted on October 5, 1970—shouting at Sarge, "How come there are no blacks in this honkie outfit?" "Help," squeaked Snorkel. Walker introduced his new character by facing all the attendant problems at once. *Stars and Stripes* banned *Beetle* again because it thought the strip would cause racial tension, but Senator William Proxmire convinced the brass to reinstate the world's most famous private. Elsewhere, *Beetle* picked up a hundred additional papers over the next twelve months.

Surprisingly in a strip with so large a cast, Beetle is still the star. The personality of the title character in populous strips often fades away, typically eroded by the attention given to other characters. But Beetle's quirks are as pronounced today as ever—and as central to much of the strip's humor. "He subscribes to the philosophy, 'Whenever the urge to work comes over me, I lie down until it goes away,'" Walker once noted. Consequently, when Beetle enlisted, "he was rapidly assimilated into army life. Instead of dorm matters, he simply

switched to barracks buddies. Instead of professors who gave him trouble, he had sergeants. Instead of institutional food in the cafeteria, he got his heartburn in the mess hall. He fell right into it—especially the bed."[8]

But *Beetle Bailey* is not really a strip about army life. Says Walker: "The truth is, it's just a strip about a bunch of funny guys. They could be policemen, factory workers, college students, whatever. The army is just a convenient setting that everyone understands. The pecking order doesn't have to be explained, and the role of the poor guy at the bottom of the ladder is a classic in literature."[9] Sociologists who study the strip for the way it represents authority are close to the heart of the matter. Walker's army is simply a version of society, which sustains its essential order through a hierarchy of authority. From the point of view of most of us in a social order, the flaws in the system are due to the incompetence of those who have authority over us. *Beetle Bailey* encapsulates this aspect of the human condition and gives expression to our resentment of authority by ridiculing traditional authority figures. But the ridicule is gentle: it takes shape as Walker repeatedly shows us that everyone in his army—authority figure or not—is but a bundle of personality quirks. Hence, the strip is a great leveler: we're all equal. We all have our frailties, our entirely human foibles.

In his *Backstage at the Strips* (still probably the best book around about the life of a cartoonist), Walker discussed his attitude toward humor. He disagreed with Jules Feiffer, who, he said, believes "you have to hate to be funny. Humor, Feiffer says, comes from dissatisfaction with things; you attack, ridicule, and destroy what you don't like with humor." Some humorists do. But, Walker

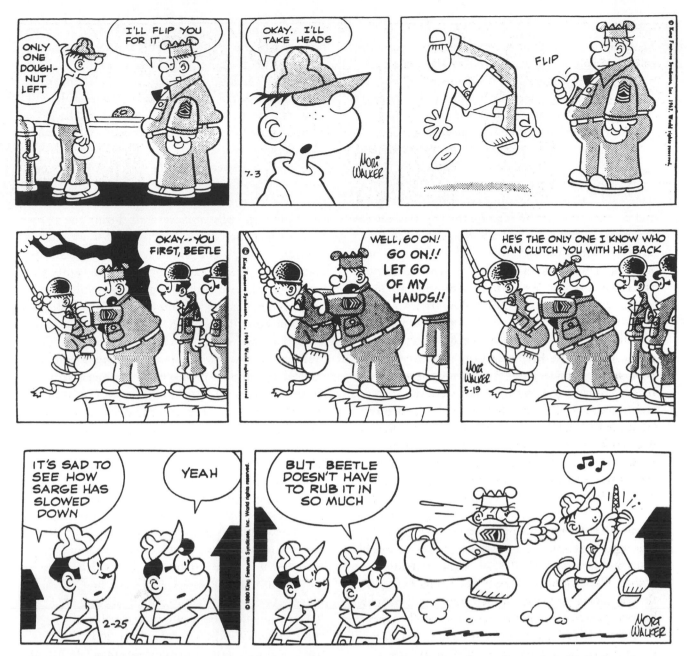

Figure 113. *Although vastly outnumbered by his supporting cast, Beetle remains the undisputed and fully functioning star of the strip—no wallflower, he. Note Beetle's abstracted leg construction in the middle strip; ditto Sarge's legs in the bottom example.*

said, he's more comfortable with Leo Rosten's notion that "humor is an affectionate insight into the affairs of man."

"*Affectionate* is the word that won me," Walker explained. "I like people. I like their absurdities, their aberrations, their pretensions. If you catch a guy exaggerating, you don't ridicule him: you *understand* him."[10] Walker's strip is, indeed, just about "a bunch of funny guys." All of us. And that is the universal appeal of the strip—its foundation in the fundamental human condition. True, in the early years, a large proportion of the gags were built on army customs, duties, and regulations. But the longer the strip lasted—and the greater its circulation grew—the more the gags sprang from the personalities of the characters rather than the institutions of the army. It was a wholly natural development, the outcome we would expect in a strip with a large cast. As the army as an institution faded away, the common condition of humanity remained, and the strip thus established its universality.

For the student of the art of the comic strip, *Beetle Bailey* is something more than a strip with universal appeal. Although Walker's accomplishments were recognized by his peers as early as 1953 when the National Cartoonists Society gave him a Reuben as cartoonist of the year, he has, oddly, never been credited enough in critical circles for his complete mastery of the medium. And his is scarcely an unconscious talent.

"An editor told me a long time ago," Walker once said, "that if you could cover up the drawing and still get the gag by reading the caption, then you were a writer and not a cartoonist. With that advice, I've always tried to get as many funny pictures into my work as possible."[11] To a greater extent than many of his trendier contemporaries—Johnny Hart, Brant Parker, Jeff MacNelly, Garry Trudeau (and his imitators)—Walker and his crew of assistants make the humor in *Beetle* visual as well as verbal. To understand the joke, we must grasp the implications of the pictures as well as the meaning of the words. In blending the verbal and the visual, Walker is firmly in the tradition of comic strip art at its finest, using the resources of the medium to their fullest.

In visual terms alone, *Beetle* achieves a high-water mark in the art of cartooning. Over the years, Walker's style has evolved. At first, he drew in a simple big-foot style that seemed a mix of John Gallagher and Tom Henderson, two great magazine cartoonists of the fifties. (Walker says his style was absorbed from Frank Willard, Walter Brendt, Chic Young, Milton Caniff, and Al Capp; so what do I know? Just that where there's smoke, there's something to make your eyes smart.) But as the years rolled by, Walker refined his style, streamlining simplicity into a distinctive comic abbreviation.

Some simplification was required to meet necessity. As strips were reproduced smaller and smaller, Walker stopped drawing elaborate crowd scenes. And he stopped using Benday gray tones to shade uniforms, instead relying entirely on judicious spotting of solid blacks to add visual variety in his strip. (The drab, monotonous setting of army life still bothers Walker, and he continually struggles to insinuate telling graphic contrasts into each daily installment.) Walker also shrank his figures to fit the smaller panels. Heads stayed about the same size, though, so the proportions changed:

heads became larger in relation to bodies than they had been in the fifties, one effect of which was to make his people cuter. At the same time, everything—heads, noses, bodies, hands, fingers—got rounder. Sarge got rounder and fatter as he grew shorter, finally becoming almost cuddly (a dubious trait for the top sergeant of tradition, but with Sarge, it works).

By the late fifties and early sixties, Walker's patented stylized forms had emerged. Not since Cliff Sterrett surrealized human anatomy in the futuristic manner in *Polly and Her Pals* during the 1920s have we had such charming comic abstractions of the human form. The simplest shapes suggest human dimensions. A cantaloupe gives us Beetle's head; a giant pear, Sarge's. Upon these pulpy craniums, Walker's grafts billiard balls for noses. Bodies in repose hang limply from these heads like uninhabited suits of clothes weighted to the ground by monster shoes (not feet), and hands are doughy wads, dangling at the ends of empty sleeves. Clothing shows no wrinkles: sleeves and pantlegs are simple geometric shapes vaguely approximating arms and legs.

Anatomy is wonderfully elastic in Walker's hands. A bent arm or leg is longer than the limb when straight (you need length to show a bend). The illusion of the body in motion is achieved by means of a carefully orchestrated series of wild distortions. A person walking has only one leg—the one in front, which trails a second foot behind as if it were growing out of the lead leg's ankle. Running figures are all elbows and knees, perfect comic abstractions. The flexibility of Walker's abstracted simplicity is capable of extreme exaggeration for comic effect. Indeed, much of the humor in many strips arises from the antic visuals as much as from the situation depicted.

If I were in a poetic mood, I'd be tempted to say that Walker's style evolved to suit his subject. His representations of humanity are as abstracted as is his microcosm of society. But that's poetry, not fact. The fact is that the drawings are the way they are so that the visuals will be funny. The pictures help the words achieve comedy by blending the visual and the verbal. But the pictures are comic in themselves, too.

Walker didn't conduct *Beetle Bailey* single-handedly for long. For most of its run, the strip

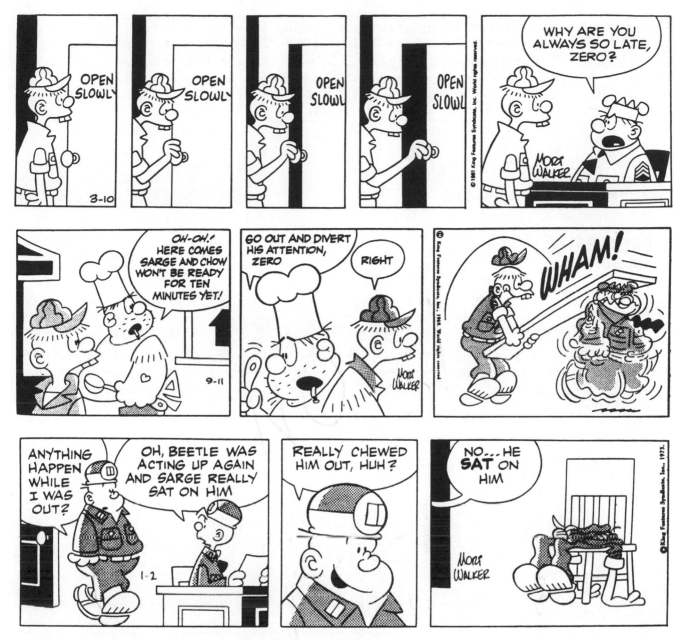

Figure 114. *The humor in* Beetle Bailey *consistently depends upon visual as well as verbal content; neither words nor pictures make complete sense without the other.*

was produced by a comic art "shop" that was as production-oriented as any of the shops of writers and artists of the forties that rolled comic book features off the line in record time. Called (tongue in cheek) King Features East, the shop was Walker's collection of cartooning assistants in Greenwich, Connecticut. Walker and his half-dozen associates were responsible for as many as nine comic strips (two numbered among the top twenty in circulation), a comic book, and numerous special publication projects. And they were indirectly involved in a tenth comic strip (also among the top twenty).

Walker started his second strip in 1954 because the hostilities ended in Korea. Fearing that reader interest in military matters would flag when the war ceased, Walker toyed with the idea of taking Beetle out of the army and returning him to family life. He tested the waters by having Beetle go home on furlough for two weeks in April 1954, but his readers voiced their disapproval: they wanted Beetle in the army. So Walker left him there. But

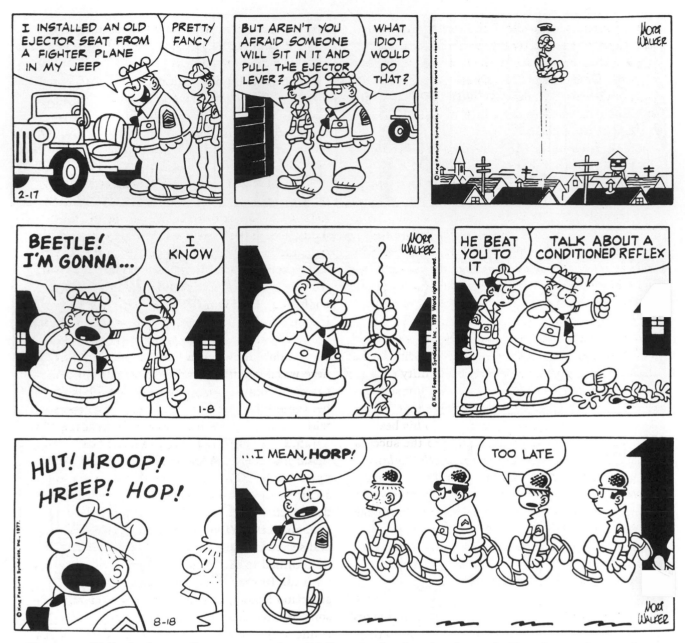

Figure 115. *Walker's abstracted anatomy permits wild distortion for the sake of comedy. Note the way legs are depicted with Sarge in the top strip, second panel, and in the second panel of the bottom strip.*

in the meantime he'd introduced two new characters, Beetle's sister Lois and her husband Hi (along with their children), and Walker found he liked doing family gags. In order to continue doing them, he redesigned the couple and launched *Hi and Lois*. To do the drawing, he engaged Dik Browne, who had been doing cartoon ads for the Johnstone and Cushing agency. The strip began October 18, 1954, and by the end of the 1980s it stood eleventh on the *Editor & Publisher* listing of comic strips by circulation.

In 1961 Walker added the short-lived *Sam's Strip* to his string, and on March 11, 1968, his shop began producing *Boner's Ark*, a funny animal strip. Sam eventually returned on April 18, 1977, in *Sam and Silo*. And on March 29, 1982, another short-run strip called *The Evermores* started. Then came *Betty Boop and Felix* (November 19, 1984) and *Gamin and Patches* (April 27, 1987), neither of which enjoyed long runs. Another venture, *Mrs. Fitz's Flats*, had debuted in 1957, and although it lasted several years, it never achieved a long list of client papers. Meanwhile, Dik Browne (caught up, doubtless, in the creative spirit of the fecund enterprise that surrounded him) concocted *Hagar the Horrible*, which began publication February 4, 1973, and crossed the thousand-paper threshold in less than ten years, ranking fifth in circulation by the end of the eighties.

At one time in the early 1980s the production lineup worked as follows. Walker, his son Greg, Bud Jones, Bob Gustafson and Jerry Dumas wrote gags for *Beetle Bailey* (penciled by Walker), *Hi and Lois* (penciled by Dik Browne and his son Bob), and *Boner's Ark* (drawn by Frank Johnson, who also inked *Beetle* and *Hi and Lois*). Dumas also wrote and drew *Sam and Silo*; Gustafson, the comic book; and Johnny Sajem, *The Evermores*. It was a gag writer's paradise—an outlet for virtually any kind of gag conjured up. The group met every Monday to review, accept, reject, or polish the gags its members had generated during the preceding week.

There is no denying that the community of humor with which Walker surrounded himself created a mutually energizing atmosphere that spurred each member of the crew to do his best. And that contributed immeasurably to the success of the shop's creations. But as for *Beetle Bailey*, the shaping hand, the informing intelligence, and the selective sense of humor are clearly Mort Walker's. And *Beetle Bailey* has improved with age as Walker has expanded on his subject and honed his graphic style. By the early 1990s the strip was (and had been for many years) the consummate comic strip, a masterful performance.

Although both *Beetle Bailey* and *Peanuts* tell jokes and are simply drawn, the two strips are not otherwise at all alike. Particularly when they began in the fall of 1950: *Beetle* was then—and has remained—pretty much a traditional comic strip. Much of the comedy sprang from the personalities of Walker's characters, but the humor itself and the ways it was generated from panel to panel to punch line was firmly rooted in the durable comedy routines of stage and screen. *Peanuts*, in contrast, broke new ground; the sense of humor on display in Charles Schulz's strip was different, more subtle, than could be found elsewhere on the comics pages. Even the drawings in *Peanuts* added a new dimension to comic strip art, something *Beetle* did not achieve until its stylistic streamlining reached

comic abstraction. And there was another difference: Walker liked the name of his feature; Schulz decidedly did not—and still doesn't.

"*Peanuts* is the worst title ever thought up for a comic strip," Schulz has said on numerous occasions.[12] The strip was christened by the editors at United Feature Syndicate, who didn't like Schulz's name for the feature, *Li'l Folks* (which was, moreover, too much like the name of a retired strip, *Little Folks*, by Tack Knight). The syndicate editors thought *Peanuts* was the perfect name for an all-kids strip—and it fit their marketing scheme perfectly, too, as we'll soon see. But Schulz hated the title and has resented it his entire career. "I don't even like the word," he said. "It's not a nice word. It's totally ridiculous, has no meaning, is simply confusing, and has no dignity. And I think my humor has dignity. The strip I was going to draw I thought would have dignity. It would have class. They didn't know when I walked in there that here was a fanatic. Here was a kid totally dedicated to what he was going to do. And then to label something that was going to be a life's work with a name like *Peanuts* was really insulting."[13]

Schulz followed a path to syndicated cartooning much like the one Walker followed. Schulz grew up in St. Paul, Minnesota, the shy and only son of a barber. He took a course in art from a correspondence school, the Federal School, based in Minneapolis. Like Walker, Schulz was drafted in 1943 and served overseas in the infantry. After V-J Day, he returned to the Twin Cities and took a position with the Federal School, now called the Art Instruction School, correcting mailed-in student lessons. He free-lanced in his spare time, lettering comic strips for a locally produced Catholic magazine and eventually producing a cartoon feature called *Li'l Folks* for the *St. Paul Pioneer Press*. The feature ran once a week, a collection of single-panel cartoons about the antics of little children who seemed a bit more sophisticated than most cartoon children. The kids were cute because of the way Schulz drew them. They were all tiny, and Schulz distorted proportions—giving them round heads as big as their bodies—in a way that made them seem even more diminutive. And tiny was cute.

Schulz was also sending cartoons to national magazines. He had broken into the *Saturday Evening Post* with the submission of a single drawing

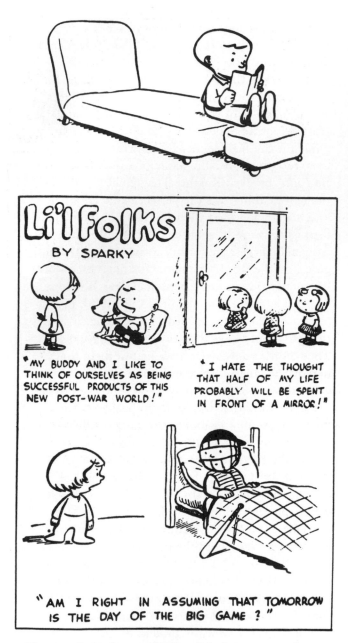

Figure 116. *At the top, the first Schulz cartoon published in the* Saturday Evening Post. *Below that, a sample of the* Li'l Folks *feature Schulz produced for the* St. Paul Pioneer Press.

of a small boy who was seated on the end of a chaise longue, dwarfed by the expanse of the seating arrangements, in order to prop his feet up on a footstool. It was John Bailey who bought the cartoon, and Schulz was grateful to Bailey. "Later, when I began to submit batches of roughs on a regular weekly basis, John Bailey once clipped little notes to each rejected idea, telling me why it wasn't acceptable," Schulz once said. "This was

extremely considerate of him and, of course, was one more reason why he was so well appreciated by cartoonists."[14]

While submitting gag cartoons to magazines, Schulz also submitted ideas for feature cartoons to syndicates. Early in 1950 United Feature Syndicate indicated interest in *Li'l Folks*, and when Schulz journeyed to New York for a conference, they decided a strip format would be better than the panel format. Schulz delivered a set of strips about his little kids, and the syndicate bought the feature. The editors saw in Schulz's tiny figures a novel marketing ploy. At the time, newspaper editors were restive about the amount of precious newsprint paper they devoted to comic strips every day and were looking for ways to reduce the size of comic strips. Because Schulz's characters were small, the editors decided to tailor the strip's dimensions to the kids' size—a maneuver that would, they believed, appeal to editors seeking to conserve space. Schulz's strip would have the same horizontal dimension as all strips but would be shallower vertically. It would therefore take up less room. And then the editors added yet another marketing ingredient: the strip should always be drawn in four equal-sized panels, an arrangement that would give editors great flexibility in running the strip. They could run the strip in one column with the four panels stacked vertically, or they could divide the strip in half, the first two panels stacked on top of the other two panels, and run it as a two-column box. The syndicate's promotional brochure for the strip touted these aspects of the strip's design—and its tiny size. "The Greatest Little Sensation Since Tom Thumb!" the brochure trumpeted. For such a feature, *Peanuts* was the perfect title.[15]

"Peanuts" suggested something small. But to Schulz, it suggested something insignificant—"something with no color," he muttered, "or else it might be the nickname of a ball player or some little kid." He pointed out that readers would assume the strip was named after one of the characters: "They're going to confuse Charlie Brown with the name." The editors assured him that wouldn't happen. "Then throughout the first year," Schulz said, "I got letters saying, I love this new strip with Peanuts and his dog. Geez!"[16]

The editors mistakenly supposed that *peanuts* was a common term for little children. This aston-

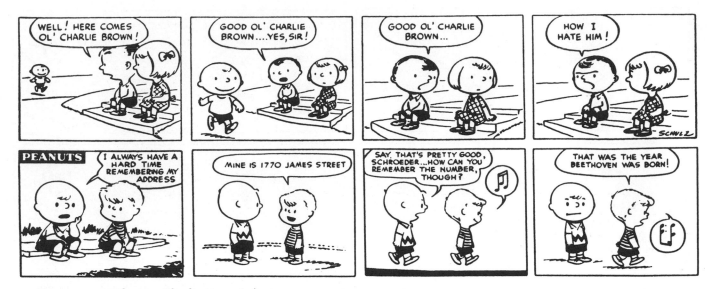

Figure 117. *At the top, Charlie Brown's first appearance.*

ishingly wrongheaded conclusion was not based upon anything in their own life experiences, apparently; instead, it was drawn entirely from a popular kids' television program of the day, *The Howdy Doody Show*. The show's principals were marionettes, and the puppet show was performed before a live studio audience of children. The audience seating area was called "the peanut gallery" by everyone on the show, and every time "the peanut gallery" was mentioned, all the kids cheered with gusto. Schulz wasn't convinced; he knew kids are never called "peanuts."[17]

Despite the gimmicky packaging, the strip got off to a slow start. But after a year it was picking up client papers steadily. And it continued to increase circulation at a modest rate through the decade. Then in the 1960s it took off. Even by the mid-1950s, though, Schulz had found his footing. He had begun to develop the idiosyncratic personalities of his characters. Charlie Brown had become the archetypal mid-century American man in search of his identity, and his dog Snoopy had started to fantasize an assortment of heroic roles for himself. Schroeder had established Beethoven as the strip's icon. And Lucy Van Pelt had made a name for herself as a world-class fussbudget.

Reflecting on the strip's development, Schulz said: "When Lucy came into the strip, around the second year, she didn't do much at first. She came in as a cute little girl, and at first she was patterned after our own first daughter. She said a lot of cute, tiny kid things, but I grew out of that whole 'tiny' world quickly, and that's when the strip started to catch on. . . . As Charlie Brown got more defensive, as Snoopy [became] a different kind of dog, as Lucy started to develop her own strong personality, I realized I was really on to something different. And I think the security blanket really was *the* major breakthrough."[18] Linus, Lucy's baby brother and owner of the famous blanket, didn't talk when he first appeared in the strip; he was too young. But as he grew older, he talked plenty—profoundly, even: he became the strip's scholarly idealist and philosopher. En route, he clutched his flannel baby blanket and sucked his thumb. And when Schulz called it a "security blanket," he not only added a term to the American lexicon but struck a chord with readers everywhere. Suddenly, everyone identified with one or more of the *Peanuts* gang.

In 1962 Schulz produced a book of aphorisms called *Happiness Is a Warm Puppy*. It was an immediate best-seller, confirming a growing suspicion: the American public had Peanuts mania. In April 1965 *Time* did a cover story on Schulz and his strip (April 9). And in October Snoopy climbed on top of his doghouse and flew it into the skies of World War I for an epic battle with the Red Baron. The list of subscribing newspapers grew by leaps. And then that Christmas the first television special was unveiled, "A Charlie Brown Christmas." *Peanuts* was undeniably big time. By the early 1990s the strip was being published in over two thousand newspapers in sixty-eight countries.

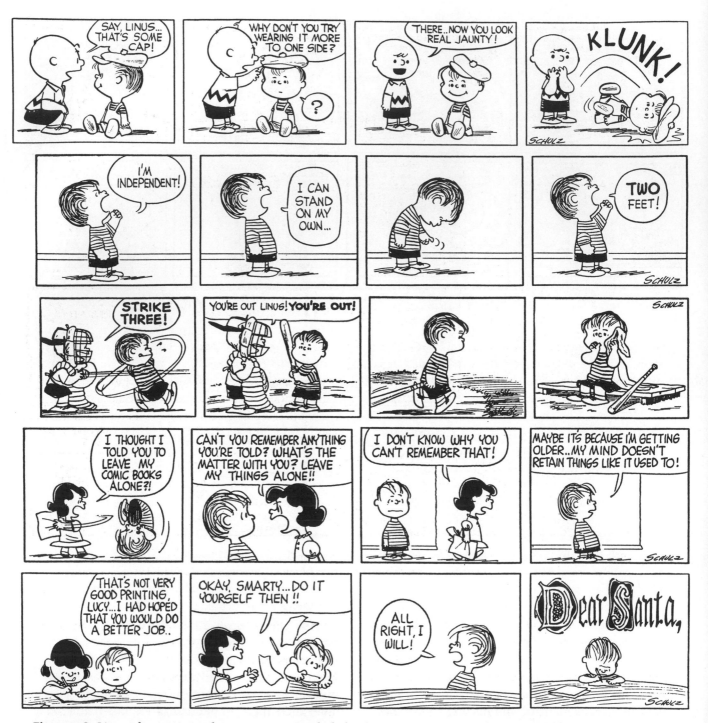

Figure 118. *Linus, the strip's resident genius, gave Schulz his first overt measure of success with the "security blanket." When he first appeared, Linus was too young to talk; that soon changed.*

There had been thirty television specials, four feature films, and a Broadway play, *You're a Good Man, Charlie Brown*. And Schulz, thanks to the merchandizing of his characters, was many times over a millionaire. *Peanuts* may well be the world's most popular comic strip.

And its popularity made it a candidate for imitation. In spite of the strip's undeniable originality,

Peanuts has served as a model for a great variety of new strips. Aspects of it can indeed be easily aped. The "show" in *Peanuts*, albeit brilliant, is not as obvious a dazzling and highly individual combination of ingredients as is, say, *Pogo*. For one thing, the surface elements of *Peanuts*, its most apparent features, lend themselves easily to adaptation by others, who shape those elements into an expres-

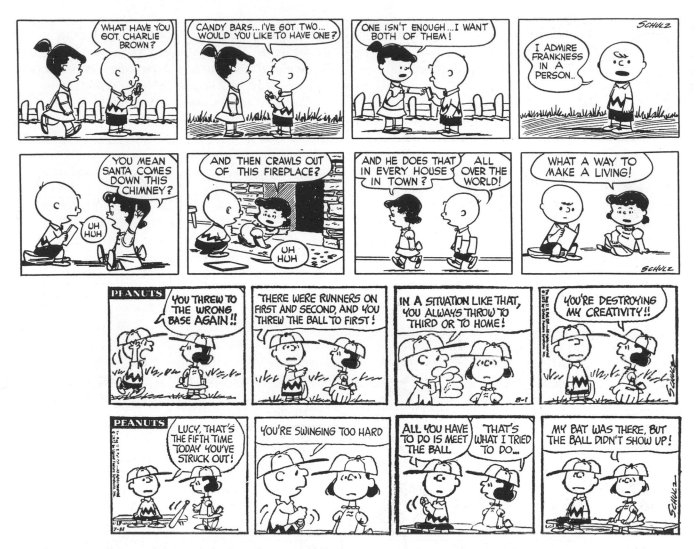

Figure 119. *The punch lines of the first three strips illustrate* Peanuts' *basic principle of humor: the application to the concerns of children of adult cant. The bottom strip reverses the formula, presenting a childlike response to adultlike coaching.*

sion of their own talents—and this without risking the charge of shameless imitation. After all, there have always been gag strips about kids, but there have been few satirical allegorical gag strips featuring animals who speak a curiously comic southern dialect. Moreover, certain facets of the humor in *Peanuts* are not peculiar to a strip about kids and can therefore be handily applied to a host of other situations. And so *Peanuts* has been more successful in establishing new standards in the medium than has *Pogo* because *Peanuts* is more serviceable as a model upon which new strips can be patterned.

Once the strip became popular, its simple graphic treatment began to set a new fashion for gag strips. Gag strips had always been drawn in the comic rather than the illustrative manner, but

even so the traditionally rendered comic characters bore more resemblance to real people than do the characters in *Peanuts* with their tiny bodies and big, round heads. Like Walker, Schulz drew in a "magazine cartoon" style, but his work was more abstract at the start than Walker's. Since *Peanuts*, a number of gag strips have been drawn with similarly stylized simplicity, often so simple as to appear crude. But such simplicity can become a vital aspect of a strip's humor: it permits a flexibility in the rendering of characters' expressions that would be impossible in a more conventionally drawn strip. The wild exaggeration that was acceptable in the wake of *Peanuts*' popularity gave a new dimension to the humor of the gag strip. Just as Charlie Brown can somersault backwards, head over heels, in reaction to some absurdity in the strip, so can

Sarge beat Beetle into a tangle of squiggly lines at the bottom of an installment's concluding panel.

The humor of *Peanuts* also set new standards. Almost from its beginning, the strip appeared quite simply to be about children who often spoke in a remarkably adult way. The humor arose from the dichotomy between the speakers and what they said, between the visual and the verbal presentations. This stratagem could be modified in a number of ways. Each daily strip established its characters in a childhood situation for two or three frames, then concluded with a punch line that supplied an adult interpretation or response to the situation. The punch line might be cast in psychological, sociological, or philosophical terms, or it might consist of an unusual application of adult cant. A simple reversal of the situation (children expressing adult concerns for two or three frames, then responding childishly) offered another set of options that admitted of every possibility present in the first arrangement (figure 119).

To this, Schulz brought a unique cast of characters, each with a distinct personality trait or quirk that offered additional possibilities for variation on the initial themes. Schroeder had a fixation on Beethoven. Lucy was a chronic complainer. "Pig Pen" was a kid who couldn't stay clean: no matter what he did, he wound up dirty from head to toe. And Charlie Brown was a loser. But he didn't start that way. "I didn't know he was going to lose all the time," Schulz once said. "He certainly wasn't [at first] the victim [he became]. When he began, he had a personality a lot like Linus. He was slightly flippant, a kind of bouncy little character. He was able to come back with a wise saying to the other characters."[19] But Charlie Brown was unpopular with the rest of the cast from the very beginning. He was often annoyingly clever. And he wanted to be "perfect," as he sometimes confessed. And from these ingredients, Schulz eventually fashioned the epitome of the loser, Charlie Brown the culture hero.

Schulz could parlay the personalities of his cast into strings of gags. A given situation—say, Linus getting ready to leave for summer camp—can be presented for several days, and on each day a different character reacts to the situation in his or her own individualistic way. This method, in turn, lends itself to the creation of set pieces that can be repeated with endless permutations. Schulz once identified twelve such devices, routines to which

he attributes the popularity of the strip: (1) the kite-eating tree that frustrates Charlie Brown's every attempt to fly a kite; (2) Schroeder's music, the elaborate visual of a stanza of classical music, and Beethoven; (3) Lucy's psychiatry booth from which the fussbudget delivers her pragmatic and unsympathetic verdicts; (4) Snoopy's doghouse, the vehicle for the beagle's overactive imagination; (5) Snoopy himself, another example of a second banana taking over a strip; (6) the bird Woodstock, Snoopy's sidekick; (7) the Red Baron, symbolizing Snoopy's emergence into stardom; (8) the baseball games that Charlie Brown always loses; (9) kicking a football, an annual exercise in which Lucy tricks Charlie Brown into trying to kick the football she holds then yanks it away at the last moment, landing the hapless Charlie Brown flat on his back; (10) the Great Pumpkin, Linus's yearly search for confirmation of his spiritual sincerity; (11) the little red-haired girl with whom Charlie Brown is hopelessly in love; and (12) Linus's blanket, about which one of Schulz's biographers wrote:

> The blanket has been another wellhead of visual humor. Linus wields it like a whip, folds it into improbable shapes, and wages titanic struggles with Snoopy for it. The regenerating blanket has been cut up, ripped, stomped on, tailored into sports coats, and nearly incinerated. . . . Linus's unflagging resistance to outside pressure to give up his blanket has characterized [this] theme.[20]

The repetition of set pieces produces a peculiar kind of continuity in the strip, as well as serving to reestablish again and again in the reader's mind the personalities of the characters. Out of this emerges another distinctive feature—the running gag. A particular situation, an individual personality trait, or a characteristic response acquires the status of punch-line humor in itself and can be repeatedly introduced in different settings or situations. To the occasional reader of *Peanuts*, Charlie Brown's remarking "Good grief" at the end of a strip is not terribly funny; but for regular readers of the strip that simple phrase has taken on a significance of uproarious proportions. The running gag is hardly a new invention with Schulz, but he stretched it further than most comic strip artists had done previously.

Much of the humor in *Peanuts* arises from ordinary, trifling daily incidents, and it is here that Schulz believes he did something new. "I intro-

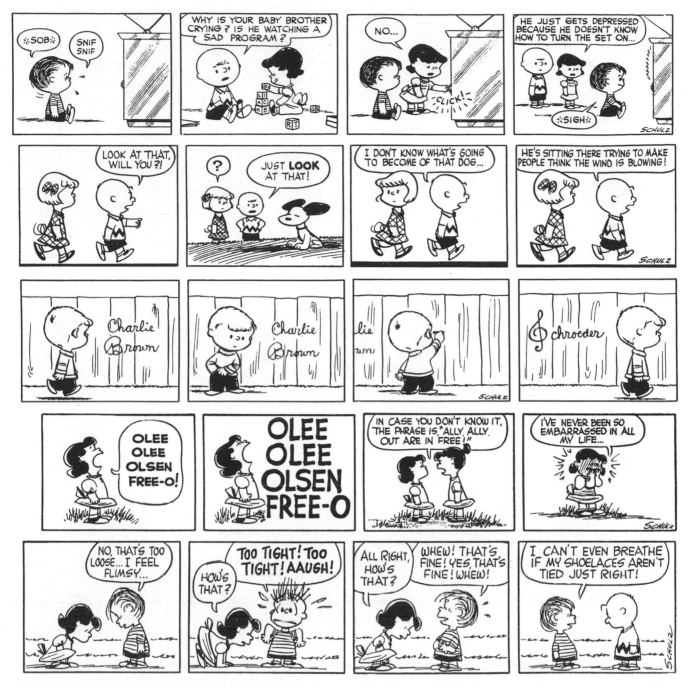

Figure 120. *Schulz perfected the humor of the "slight incident."*

duced the slight incident," he said. "I can remember creating it sitting at the desk . . . what would happen in the three panels that I was drawing at that time was a very brief and slight incident. No one had ever done that before in comic strips. Older kid strips were of the 'What shall we do today?' school. I changed all of that. I remember telling a friend that I knew I was really on to something good."21 Percy Crosby in his great kid strip *Skippy* had done something similar, Schulz acknowledges;

but Crosby's kids haven't the idiosyncratic personalities that Schulz's kids have.

The "slight incident" acquires comic impact only in conjunction with the pronounced personality of one of the strip's characters. Until Schulz showed how to combine these elements with a different emphasis, gag-strip humor had been chiefly situational: the comedy sprang more from the situation than from the characters. The characters had personalities, and they behaved "in character"

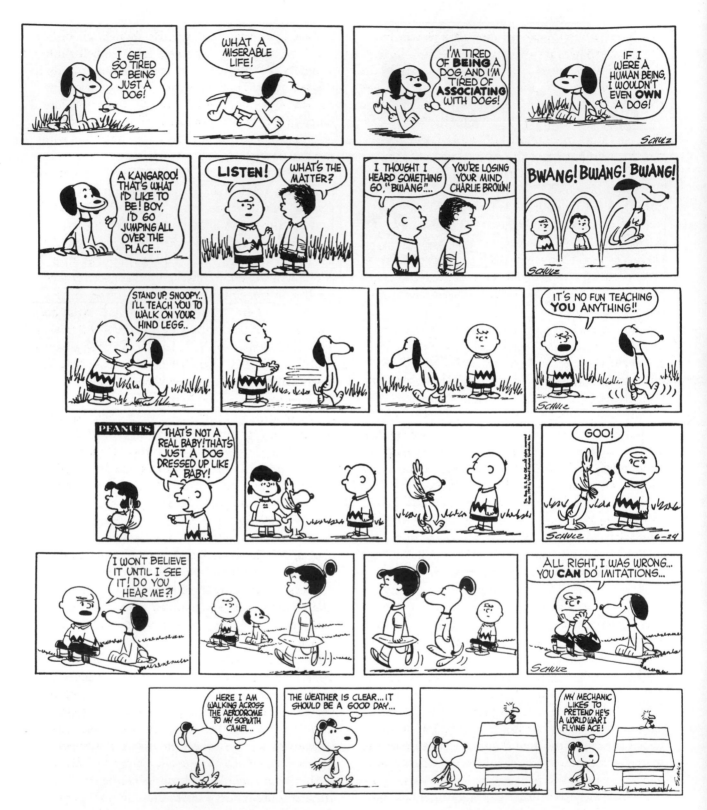

Figure 121. *Snoopy evolved from a dog who hated being a dog to a dog who could be anything his imagination required.*

in whatever circumstances they were placed, but the emphasis was on the situation. Schulz shifted the focus. He showed his characters reacting to the most mundane situations imaginable, but because their personalities were so convincingly developed, he could create comedy. When Charlie Brown coaches Linus in penmanship and Linus demonstrates an impressive calligraphic style at his first try, the incident (using a pen for the first time) is less important to the humor than Linus's personality (he's an unqualified genius). In similar fashion, Schulz can wring laughter out of Snoopy scowling at Lucy or licking her face, or Linus's shoelaces being too tight. And once Schulz had demonstrated how singular personalities can generate humor in a strip, other cartoonists began mining the same terrain.

While the essential element of the strip's humor arises from the dichotomy between the speakers and what they speak, between the world of children and that of adults, the charm of *Peanuts* and its introspective greatness lie not in its pointing to the difference between adults and children, but in its emphasizing the similarity. Charlie Brown and his friends may sound precocious, but the strip nonetheless preserves the innocence, the dreams, and the aspirations as well as the trials of childhood. The effect of the combination is that those childhood aspirations and trials do not appear much different from our own. We escape from our frustrations momentarily when Charlie Brown shares them with us. But *Peanuts* makes childhood universal without making it adult—as does *Miss Peach*, for example, in which the precocious kids sometimes sound as cynical as we are led to believe all adults become. In *Peanuts*, though, the kids never become cynical.

Snoopy embodies the strip's ever-questing spirit better than any of the other characters. During the sixties, Snoopy rose to such prominence that he threatened to take over the strip. The humor here springs from the dog's preoccupation with pursuits normally followed by humans; again, a dichotomy is at the core of the comic mechanism. And, again, it is the dichotomy of the non sequitur: from the evidence presented to our eyes (a dog), it does not follow that we will be witnessing activity usually associated with humans (flying an airplane, writing a novel). We were not always privileged to know Snoopy's thoughts. At first, he was a dog like all dogs. He barked; he didn't write novels.

But then he began thinking. He thought about how much he disliked being a dog. He tried being other animals—an alligator, a kangaroo, a lion lurking in the tall grass. Then he began doing imitations of humans—of Lucy, Violet, even Beethoven. Before long, he was walking on his hind legs. And then he started flying his doghouse into dogfights with the Red Baron.

Mort Walker watched Snoopy's development into something other than a beagle with growing dismay—then wonderment. "When Charlie Schulz first did Snoopy in a helmet sitting on top of the dog house pretending he was fighting the Red Baron, I thought Schulz was going to ruin the strip. I could believe Snoopy sitting up there sort of pretending or imagining he was a vulture or something, but where did he get the helmet? What does a dog know about World War I or the Red Baron? And then he showed bullet holes in the dog house. I said, Good golly—this has gone beyond the pale. Then when it became so popular, I said, It just shows you—comics, as Rube Goldberg used to say, are an individual effort that is so beyond explaining that nobody could ever mastermind it."[22]

Schulz sees Snoopy as the fantasy element of the strip. "He is the image of what people would like a dog to be," he told *Time*.[23] Maybe not all people; maybe just children. In his role-playing, Snoopy clearly does what little kids normally do: he imagines adventures in which he is the hero. His charm, Schulz recognizes, resides in the childlike combination of innocence and egotism that define his personality and propel him into new and unlikely circumstances again and again. He never tires, never gives up. And neither does Charlie Brown.

Despite Snoopy's bid for stardom in the strip, the strong personalities of the other characters kept reasserting themselves. And Schulz kept inventing more distinctive personalities—Peppermint Patty, Marci. But he always came back to Charlie Brown. "All the ideas on how poor old Charlie Brown can lose give me great satisfaction," Schulz once said. "But of course his reactions to all of this are equally important. He just keeps fighting back. He just keeps trying. And I guess that particular theme has caught the imagination of a lot of people nowadays. We all need the feeling that somebody really likes us. And I'm very proud that somehow all these ideas about Charlie Brown's struggle might help in some very small way."[24]

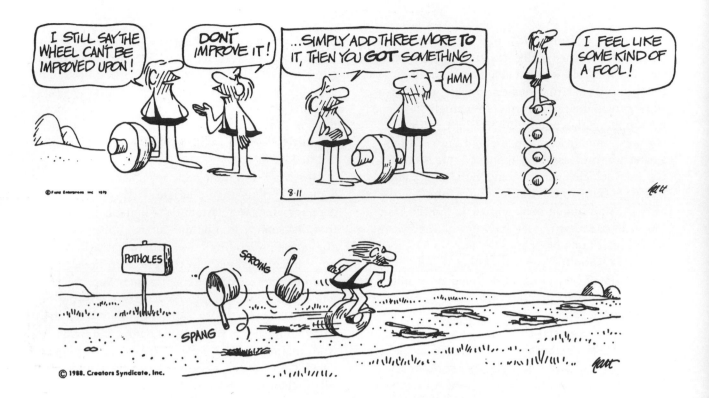

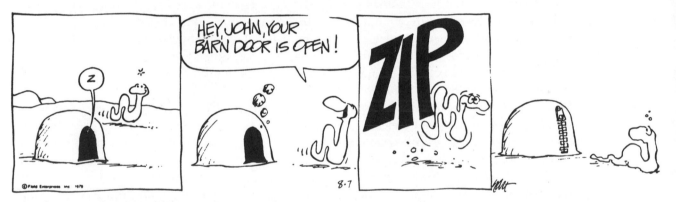

Figure 122. *In B.C., Johnny Hart offers anachronistic humor, comedy that derives from the dichotomy between the prehistoric setting of his strip and the modern preoccupations of his characters, between the visual and the verbal.*

Humor arising from a dichotomy, or "non sequitur humor," is another characteristic of *Peanuts* that set a comic strip fashion. Or, if it did not exactly set the fashion (a debatable point since the "sick jokes" and "elephant jokes" of the fifties turn on a similar comic device), it was at least the first strip to capture and capitalize on a mode of humorous thinking then in the air. Two other strips that have at their core some adaptation of the principles of non sequitur humor are *B.C.* and *Tumbleweeds*. In each strip, as in *Peanuts*, the adaptation is original, inventive, and highly individual, and in each strip the reader finds again the devices and techniques made familiar to him in *Peanuts*—artwork deceptively simple, personality traits sharpened nearly

to the point of eccentricity, repetition of set pieces, the running gag, animals with human aspirations.

When Johnny Hart's *B.C.* began on February 17, 1958, the comedy at first sprang from our recognition of a discrepancy between the visual and the verbal, between the setting of the strip and the concerns of its characters. The setting is prehistoric; the concerns, the preoccupations, are ours of the twentieth century. Hence, even in this unlikely setting, we are delightfully surprised to discover—ourselves. But with a difference. Man, as always, is the inventor, the discoverer. And there is a childlike (and therefore entirely human) delight in discovery, invention, novelty. But an invention

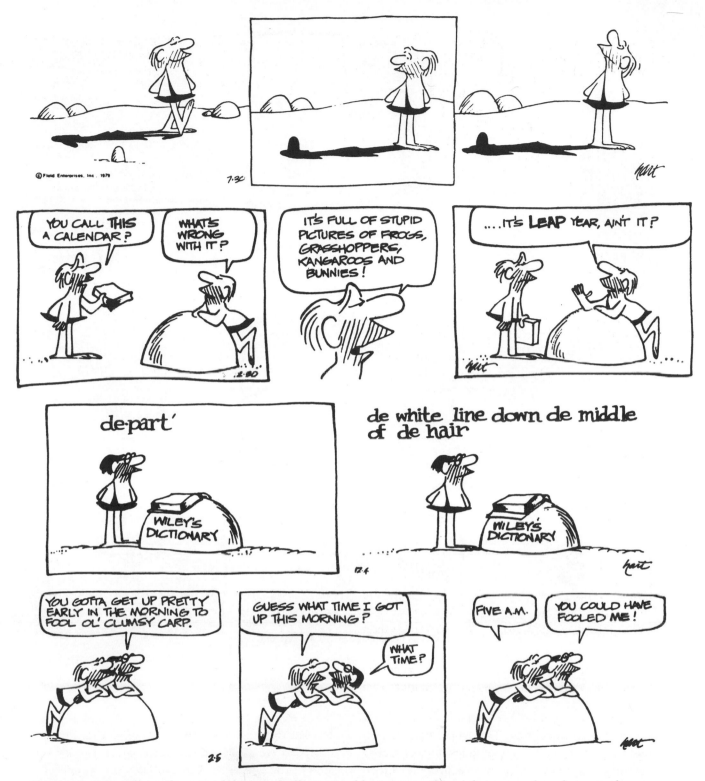

Figure 123. B.C. *still retails some of the most brilliant visual humor around (top), but more often than not, the humor is essentially verbal.*

lands in the world of *B.C.* full-blown, without having evolved from a need. Like children, the prehistoric characters in *B.C.* fasten on some new device without fully understanding its function or the principles upon which its operation rests. (The railroad train in our example in chapter 1 is typical.) The result is that newly discovered devices are not put to their proper use: they remain novelties, oddities, things that fit into our world, but not quite into theirs. Thor's invention of the

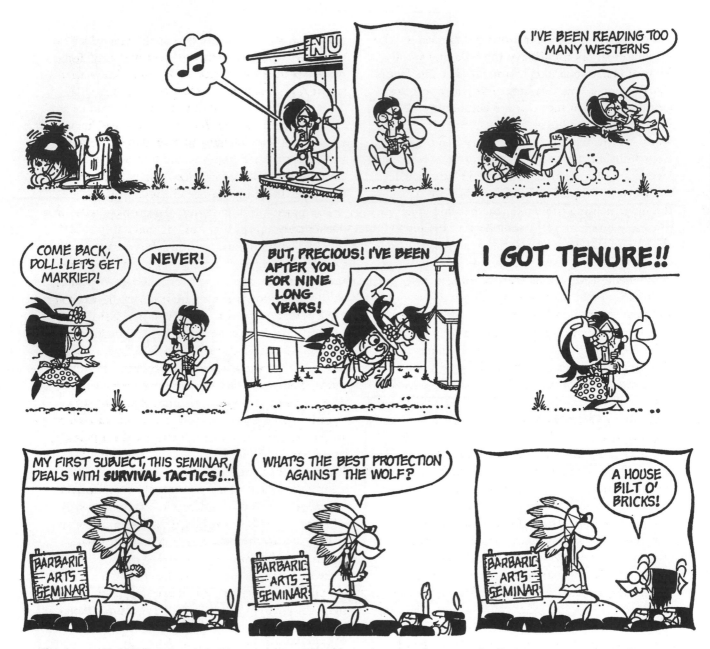

Figure 124. *Tom K. Ryan's comic Western fantasy,* Tumbleweeds, *is another example of a contemporary strip that builds its comedy upon a discrepancy, in this case, the discrepancy between the Hollywood expectations of his cowpokes and the reality of life in the not-so-glamorous old West.*

wheel is a prize specimen. The wheel he is so proud of isn't attached to a vehicle: it's just a circular stone that Thor rides by straddling it as if it were a horse. *B.C.* evolved into something else over the years, however, and its humor eventually depended less and less upon anachronism.

In *Tumbleweeds*, which began in September 1965, Tom K. Ryan builds up the ideal of the Old West and then punches holes in it. Here the discrepancy or dichotomy is between the myth of the Old West and its reality. Ryan's diminutive charac-

ters set the stage with their cuteness: they are so cute that we expect to encounter a child's rosy version of the Old West. Ryan inflates the speech of his characters to match the yearnings that the pictures seem to express, but the facts of life then deflate this scenario. The dialogue abounds in the clichés and doggerel mythology of the dime-novel Western, but reality is seldom as high-flown as the prose. The title character's mount is not the noble steed of yesterday's Roy Rogers movie: he's a moth-eaten army surplus cayuse, and he can never quite live up to the aspirations of his master, who celebrates in his mind's eye the wild and woolly West of Hollywood, not historical fact. The fact is that his horse Epic can never jump across those gullies that yawn like chasms before him. Tumbleweeds, despite his aspirations, must live in this world, not in his dreams. On every hand, expectations built on the Old West of motion picture and legend are disappointed. The sheriff can capture the town hoodlum but can't lock him up in jail; the judge is blind to justice; the heroine is not a modestly blushing shy young desert blossom— she's painfully plain and aggressively desperate to catch a man. Not even the Indians live up to our Hollywood expectations: hardly savages, they must go to school and take evening classes in the theory and practice of bloodthirsty warfare.

Still, even if our fond anticipations are destined to be blighted, the lesson of the strip is not bleak. Tumbleweeds's dreams may be doomed to disappointment, but there is no bitter disillusionment here—only a remarkable resilience. The characters turn quickly from their fancies to the facts and embrace reality. Hildegarde may want Tumbleweeds as her husband, but, in the last analysis, any man will do. The realities do not crush these pint-sized dreamers—nor do they quite wake them up.

The humor in these new strips is more sophisticated than comic strip comedy had been in the past. The humor of *Blondie* was, and is, humor appropriate to the setting in which the characters are developed and appropriate to the characters themselves: the success of the punch line does not rest on our ability to recognize a dichotomy or discrepancy between characters and setting, dialogue and action. The humor of *Bugs Bunny* or of *Donald Duck* does not originate in their being animals that behave like humans, as it does with Snoopy in *Peanuts*. Nor, in these two strips, does the comedy come from the animals behaving like animals, as it sometimes does in *Pogo* or in *Animal Crackers*. The humor in the strips of this new tradition —*Pogo, Peanuts, B.C., The Wizard of Id, Tumbleweeds, Animal Crackers*, to name a few—is more sophisticated because it depends on our recognizing something that is only implicit in the strip. We laugh at *B.C.* because we are shown childlike men, men just beginning to be men, trying out civilization, and we see what they do not: like a suit that's too large, civilization doesn't quite fit. We laugh at *Tumbleweeds* much of the

time because we recognize that the real Old West was quite different from the West that tiny Tumbleweeds tries to reenact. If we didn't know that trains run on round wheels along smooth rails, Thor's choo-choo wouldn't appear funny to us at all. If we didn't know that most cowboys' horses don't jump wide chasms in a single bound, Tumbleweeds's dashed hopes would be tragic instead of comic. But we do know these things, and upon that knowledge the humor of these strips is built.

The humor of dichotomy—because it points to a discrepancy, a non sequitur—is inevitably sobering. In *Tumbleweeds*, for example, it isn't just the Old West that the characters try to create with their language, and it isn't just the Old West that can't live up to its poetry. Man hovers between the lines here, and he is a bit short of his vision of himself, too, just as he is in *B.C.* and in *Pogo*.

The artwork in *Beetle Bailey* and *Peanuts* was as influential as the nature of the humor in the strips. The simplicity of each style opened the door to a range of graphic techniques that were equally uncomplicated. And as the size of comic strips steadily shrank (ironically, by the 1980s all comic strips were about the size of the first year's *Peanuts*), only simply rendered pictures could be clearly discerned in the tiny panels. But the general acceptance of this style of drawing led down a slippery slope. Newspaper editors are scarcely art critics, and to their relatively undiscriminating eyes a crudely drawn comic strip was much the same as a simply drawn one. Moreover, once the joke became the most important aspect of a comic strip, the manner of rendering the pictures seemed not to matter at all.

Accordingly, by the end of the eighties the nation's comics pages were thoroughly infected with drawings of dubious quality. When Schulz and Walker started their syndicated careers, they decided, deliberately, to draw simply; they had the facility to draw more realistically, but they chose to render their strips in an unembellished, abstract fashion. The same cannot be said for some of those who followed in their footsteps. These are the cartoonists of what Schulz calls "the high school yearbook school of drawing"; they are amateurs. In their pictures, these cartoonists are obviously groping for the right lines. Their perspective is either off or nonexistent, their knowledge of anatomy is faulty, and their skill with pen or brush is rudimentary at best. Many of this new

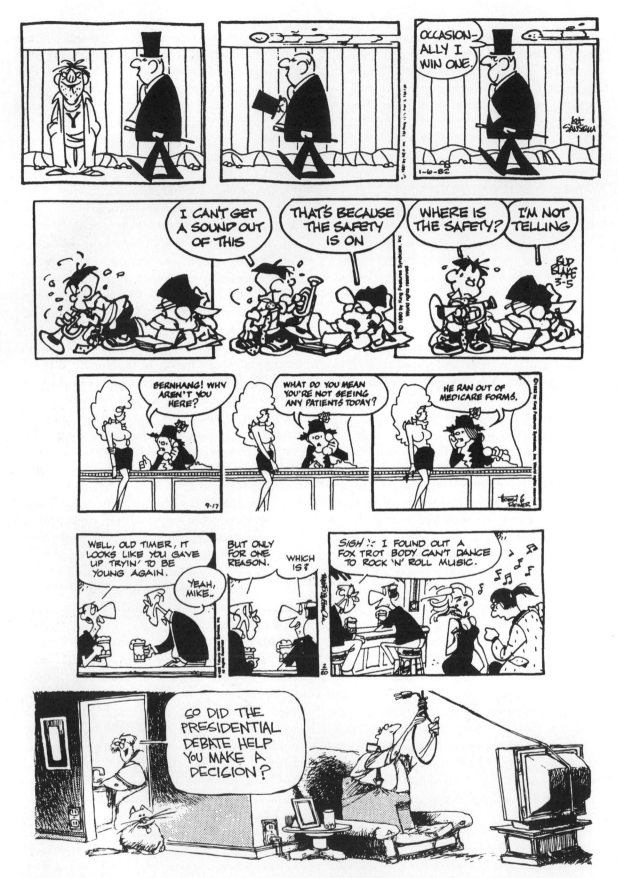

Figure 125. *A sampler of well-drawn strips from the 1980s and 1990s. From the top down:* The Born Loser *by Art Sansom,* Tiger *by Bud Blake,* Agatha Crumm *by Hoest and Reiner,* Motley's Crew *by Ben Templeton and Tom Foreman, and* Non Sequitur *by David Wiley Miller. "Wiley" compensates for the absence of timing in his one-panel "strip" by spreading the information essential to his gag across the entire picture: to comprehend his jokes the reader must "read" the entire "strip" left to right, as if it were a sequence of panels.*

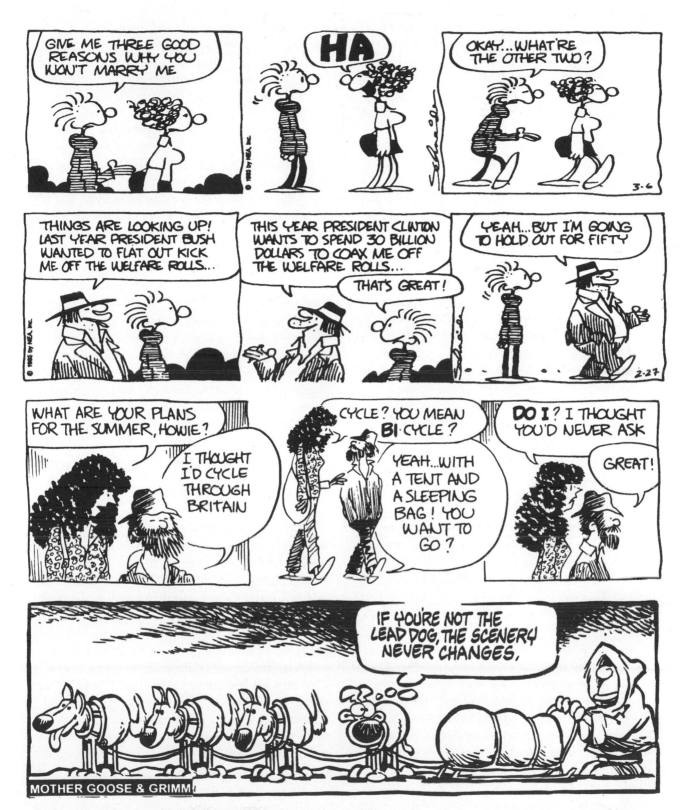

Figure 126. *Howie Schneider's* Eek and Meek *(top two strips) displays the cartoonist's confidence in linework, thereby betraying a skill not otherwise in evidence. In the mid-1980s Schneider did an autobiographical strip,* Howie, *for which he used a more sophisticated style (third from the top). Mike Peters's strip (bottom), the ultimate "dog strip," is another example of a well-drawn strip.*

breed have an acute sense of humor, brilliantly satirical in perception and bent. But the manner in which they draw offends the eye of the art lovers of yore who worship at the altar of a graceful line and a well-drawn tableau.

Walker's graphic style was perpetuated in all the strips that emerged from his shop. And Dik Browne added a finely felt texture to *Hi and Lois* and, later, to *Hagar*. And many other strips that debuted in the sixties and seventies were drawn in a similar "magazine cartoon" style—Art Sansom's *Born Loser*, for example, drawn in a manner so refined that it was dazzling in its purity. Equally elegant rendering can be found in *Boomer*, *Wright Angles*, *Motley's Crew*, *Agatha Crumm*, and *Eb and Flo* (a *Hi and Lois* approximation). *Peanuts* initially inspired a parade of strips about kids, all drawn with big heads and little bodies. Among the first of these was Mel Lazarus's *Miss Peach*, introduced February 4, 1957. Lazarus took Schulz's style a step further: the kids in Miss Peach's classroom have bodies that are infinitesimal, mere squiggles, and their gigantic heads are crowned with bulbous noses that grow out of their foreheads in a deformed caricature of childhood. Morrie Turner restored more realistic proportions in early 1965 with his multiracial *Wee Pals*, but the Schulz model was followed pretty faithfully in such strips as *Winthrop* and Bud Blake's *Tiger* (a symphony of black solids and quirky, lilting line).

To the extent that Schulz's stylized and simplified anatomy inspired Johnny Hart in *B.C.*, then Schulz as well as Hart can be detected in such strips as *The Wizard of Id* (written by Hart and drawn by Brant Parker), *Animal Crackers*, *Catfish*, *Inside Woody Allen*, *Frank and Ernest*, and *Eek and Meek*. All these are drawn in a simple but relatively sketchy manner. Howie Schneider's style in *Eek and Meek* is perhaps the least refined of the styles represented in these strips, but, like Schulz and Walker, Schneider chooses to draw this way. That genuine skill at drawing underpins his style can be readily ascertained by comparing the confidence of Schneider's linework with the gawky tentative scrawl of Kevin Fagan's work in the early *Drabble* or the wooden minimalism of Scott Adams in *Dilbert*. But the way to *Drabble* and *Dilbert* was paved as much by Garry Trudeau as by Schulz and Hart. Trudeau's *Doonesbury* arrived in twenty-eight papers on October 26, 1970, and within a very few years, its popularity—notoriety,

even—had established the legitimacy of bad drawing, apparently for the rest of the century.

Doonesbury had a trial run during Trudeau's college days at Yale. Under the title *Bull Tales*, it appeared in 1968 in the *Yale Record*, an irregularly published magazine (edited, for a time, by Trudeau), and, starting September 30 that year, in the campus newspaper, the *Yale Daily News*. Trudeau was influenced by Jules Feiffer, who had attracted a cult following with the weekly cartoon he had been doing for the *Village Voice* since 1956. Drawing in a simple, sketchy style, Feiffer specialized in the angst of modern America. His cartoon is mostly talk. Indeed, his characters are psychotic about talk. In agonizingly introspective monologues and dialogues, they explore their psychological or sexual anguish, invariably tripping over their own shortcomings as they unintentionally reveal their personality disorders and character flaws in the progress of their discourse. Visual-verbal blending is minimal in Feiffer's cartoon: although the pictures sometimes underscore the irony of the characters' self-revelatory remarks, they primarily serve to pace the talk. Feiffer had a good ear for the way people talk, and in capturing their speech and pacing it, he gave his cartoon a unique rhythm, a cadence that led inexorably to a punch line of revelation.

Trudeau drew in Feiffer's sketchy fashion, even eschewing speech balloons by clustering his characters' verbiage near their heads like Feiffer did. But his college kids did not whine in endless self-analysis. Instead, they commented, directly or indirectly, on aspects of campus life. Trudeau's humor was not of the bemused non sequitur sort; it was attack comedy, sharp and barbed. Trudeau was incisive and witty, his insights often powerfully satirical and always irreverent. It was an age of collegiate irreverence. It was the age of protest—against the Vietnam War, against the establishment, against authority of all kinds. The temper of the times fostered among some young cartoonists a revolutionary counterculture, and they expressed their disdain for mainstream America by producing "underground comix," comic books that championed the drug culture and assaulted conventional sexual mores with graphic gusto. Trudeau was not so blatant as his underground compeers, but he was every bit as perceptive and angry. He attracted the attention of the Universal Press syndicate, and

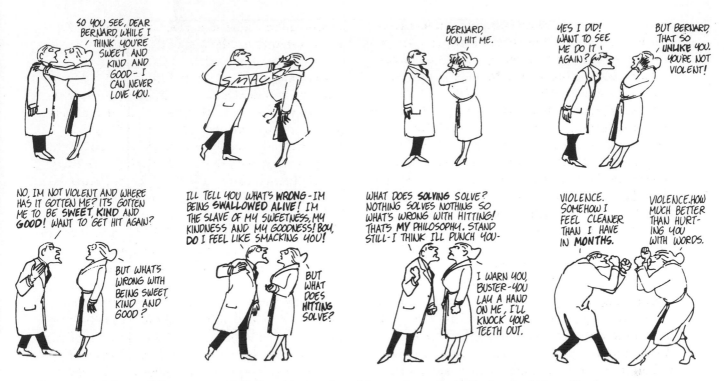

Figure 127. *Jules Feiffer's cartoons, in both subject and graphic treatment, probably inspired Garry Trudeau.*

after Trudeau graduated with a masters in art in 1970, *Bull Tales* was reincarnated as *Doonesbury*, Trudeau appropriating the name of the strip's would-be Lothario for the new title. As a syndicated feature, *Doonesbury* continued Trudeau's satiric attack but extended his range of targets to include society at large as well as campus life. And when Richard Nixon committed Watergate, Trudeau had a field day. *Pogo* was still being published, but it was on its last legs; Walt Kelly was mortally ill, and Trudeau unceremoniously donned his mantle as the most pungent political satirist on the comics page.

Unlike Kelly, Trudeau used the real names of his targets. Although he didn't draw pictures of Nixon, he drew the White House and lettered outside its windows speeches that only Nixon and his embattled aides could have uttered. In one of the most famous strips of the period, Trudeau contrived for one of his characters, Mark Slackmeyer, to pronounce John Mitchell guilty while at the same time pretending to allow the former U.S. attorney general the presumption of innocence (figure 129).

For a long time, I was not much impressed by Trudeau's work. It was his drawing ability, or lack thereof, that turned me off. Yes, I am one of those art lovers I invoked a few pages ago, one of those

who is distressed by ugly, amateurish artwork. In Trudeau's case, I was put off mostly by his habitually static visuals: panel after panel, the pictures stay the same while the political commentary drones on. Dull. In a medium in which the visual and the verbal should blend, neither making complete sense without the other, it seemed to me that Trudeau's visuals did little more than establish the setting and identify the speakers. Scarcely high art. But then I spent a weekend poring over *The Doonesbury Chronicles*, a reprint collection of strips from the feature's first four years, and the experience altered my opinion. While it is often true that once the setting is established by the opening panel, the sense of the words is largely independent of the pictures, there is, I realized, a tension between word and picture that adds a layer of meaning to the strip.

Imagine a typical Trudeau sequence: a shot of the White House (repeated without alteration throughout the strip), or of Michael Doonesbury watching TV motionlessly. To begin with, the unchanging pictures act to mute the impact of the words—the strip's only "action." Without much visual activity, the tone of the strip is rigorously restrained. And in those strips in which the last panel incorporates some minor visual change (Zonker looking helplessly out at the audience in

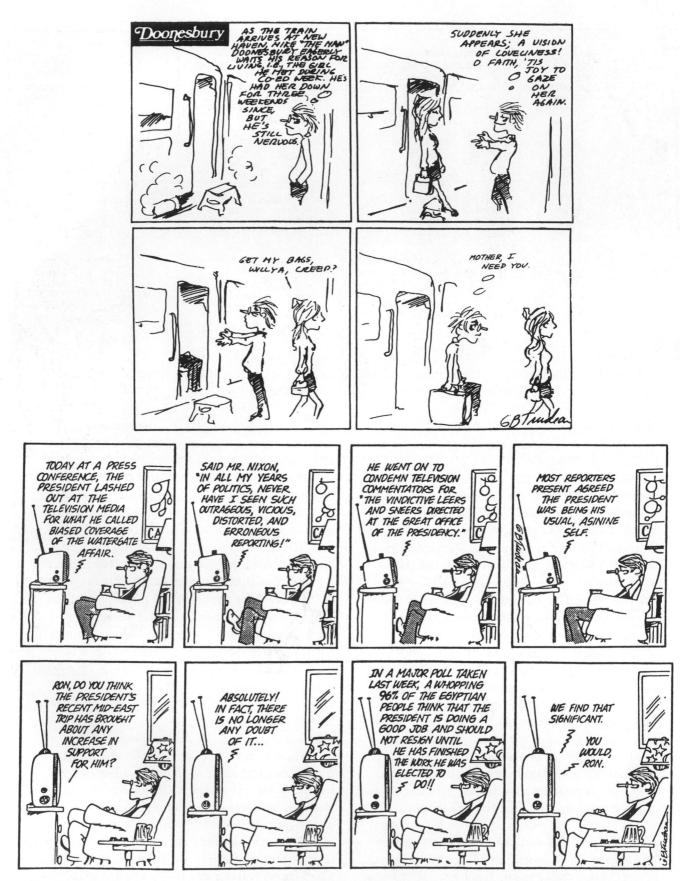

Figure 128. *Trudeau's early drawing style was extremely sketchy, in the manner of Jules Feiffer (top), although later it became somewhat more refined (bottom two strips). Typical of Trudeau's presabbatical work, the static visuals of these two strips make dull viewing; but here, the medium is the message.*

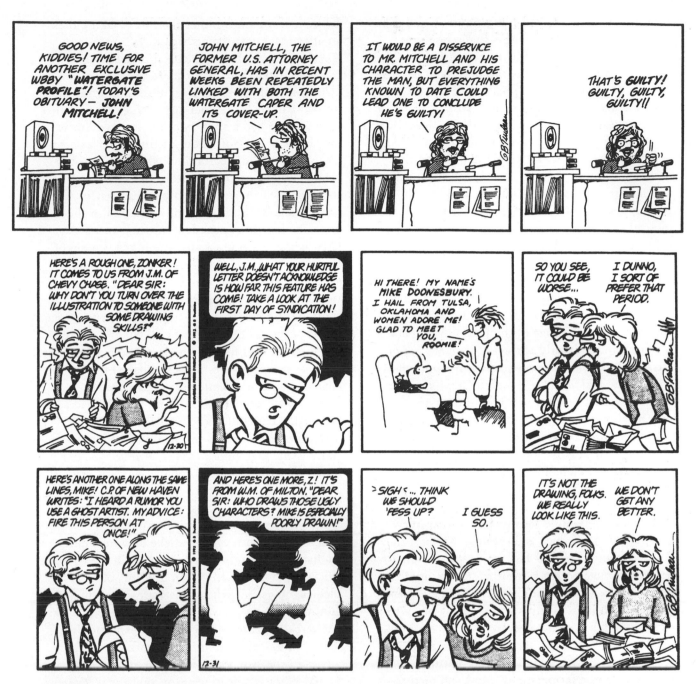

Figure 129. *At the top is Trudeau's celebrated verdict on John Mitchell's guilt in the Watergate scandal. The next two strips, from 1992, show Trudeau's postsabbatical drawing style—variety in camera distance and compositions, use of silhouettes, and flowing, flexible linework by Don Carlton.*

frustration or Michael starting to smile), that change—however slight—gains greatly in dramatic import. Since the fourth-panel alteration is the only thing "happening" in the strip, it draws attention to itself way out of proportion to the intensity of the "action" itself. Thus, a single fourth-panel variation in an otherwise repetitive series of panels becomes a powerful device for Trudeau's edi-

torializing. Under these circumstances, even a lifted eyebrow can tell us how we are to interpret the verbal message: ironically, seriously, mockingly, whatever.

A reverse effect is achieved in those strips in which the fourth panel presents no variation, in which all four panels are visually identical. In these strips, there is no editorial comment whatsoever. The verbal message is presented, and it has no effect, no impact, on the visuals. Nothing changes. Thus, there seems to be no relationship between the words and the pictures. And because we expect a relationship, its absence constitutes the message of the strip. In such strips, the words may suggest some political or merchandising high jinks, some grossly self-serving enterprise. Because there seems to be no relationship between the words and the pictures, it is as if the strip is presenting us with two worldviews. The visuals portray "our" world; concrete details make it recognizable to us. The words, however, suggest another world—the absurd extremity that results if we extend the logic of our politics or social customs or merchandising practices. These worlds run parallel to each other, but neither seems to have any real effect upon the other. And that, in fact, is the existential message of the medium as practiced by Trudeau: the world we seem to create out of custom and mores has no bearing upon or relationship to the real world of concrete details in which we all dwell. The ideal to which our customs aspire has become absurdly out of touch.

Visually, the *Doonesbury* of this period was about as dull as it is possible for a comic strip to be. But to do as I had been doing (to look for a blending of word and picture in which the sense of each is dependent upon the other) was to fall short of grasping the whole meaning of *Doonesbury*. Still, the method does yield results—even if they are unexpected results. The words and the pictures in *Doonesbury* do work together. One comments on the other—while each retains an independent (albeit sometimes absurd) sense of its own. With this deployment of the resources of the medium, Trudeau has taken the art of the comic strip a step further. He has made the very nature of the medium—the relationship of word and picture—the vehicle of his humor and his comment. In a much more specific sense than in other strips, in *Doonesbury* the medium is message.

In daring, Trudeau is certainly Walt Kelly's equal. But he falls far short of Kelly's artistry. After all, despite the existential tension between word and picture in the static panel installments, Trudeau's strip is mostly a verbal exercise: it makes its satiric thrusts with words rather than by blending word and picture in fine-tuned concert. And the power of *Doonesbury's* humor is rooted in the strip's penchant for calling its political villains by their real names rather than by cloaking them in allegorical costume as was Kelly's practice. There's less art than audacity in *Doonesbury*.

Equally audacious was the unprecedented twenty-month sabbatical Trudeau took from January 1983 until September 1984. When he returned, *Doonesbury* had a slightly different look. Static panels were not trotted out as frequently as before. The artwork had a certain polish this time out, thanks in part to Don Carlton, the artist who inked Trudeau's penciled strips. Years earlier, Trudeau had given up inking the strip; and in the 1980s he faxed his penciled drawings to Kansas City, where Carlton created the inked version of the strip. Together, Trudeau and Carlton now sought greater visual variety in every daily installment. They varied camera distance and angle and spotted solid blacks dramatically. The appearance of the strip was much improved, but the existential message was forfeit. Too late: the previous years of static pictures had established the "photocopied" panel as a legitimate artistic mode. In graphic style as well as content, Trudeau had set a precedent that could not be recalled.

Doonesbury ushered in the era of poorly drawn comic strips. *Drabble, Dilbert, Arnold, Sally Forth, Foxtrot,* and the autobiographical *Cathy* (flat and gray as a TV test pattern in black and white). The humor in such strips was often of the highest order—witty, trenchant, insightful, the satiric embodiment of Truth even. But the drawing ability on display was embarrassingly unskilled. Syndicate officials and salesmen got around this obvious inadequacy by saying the strips were drawn in a new minimalist style: they had a "contemporary look." But verbal equivocation could not expunge the shortcomings of amateurish artwork.

Not all the new strips looked quite so contemporary. When Trudeau went on sabbatical, *Doonesbury's* place in the lineup on many comics pages was taken by Berke Breathed's *Bloom County*. Echoing *Doonesbury* when it debuted on December 8, 1980, Breathed's strip soon proved to have a unique flavor of its own. A fantasy tangy with social commentary and satire, it was drawn in somewhat the same sketchy manner as *Doonesbury*, albeit with the confident flair of a greater artistic competence. Another fantasy strip was Mike Peters's 1984 entry, *Mother Goose and Grimm*. Initially, the strip's comedy sprang from anachronistic fairy-tale allusions, but when Peters settled in for the long haul, he focused on Mother Goose's manic dog Grimm and developed the ultimate "dog strip." Drawing in bold brush strokes with great verve and dash, Peters demonstrated consistently the comic efficacy of the medium's classic blend of verbal and visual content. But before the ultimate "dog strip" came along, there was the ultimate "cat strip."

Jim Davis had been assisting Tom Ryan on *Tumbleweeds* while he tried to sell a comic strip about anthropomorphic insects. After five years of rejections, he shifted to an anthropomorphic cat, and *Garfield* was introduced on June 19, 1978. In giving the center of his stage to a fat cat, Davis created comedy out of laziness, selfishness, a voracious appetite, and a colossal ego. Garfield, Davis once said, is "a very selfish animal, someone out for his own creature comforts; someone very egotistical yet so honest people can't dislike him."[25] In fact, they liked him very much. *Garfield* became a phenomenon. Within five years the strip was in over a thousand papers; within a dozen years, more than 2,100 worldwide, catching (if not surpassing) *Peanuts*. Books reprinting the strip made the *New York Times* best-seller list for weeks, sometimes several of them at the same time. As the 1990s dawned, *Garfield* had become as large a cottage industry as *Peanuts*. Davis employed a staff of forty to produce the strip and merchandise the character (mercilessly—through some four hundred licensees that produce the paunchy feline's face and form on everything from lunchboxes to Christmas tree ornaments).

In spite of all the mercantile enterprise, Davis remains in control of the strip. The final artwork is produced by Gary Barker, who pencils the strip, and Valette Grene, who inks it. But Barker begins with sketched gags supplied by Davis. Judging from the evidence of the strip alone, it's clear that *Garfield*, regardless of the number of hands that produce it, still reflects a single creative intelligence. The humor of the strip has a certain style, and that style is not one that is easily imitated. More than many of its contemporaries on the funnies pages, *Garfield* is a visual strip. Most of its gags depend upon the pictures: before we can comprehend the joke, we must understand the pictures. And many of the gags are sight gags, entirely visual. Movement—action, usually of the swiftest sort—characterizes many of the installments. In this respect, *Garfield* has about it the nimbus of a classic Tex Avery animated cartoon—wild, improbable action yielding highly comic results.

Garfield was rare in another respect during the eighties: it was not the product of market research or demographic studies. The decade was awash with comic strips aimed at distinctly defined audiences. Thinking of a newspaper as the conveyance of advertising, syndicate officials began to concoct comic strips that would appeal to specific segments of the buying public. Such strips could be sold to newspaper editors as the attractions that would bring these buyers to the newspaper—and to the ads in the papers, and, subsequently, to the stores that placed the ads. Before long, every special interest group in the demographic hopper had a strip tailored for it—working mothers, single fathers, blue-collar workers, sports fans, racial minorities, baby boomers, retirees, and career women of all descriptions. Although some of these contrivances managed to acquire gifted cartoonists or artist and writer teams and were consequently lively and entertaining, many were flat and lifeless, the result of the uninspired calculations of demographers rather than the creations of honest artistic sensibilities. In many of these endeavors, the classic blending of the medium's visual and verbal elements all but disappear. Many such strips are entirely verbal: the pictures do no more than identify the characters who are speaking. To the extent that a gag may spring from the personality of a particular character, then the humor is dependent upon the pictures, but this kind of dependency is a far cry from the dramatic blending that distinguishes the best of the medium. Thus, the strip form itself—the sequencing of action in a series of panels—is used solely as a way of timing the delivery of a verbal gag.

What with the ugliness of strips boasting a "contemporary look" and the cobbled-up contraptions of market research and the vapid verbal humor that undermined the function of pictures in the medium, comic strips seemed an endangered species. And then, in November 1985, a breath of genius blew across the land.

It was a new strip that was drawn from panel to panel instead of being a parade of photocopied pictures. Every panel was different. Even more astonishing—and gratifying beyond expression—the cartoonist doing this comic strip could draw.

He could draw his characters in more than one position and with more than one expression. And he could draw a lot of things—not just his characters but also houses, animals, landscapes, street scenes. Anything. And he wasn't doing the strip by demographic prescription. "I just draw for myself," Bill Watterson said.[26]

For himself—and for millions of readers who took *Calvin and Hobbes* to their hearts in record time. Watterson's profession did the same: before the strip was two years old, Watterson had won the National Cartoonists Society's coveted Reuben Award, the accolade of his peers as best cartoonist of the year. He won it again two years later. Unprecedented. And Watterson wasn't even a member of the organization. Even before the first Reuben, though, it was clear to Watterson and his syndicate, Universal Press, that he had a hit strip on his hands. And at that point, Watterson once again indulged a maverick tendency. The merchandising hustlers began to pester him about licensing his creation for T-shirts, greeting cards, toys of all sorts, jewelry, coloring books, TV appearances—all that stuff that earned fortunes for Schulz and Davis—but when they came knocking on Watterson's door, he kept the door closed.

He explained his reasons in one of the few interviews he's given. "I'm convinced," he said, "that licensing [the characters] would sell out the soul of *Calvin and Hobbes*." He sees his strip as more than a gag strip; it does more than tell a joke: "The humor is situational, and often episodic. It relies on conversation, and the development of personalities and relationships. These aren't concerns you can wrap up neatly in a clever little saying for people to send each other or to hang up on their walls."[27]

The idea of a Hobbes doll, for example, is "especially noxious." Such a product would "take the character out of the world for which he was intended. If you stick thirty Hobbes dolls on a drugstore shelf, you're no longer talking about a character I created. At that point, you've transformed him into just another overpriced knickknack." And this would do serious violence to the very heart of the strip: "The whole intrigue of Hobbes is that he may or may not be a real tiger. The strip deliberately sets up two versions of reality without committing itself to either one. If *I'm* not going to answer the question of who or what Hobbes is, I'm certainly not going to let Dakin an-

swer it. It makes no sense to allow someone to make Hobbes into a stuffed toy for real, and deprive the strip of an element of its magic."[28]

In the last analysis, Watterson fears that merchandising the strip would destroy the relationship that must exist between a creator and his creation if the work is to have a life of its own. "I'm happy that people enjoy the strip and have become devoted to it," he said. "But it seems that with a lot of the marketing stuff, the incentive is just to cash in. [The merchandised gimmicks] are not trying to do the job of the comic strip; they are not giving jokes or developing characters. . . . Calvin and Hobbes will not exist intact if I do not exist intact; and I will not exist intact if I have to put up with all this stuff."[29] Watterson believes that books reprinting the strip are the only legitimate byproduct of his work. But he won't even flog the books. When the publisher of the first collection of reprints, *Calvin and Hobbes*, asked Watterson to embark upon a national public appearance tour to promote sales of the book, he said no.

Watterson had heard "no" a lot until 1985. After graduating from Kenyon College in Ohio in 1980, he found a job as the political cartoonist for the *Cincinnati Post*. But it didn't work out. Watterson's comic sensibilities were not suited to political cartooning; he was fired after a few months. He then spent the next five years trying to sell one comic strip idea after another to an assortment of syndicates. After six failures, he hit upon a seventh that eventually resulted in *Calvin and Hobbes*.

Ostensibly, the strip is built on the premise that the relationship between an imaginative young kid (a six-year-old, to be precise) and his favorite stuffed animal will produce situations to amuse readers. Indicative of the kid's imaginative prowess is the strip's visual gimmick: when the kid Calvin is alone with his toy tiger, Hobbes appears as a real tiger, walking and talking and all the rest of it; but whenever adults are on the scene, the tiger is depicted merely as a stuffed animal. This treatment is evocative of *Barnaby* of the 1940s, in which a boy of Calvin's age acquires a fairy godfather who his parents think is wholly imaginary. We, however, know better because we *see* Mr. O'Malley, as he is called. (Moreover, we recognize in him a con man of the W. C. Fields persuasion.) But Watterson arrived at his conception by his own route: born in 1958, he hadn't heard of Crockett

Johnson's famed strip or seen it until after *Calvin and Hobbes* was launched.

At the beginning of the strip's run, the novelty of Watterson's approach was useful: it served to remind us of just how active Calvin's imagination is. (To say it is hyperactive is putting it mildly.) But even then, very few of the gags depended on our knowing that Hobbes is a stuffed animal. And once the strip was thoroughly launched, Watterson made less and less use of the ploy. He focused more on Calvin as a personality and less on the relationship between the boy and his stuffed tiger. Consequently, although Hobbes appears with about the same frequency as he did at the beginning, he appears almost always as the "live" creature of Calvin's imagination, not as the stuffed toy.

And that is just as it should be, because the strip is really about Calvin. The comedy arises from the outrageousness of his assault on the real world—the world of adults. Our world. Lost in the world of his imagination, Calvin is Spaceman Spiff confronting a bug-eyed Graknil for the first three panels of the strip. In the last panel, the veil is drawn aside, and we find Calvin at his desk in school; the alien monster is really Miss Wormwood, his somewhat intimidating teacher, who stands before him demanding his book report. But Calvin, reportless, smiles the tolerant and superior smile of Spiff, knowing that the Graknil's moments are numbered.

With increasing mastery of his supple brush, Watterson made credible even the most fantastic of Calvin's daydreams. Dinosaurs tower and lurch menacingly through the panels until Calvin is brought back to this century's reality; alligators float ominously in the swimming pool, eyes heavily lidded with sinister appetite. Drawn convincingly, with scrupulously accurate anatomy, the dinosaurs and alligators make Calvin's fantasies real—an illusion integral to the unfolding joke. And Watterson's landscapes—whether pastoral fields or lush forests or fantastic, surreal alien planets—are just as authoritatively rendered and just as essential to the strip's comedy.

Calvin is the personification of kid-dom. He's entirely self-centered, devoted wholly to his own self-gratification. In pursuit of this completely understandable childhood goal, Calvin acknowledges no obstacle, no restraint. His desire and its satisfaction are all that matter to him. His face grotesquely contorted, Calvin the Zombie searches for food. "Horribly, the dead feed upon the living," he says. Then he smears his face with peanut butter and jelly, letting clots and globules of it drip down his chin. "Although in a pinch, PBJ will do," the zombie intones, "if you eat it messily enough." On another occasion, playing in his bath, Calvin cannonballs into the tub, effectively emptying its contents onto the bathroom floor.

He is childhood unbound.

But Watterson has given his portrait of childhood a special twist. Calvin doesn't talk like a little kid. He talks like an adult. Or, perhaps, like a true child of the television generation—a kid who has watched too much prime-time TV. Discovering that his library book is two days overdue, Calvin panics: "What will they do?" he asks his mother frantically. "Are they going to interrogate me and beat me up? Are they going to break my knees? Will I have to sign some confession?" His mother assures him that he'll just have to pay the fine. Calvin is considerably calmed by the news. "The way some of those librarians look at you," he says, "I naturally assumed the consequences would be more dire."

Schulz gives us little kids with adult vocabularies, too, but Calvin is not a character in *Peanuts*. Charlie Brown and Lucy and the other Schulz kids are motivated by adult concerns, or so it seemed then (and, to a large extent—whenever Snoopy leaves the stage to the humans these days—even now). Calvin, on the other hand, is motivated entirely by his childhood fantasies and desires. But he talks about these objectives with adult sensibilities. Coming home from school, Calvin asks his mother if she's fed Hobbes that day. With a tolerant grimace, she confesses she hasn't. "Thanks, Mom," Calvin says: "You wanna just douse me in steak sauce before I go to my room?"

He's a kind of superkid. He does what we imagine a kid would want to do, but he does it by using adult language and intelligence. He is therefore empowered to an extent that an average kid is not. He is better equipped to achieve his goals. Calvin is terrified during a routine visit to his doctor, and he keeps up a running monologue that's clearly designed to make his mother (who is waiting outside the room but within earshot) feel guilty for taking him to the doctor: "Hey, doc, why are you rubbing my arm with cotton? Are you going to put a leech there? Are you going to bleed me? You're not going to amputate, are you? *Are* you? What's that? Is

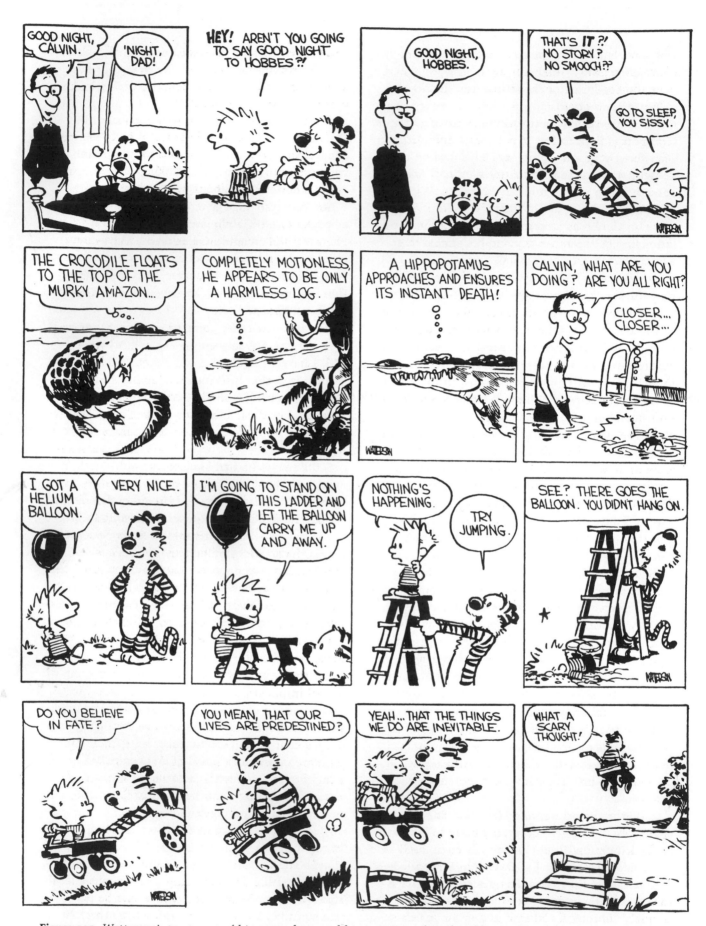

Figure 130. *Watterson's treatment of his young hero and his imaginary friend Hobbes makes deft use of visual-verbal blending: nothing makes much sense unless we comprehend both the words and the pictures. At the bottom, one of the strip's occasional soaring flights of philosophical fantasy.*

that a shot? Are you going to *Aaughh! It went clear through my arm!! I'm dying!* I hope you've paid your malpractice insurance, you quack! *Where's my Mom?"*

When Hobbes asks him why he's getting so many magazines in the mail lately, Calvin explains that he went to the library and filled out all the subscription cards he could find that said "Bill Me Later."

Whenever he takes his bath, Calvin explains to Hobbes, he always puts his rubber duck into the water first. "For companionship?" asks Hobbes. "To test for sharks," replies Calvin.

Calvin wants to take Hobbes with him on a trip to the store, but his mother initially says no. Calvin roars at the top of his lungs: "But I want him to come with us!" The bold black lettering fills the panel. His mother relents. In an aside, Calvin explains: "If you can't win by reason, go for volume."

In short, Calvin is a terror. A brash young assault force.

In a sense, of course, he's not really a kid at all. He's Watterson being a kid—or, rather, Watterson imagining himself a kid but with his adult abilities intact so that he can not only achieve his wildest imaginings but enhance those imaginings with the empowering energy of mature creativity. When Calvin and Hobbes put the loose end of the roll of toilet paper into the toilet and flush, delighting hysterically in the frantic revolutions of the roll of tissue as it unrolls, its entire length pulled inexorably in the maelstrom by the cascading water, they are implementing a highly sophisticated scheme. It's not a kid's prank; it's an adult's.

But Calvin can be an ordinary kid, too, motivated by a wholly juvenile mentality—when, for instance, he holds his nose while sneezing because he's trying to blow his shoes off. An annoying kid, perhaps, but also vaguely endearing. He complains that his bath water is too cold. His mother adds some hot water. Now it's too hot, Calvin says. She adds cold water. "Now it's too deep," he says, deadpan.

In obeying every impulse that flits into his consciousness, Calvin is something more than a kid. He's id, animated solely by his desire to gratify his every imagined wish. As Watterson himself says, "He has no sense of restraint; he doesn't have the experience yet to know the things that you shouldn't do." And to some extent, Hobbes is su-

perego. "Hobbes," Watterson goes on, "is a little more restrained, a little more knowledgeable. . . . [He] has a little bit of that sense of consequence that Calvin lacks entirely."[30]

Careening down a hill on with Calvin on his sled, Hobbes is a typical backseat driver: "Watch out for those trees . . . Look out for that rock! . . . Not so close to the edge . . ." When Calvin brings home a new record album by a rock group whose songs (he says) "glorify depraved violence, mindless sex, and the deliberate abuse of dangerous drugs," it's Hobbes who cautions: "Your Mom's going to go into conniptions when she sees this lying around." (That, of course, is exactly what Calvin hopes for: "Well," he says, "I sure didn't buy it for the music.")

Calvin holds a filled water balloon as he comes up to Hobbes. "You see," he explains, "I have a water balloon, and you don't. I therefore have offensive superiority, so you have to do what I say. What do you think of that?" Hobbes says: "I think I'll take this stick and poke your balloon." The last panel closes in on a drenched Calvin, who says: "That's the trouble with weapons technology: it becomes obsolete so quickly."

As Pat Oliphant observes (in the introduction to *Something under the Bed Is Drooling*, the second volume of *Calvin and Hobbes* reprints), Hobbes "leavens" Calvin's brashness "with a wry, endearing wisdom." Most of the time, Hobbes is—appropriately—the passive companion, innocently going along with whatever scheme Calvin has hatched. Sometimes Hobbes acts as a sort of counselor, giving useful advice, even if sometimes he's a rival, a competitor at their childish games. Always, though, he's Calvin's best friend.

But there are philosophical as well as psychological implications in the strip. A political science major in college, Watterson named his stars after John Calvin, the Protestant reformer of the sixteenth century, and Thomas Hobbes, the seventeenth-century social philosopher. "It's an inside joke for poli-sci majors," Watterson says. But he doesn't explain the joke. No professional humorist explains his jokes.

I, however—lacking professional standing—am scarcely daunted by such trifles. John Calvin, you'll remember, advocated predestination and election: at the dawn of time, God determined who would be damned and who would be saved (the so-called Elect). No one can know which he is,

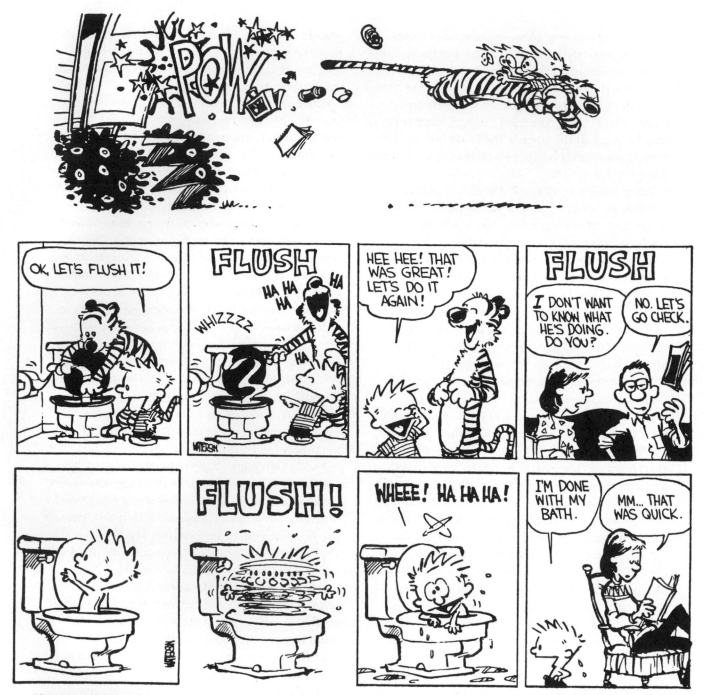

Figure 131. *Watterson's pictures are often vibrant with the energy of his characters. At the top, a typical display, with Hobbes "greeting" Calvin as the latter gets to the front door upon returning from school. And Watterson makes visual comedy out of this energetic action: Hobbes's tail streaming behind his flying body lends the appearance of great velocity to the lunge of his ambuscade. And for comic touches to emphasize the impact of the tiger on the boy, Watterson adds trailing debris—Calvin's lunchbox smashed open, its contents airborne, his notebook akimbo, one of his shoes aloft—and finally, in an inspired fillip, Calvin's eyes bugging out and out and out, in strobe-lighted stages that trace his flight. Delicious. (Incidentally, toilet jokes aren't as frequent in the strip as this sampling suggests, but these two seemed so remarkably inventive I had to include them.)*

and good works don't affect the outcome. Oddly, instead of fostering massive discouragement among his followers, this notion fired zealous undertakings. The righteous deluded themselves into believing they were among the Elect, not the damned. Thus, they didn't see themselves as helpless before an arbitrary God; they saw themselves as his instruments. In the grip of such conviction, men who had inherited Calvin's tradition conquered a continent and raised a democratic form of government. If a single term could describe John Calvin, it would be *certainty*. He was certain of his theology, of himself—and of his being among the Elect. For his part, Thomas Hobbes theorized that humankind in a hypothetical state of nature was constantly at war, each individual fearful of all others. Primitive life, before social organization, was lawless, violent, and fearful; in Hobbes's most famous phrase, it was "nasty, brutish, and short."

Watterson's tiger is doubtless a symbol of the state of nature. He is a jungle creature, a brute. But as I've pointed out, he is scarcely brutish. In fact, he is more civilized than his young owner: as superego, Hobbes is the unconscious product of social organization. Calvin, on the other hand, is nasty, brutish, and short. Well, nasty and short anyhow. But there isn't a perfect reversal in Watterson's allusions. Calvin is clearly among the Elect. He is certain of his rightness, so he can misbehave without fearing the consequences: he is already saved; his deeds cannot affect his fate.

So much for in-group poli-sci jokes. It's hard to know where to laugh.

But nobody reads a comic strip for its historical allusions. Most of us read the comics for entertainment, pure and simple. And in a visual art form, much of the entertainment arises from the pictures themselves. That, at least, is the way it should be. And that, in *Calvin and Hobbes*, is surely the way it is. The quick and short of it is that Watterson draws comic strips the way they should be drawn. Much of his humor lies in the pictures, and in many of the individual strips, the words alone make no comic sense at all without the pictures.

Watterson is well aware of the way his medium functions. At the Walt Kelly celebration at Ohio State University in the summer of 1988, he gave a short talk in appreciation of Kelly's work, remembering *Pogo* as a strip in which the verbal and the visual blended for powerful effect. Most strips today, Watterson said, are simply illustrated jokes: the gag is the same regardless of the characters used in the situation. A lamentable state of affairs, although happily it doesn't exist in *Calvin and Hobbes*. Not only does the humor usually emerge from the words and pictures in tandem: the pictures alone, without words, are funny. Their energy makes them funny. Watterson's action sequences in particular are comically imaginative and inventive.

Hobbes loves to ambush Calvin when the latter arrives home from school, and when he lunges from concealment at the boy, the tiger is a striped rocket streaking across a panel. On a memorable Sunday page, Hobbes flits from place to place in the house, seeking the perfect spot to hide—once flitting so rapidly that he leaves his stripes behind him in midair. Chasing through the house after each other in a game of cops and robbers, Calvin and Hobbes create a shambles, upsetting furniture right and left as they tear through the rooms. But they stop in terrified anxiety, eyes like saucers, fists frozen at the apogee of their swings, when Calvin's mother screams, "Calvin!"—a clarion call for order. Childhood fear of parental reprisal was never so perfectly captured in ink on paper.

Another time, Calvin plays at being a monster, grimacing horribly, one eyeball large and round, the other squinted shut and tiny, his mouth a gaping maw. His mother tells him to be careful or his face will freeze like that. Calvin stops in his tracks. "Wow," he says to himself, the appeal of the proposition nearly overwhelming. Then there was the hysterical sequence of a week or so in which he slicked his hair—usually spiky in disarray—into sleek horns in order to make his school picture interesting.

And there's an evocative piece of business Watterson does every so often with a wagon or a sled, reminiscent of Percy Crosby's *Skippy*. Calvin at the helm, Hobbes a sometimes terrified passenger, the wagon plummets downhill like a guided missile, Calvin idly philosophizing as they hurtle on:

"Do you believe in Fate?" he asks Hobbes.

"You mean, that our lives are predestined?" says Hobbes.

"Yeah—that the things we do are inevitable."

And at this critical moment, the wagon with its passengers reaches the end of a dock or the edge of

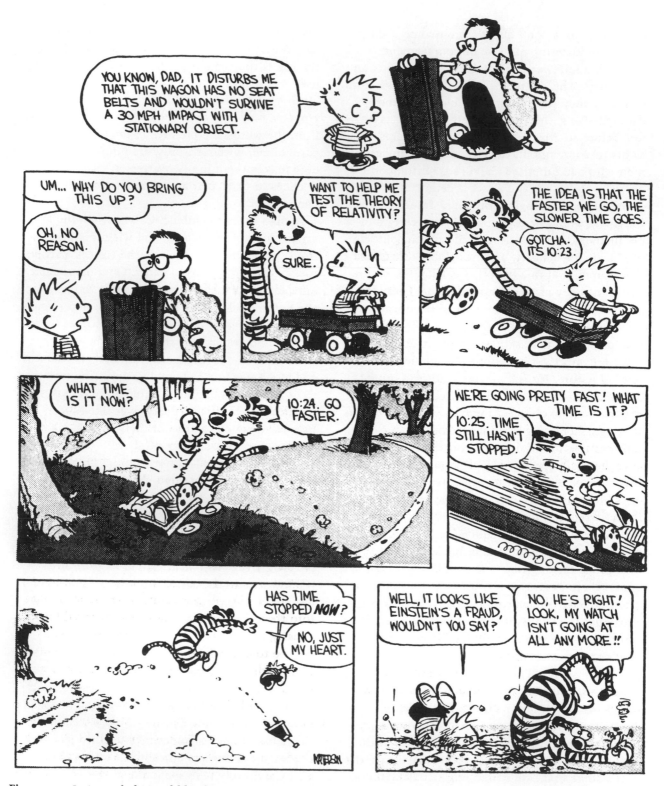

Figure 132. *In its verbal-visual blending and in the cleverness of its gag, this is surely a classic Sunday page.*

a bluff and soars off into space, a tiny speck in the panel. "What a scary thought," murmurs the tiger as they slip loose the surly bonds of earth.

The picture convinces us that such a voyage could really happen. And we enjoy the ride, too. We always do in comic strips that are so skillfully drawn as to make the journey a treat for the eyes as well as a feast for the funny bone.

Meanwhile . . .
An Ending to Begin With

We can't ask for a better place to stop than the trajectory of Watterson's fantasy. Hanging here in midair, momentarily poised at the apex of his visual flight, we have an excellent opportunity to view the surrounding landscape and to take stock as our lives flash before us. And the prospect is encouraging despite its hazards. The triumphant march of *Calvin and Hobbes* across the funnies pages of the nation has been emblematic: it has asserted the importance of the visual aspects of the medium at a time in its history when the verbal seemed ascendant. And Watterson has not been alone in endeavoring to redress the imbalance. In 1992, for instance, "Wiley" (David Wiley Miller) introduced *Non Sequitur*, a single-panel comic strip that aggressively reaffirms the vital role of the visual in comics. Believing that too many of his colleagues had become overly verbal in their humor, Wiley deliberately made his punch lines dependent upon the pictures. He often used words to set up the gag, and he composed his strip-wide panel so that it must be "read" its entire length, from left to right, from verbal setup at the left to the visual punch line at the right (see figure 125, last chapter). Or vice versa. And he often insinuated sight gags into his drawings, little bits of comedy only vaguely related to the main joke—pictures of manic house cats or malevolent children or bored bystanders. *Non Sequitur* became a top seller virtually overnight, attesting to the potent appeal of Wiley's approach.

In the last analysis, though, we need not fear for the vitality of the medium. The form itself is a curiously robust and persuasive advocate for the interdependency of the visual and the verbal. Even in strips like *Dilbert* and *Cathy*, where the drawings veer toward technical incompetence, the visuals are a powerful component of the form: it is difficult to imagine either of these strips drawn in any other way, so thoroughly have we been lured into the toils of their unique visual-verbal blends. Clearly, as long as there are cartoonists, stories will be told in which the pictures and the words blend indivisibly to achieve their narrative purposes.

Meanwhile, we can take heart from the successes of *Calvin and Hobbes*, *Non Sequitur*, even *Dilbert* and *Cathy*. Each of these works is a highly eccentric achievement that affirms through its uniqueness the pivotal role of individual creativity in cartooning. This medium, more than almost any other in the entertainment industry, responds to the individual's impulse for self-expression. And its vitality is perforce a resounding celebration of the worth of the individual.

NOTES

CHAPTER 1

1. Roy L. McCardell, "Opper, Outcault and Company," *Everybody's Magazine*, June 1905, p. 765. Most histories of American journalism recognize in the Yellow Kid the origins of the term "yellow journalism." McCardell adds to this general knowledge the language people used in discussing the circulation battle—"the Yellow Kid journals," "yellow journals." "And so," McCardell continues, "from Mr. Outcault's creation has come the term 'yellow journalism,' with all that it implies of good and evil." McCardell was, himself, one of those watching from the sidelines, but he was scarcely a disinterested bystander. He had been on the *World* staff in the early 1890s, and later, as a member of the *Puck* staff, he had recommended Outcault to Goddard when the latter asked him if he knew of any comic artists whom he might hire to produce a weekly comic "magazine" like *Puck* and *Judge* as a Sunday supplement. Moreover, McCardell claims that the idea of the weekly colored comic supplement was his own: "In 1891, the present writer, then on the *World*'s staff, suggested to Ballard Smith, the managing editor, that as the American public worried mostly about being amused, it might be well to try the effect on them of a comic colored supplement to the Sunday paper; but it was not until three years later that a color press was produced that would print and register properly" (p. 763). Presumably, McCardell watched the battle for readers with almost parental pride. Incidentally, he notes that the Yellow Kid had a name—Mickey Dugan (p. 764).

2. Edwin Emery, *The Press in America: An Interpretive History of the Mass Media*, 3d ed. (Englewood Cliffs, N.J.: Prentice-Hall, 1972), p. 443.

3. Stephen Becker, *Comic Art in America* (New York: Simon and Schuster, 1959), p. 13.

4. Tappan W. King, "The Image in Motion," *Crimmer's*, Winter 1975, p. 15.

5. Kressy's letter offering this explanation for the irregularity is printed in Dave Holland, *From Out of the Past: A Pictorial History of the Lone Ranger* (Granada Hills, Calif.: Holland House, 1988), p. 163.

The following works were also consulted:

Craven, Thomas. *Cartoon Cavalcade*. New York: Simon and Schuster, 1943.

Robinson, Jerry. *The Comics: An Illustrated History of Comic Strip Art*. New York: G. P. Putnam's Sons, 1974.

Waugh, Coulton. *The Comics*. New York: Macmillan, 1947.

CHAPTER 2

1. All dates and biographical facts have been drawn from John Canemaker's *Winsor McCay: His Life and Art* (New York: Abbeville Press, 1987).

2. Ibid., p. 82.

3. Ibid., p. 85.

4. Ibid., p. 212.

5. M. Thomas Inge, *Comics as Culture* (Jackson: University Press of Mississippi, 1990), p. 33.

6. Quoted in Canemaker, *Winsor McCay*, p. 211.

7. Ibid., p. 139.

8. Ibid.

9. Ibid., p. 156. *The Sinking of the Lusitania* was McCay's other early masterpiece: "a monumental work," Canemaker calls it, even if it did not revolutionize the medium.

10. Ibid., p. 185.

The following works were also consulted:

Marschall, Richard, ed. *Dreams and Nightmares: The Fantastic Visions of Winsor McCay.* Westlake Village, Calif.: Fantagraphics Books, 1988.

McCay, Winsor. *The Complete Little Nemo in Slumberland.* 5 vols. Westlake Village, Calif., and Seattle: Fantagraphics Books, 1989–91.

———. *Dreams of the Rarebit Fiend.* 1905; rpt. New York: Dover, 1973.

CHAPTER 3

1. The strip nonetheless continued to appear in the paper sporadically until its final publication on June 7, 1904 (Paul Leiffer and Hames Ware, "American Comic Strips: A Chronological Listing," *The Comics Buyer's Guide,* April 27, 1984, p. 20). In recounting the episode in his autobiography, *King News* (Philadephia: F. A. Stokes, 1941), Koenigsberg says that only eighteen daily strips were prepared, a three-week run; he further implies that only those strips were published before the idea was abandoned because of Hearst's passion for decency and decorum in the pages of his papers (pp. 381–85). But Bill Blackbeard has reported that the strip can be found in the *Chicago American* at irregular intervals for several months after daily publication ceased ("The Forgotten Years of George Herriman," *Nemo* 1 [June 1983]: 53). On the basis of this fact, Blackbeard speculates that Koenigsberg's version of the history of *A. Piker Clerk* is "fanciful," arguing instead that the idea died because it didn't stimulate sales of the newspaper at a sufficient rate. And it didn't, he goes on, because Koenigsberg failed to print the strip every day in every one of the twelve editions of the *American*; under the circumstances, regular readership was impossible because readers didn't know which edition of the paper to buy for *Clerk.* Koenigsberg, however, is unequivocal in claiming that the strip was a successful circulation-building device: "*A. Piker Clerk* scored an instantaneous hit," he asserts; "it was reflected in the *Chicago American's* circulation reports" (p. 384). Regardless of which version of the story is accurate, the crucial facts for my purpose are undisputed: (1) *A. Piker Clerk* was the first daily comic strip, but (2) it didn't last.

2. Coulton Waugh, *The Comics* (New York: Macmillan, 1947), p. 28.

3. In "The Forgotten Years of George Herriman," Blackbeard maintains that Fisher must have known about Briggs's strip (p. 54). Although the internal evidence of Fisher's offering surely supports this contention, there is no other basis for it aside from the similarities between the two strips (similarities that will become apparent herein). Blackbeard also says that George Herriman knew about the Briggs experiment in Chicago (p. 52), and since Herriman was on the staff of another Hearst paper, the *New York American*, in the spring of 1904, it is at least likely that he'd seen exchange copies of other papers in the Hearst empire. It is certain that when Herriman came to Los Angeles and found work on Hearst's *Examiner*, he produced a two-week run of daily strips about a horse race gambler called *Mr. Proones the Plunger.* But it is not certain whether Herriman's inspiration was Briggs or Fisher: *Proones* started December 10, 1907, not quite a month after Fisher's strip debuted a few hundred miles to the north and just a day before Hearst's *Examiner* in San Francisco launched *A. Mutt* with the usual ballyhoo. Hearst had shanghaied Fisher away from the *Chronicle* by offering a higher salary (as we'll see anon); the publisher's desire to have Fisher's popular tout strip may well have prompted his editors in Los Angeles to urge Herriman to produce an imitation for local consumption.

4. Waugh gives the year of Fisher's birth as 1884 (*The Comics*, p. 28); but John Wheeler, "A Captain of Comic Industry," *American Magazine* (n.d.; c. 1916), p. 49, says Fisher was born in 1885. (Wheeler's article was acquired at a flea market in the form of a clipping; none of the clipped pages carry dates, but from internal evidence I have estimated the date of publication.)

5. William E. Berchtold, "Men of the Comics," *New Outlook*, April 1935, p. 39.

6. Bud Fisher, "Confession of a Cartoonist," *Saturday Evening Post*, July 28, 1928, p. 10. This article was the first of four parts that ran in subsequent weekly issues of the *Saturday Evening Post* (August 4, August 11, and August 18).

7. Eric Partridge, *Slang Today and Yesterday*, 3d ed. (New York: Bonanza Books, n.d.), p. 450.

8. Bud Fisher, "Confession," July 28, p. 10. Fisher gives an example of how a horse's name can inspire a joke: "To illustrate, I remember that someone had beaten up Mutt in the preceding day's strip, and he was in the hospital in bad shape. There was a horse entered in the third race named Bright Skies, and I had Mutt looking out the hospital window at the well-known California sunshine. He saw the clear heavens and looked at the paper. 'Bright Skies,' he said. 'That's a hunch.' So he tore off his bandages, threw away his crutches, jumped through the hospital window, and swam across the bay to bet five dollars on Bright Skies."

9. John Wheeler, *I've Got News for You* (New York: E. P. Dutton, 1961), p. 145.

10. Bill Blackbeard, "The Man Who Made Millions," introduction to *A. Mutt* (Westport, Conn.: Hyperion Press, 1977), p. ix; also noted in the introductory matter of *The Mutt and Jeff Cartoons* by Bud Fisher (1910; rpt. Greenfield, Wis.: Arcadia Publications, 1987), n.p.

11. Fisher, "Confession," August 4, p. 113.

12. Fisher, "Confession," July 28, p. 11. Not content with the protection this single maneuver gave him, Fisher had the same copyright notice published with the first two strips that appeared in Hearst's *San Francisco Examiner* on December 11 and 12, 1907.

13. Wheeler, *I've Got News for You*, p. 139.

14. Blackbeard, in "The Man Who Made Millions" (p. xiii) says it was Liverpool. But Wheeler, who was on intimate terms with Fisher all his life—even serving as ex-

ecutor of his will—says it was Ed Mack (*I've Got News for You*, p. 141). Richard Marschall, writing the Al Smith entry in *The World Encyclopedia of Comics* (New York: Chelsea House, 1976) says it was Mack from about 1918 on and Liverpool and others prior to 1918 (p. 625). I assume Wheeler to be the most reliable of the sources and name Mack in subsequent references to the circumstance.

15. The details of Fisher's legal battles can be pieced together from Bill Blackbeard's Bud Fisher entry in *The World Encyclopedia of Comics* (p. 508) and his comments in "The Man Who Made Millions" (p. xi), from Wheeler's autobiography (*I've Got News for You*, p. 141), and from Fisher's own description in "Confession," August 4, p. 110 and p. 113.

16. Stephen Becker, *Comic Art in America* (New York: Simon and Schuster, 1959), p. 34.

17. Ibid.

18. Wheeler, *I've Got News for You*, p. 150–51.

19. Ibid., p. 147.

20. Ibid., p. 145.

21. I rely here on Bob Dunn's description of a visit he and Rube Goldberg made to Fisher during the last few months of Fisher's life; see "Said and Dunn," Dunn's column in *Cartoonist PROfiles* 22 (June 1974): 60–61. Dunn's reminiscence is supplemented by Art Wood in *Great Cartoonists and Their Art* (Gretna, La.: Pelican Publishing, 1987) in which Wood gives an account of his visit as a young man with Fisher (p. 70).

22. Blackbeard, "The Man Who Made Millions," p. ix.

23. Ibid., p. vii. Incidentally, it is this volume, *A. Mutt*, reprinting the first year of the strip, that makes possible the discussion and analysis of this chapter. The convenience of such a publication for the researcher and critic, while obvious, is not acknowledged often enough.

24. Oddly, there has been some confusion about the actual date of Jeff's debut in the strip. In his introduction to *A. Mutt*, Blackbeard gives the date as March 27, but in the strip itself, during a special commemorative series drawn nearly five decades later, Fisher (or his assistant at the time, Al Smith) says it was March 29 (in the installment for January 10, 1952). Blackbeard observes this discrepancy himself in "Mutt and Jeff's Family Album," *Nemo* 10 (December 1984), p. 46. The March 27 starting date is also given in the introductory matter of *The Mutt and Jeff Cartoons*; this material, however, appears to have been added to the original 1910 document by its 1987 editors. The strips of March 1908 as reprinted in the *A. Mutt* volume are no help: they are not dated. (Dating daily strips was a practice that did not begin until some years later.) Moreover, for some reason, the strip in which Jeff first appears *is omitted from the Hyperion Press collection*. In fact, the book leaves out six strips from this critical period—those for March 24 through March 29. The strip in which Jeff makes his first appearance in the book (on page 50) was actually published April 1, 1908, five days after he was introduced to readers of the *San Francisco Examiner*. To ascertain the actual date of Jeff's first meeting with Mutt, I viewed the microfilm of the *Examiner* for March 1908.

25. Blackbeard, "The Man Who Made Millions," p. xi.

26. Bud Fisher, "Seven Tips I Have Picked Up on the Way," *American Magazine*, May 1920, p. 20.

27. Ibid.

28. Ibid.

29. The strip's seventy-fifth anniversary was celebrated in "Mutt and Jeff," *Cartoonist PROfiles* 56 (December 1982): 54–57. The strip ceased, however, shortly thereafter. George Breisacher was the last cartoonist on the feature. He took over when Al Smith retired in 1981. With the help of his assistant, Jim Scancarelli, he gave the venerable strip a fresh look by using a brush and a bolder, more flexible line—all without sacrificing the essential "feel" of the strip.

30. Bill Blackbeard, "Knocking Down Father," introduction to *Bringing Up Father* by George McManus (Westport, Conn.: Hyperion Press, 1977), p. v.

31. Dates and biographical information throughout the remainder of this chapter are derived from Blackbeard (see note 30) and from a three-part article written by McManus (with Henry La Cossitt) published in *Collier's* in 1952, "Jiggs and I" (January 19, January 26, and February 2).

32. See Lucy Shelton Caswell and George A. Loomis, *Billy Ireland* (Columbus: Ohio State University Libraries, 1980).

33. "Jiggs and I," January 19, p. 67.

34. Ibid.

35. "Jiggs and I," February 2, p. 39.

36. Ibid., p. 41.

37. Ibid., p. 39.

38. Ibid.

39. Ibid.

40. Ibid., January 19, p. 67.

41. Ibid., February 2, p. 31.

42. Ibid., January 19, p. 9.

The following works were also consulted:

McManus, George. *Jiggs Is Back*. Berkeley, Calif.: Celtic Book Co., 1986.

———. *Bringing Up Father*. New York: Scribner's, 1973.

CHAPTER 4

1. Neil M. Clark, "Sidney Smith and His Gumps," *American Magazine*, March 1923, p. 72.

2. Quoted in Ibid., p. 76.

3. The history of syndication (and the figures cited here) can be found in Elmo Scott Watson's *A History of Newspaper Syndicates in the United States: 1865–1935* (Chicago: Publishers' Auxiliary, 1936).

4. Quoted in Jerry Robinson, *The Comics: An Illustrated History of Comic Strip Art* (New York: G. P. Putnam's Sons, 1974), p. 68.

The following works were also consulted:

Emery, Edwin. *The Press and America: An Interpretive History of the Mass Media*. 3d ed. Englewood Cliffs, N.J.: Prentice-Hall, 1972.

Galewitz, Herb, ed. *Sidney Smith's The Gumps.* New York: Scribner's, 1974.

McGivena, Leo E. *The News: The First Fifty Years of New York's Picture Newspaper.* New York: News Syndicate, 1969.

Tebbel, John. *An American Dynasty.* New York: Doubleday, 1947.

CHAPTER 5

1. Gene Byrnes, *A Complete Guide to Professional Cartooning* (Drexel Hill, Pa.: Bell Publishing, 1950), pp. 71–72.

2. Bill Blackbeard, "When Thud and Blunder Became Blood and Thunder, and the Comic Strips Ran Red," introduction to *Bobby Thatcher including Phil Hardy* by George Storm (Westport, Conn.: Hyperion Press, 1971), p. vi.

3. My recollection of Kane's talk, San Diego Comic Convention, August 1992.

4. Quoted in Richard Marschall, "Mail Order Success," *Cartoonist PROfiles* 30 (June 1976): 27.

5. Ron Goulart, *The Adventurous Decade* (New Rochelle, N.Y.: Arlington House, 1975), p. 28.

6. My taped interview with Milton Caniff, March 1984.

7. Goulart, *The Adventurous Decade*, p. 31.

8. Coulton Waugh, *The Comics* (New York: Macmillan, 1947), p. 176.

9. Bob Zschiesche, "Roy and Les," *Cartoonist PROfiles* 41 (March 1979): p. 59.

The following works were also consulted:

Becker, Stephen. *Comic Art in America.* New York: Simon and Schuster, 1959.

Campbell, Gordon, and Jim Ivey, eds. *Roy Crane's Wash Tubbs: The First Adventure Comic Strip.* New York: Luna Press, 1974.

Crane, Roy. *The Complete 1942–1943 Wash Tubbs & Captain Easy.* 18 vols. New York: Nantier, Beall, Minoustchine, 1987–92.

CHAPTER 6

1. Quoted in Martin Sheridan, *Comics and Their Creators* (1944; rpt. Brooklyn, N.Y.: Luna Press, 1971), p. 53.

2. Most histories of the medium give a much later starting date for *Gasoline Alley.* But when I researched the *Chicago Tribune,* I found that the panel first appeared on the date given here.

3. Quoted in Herb Galewitz, ed., *Great Comics Syndicated by the Daily News–Chicago Tribune* (New York: Crown Publishers, 1972), p. ix.

4. Quoted in Sheridan, *Comics and Their Creators,* p. 220.

5. Patterson's letter appears in Jerry Robinson, *The Comics: An Illustrated History of Comic Strip Art* (New York: G. P. Putnam's Sons, 1974), p. 85.

6. Taped interview conducted with Ferd Johnson by Shel Dorf, August 20, 1991, a copy of which is in my possession.

7. Stephen Becker, *Comic Art in America* (New York: Simon and Schuster, 1959), p. 68.

8. Quoted in Bruce Smith, *The History of Little Orphan Annie* (New York: Ballantine Books, 1982), pp. 8–9.

9. Quoted in Ellery Queen, "The Importance of Being Earnest; or, the Survival of the Finest," introduction to *The Celebrated Cases of Dick Tracy,* ed. Herb Galewitz (New York: Chelsea House, 1970), p. xvii.

10. Quoted in Sheridan, *Comics and Their Creators,* p. 121–22; see also John Culhane, "Dick Tracy: The First Law and Order Man," *Argosy,* June 1974.

11. Quoted in Culhane, "Dick Tracy," p. 44.

12. Quoted in Sheridan, *Comics and Their Creators,* p. 122.

13. Culhane, "Dick Tracy," p. 45.

14. Quoted in Herb Galewitz, "Interview with Chester Gould," *The Celebrated Cases of Dick Tracy,* p. viii.

15. Ibid.

16. Quoted in Sheridan, *Comics and Their Creators,* p. 75.

17. The incident is related by Mosley in his autobiography, *Brave Coward Zack* (St. Petersburg, Fla.: Valkyrie Press, 1976), p. 26.

18. Ibid., p. 44.

19. Dorf interview with Johnson, August 20, 1991.

The following works were also consulted:

Allen, Frederick Lewis. *Only Yesterday: An Informal History of the 1920s.* New York: Harper and Row, 1964; originally published in 1936.

Gies, Joseph. *The Colonel of Chicago.* New York: Dutton, 1979.

McGivena, Leo E. *The News: The First Fifty Years of New York's Picture Newspaper.* New York: News Syndicate, 1969.

Swanberg, W. A. *Citizen Hearst: A Biography of William Randolph Hearst.* New York: Scribner's, 1961.

Waldrop, Frank C. *McCormick of Chicago.* Englewood Cliffs, N.J.: Prentice- Hall, 1966.

Wendt, Lloyd. *The Chicago Tribune: The Rise of a Great American Newspaper.* New York: Rand McNally, 1979.

CHAPTER 7

1. Arn Saba, "Harold R. Foster: Drawing upon History," *The Comics Journal* 102 (September 1985): 62.

2. Quoted in William F. Nolan, "Some Kind of Gumshoe," introduction to *Dashiell Hammett's Secret Agent X-9,* ed. Tony Sporafucile (New York: Polygonics, 1983), p. viii.

3. Ibid., p. x.

4. Ron Goulart, *The Adventurous Decade* (New Rochelle, N.Y.: Arlington House, 1975), p. 64.

5. Stephen Becker, *Comic Art in America* (New York: Simon and Schuster, 1959), p. 227.

6. Coulton Waugh, *The Comics* (New York: Macmillan, 1947), p. 254.

7. Becker, *Comic Art in America,* p. 228.

The following works were also consulted:

Dille, Robert C., ed. *The Collected Works of Buck Rogers in the 25th Century.* New York: Chelsea House, 1969.

Foster, H. *Tarzan in Color.* Vol. 1. New York: Nantier, Beall, Minoustchine, 1992.

Raymond, Alex. *Flash Gordon.* Vol. 1. Princeton, Wis.: Kitchen Sink Press, 1990.

———. *Flash Gordon into the Ice Kingdom of Mongo.* New York: Nostalgia Press, 1967.

———. *Flash Gordon into the Water World of Mongo.* New York: Nostalgia Press, 1971.

———. *The Official Jungle Jim.* Vol. 1. Las Vegas: Pioneer Press, 1989.

Raymond, Alex, and Dashiell Hammett. *Secret Agent X-9.* New York: Nostalgia Press, 1976.

Robinson, Jerry. *The Comics: An Illustrated History of Comic Strip Art.* New York: G. P. Putnam's Sons, 1974.

CHAPTER 8

1. Milton Caniff, "On Sunday You Can See the Blood in Color," *The Magazine of Sigma Chi*, February–March 1945, p. 85 (rpt. *The Quill*, 1937).

2. From my copy of the typescript, in the "Appendix," p. 2.

3. Coulton Waugh, *The Comics* (New York: Macmillan, 1947), p. 267.

4. "Escape Artist," *Time*, January 13, 1947, p. 62.

5. Milton Caniff, "Terry, the Pirates and I," introduction to *Terry and the Pirates*, by Milton Caniff (New York: Nostalgia Press, 1970), n.p.; see also "Shop Talk with Milton Caniff," interview by Will Eisner, *The Spirit* 35 (June 1982): 37.

6. Quoted in Gene Byrnes, *A Complete Guide to Professional Cartooning* (Drexel Hill, Pa.: Bell Publishing, 1950), p. 75.

7. My taped interview with Caniff, November 1984.

8. Quoted in John Paul Adams, Richard Marschall, and T. Nantier, *Milton Caniff: Rembrandt of the Comic Strip* (New York: Flying Buttress Publications, 1981), p. 40.

9. Steinbeck's letter is on file at the Research Library for Cartoon and Graphic Art, Ohio State University.

10. My taped interview with Caniff, March 1984.

11. Arn Saba, "I'm Just a Troubadour Singing for My Supper," *The Comics Journal* 108 (May 1986): 81.

The following works were also consulted:

Caniff, Milton. *The Complete Dickie Dare.* Agoura, Calif.: Fantagraphics Books, 1986.

———. *Terry and the Pirates.* 12 vols. New York: Nantier, Beall, Minoustchine, 1984–87.

Harvey, Robert C. *Meanwhile: The Life and Art of Milton Caniff.* Unpublished authorized biography, 1990; copy archived at the Cartoon and Graphic Arts Research Library, Ohio State University.

Sickles, Noel. *Scorchy Smith.* 2 vols. New York: Nostalgia Press, n.d. (c. mid-1970s).

CHAPTER 9

1. The total number of daily newspapers had declined from its peak of 2,200 in 1910 to 1,942 in 1930, according to Edwin Emery in *The Press in America: An Interpretive History of the Mass Media*, 3d ed. (Englewood Cliffs, N.J.: Prentice-Hall, 1972), p. 443.

2. Elmo Scott Watson, *A History of Newspaper Syndicates in the United States: 1865–1935* (Chicago: Publishers' Auxiliary, 1936), notes that there were 130 feature syndicates in 1936, supplying over 1,600 different features (p. 35).

3. The argument in this paragraph is offered by Robert S. McElvaine in *The Great Depression: America, 1929–1941* (New York: Times Books, 1984).

4. Quoted in Martin Sheridan, *Comics and Their Creators* (1944; rpt. Brooklyn, N.Y.: Luna Press, 1971), p. 213.

5. Coulton Waugh, *The Comics* (New York: Macmillan, 1947), p. 197.

6. Ibid., p. 199.

7. Ibid.

8. Bill Blackbeard, "The First (Arf, Arf!) Super Hero of Them All," in *All in Color for a Dime*, ed. Dick Lupoff and Don Thompson (New Rochelle, N.Y.: Arlington House, 1970), p. 113.

9. Leonard Maltin, *Of Mice and Magic: A History of American Animated Cartoons* (New York: McGraw-Hill, 1980), p. 106.

The following works were also consulted:

Allen, Frederick Lewis. *Since Yesterday: The Nineteen-Thirties in America.* New York: Harper and Row, 1972.

———. *Only Yesterday: An Informal History of the Nineteen-Twenties.* New York: Harper and Row, 1964; originally published in 1931.

Blackbeard, Bill. "E. C. Segar's Knockouts of 1925 (and Low Blows Before and After): The Unknown Thimble Theatre Period." *Nemo* 3 (October 1983): 7–19.

Sagendorf, Bud. *Popeye: The First Fifty Years.* New York: Workman Publishing, 1979.

Segar, E. C. *The Complete E. C. Segar Popeye.* Ed. Richard Marschall. 11 vols. Seattle, Washington: Fantagraphics Books, 1984–90.

———. *Thimble Theatre: Introducing Popeye.* Westport, Conn.: Hyperion Press, 1977.

———. *Thimble Theatre Starring Popeye the Sailor.* New York: Nostalgia Press, 1971.

Sullivan, Mark. *Our Times: The Twenties.* New York: Scribner's, 1936.

Susman, Warren I. *Culture as History: The Transformation of American Society in the Twentieth Century.* New York: Pantheon, 1985.

CHAPTER 10

1. Quoted in Patrick McDonnell, Karen O'Connell, and Georgia Riley de Havenon, *Krazy Kat: The Comic*

Art of George Herriman (New York: Harry Abrams, 1986), p. 15.

2. Ibid., p. 54. I doubt that anyone is bothered by the absence of a specific sexual identity in the delineation of Krazy. Certainly not poet E. E. Cummings, who, in the introduction to the first collection of *Krazy Kat* strips, said "the ambiguous gender doesn't disguise the good news that here comes our heroine" (*Krazy Kat*, New York: Holt, 1946), n.p.

3. McDonnell et al., *Krazy Kat*, p. 73.

4. Quoted in Ibid., p. 71

5. In our conversation, Cook also told me that Ishmael Reid elaborated on the matter in one of his books. *Mumbo Jumbo* is dedicated to George Herriman.

6. Walt Kelly, *Ten Ever-Lovin' Blue-Eyed Years with Pogo* (New York: Simon and Schuster, 1959), p. 41.

7. Quoted in *Festival of Cartoon Art* (Columbus: Ohio State University Libraries, 1986), p. 24.

8. A description of "action analysis" can be found in Richard Schickel, *The Disney Version* (New York: Simon and Schuster, 1968), pp. 179–80.

9. Hank Ketcham, *The Merchant of Dennis* (New York: Abbeville Press, 1990), p. 60.

10. Kelly, *Ten Ever-Lovin' Blue-Eyed Years with Pogo*, p. 9.

11. Selby Daley Kelly and Steve A. Thompson, *Pogo Files for Pogophiles: A Retrospective on Fifty Years of Walt Kelly's Classic Comic Strip* (Richfield, Minn.: Spring Hollow Books, 1992), p. 43.

12. Quoted in Ibid., pp. 189, 195.

The following works were also consulted:

The Best of Pogo. Edited by Mrs. Walt Kelly and Bill Crouch, Jr. New York: Simon and Schuster, 1982.

George Herriman's Krazy and Ignatz: The Komplete Kat Komics. 9 vols. (1916–24). Forestville, Calif.: Eclipse Books and Turtle Island Foundation, 1988–92. This series begins a complete reprinting of the "Sunday" (or weekend) *Krazy Kat* pages.

George Herriman's Krazy Kat. New York: Madison Square Press and Grosset & Dunlap, 1969.

Herriman, George. *The Komplete Kolor Krazy Kat.* Edited by Rick Marschall. 2 vols. Abington, Pa.: Remco Worldservice Books, 1990, 1991.

———. *The Family Upstairs: Introducing Krazy Kat, 1910–1912.* Westport, Conn.: Hyperion Press, 1977.

Kelly, Walt. *Pogo.* New York: Simon and Schuster, 1951.

———. *The Pogo Papers.* Boston: Gregg Press, 1977; originally published c. 1953.

Manchester, William. *The Glory and the Dream: A Narrative History of America 1932–1972.* New York: Bantam, 1975. (See especially pt. 3, "Sowing the Wind, 1951–1960.")

Phi Beta Pogo. Edited by Mrs. Walt Kelly and Bill Crouch, Jr. New York: Simon and Schuster, 1989.

Pluperfect Pogo. Edited by Mrs. Walt Kelly and Bill Crouch, Jr. New York: Simon and Schuster, 1987.

Pogo Even Better. Edited by Mrs. Walt Kelly and Bill Crouch, Jr. New York: Simon and Schuster, 1984.

Outrageously Pogo. Edited by Mrs. Walt Kelly and Bill Crouch, Jr. New York: Simon and Schuster, 1985.

CHAPTER 11

1. By the end of the 1980s Jim Davis's *Garfield* would rank with these three, and by the mid-1990s Bill Watterson's *Calvin and Hobbes* would join them.

2. Clipping from *Time*, no date or page number, although internal evidence dates it to 1950.

3. *Saturday Review of Literature*, December 16, 1950, p. 33.

4. Mort Walker, *Backstage at the Strips* (New York: Mason/Charter, 1975), p. 195.

5. *Editor & Publisher*, March 3, 1984, p. 64.

6. Mort Walker, *The Best of Beetle Bailey* (Bedford, N.Y.: Comicana, Inc., 1984), n.p. The subsequent descriptions of other characters are all drawn from this book.

7. Walker, *Backstage at the Strips*, p. 228.

8. Walker, *The Best of Beetle Bailey*, n.p.

9. Ibid.

10. Walker, *Backstage at the Strips*, p. 230.

11. Walker, *The Best of Beetle Bailey*, n.p.

12. Rick Marschall and Gary Groth, "Charles Schulz Interview," *Nemo* 31 (January 1992): 11.

13. Ibid., p. 12.

14. Quoted in Rheta Grimsley Johnson, *Good Grief: The Story of Charles M. Schlulz* (New York: Pharos Books, 1989), p. 21.

15. Ibid., p. 26.

16. Marschall and Groth, "Charles Schulz Interview," p. 12.

17. Ibid.

18. Lee Mendelson, *Charlie Brown and Charlie Schulz* (New York: New American Library, Signet Book, 1971), p. 54.

19. Ibid.

20. Johnson, *Good Grief*, p. 75. For a discussion of the twelve devices, see pp. 74–83.

21. Shel Dorf, "Charles Schulz," *Comics Interview* 47 (1987): 9; see also Johnson, *Good Grief*, p. 23.

22. Shel Dorf, "The Fantasy Makers: Interview with Mort Walker," *The Buyer's Guide*, n.d., n. pag.

23. "Good Grief," *Time*, April 9, 1965, p. 81.

24. Quoted in Mendelson, *Charlie Brown and Charles Schulz*, pp. 128–29.

25. James Van Hise, *Calvin and Hobbes, Garfield, Bloom County, Doonesbury, and All That Funny Stuff* (Las Vegas: Pioneer Books, 1991), p. 76.

26. Richard Samuel West, "Interview: Bill Watterson," *The Comics Journal* 127 (March 1989): 57.

27. Ibid., p. 68.

28. Ibid.

29. Paul Dean, "Calvin and Hobbes Creator Draws on the Simple Life," *Los Angeles Times Ideas* April 1, 1987, p. 1.

30. Ibid., p. 4.

The following works were also consulted:

Browne, Dik. *The Best of Hagar the Horrible*. Bedford, N.Y.: Comicana, 1985.

Hurd, Jud. "Garfield." *Cartoonist PROfiles* 71 (September 1976): 12–19.

Robinson, Jerry. *The Comics: An Illustrated History of Comic Strip Art*. New York: G. P. Putnam's Sons, 1974.

Trudeau, Garry. *The Doonesbury Chronicles*. New York: Holt, Rinehart, and Winston, 1975.

Wagner, Charles A. "Tumbleweeds." *Cartoonist PROfiles* 37 (March 1978): 36 39.

Watterson, Bill. *Calvin and Hobbes*. Kansas City, Mo.: Andrews, McMeel and Parker, 1987.

———. *Something under the Bed Is Drooling*. Kansas City, Mo.: Andrews and McMeel, 1988.

INDEX